BOUND LIVES

BOUND LIVES

AFRICANS, INDIANS, AND THE
MAKING OF RACE IN COLONIAL PERU

Rachel Sarah O'Toole

UNIVERSITY OF PITTSBURGH PRESS

Published by the University of Pittsburgh Press, Pittsburgh, Pa., 15260
Copyright © 2012, University of Pittsburgh Press
All rights reserved
Manufactured in the United States of America
Printed on acid-free paper

10 9 8 7 6 5 4 3 2 1

Library of Congress Cataloging-in-Publication Data

O'Toole, Rachel Sarah.
  Bound lives : Africans, Indians, and the making of race in colonial Peru / Rachel Sarah O'Toole.
    p. cm.
  Includes bibliographical references and index.
  ISBN 978-0-8229-6193-2 (pbk. : alk. paper)
  1. Indians of South America—Peru—Government relations. 2. Indians of South America—
Peru—Colonization. 3. Africans—Peru—Government relations. 4. Africans—Peru—Colo-
nization. 5. Slavery—Peru—History. 6. Caste—Peru—History. 7. Peru—Colonization. 8.
Peru—Foreign relations—Spain. 9. Spain—Foreign relations—Peru. 10. Spain—Colonies—
America—Administration. I. Title.
  F3429.3.G6O9 2012

  305.800985—dc23   2012001782

For a true criollo, Guillermo Luis Meza Arrieta (1954–2009)

CONTENTS

ACKNOWLEDGMENTS   IX

INTRODUCTION: Constructing Casta on Peru's Northern Coast   1
CHAPTER 1. Between Black and Indian: Labor Demands and the Crown's Casta   17
CHAPTER 2. Working Slavery's Value, Making Diaspora Kinships   35
CHAPTER 3. Acting as a Legal Indian: Natural Vassals and Worrisome Natives   64
CHAPTER 4. Market Exchanges and Meeting the Indians Elsewhere   88
CHAPTER 5. Justice within Slavery   122
CONCLUSION. The Laws of Casta, the Making of Race   157

APPENDIX 1. Origin of Slaves Sold in Trujillo over Time by Percentage (1640–1730)   171
APPENDIX 2. Price Trends of Slaves Sold in Trujillo (1640–1730)   172
EXPLANATION OF APPENDIX DATA   173

NOTES   175
GLOSSARY   223
BIBLIOGRAPHY   227
INDEX   251

ACKNOWLEDGMENTS

THIS PROJECT BEGAN WITH ASKING how race and racism worked in colonial Latin America. Although (in my own estimation) I have not completely answered my questions, I have learned a great deal in the process.

I thank the archivists and librarians who allowed access to the numerous materials from which this book is written. First, I thank the wonderful and caring staff of the Archivo Regional de La Libertad in Trujillo (ARLL), including Director Napoleón Cieza Burga, Silvia Romero Benites, Alfonso Acuña Suarez, the late Helio Walther Arteaga Liñan, and the ever faithful (and very funny) Martha Chandaví de Arteaga. I also thank the staff of the Archivo General de la Nación (AGN) in Lima (particularly the astute Yolanda Auqui Chávez and Silvia Montesinos Peña), Imelda Solano Galavetta of the Archivo Arzobispal de Trujillo (AAT), and Laura Gutiérrez Arbulú and the staff of the Archivo Arzobispal de Lima (AAL). I thank the warmly welcoming staff of the Archivo Regional de Lambayeque (ARL) and those of the Biblioteca Nacional del Perú (BNP) for their assistance as well as the parish secretaries and priests of the Archivo Parroquial de Cartavio (APC) and Archivo Sagrario de Trujillo (AST) for their accommodation. In Spain I thank the staff of the Archivo General de Indias (AGI) and the Archivo Histórico Nacional (AHN), and in Rome the staff of Archivum Romanum Societatis Iesu (ARSI), who guided me with efficiency and cheer.

In the United States I thank the staff of the following institutions, where I am grateful to have received support: the John Carter Brown Library Post-Doctoral Research Fellowship, funded by the National Endowment for the Humanities (2004); the Beinecke Rare Book and Manuscript Library John D. and Rose H. Jackson Post-Doctoral Research Fellowship (2004); and the Newberry Library Short-Term Resident Fellowship (2003).

During 2006 and 2007, I benefited from a Humanities, Arts, Science, and Technology Advanced Collaboratory (HASTAC) Residential Research Fellowship of the Law in Slavery and Freedom Project at the Institute for the Humanities at the University of Michigan. In 2004, I enjoyed a Villanova University Faculty Summer Research Fellowship and Research Support Grant. An Albert J. Beveridge Grant for Research in the History of the Western Hemisphere from the American Historical Association in 2003 allowed me to conduct research in Peru. A Short-Term Research Fellowship from the International Seminar on the History of the Atlantic World at Harvard University in 2003 allowed me to conduct research in Spain. I was able to finish the final research and writing of this book with a 2010 Faculty Career Development Award from the University of California, Irvine, a 2007 University of California Pacific Rim Research Mini-Grant, a 2007 University of California, Irvine Academic Senate Council on Research, Computing and Library Resources (CORCLR) Cultural Diversity Grant, and a Publication Subsidy Award from the UCI Humanities Center. Some of this funding went to the superb research assistance of Professor Nelly Graciela Cárdenas Goyena (at the Universidad Nacional de Trujillo) and Ernesto Bassi (graduate student at the University of California, Irvine), whose friendships I value even more than their attention to detail!

As a graduate student, I benefited from the following fellowships and awards: a J. William Fulbright Dissertation Fellowship (Peru), an Off-Campus Dissertation Fellowship from the Graduate School at University of North Carolina at Chapel Hill, a Ford Foundation Dissertation and Pre-Dissertation Fellowship from the Institute of Latin American Studies Peruvian Consortium/Duke–University of North Carolina at Chapel Hill Program, the Mowry Research Awards from the Department of History at the University of North Carolina at Chapel Hill, and an Andrew W. Mellon Fellowship at the Vatican Film Library at Saint Louis University.

I have enjoyed conversations and exchanges with fellow historians in Peru, and I thank the Instituto de Estudios Peruanos for often providing a home away from home, especially Carlos Contreras and Vicky García. I am glad for the good advice, clear suggestions, and warm encouragement of Luis Miguel Glave, Jorge (Tito) Bracamonte, Susana Aldana, María Emma Mannarelli, Luis Millones, Maribel Arrelucea Barrantes, Jesús Cosamalón Aguilar, and Juan Carlos Guerrero in Lima. In Trujillo, Juan Castañeda Murga has been a steadfast colleague. At the Museo Afroperuano in Zaña, I thank Sonia Arteaga Muñoz and Luis Rocca. In Chiclayo I thank Ninfa Idrogo and Guillermo Figueroa. I thank Karoline Noack, Karen Graubart, and Susan Ramírez for their many questions and corrections on the history of the Peruvian northern coast.

The research for this book began under the kind direction of my graduate adviser, Sarah Clarke Chambers (now at the University of Minnesota), who allowed me to pursue the ideas that most interested me. At the University of North Carolina at Chapel Hill, I was lucky to have been taught by the formidable Louis A. Pérez Jr., who tolerated the Andes with good humor. John Chasteen tried to teach me how to write. Kathryn Burns provided an intellectual model. Nancy A. Hewitt (then at Duke University, now at Rutgers University–New Brunswick) asked me to think comparatively. Sarah Shields showed me how to be a teacher. Theda Perdue modeled political professionalism. Judith MacKenzie Bennett (now at University of Southern California) previewed what was to come. Jerma Jackson asked many good questions.

At Villanova University, I was mentored by Seth Koven (now at Rutgers University–New Brunswick), Marc Gallicchio, and Adele Lindenmeyr. I was lucky to have won the friendship of Charlene Mires (now at Rutgers University–Camden), Judy Giesberg, and Rebecca Lynn Winer. At the University of California, Irvine, I have found a true intellectual home. My colleagues Heidi Tinsman, Steven Topik, Anne Walthall, Carolyn Boyd, and Laura Mitchell are wise and supportive. My friend Bob Moeller survived the late seventeenth-century wheat blight and still talks to me. For too short of a time Tom Sizgorich reminded me that being funny was not antithetical to being smart. I thank my colleagues Nancy McLoughlin, Jessica Millward, and Vinayak Chaturvedi for reading and discussing (too) many drafts of this book.

I am most grateful for those who "voluntarily" read and commented on my work. I thank Anne Marie Choup and Lesley Bartlett for being there at the beginning and taking me across the finish line. Leo Garofalo and Joan Bristol believed in these ideas when I did not want to anymore. Sherwin Bryant and Herman Bennett tried to catch my mistakes. Christine Hünefeldt and

Marisol de la Cadena revealed themselves as the readers for the University of Pittsburgh Press and have been long-standing inspirations for how to write Peruvian history with attention to race and power. David Kazanjian asked me to say what I mean, and Kathryn Burns warned me to take everyone off at the right exit. I thank the participants of the Workshop on Difference in Colonial Latin America at Connecticut College (in 2003, 2004, and 2005), especially Jeremy Mumford and Charles Beatty Medina. I thank Joshua Shanholtzer at the University of Pittsburgh Press for his speedy and steady oversight.

I am very appreciative to the following individuals for comments, lecture invitations, interest, and many conversations: Mary Weismantel, Charles Walker, Linda Sturtz, Rebecca Scott, Elizabeth Kuznesof, Doug Cope, Jaime Rodríguez, Gabriela Ramos, Nicanor Domínguez, Cathy Komisaruk, Ben Vinson III, Kris Lane, Pamela Voekel, Pete Sigal, Jocelyn H. Olcott, Marcela Echevarri, Annie Valk, Kym Morrison, Michele Reid-Vazquez, Adam Warren, Michelle McKinley, Will Jones, Amy Ferlazzo, Bianca Premo, Jessica Fields, Yanna Yannakakis, Irene Silverblatt, Kevin Sheehan, Paula De Vos, Bill Van Norman, Peter Blanchard, and Martin Klein. Florencia Mallon, the late Jeanne Boydston, and Frank Salomon encouraged me as an undergraduate at the University of Wisconsin–Madison to pursue graduate studies, and I am still grateful! I also thank my students, every day, for challenging me to think outside of many boxes.

Most important, it's good to have good company. My parents, Tom and Ann O'Toole, opened the door to the world to me and then encouraged me to walk through it. My grandparents, Dorothy Ann Trautt (1917–2009) and Phil Joseph O'Toole (1909–2001), taught me how to work hard when I got there. With fierce love, la familia Guevara (Mónica, Helder, Jean-Paul, Mirjam, Pier, Blanca, and Leonardo with tía Ruth) put me on this path. My tíos and tías—Andy Marshall, Carmen Alarco, Janice Baker, and Frank Zappalá—always let us stay with them. Nasreen Mohamed and Christine Williams have kept me laughing, especially at myself. Soledad (Choli) Marroquín Muñoz and her late partner, Guillermo Luis Meza Arrieta ("el Doctor Tienes Que"), taught me how to make the most of Sundays in Lima. Most especially, I thank my brilliant and handsome spouse, Ann M. Kakaliouras, for being the moral and intellectual center of my life.

BOUND LIVES

Introduction

Constructing Casta on Peru's Northern Coast

HOW DID AFRICANS BECOME "BLACKS" and Andeans become "Indians" during the "long" seventeenth century that spilled from the 1600s into the 1700s?[1] Named as "Indians," indigenous people were considered by the crown as vassals and therefore corporate members of colonial society. In this capacity coastal Andeans were expected to pay tribute, serve labor obligations, practice Catholicism, and (in some cases) function as rural authorities. Similar obligations and protections were not uniformly extended to Africans and their descendants, who, even if considered Catholic, were afforded a much more limited corporate location.[2] Africans and their descendants in rural areas were far from ecclesiastical courts and had limited clerical contact. As a result, they were often excluded from protections articulated by Catholic authorities and left to negotiate with slaveholders and, in a few instances, colonial authorities.[3] As a result, enslaved men and women sold from West and West Central Africa to Peru created kinships and their own sense of justice within slavery, in addition to what they could

1

gain judicially. Simultaneously, on the northern Peruvian coast, Africans and Andeans developed trading and kinship relations apart from their assigned *casta* locations of black or Indian. The goal of *Bound Lives* is to understand these processes of exclusion and exchange in order to illuminate how coastal Andeans and enslaved Africans with their descendants understood their legal casta in their everyday lives.

As recorded in colonial trial records, Africans and Andeans could act from within their juridical locations of "black" and "Indian," or their castas of "black" and "Indian." One of the main contributions of this book, therefore, is to understand how casta terms communicated legal locations—not solely race and class, or how historians have previously glossed these categories.[4] Demonstrating how allegedly separate groups—Africans and Andeans—interacted from their assigned colonial positions of black and Indian, illustrates lived definitions of casta. In addition, inhabiting or using casta terminologies implies an undoing. More recently, scholars have emphasized how lineage formed the basis for a racial hierarchy or a "caste system," however unstable or socially constructed.[5] This book continues to destabilize fixed notions of casta. By understanding which components within casta categories bound Africans and Andeans to colonizers' or slaveholders' demands and which elements could be negotiated, the aim is to explore the construction of casta from the bottom up.

In addition, focusing on multiplying differences within the categories of "Indian" and "black" (including transatlantic and Diaspora terms such as *bran* or *mina*) reveals the instability of casta categories as employed by powerful landholders, threatened indigenous villagers, and protesting enslaved laborers. Irregularity, however, did not mean a lack of consequences. Crown obligations and labor demands were rooted in the inequities of casta between Africans and Andeans. Shifting the focus away from identity categories to legal locations that Africans, Andeans, or their descendants could claim, or were denied, reveals how casta took its meaning in the interplay between colonial law and daily practice. Most important, by examining Africans and Andeans simultaneously, I argue that indigenous people—as Indians—were awarded more legal access than enslaved people. This is not to say that enslaved men and women did not struggle to gain legal recognition. My point is that Africans and Andeans shared legal agency but were not considered as equals within all permutations of colonial law.

Bound Lives adds to a scholarship that challenges an image of the rural Andes as solely an indigenous society colonized by the Spanish. Historians of Peru's coastal valleys have discussed the significant populations of Africans and their descendants but focused on the rise of landholders and the system of slavery rather than the perspectives and actions of enslaved men and women.[6] Although there were glimpses into the daily lives of rural slaves and the strategies of fugitives in the countryside, historians focused on urban areas—especially in the eighteenth and nineteenth centuries—to reveal how enslaved people resisted, manumitted themselves and their families, and eventually brought about emancipation.[7] As for the highlands, African-descent populations are beginning to be documented.[8] Still, most historians of the colonial Andes have extensively discussed indigenous communities in the rural sierra, but not explored their contact with Africans and their descendants.[9]

With few exceptions, accounts of the Andean past remain divided between histories of indigenous people and histories of enslaved Africans and their descendants.[10] For example, the encyclopedic study of slavery in colonial Peru by historian Frederick Bowser emphasized that Spanish colonial law separated blacks from Indians.[11] *Bound Lives* dismantles an assumption in Peruvian historiography that indigenous and African people did not interact and, when they did, the exchange was marked with violence and conflict.[12] Regardless of royal mandates to the contrary, I found that local criminal and civil trials, appeals cases to the viceregal capital or the imperial Spanish courts, as well as sales, wills, and inventories, provided evidence of enslaved and free people who traded, celebrated, drank, ate, and fought with indigenous men and women into the eighteenth century. In state and ecclesiastical archives in Lima and on the northern coast as well as in Spain's Archivo General de Indias, copious judicial and notarial documentation attested to dynamic, multiple, and diverse exchanges among Africans and Andeans.[13] In this sense, this book is part of the scholarship of inserting Africans and their descendants into the histories of such Andean cities as Cuzco, La Paz, Lima, and Quito.[14] By moving the focus to the rural and provincial environments, however, I correct previous assumptions that indigenous-African relations tended to be hostile, since blacks were perceived to have served Spanish colonizers.[15] As a result, this book contributes to a history of the highland and coastal Andes, where indigenous people with Africans and their shared descendants were enemies as well as kin, friends *and* foes—sometimes simultaneously.

Critically, I argue that African–Andean interactions occurred within the impositions of colonialism and slavery. I seek to understand, first, the distinct legal locations of indigenous and African people in colonial Latin American society and, second, to explain how these juridical positions informed strategies of resistance and adaptation to colonial rule and landholder demands. In this sense, the book builds on scholarship that compares the locations of indigenous and black people in the Americas. Some scholars have found that African and African-descent people occupied separate locations in colonial Latin American society, which meant in some cases that blacks served as intermediaries between natives and Spaniards while in others they worked in the most dangerous and menial positions.[16]

Other scholars concluded that Spanish perceptions and colonial constructions of indigenous and African people also reveal imposed and idealized hierarchies, which in some instances meant that Indians were awarded protection from blacks while in others meant that indigenous people endangered colonial order.[17] All of these positions may be possible, but it does us a disservice to understand Indian-black relations as unchanging. I argue that the colonial constructions of Indian versus black affected each other and the way that Andeans and Africans would act within (and outside) of colonialism and slavery. The main contribution of Bound Lives is to understand how Africans and Andeans shaped the constructions, categories, and expectations of property and vassalage that bound them. The point is to illustrate how these locations shifted according to economic realities or particular demands. The contribution is two-fold. The impositions of casta may have been clear, but what people did with them was not. Relations between Africans and Andeans were not static, therefore neither were definitions of casta.

The demands of the colonial state limited the possibilities of Africans and Andeans but did not secure their locations within hierarchies according to casta. To explain, I draw on the work of U.S. historians who have endeavored to understand the conflicting and contradictory nature of indigenous-African relations and identities within larger structures of slavery, colonialism, and nation-state expansion.[18] Context, in this case, is critical. Expanding estates imposed on indigenous villages and rural slavery dictated Africans and their descendants disputed labor practices in the northern coastal valleys (Trujillo, Chicama, Jequetepeque, Saña, and Lambayeque). In these conditions, I explore how Africans, as trading partners or fellow laborers, were integral to economic and social transformations of indigenous Andean communities. In turn, Andeans witnessed the violence of slavery but also served as rural justices primarily to defend their communities, and in the process they supported and maintained slavery. There was a continual back-and-forth. Africans and their descendants stole from Andean neighbors, but also relied on trade with the same members of colonial reducciones for sustenance on the rural estates. Also, Andeans assaulted Africans who mistakenly joined special community meetings but defended enslaved men who were unfairly punished by their owners. There are many ways to understand the shifting terrain of these actions, responses, and strategies. Within the parameters of colonization and slavery, Africans, Andeans, and their descendants employed colonial racial categories or casta terms to mark their distinctions from others but not to simply fit into their place in the hierarchies of casta.

Lastly, this book corrects a common interpretation in colonial Latin American history that African and African-descent people replaced indigenous populations in coastal and lowland regions. On the northern Peruvian coast, scholars have documented that indigenous populations declined throughout the sixteenth and seventeenth centuries as a result of epidemics, labor demands, and colonial resettlement.[19] Elsewhere in the Andes, however, these same processes prompted indigenous adaptation to colonial rule—not the disappearance of Andean societies. For example, demographic shifts reflected Andean migration as indigenous people developed new communities in towns, cities, and estates, or incorporated newcomers into their villages.[20] Andeans also developed colonial or urban identities by maintaining regional distinctions or coalescing into pan-Indian collectivities.[21] In other cases, Andeans increased their market interactions and cohabitation with Africans, and in some cases they intermarried or developed shared religious practices as described by historians Jane Mangan, Jesús Cosamalón Aguilar, and Leo Garofalo for colonial Potosí and Lima.[22] Along the northern coast the Spanish established settlements and expanded estates, displacing indigenous landholdings particularly in the Trujillo, Chicama, and Saña valleys. Fewer in number, but certainly still present, northern coastal Andeans transformed their communities, adapted to Spanish colonial demands that included slavery, and developed sustained relationships with Africans and their descendants (as well as Spaniards and creoles).

Both colonized Andeans and enslaved Africans with their descendants made sense of the obligations and the expectations imposed on them because of their social locations and expressed their understandings through their uses of casta. Spanish colonial authorities created legal distinctions that made Africans into "blacks" and transformed Andeans into "Indians," but they could not dictate how colonial inhabitants would enact these terms in everyday life. Analyzing how enslaved and free, indigenous and African acted out their assigned positions in relation to each other also demonstrates the entangled ways in which Africans and Andeans claimed their locations within Spanish colonialism. Africans were excluded from official locations of native vassalage on an everyday basis, partly because Andeans continually claimed their "rightful" place as the crown's subjects. Even when the regional economies shifted on the northern Peruvian coast and slaveholders privatized communal indigenous landholdings, Andeans continued to articulate their official locations as Indians even as they developed lasting ties with Africans and their descendants. When understood from the perspectives of indigenous or enslaved people, casta categories were legal terms that provided or elided access to royal protections or elite concerns. Casta as practiced was not fixed or a stable marker of identity, but could be employed as a powerful marker of distinction.

The Northern Peruvian Coast: "Between Cold Mountains and a Turbulent Sea"

The northern coast of Peru is located between the sharp rise of the western Andean Cordillera and the turbulent Pacific Ocean.[23] Rivers descending from the mountain peaks wind their way into coastal valleys, and during the rainy season many swell to make their way to the ocean. The fertile, irrigated lands still reach, like fingers, between the sandy expanses and the sparse scrub woods of carob once inhabited by foxes, lions, and deer.[24] Built by coastal people more than thousands of years ago, there is still evidence of a system of managed streams and earthen canals that crisscrossed the valleys of Virú, Trujillo (including Santa Catalina), Chicama, Jequete peque, Saña, and Lambayeque, the major valleys of the northern Peruvian coast as depicted in figure I.1. The Spanish quickly took advantage of the diverse resources available in the northern valleys. On the ocean, such coastal villages as Eten in the Lambayeque valley and Santiago de Cao in the Chicama valley supplied local markets with a wide variety of fish and shellfish.[25] Indigenous lands and (by the colonial era) private farms in the middle and upper valleys were devoted to the cultivation of corn, potatoes, and garbanzo beans as well as cucumbers and peppers.[26] Spanish and indigenous wheat farms and cattle ranches soon complemented local crops. Scrub forests of carob provided pasture for sheep, goats, pigs, and occasionally cattle.[27] At the high end of the valleys close to the Andean foothills, herders tended their animals while fugitive slaves sometimes took refuge in the dry canyons that quickly ascend into the mountains.

Throughout the colonial period, mule trains connected the coast with northern Andean regional economies surrounding Loja and Quito (in today's Ecuador) as well as Cajamarca and Chachapoyas in the northern Peruvian highlands. Muleteers also complemented the trade along the northern coast by connecting Trujillo and Lima especially when the ocean currents and winds were not amenable to seafaring.[28] Though the northern coastal ports such as Huanchaco (in Trujillo), Malabrigo (in Chicama), and Chérrepe (in Saña) lacked sheltered anchorage, landholders still employed them to ship out flour, wheat, soap, hides, preserves, and sugar from the coastal valleys to Pacific markets.[29] In return, coastal valley inhabitants and other

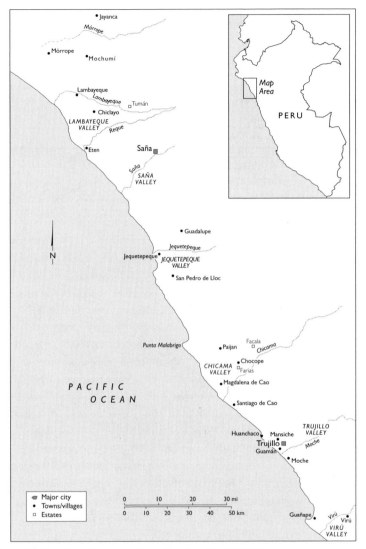

Figure I.1. Northern Peruvian Coast. Rendered by Bill Nelson.

entrepreneurs purchased slaves, textiles, and wine in the ports of Panama and Callao (Lima).[30] These cities figured prominently within colonial bureaucracy and also in the essential silver shipments from the highland mines to the Caribbean and then transported across the Atlantic. Exports from the Peruvian northern coast suffered in the first part of the seventeenth century due to unstable markets.[31] In the later seventeenth century and early eighteenth century, landholders complained of a wheat blight coupled with

Table I.1. Demographic Estimates for Trujillo City and Valley, 1604 and 1763.

	Spanish and mestizos		Free and enslaved blacks and mulatos		Indians	
	Total	Percentage	Total	Percentage	Total	Percentage
1604[1]	750	27	960	34	1,090	39[2]
1763[3]	4950	63[4]	2,650	34	214	3

Notes: 1. Anómino, "Fragmento de una historia de Trujillo," 90–93.
  2. This number is inflated because it includes children.
  3. Feijóo de Sosa, Relación descriptiva, 29–30.
  4. This number is inflated because it includes children.

flooding from excessive El Niño rains that supposedly reduced crop production and dampened trade.[32] Nonetheless, the northern coast remained an essential regional economy within the Peruvian viceroyalty by supplying foodstuffs and other goods to urban areas along the critical trade routes of the Pacific until the end of this study in the early eighteenth century.

On the northern Peruvian coast, prosperity for the landholding elite rested on their ability to secure sufficient laborers to tend cattle on the ranches or plant and harvest on the wheat farms and sugar estates. After the implementation of the mita (a rotational system of forced labor) in the later part of the sixteenth century, regional elites relied on coastal and highland mitayos (Andeans serving their mita obligation) as well as contracted indigenous laborers. By the mid-seventeenth century the labor demands of coastal landholders, compounded with a crown policy of composición de tierras (the sale of vacant land), resulted in land privatization and indigenous migration throughout the Andes.[33] In the Chicama valley Andean colonial reducciones (indigenous towns created by royal orders) such as Santiago de Cao and Paiján lost arable, irrigated lands as did other communities in the Trujillo, Jequetepeque, and Lambayeque valleys.[34] The crown-appointed inspector resold these so-called vacant lands to private landholders who were mostly Spanish or creoles (Spanish-descent people born in the Americas).[35] The willingness of crown authorities to overlook the sanctity of communal land indicated that coastal Andean communities and individuals would need to defend themselves in other ways besides claiming crown protections due to them as reducción Indians.

Unfortunately, there is no comprehensive census for the northern coast. However, in 1604 the magistrate counted the inhabitants of Trujillo (the region's main city) and the immediate valley. With the exception of scattered calculations of indigenous communities to assess tribute obligations, there is no other census until 1763, when again Trujillo's magistrate counted the inhabitants of the city and its surrounding valley.[36] The thin demographic evidence, as illustrated in table I.1, suggests two points. First, between 1604 and 1763 there was a dramatic decline in Trujillo's identified "Indian" population and an increase in the numbers of Spaniards and mestizos.[37] Andeans, however, did not disappear from the northern coastal valleys; rather, they distanced themselves from reducciones. These official numbers suggest that they removed themselves from the location of "Indian" because the obligations no longer were accompanied by protections. Second, during the early seventeenth century the magistrate's count indicates that in the city of Trujillo and its surrounding farms, Africans, Andeans, and Spaniards were proportional percentages of the population. The contrast between 1604 and 1763 suggests that Africans and their descendants remained roughly 34 percent of the total population. In the city and the valley of Trujillo, Africans and their descendants were never in the majority, while the surrounding valleys may have had larger populations of Africans.

Coastal landholders did not immediately profit from their cooptation of communal indigenous lands. In 1641 the Spanish crown ended altogether its slave-trading contract with Portuguese transatlantic merchants.[38] By the early 1640s royal officials in Lima reported that the official importation of African captives had ceased into the Peruvian Pacific.[39] Contraband trade probably continued as Trujillo's slaveholders purchased captive West Central Africans from Panamanian merchants.[40] Enslaved men and women, in turn, would negotiate the experiences of multiple slave trades from the Atlantic to the Pacific by calling on slaveholders to recognize their value as slaves. Meanwhile, colonial officials from Panama to Lima identified a crisis in the labor supply throughout the 1640s as they claimed there was a lack of blacks who could be forced to perform the necessary labor.[41] In 1646 the viceroy warned that without blacks the work on rural estates would cease as well as the local production of foodstuffs and goods.[42] Simultaneously, coastal Andeans increasingly abandoned their assigned reducciones that had supplied mitayos to landholders.[43] As throughout the Andes, with less land and water but still the impositions of serving mita and paying tribute, membership in the Indian towns became more untenable.[44] In short, coastal landholders lacked enslaved Africans when indigenous communities refused (or could not) supply their required labor quota. By the 1650s, more coastal landholders were land rich but labor poor.

Within a few years there were signs that northern coastal landholders were recovering. In the 1650s prices for wheat and flour doubled in Panama, where the tropical climate made these crops difficult, if not impossible, to produce.[45] By the 1660s the Spanish crown renegotiated slave-trading licenses with new transatlantic merchants as the Dutch secured the Caribbean island of Curaçao, thus increasing the number of slaves traded into Portobelo and Cartagena.[46] Contraband trade continued throughout the 1660s as Portuguese, Dutch, and English slave traders sold Africans and criollos along the Caribbean borders of Spanish America.[47] The English, in particular, offered stiff competition. During the 1660s English ships transported captives from Jamaica and Barbados to Portobelo, where its slave-trading company maintained its agents.[48] As a result, sales of captive Africans increased in Trujillo as prices continued to climb.[49]

By 1670, Trujillo slaveholders paid on the average of 650 pesos for an able-bodied enslaved man or woman, the highest mean price in my sample of slave sales from 1640 to 1730.[50] At first, the Dutch supplied slaves from Luanda, but gradually captives from the Gold Coast and the Bight of Benin (also traded by the English) were sold into Spanish America.[51] Indicating the keen demand for enslaved laborers, Trujillo's buyers noted only whether captives were healthy and able-bodied and paid the price demanded by the renewed transatlantic slave trade.[52] By the 1690s the Trujillo and Chicama valleys prospered from demand along the Pacific for wheat and flour, which landholders supplied to such coastal cities as Guayaquil.[53] In 1720 Trujillo authorities noted that there were a sufficient number of slaves on the wheat farms, cattle ranches, and sugar estates in the region.[54]

The recovery of the slave trade into the Spanish Americas, however, did not preclude the integration of coastal Andeans into the new economies of the later seventeenth century. With the renewed growth of the slave trade into coastal Peru, sugar production expanded gradually in the northern coastal valleys. Wheat and flour remained valued exports. With more enslaved laborers, landholders planted more cane to take advantage of the rising prices for sugar.[55] Nonetheless, landholders did not completely switch to sugar.[56] Local and regional markets (in Panama and elsewhere) for flour, meat, soap, and hides were still lucrative, as suggested by the number of estates still producing wheat and cattle.[57] With these diversified markets plus the larger landholdings and access to the accompanying irrigation, private landholders intensified their encroachment onto indigenous fields in the later decades of the seventeenth century.[58]

By the late seventeenth century, indigenous towns struggled to defend land and water resources against encroaching private estates as some enslaved people took advantage of slaveholders' dependency on their labor to look for new owners. Coastal Andeans continued to migrate into colonial cities and towns to work as artisans and marketers, while others carried on in the countryside as private landholders, day laborers, and even "police." Enslaved laborers, in turn, became fugitives but also firmly defended their sense of just work rhythms to push against the demands of slaveholders in their capacity as colonial officials. Privately-owned wheat farms, cattle ranches, and sugar estates dominated most of the coastal valleys by the later part of the century.[59] Coastal Andeans as laborers, muleteers, and small landholders, however, quickly became essential to getting goods to market and even contributing their own to the Pacific shipments while enslaved laborers became central to the coastal workforce. The eighteenth-century image of black men working in tar smelting operations (from the northern Peruvian collections of Bishop Baltazar Jaime Martínez Compañón) on the cover of this book underlines how laborers and the need for labor—in addition to the legal significance—contributed to the meaning of casta categories. The rise of sugar production with the expansion of estates meant an increase in the power of slaveholders that was further solidified through their claims to local offices. By the mid-seventeenth century the crown was selling the position of the magistrate, making it an investment for local elites.[60]

On the northern Peruvian coast magistrates in all likelihood profited from their positions; they were accused of usurping indigenous lands, allowing abuses of enslaved men and women, and selling overpriced alcohol to underpaid indigenous workers.[61] Likewise, landholders and merchants employed their appointments to the municipal council to better their positions such as diverting public water resources to their sugar mills or employing civic funds in order to secure ports for commerce.[62] As such, Trujillo's regional elites were part of the diffusion or decentralization of power that supported the seventeenth-century Hapsburg kingdoms.[63] There are many implications, but the power of the regional elites would also influence African and Andean usages of casta. The Spanish crown provided a series of regulations governing the relationships and the definitions of casta categories, yet regional elites would choose at which point they would enact or follow these mandates. In some cases their ideal hierarchy of Spanish superiority followed royal expectations, while in other situations local precedent overruled royal orders.

Legal Entries into Everyday Relations

Regional elites had a stake in the implementation of casta categories, but the concern here is how distinct groups of Andeans and Africans occupied, produced, and changed the meanings of the legal colonial categories created to contain them. To understand how indigenous laborers and enslaved Africans were organized but also employed the casta terms, I examine daily interactions within the changing historical and economic contexts of the mid-seventeenth century into the early eighteenth century. Everyday relations can be found in two types of documentation: those records that reveal usual exchanges and other records that illuminate extraordinary episodes. By looking at mundane and unusual events in relation to each other, I examine what enslaved or indigenous people claimed rather than merely what they did in particular situations. Criminal and civil trials, appeals cases, and judicial rulings along with sales, wills, inventories, and other records from notarial records provide details of when, where, and how African and indigenous people interacted. The exploration of the claims-making within judicial records provides a documentary nexus between official expectations and colonized or enslaved actions.[64] An examination of everyday details combined with an investigation of official orders provides an entry into how Africans and Andeans constructed casta in the courts and, when contextualized in their lives, can illustrate distinct legal locations of enslaved Africans and coastal Andeans.

Judicial cases are critical because they were one of the few locations where, in highly mediated forms, indigenous or enslaved people articulated their demands or requests. Rather than attempting to "read against the grain" to understand what Andeans or Africans "really wanted," I attempted to read "with the grain" of the archive.[65] In other words, I read judicial cases for the evidence of how Andeans or Africans were being employed or employed judicial situations. Even if assisted by legal representatives or shunted into specific legal locations, Andeans and Africans were also presenting themselves (or being presented) as witnesses, plaintiffs, and defendants in a legal context that many of them were versed in the logistics of or would quickly learn.[66]

In these settings, I asked how indigenous or enslaved people's strategies were performative, but not in the sense that made their actions have less impact or be less real. Rather, I understood the performative quality of Andeans or Africans to be a marker of their agency. In the case of Sebastian (an enslaved foreman of casta *arara* discussed in chapter 5), his confession of defying the authority of his Spanish overseer was also corroborated by other enslaved witnesses. Obviously, Sebastian was not considered to be legally equal to the slaveholder who initiated the suit for lost damages and his testimony along with those of other enslaved witnesses could be dismissed given the customary practices of colonial courts. Furthermore, Sebastian could not make claims to defend his community as a corporate group like Andean laborers. Nonetheless, I asked how Sebastian presented himself in the case given the cultural assumptions within the parameters of a judicial case.

I also juxtaposed the events he recalled with those of other enslaved witnesses and slaveholders. Taking the court case as a performative moment allowed me to see how slaveholders attempted to employ these instances as means to display their readings of enslaved men as violent or unruly, when in fact many enslaved men appeared to have known the rules or were trying to figure out the legal mechanics in an attempt to use them to their advantage. Moreover, by merely being conscious of how black men were criminalized in colonial courts helped me to see the distinction between their location in the law and that of Andean men. Approaching criminal or civil cases as events that contain weighted descriptions of other events helped me to see how participants acted within the judicial moment by presenting, or being forced to present, their evidence or tell their side of the story. Using this approach, I show how laws both acted on and animated categories as well as expectations of casta performances.

I apply microhistorical and ethnohistorical techniques to understand how enslaved and colonized people engaged with casta in the judicial documentation as well as in the notarial records. The brevity of many criminal and civil trials in the provincial secular courts combined with the formulaic quality of most notarial entries make a microhistorical approach to any one individual a challenge. Small pieces of evidence from multiple sources need to be pulled together to explain why a particular individual acted in a particular way. I employ this microhistorical approach to see how individuals were related to a host of other individuals, communities, and practices. For instance, civil cases intended to transfer a deceased's wealth to named inheritors revealed a whole range of relations, such as the case of Pedro Esteban Peñarán, a native of a Chicama valley reducción discussed in chapter 4. By explaining how items of his inventory connected this indigenous man to individuals within his community, but also to many who inhabited non-reducción locations (combined with more evidence), I traced the emergence of Andeans who located themselves "elsewhere" in the market economies of the mid-seventeenth centuries. Following fragmentary evidence away from its intended use illuminates rural Andean and enslaved African realities based on a careful (and sometimes time-consuming) correlation of information.

I engage in the microhistorical methods of exploring the discrepancies between testimonies and interrogating multiple possibilities for a subject's actions, including my own doubts.[67] I reconstruct particular events or circumstances based on a compilation of details regarding, for instance, enslaved marketing practices or indigenous muleteer networks. The details provide the context for understanding colonized tactics and enslaved strategies as well as colonial procedures and slavery's order.[68] By reconstructing how and why men or women claimed certain terms in particular circumstances, I illuminate what Africans and Andeans meant in invoking casta categories. The point is to place individual actions within larger communities so that the rare events that were recorded in colonial documentation can suggest what was possible, probable, and expected—not just what was unique or exceptional.[69]

I use the details of everyday life within the context of the judicial documents. Rather than being a barrier to "true" events, court cases can provide evidence of distinct forms of discourse that, if taken in context, provide particular types of facts. In other words, I analyze information provided by defendants, witnesses, or prosecuting legal representatives according to their particular motivation in the court case. In addition, I take rumor, gossip, hearsay, and eyewitness accounts recorded in judicial testimony as significant forms of evidence. When employed in their documentary context, claims to casta terms or characteristics were simultaneously based on public and intimate circumstances. Small occurrences that reflect private matters could have a greater impact if discussed, enacted, or performed in public. In this way what people said happened, regardless of actual events, forms a significant part of my evidence base. These events and exchanges made up public culture where indigenous and enslaved people employed official legal discourse even from their marginal positions.[70]

In colonial Latin American society Africans and Andeans would have observed judicial expectations when edicts were announced in the main plaza, people were executed at public gallows, and the justice of the peace arrested individuals in their homes while declaring their crimes to their neighbors or kin.[71] Furthermore, enslaved and indigenous people witnessed court activities as litigants, witnesses, and accused criminals as magistrates, bailiffs, notaries, and legal representatives incorporated particular orders or mandates into legal proceedings.[72] Moreover, Africans and Andeans participated in or watched processions or other public events where they articulated their own locations within colonial hierarchies or observed others.[73] Other scholars will surely find new ways of comprehending how Africans and Andeans self-identified or understood themselves. Here, criminal and civil cases provide a framework to understand how Africans and Andeans (and their descendants) claimed and enacted casta within as well as beyond the colonial judiciary, making this book among the few employing legal records to explore how Africans became "blacks" and Andeans became "Indians."

The secular documentation that forms this evidentiary base presents two challenges. First, the criminal cases—and to a lesser extent the civil cases—that constitute the majority of the records available for the midcolonial period on the northern Peruvian coast focus primarily on the actions of men rather than women. In addition, enslaved men outnumbered enslaved women on rural estates where the labor of indigenous men was documented in terms of wages and required labor contribution. Indigenous men were often accompanied by their wives or female relatives, but women's work was assumed rather than discussed in civil or criminal cases as well as in notarized estate inventories. The challenge remains to articulate the perspectives of women, whose actions were often ignored in the official construction of casta distinctions that constitute the basis for this book. Future researchers may also wish to ask how gender distinctions influenced the ways that Andeans or African descendants, rural or urban inhabitants, criollos or Africans could employ casta categories.

Second, ecclesiastical documentation is lacking for the northern Peruvian coast. The holdings of the Archivo Arzobispal de Trujillo and the parish records for rural communities are scanty for the midcolonial period. Extirpation trials for the northern coast have been lost, leaving investigation of the records of Lima's Inquisitorial Tribunal housed in Madrid for other researchers. I have tried to compensate by incorporating the few records of religious and spiritual activity from a variety of archives (including the Jesuit archives in Rome) into the book. Nonetheless, without substantial ecclesiastical evidence that often documents the actions and beliefs of women, a women's history and a gender analysis of colonial casta will be left to future studies. Moreover, future researchers may wish to dig deeper into the type of access that rural enslaved people had to clerics and Catholic institutions to question my assertions regarding their lack of corporate standing.

Finally, I maintain an interest in how enslaved people created meanings from transatlantic casta categories such as *bran* (suggesting origins in Guinea-Bissau) and *arara* (pointing to origins along the Bight of Benin) to describe themselves and their communities in colonial Peru.[74] I built on the scholarship that has documented how the African origins of enslaved men and women in colonial Lima changed from Iberia to Senegambia and West Central Africa.[75] In this way I engaged with historians who have focused on specific cultural expressions such as how West Central Africans in Mexico or Cartagena articulated alternative forms of authority through divination, amulets, and other religious practices.[76] For the northern Peruvian coast, this approach—revealing continuities of religious, warfare, and kinship practices in the Americas—has proved challenging since the necessary ecclesiastical documentation has not survived for the seventeenth-century northern Peruvian coast.[77]

In contrast to following the articulations of one African casta, this book focuses on the multiple passages, the repeated market transactions, and the diversity of the African Diaspora populations in the region to illuminate multiple identities.[78] I integrate the discussion of diasporic casta in my consideration of colonial casta in order to reveal how Africans used overlapping identities rooted in particular African societies and experiences in the Americas to claim political, commercial, and social collectivities depending on particular historical circumstances.[79] Regardless of what they were called by slave traders or slaveholders, enslaved peoples' adaptations illustrate their employment of mutual languages or shared experiences of the slave trade to establish diasporic kinships that fit and did not fit within the colonial or slave trade assignations of casta. Still, there is much more to ask about how transatlantic castas, African Diaspora identities, and colonial castas worked or did not work together. Even more pertinent is asking how men and women employed these terms while they created and sustained kinship networks and communities in the Americas. I challenge myself and others to continue in the work of uncovering this African Diaspora past in the Andes.

1. Between Black and Indian

Labor Demands and the Crown's Casta

IN THE EARLY SEVENTEENTH CENTURY, Father Bernardino de Cárdenas lamented that indigenous people in the viceroyalty of Peru were treated as slaves. He warned that Spaniards forced "poor Indians" to work in the highland mines. Indians, declared the Franciscan, were free people and as such their labor should be compensated.[1] Implicitly, Cárdenas suggested a comparison with Africans and their descendants—as slaves—who were not paid. He echoed ongoing royal concerns with the exploitation of indigenous workers and repeated Spanish anxieties over the sustainability (perceived or actual) of indigenous labor. The cleric also recalled an episode of an African mistreating an indigenous leader (cacique). In Cárdenas's account, a priest arrived and ordered the "black slave" to "leave the Indian alone; realize that you are a slave, and the Indian [is] free." According to Cárdenas, the black replied that "he was a slave of one single master, but the Indian was a slave of all the whites and blacks" and therefore could be beaten and insulted—even by a black.[2]

Cárdenas's account employed a number of stereotypes that circulated throughout the Americas in the colonial period, including a defiant black, a pedantic cleric, and a pitiful Indian. He invoked these figures in a particular context. As he finished his account in 1632, colonial officials were renewing their efforts to collect revenues from indigenous populations, including migrant laborers, in response to fiscal pressures from the crown.[3] As Andean communities declined in numbers or refused to serve mita, colonizers wondered whether enslaved laborers or another form of indigenous labor would fulfill their demands. Given these circumstances, the exchange described by Cárdenas suggests a commentary on ongoing debates of whether black or indigenous labor would be suitable for the highland mines, as well as whether forced labor or wage labor was the most efficient or morally appropriate for the viceroyalty. By having compared Indian and enslaved labor, Cárdenas's account suggested how the enslavement of African laborers could be considered as equivalent in some senses with the requirement of mita labor service from Andean populations. At the same time, the Franciscan underlined a colonial maintenance of critical differences between blacks and Indians.

Cárdenas's usage points to royal intentions to separate Indians from blacks while conceding that both provided a similar type of labor. On one hand, official discourse contrasted the qualities of blacks and Indians to justify Spanish colonialism. If Indians were weak and miserable (meaning impoverished and lowly), then the crown was needed to provide protection from supposedly predatory colonizers and, hypothetically, dangerous black men. Colonial authorities emphasized what they perceived to be distinctions between "black" and "Indian" often to depict indigenous people as constantly under threat. By doing so, the crown could continue to promote itself as fulfilling its religious obligations to convert and to protect its "native vassals" while underplaying the fact that Spanish colonizers exploited indigenous laborers. The differences implied by separation, however, did not mean that Indians were incapable of the same labor as blacks. In particular moments of crisis when laborers were lacking during the seventeenth century, viceregal and regional authorities also considered the interchangeability of blacks and Indians, further illustrating the constructed nature of their differences. Those defending the continuation of the mita to Potosí in the early seventeenth century claimed that replacing Indians with black slaves would be too costly.[4] Others argued that blacks were unsuited to the altitude of the highland mining areas while Indians were more adept than blacks at producing silver.[5] Unquestionably, the cost of transporting enslaved people to the highland mines may in fact have been prohibitive, but Africans were certainly capable of adapting to the climate. The point is that even within clerical texts and colonial mandates, casta divisions and contrasts were mal-leable, especially when labor was in demand.

Throughout the viceroyalty, landholders and others eagerly appropriated Andeans and Africans as laborers no matter what their casta. In 1634, during a period of increasing disparity, mine owners called on the crown to favor their enterprises with more generous allocations of Indians to serve mita. Already, the landholders purchased black slaves to replace indigenous labor-ers lost as a result of exploitative working conditions.[6] After the 1640s, when the expansion of Spanish estates and the reduction of indigenous landhold-ings corresponded with the cessation of the legal slave trade into Spanish America, landholders, mine owners, and others demanded the labor of both blacks and Indians.[7] In the mid-seventeenth century the crown extorted more revenue, but indigenous refusal combined with the dramatic end in the crown-sanctioned slave trade heightened elite anxieties about the supply of labor and influenced the rhetorical construction of all laborers' casta.

Official discourse did not necessarily follow economic realities. For lo-cal authorities, as the crown-sanctioned slave trade within Spanish America surged in the late seventeenth century, a need for any laborer, coupled with the erosion of indigenous *reducciones*, lessened the distinctions made between castas. The repeated attempts to restructure the failing mita (including the reforms of the viceroy Duque de la Palata) only confirmed the perception that enslavement of black men and women was more necessary than before.[8] These shifting policies illustrate how casta categorization and expectations were remade and recast according to changing economic conditions and changing labor demands of the viceroyalty.

Only recently have scholars articulated how blacks were conceptualized in relation to Indians, but these treatments tended to focus on the abstract constructions of elite concerns.[9] Here, I explore official mandates in order to understand how the castas of Indian and black were articulated in rela-tion to each other. Moreover, this chapter grounds shifting administrative orders in relation to the end (in the 1640s) and then return (in the 1660s) of the official slave trade when both crown and viceregal officials consid-ered a perceived interchangeability of black and Indian laborers in Peru, thus undermining the specific differences between them that had previously been created. The distinctions between black and Indian, even in official discourse, would eventually dissolve, when the crown could no longer point to a geographically-contained indigenous population within assigned colo-nial towns in the late seventeenth century. Before examining how Andeans and Africans negotiated, contested, and utilized casta characteristics, this chapter explores how the crown, clerics, and local authorities contradicted and contested each other as they constructed the categories of Indian and black. By locating official articulations of black and Indian within colonizers' anxieties about labor, this chapter demonstrates how the discussions of casta categorization were rooted in shifting material realities and the contradictory discourses of a crown checked by colonizers' labor demands.

Protecting Indians

Since the sixteenth century, the Spanish crown had declared that native peoples of the Americas who agreed to be ruled would be protected from Spanish colonizers in the Americas, corrupt officials, and blacks as well as other people of mixed descent. In their capacity as Indians complying with crown mandates, indigenous people in the Andes paid tribute and provided labor by serving mita. In exchange, well into the seventeenth century the viceroy and the Real Audiencia in Peru continued to proclaim that indigenous laborers would be protected from Spanish colonizers, including mine owners and landholders.[10] The Real Audiencia also ordered owners of textile workshops, sugar mills, and mines to pay their indigenous workers a just jornal (a day's pay).[11] In one sense the requirement that labor be compensated with wages illustrated the crown's dedication to an ideal that vassals were free from unjust coercion, including indigenous people. In another sense the crown required payment of indigenous wages so that Indians could pay tribute, an essential royal revenue throughout the seventeenth century.[12] Protecting Indians was a means for the crown to protect a source of income while prohibitions against Indian slavery bolstered the crown's overall moral justification as custodian of indigenous people.

The language of enslaving indigenous people was entangled with the crown religious and legal commitment to defend its native vassals. Since the sixteenth century, the crown (with its viceroys) had attempted to revoke colonial enslavement of native people who resisted or in other ways earned the designation of "barbarous."[13] Royal jurists explained that indigenous people as vassals could not be named as or be assumed to have qualities of slaves.[14] In an invocation of royal mandates, fray Alonso Gravero of La Paz (in today's Bolivia) reminded the crown that the "poor natives" were innocent "Christian sheep" who should not be enslaved.[15] The moral mandate had practical consequences. In 1662, Peru's viceroy warned that the continued warfare and enslavement of indigenous Chileans would push them to revolt.[16] In 1669, Santiago's bishop informed the crown that because the local governor had forced indigenous men and women out of their communities to work on Spanish ranches, the Indians had taken up arms to free themselves.[17] These and other mandates warned that without virtuous colonial officials, the crown's mandates to protect Indians had gone unheeded. Indeed, the crown protections of indigenous communities in the central and southern Andes had been repeatedly violated by inspectors and other authorities marking a deterioration of royal authority by the mid-seventeenth century.[18]

The loose hold of colonial governance coincided with royal comparisons between Indians and blacks using the language of enslavement in the late seventeenth century. In 1681 the viceroy attempted to explain to the crown why indigenous people had abandoned their assigned colonial towns. He claimed that indigenous leaders (caciques) had enslaved Indians and forced them to work to such an extent that they had fled. Rather than examine the extreme pressures on indigenous communities of tribute and mita that could not be resolved, and keep the colonial treasury solvent, the viceroy's choice of language described slavery as being forced to work without pay, day and night.[19] The same year, the crown had disapprovingly reported that Indians were treated worse than slaves on estates.[20] The royal concerns with the repressive treatment of Indians were reiterated on Peru's northern coast. In the required investigation of Trujillo magistrate's retirement in 1672, witnesses were asked if the colonial officials had treated Indians "as if in slavery," including executing public physical punishments or placing them in the stocks.[21] In the same period, a Dominican observed that Indians had become "perpetual slaves of the magistrates."[22] Andeans, however, had not become enslaved in the seventeenth century. Instead, many indigenous communities, particularly those subjected to the Potosí mita, had reached a crisis point in the late seventeenth century as the exactions of magistrates from rural Andeans became more excessive.[23] Colonial authorities expressed the nature of these payments as forms of local slavery in ways that played down the ongoing demands of a colonial government that required more revenue due to Spain's ongoing debt and fiscal crisis.

A repetitive language about Indian enslavement contrasts with a silence regarding the experiences of enslaved African and African-descent people, who regularly endured violent punishment and were uncompensated for their labor. The implicit suggestion was that while blacks were expected to suffer the conditions of slavery, Indians were not. For clerics, blacks became a standard image to argue for increased protection of Indians. The Franciscan Bernardino de Cárdenas suggested that Indians were more ignorant of Catholic doctrine than slaves.[24] Likewise, Santiago's bishop complained that Indians were being taken from their parishes and forced to continuously work "like black slaves" to suggest a correlation between lack of clerical supervision and labor demands.[25] The clerics even suggested that Indians were in worse positions than enslaved blacks. Santiago's bishop explained that once removed from their parishes, Indians had no one to take care of them. In contrast, he explained, owners fed, attended to illnesses, and buried slaves in order to protect their property.[26] By speaking of slavery but not enslaved Africans, the clerical discourse suggested that black slaves were better off than indigenous people.

Cárdenas suggested that Indians were enslaved to everyone.[27] For clerics, these statements bolstered their case that further evangelization of indigenous people was necessary. In most parts of the Andes, indigenous people were assigned to dedicated parishes and specific clerics. In contrast, enslaved men and women in urban areas were to attend the general, Cathedral parishes and in the rural areas make do with itinerant clerics. The Catholic practices of Africans and their descendants (or even their lack) were not in discussion. Instead, colonial authorities and Catholic clerics employed blacks as discursive objects to construct their relationship with Indians and justify an expansion of their positions even during various fiscal crises of the seventeenth century.

The crown also was charged with a religious obligation of evangelizing native people of the Americas that in many ways supported colonial economic goals. Falling within this moral parameter, the crown was to provide "good treatment" to Indians who, although they were "free vassals," were supposedly too facile for self-governance.[28] For the judge (oidor) of the Real Audiencia of Lima, Spanish rule and even work demands would liberate "miserable" (or vulnerable) and "naturally lazy Indians" from their condition.[29] In the Andes crown officials echoed the Consejo de Indias's declaration that Indians, "pusillanimous by nature," lived in a "wretched" or "miserable" state that made them susceptible to a variety of exploiters.[30] By depicting indigenous people as Indians who were unable to defend their communities from "predators" who demanded their work, the legal discourse allowed that colonizers would continue to exploit indigenous laborers and created an indispensable role for colonial officials even as they were increasingly unable to deliver coveted indigenous mitayos and, by the 1640s, captive blacks through the official slave trade to Peru. In many ways royal and viceregal officials abdicated their responsibility by allowing Spanish colonizers to claim all sorts of labor from indigenous vassals, but by constructing Indians as needing oversight, the crown justified royal rule.

In an effort to bolster their roles as protectors of Indians, the crown and its officials constructed forces that threatened indigenous people. Those described as preying on indigenous people (in official discourse) therefore should be understood as part of the authorities' construction of their own status. In crown orders to protect Indians, the devil played a primary role, as did pirates, Jews, and Protestants.[31] The crown also pointed to the danger of Spanish colonizers, including mestizo intermediaries who preyed on Indians.[32] Likewise, crown authorities portrayed Africans and their descendants as dangerous to indigenous communities and disruptive to the social harmony of colonial Spanish society. Secular and ecclesiastical officials repeatedly shared their concerns with protecting Indians from blacks. In 1609 the crown ordered the viceroy of Peru to settle the large numbers of "*mulatos, zambiagos* [African and indigenous-descent men], free blacks and mestizos" into Spanish towns, away from Andean reducciones.[33]

In part, the motivation was financial. By confining free people of color to urban areas, the crown hoped to be able to collect tribute as they did from indigenous communities. The viceroy resisted, pointing to the enormity of the task, but agreed that the multitudes of free mulatos, blacks, and zambiagos needed to be contained, because otherwise they would enter the Indian towns and do more harm.[34] In the meantime, Andeans were also mixing with Africans and their descendants by migrating to urban and mining centers as well as to estates in search of wage work.[35] Therefore, in addition to providing evidence that many types of people moved throughout the viceroyalty, the repetition of orders to separate blacks from Indians evinces that secular and ecclesiastical officials constructed a danger for their own purposes, instead of being a danger truly faced by Andean people.

The constructed nature of Indian-black hostility was more visible in official language when contrasted with local realities. In 1607, Trujillo's magistrate executed a mandated inspection of cattle ranches, sugar mills, and indigenous towns (including other crossroad settlements) in the nearby Chicama valley on the northern Peruvian coast. According to the crown, local officials were required to ensure that indigenous laborers were paid and did not grind sugar cane or boil juice into sugar.[36] Royal authorities had deemed this work to be too dangerous for indigenous laborers.[37] Based on the royal concerns of protecting indigenous people, the questions in the inquiry focused on whether Indians worked in sugar fields or mills or "anything else that was dangerous" and were paid.[38] The investigation implicitly compared Indians with black laborers who were not paid, worked long hours, and suffered the dangers of laboring in the sugar mills. The scripted inspection document included questions for indigenous laborers, and their formulaic responses, regarding whether blacks and overseers seized horses or chickens without paying.[39]

Most of the witnesses explained that they had been compensated and did not mention any type of harassment. Given that indigenous laborers provided their testimony in front of an estate owner or overseer, their responses were not surprising. Indicative that Indian-black hostility was assumed by colonial officials but not experienced, indigenous witnesses from Paiján explained that *yanaconas* (hired indigenous laborers) on the local estate planted nearby fields but did not help in cleaning the irrigation canals.[40] As Indians on a reducción, their conflicts were more likely with indigenous laborers from nearby estates than with enslaved Africans. The indigenous laborers on the Morales Tinoco vineyard were more explicit when questioned by the colonial official, explaining that they had not been "aggravated by any Spaniard or black."[41] The absence of complaints against Africans and their descendants by indigenous people points to a sharp contrast between official expectations of hostility and lived experiences of mutual coexistence.

Indigenous accusations that surfaced against Africans were part of a larger strategy to obtain relief from local landholders or to secure justice from colonial officials. During the same inspection tour, one complaint emerged against an African-descent person. Three resident indigenous laborers (yanaconas) on the sugar estate of Facalá explained that the black foreman, Manuel, had mistreated them, made them work in fields without providing a place for their gardens, and neglected attending to their illnesses.[42] They also complained that the owner of the estate had not paid them, so that they in turn had been unable to pay their required tribute. In addition, the yanaconas protested that the mules from the estate had eaten their crops and they had not been paid for the damage. If Manuel had been abusive or negligent, the yanaconas made clear that his owner was equally so. In many ways these grievances indicate how Facalá's indigenous laborers seized on the opportunity of a colonial inspection to file their complaints regarding their treatment on the estate that had very little to do with their relations or treatment by "blacks" but more to do with Spaniards.

The official rhetoric may have provided an opening, but their responses to the questions indicate that Facalá's indigenous laborers faced a severe crisis. They had been unable to secure justice from the most immediate authorities and without cash or crops, they faced debt and hunger. Like many other Andeans in the early seventeenth century, Facalá's indigenous laborers had left their reducción, joined the labor market, and in some cases suffered the economic consequences. Nonetheless, in this instance they could call on their juridical status as Indians and insert themselves into the crown's concern for its indigenous vassals. Even when they reported how slaves from the sugar mill had taken their corn, the indigenous laborers blamed the Spanish overseer who had allowed and then not righted the injustice. Facalá's indigenous laborers employed the mandated inspection tour to present their complaint to a colonial official that had been ignored by local authorities. In other words, they employed an available judicial avenue to achieve resolution for a local problem. Rather than an affirmation that blacks preyed on Indians, as suggested by the questions of the official inspection, the rare testimony of Facala's indigenous laborers provides evidence that the crown's construction of black aggression toward Indians was a potent official discourse that did not necessarily reflect reality.

Labor Demands, Labor Distinctions

Calls for particular types of laborers were connected to political or economic strategies or circumstances. When faced with the resistance of Andean laborers or their demographic decline, royal authorities issued declarations about replacing indigenous laborers with black slaves. By the early seventeenth century, Africans and their descendants were not intended to only complement indigenous laborers. In a compilation of royal jurisprudence, an official chronicler of the crown (Antonio de Herrera) and an influential jurist (Juan de Solórzano Pereira) suggested that black slaves could replace the diminishing number of Indians.[43] Likewise, in 1615, Peru's viceroy proposed that blacks could make up for the lack of Indians.[44] As indigenous labor became less available, Indians were no longer understood as indispensable.[45]

As previously noted, Peru's viceroy acknowledged a royal order prohibiting Indians from laboring in textile workshops (obrajes) or sugar mills due to demanding and unhealthy work conditions.[46] (These suggestions were intended to apply throughout the Andes, including sugar cultivation in Quito and gold mining in Popayán.)[47] The implication was that slaves would take the place of indigenous Andeans, as contemporary mandates suggested that blacks, not Indians, should work in sugar or gold production.[48] In one sense these propositions point to the perceived desperation of colonizers (and colonial authorities) to secure laborers for mines, estates, and other enterprises.[49] In another sense they suggest a notion that indigenous and black laborers were mutually replaceable. At the official level, when labor was in demand, casta distinctions did not matter.

The characteristics of a desired labor force were regularly recast. For example, the abrupt end of the official transatlantic slave trade heightened the equation of Indian with black labor in Peru. After the Spanish crown ended its slave-trading contract with Portuguese transatlantic merchants, royal authorities in Lima reported that the official importation of African captives had ceased into the Peruvian Pacific.[50] Contraband trade probably continued as Trujillo's slaveholders purchased captive West Central Africans from

Panamanian merchants but in much fewer numbers.[51] Nonetheless, colonial officials from Panama to Lima identified a crisis throughout the 1640s due to the perceived (or promoted) lack of captive or enslaved blacks.[52] In 1646 the viceroy warned that without blacks the work on rural estates as well as the local production of foodstuffs and goods would stop.[53] A serious threat, these staples fueled the mining economy that was still producing valuable revenue for a crown with an increasingly depleted treasury.[54] The rhetoric of a labor crisis was compounded with the implementation of a census, completed in 1645, proving what many had already known: that indigenous people throughout the Andes had experienced a radical demographic decline and many had become migrants from their assigned communities.[55] Whether promoting the slave trade or shoring up the crown's position to protect the Indians, by declaring an inability to produce or profit without black slaves, colonial authorities warned that indigenous people would soon cease to be a viable labor source.

For colonial authorities the perceived need and the diminishing number of laborers, both Indian and black, continued into the seventeenth century. In 1648 a retiring viceroy observed that the kingdom lacked blacks and that the task of preserving indigenous populations continued to pose a challenge.[56] In 1650 the next viceroy reminded the crown that Indians had been unable to provide the required mita labor because of a decline in the populations of indigenous communities, just as eight years without the importation of blacks from the transatlantic slave trade had left local estates with half of their enslaved labor force.[57] In a 1657 petition to resume the official slave trade, it was observed that Indians could not provide all of the necessary labor.[58] By 1705 the bishop of Quito and interim viceroy observed that there was a need for black slaves because Spaniards would not perform manual labor, and there were very few Indians left to work in the coastal valleys.[59] Colonial mandates and clerical declarations that made such clear distinctions between blacks and Indians became scarcer as labor demands increased.

Simultaneously, differences between Indians and blacks often highlighted complicated debates over labor. In 1640 fray Francisco de la Cruz argued that it was a financial liability to have enslaved blacks in the highland mines. According to the cleric, Indians were more useful in cold climates while blacks were most productive in hot lands doing agrarian work.[60] In 1669 the Chilean bishop underscored the perceived climatic distinctions that structured racial differences by explaining that the frigid temperatures and cold rain showers of the highlands were prohibitive to blacks in comparison to Indians.[61] In both cases the clerics explained how Indians should be protected by a reform of the labor demands, as many debates surged throughout the seventeenth century between landholders and mine owners over claims to indigenous labor forces given the high costs of importing slaves especially to the interior of the southern Andes.[62]

One reason, however, to emphasize these climatic distinctions between blacks and Indians was to capitalize on the perceived profitability of either group as laborers. If clerics, chroniclers, and other colonizers pointed to the inability for blacks (with supposed origins in tropical climates) to work in the cold mining regions such as Potosí, it could also be because trading large numbers of captives through Río de la Plata to the Andean highlands was not profitable.[63] Rather than protect indigenous people from the overexploitation of their labor, those who made the argument for climatic distinctions between Indians and blacks were implicitly urging the crown to deploy laborers where they thought they would be of the most value.

Laborers of any casta were essential to colonial profits. Regardless of metropolitan orders that distinguished blacks from Indians, colonizers and colonial authorities could also collapse the two as necessary laborers.[64] Illustrating how labor demands influenced the malleability of casta constructions, regional authorities and crown officials came to disparate conclusions regarding the midcentury labor crisis. In 1654 local authorities complained to Trujillo's magistrate that for the last ten years there had been a tremendous lack of (enslaved) blacks to work in local fields. They feared that the disparity of labor would continue indefinitely. Their solution was to demand that the magistrate bring Indians on a reinvigorated mita from the more distant northern valleys surrounding Chiclayo and the highland region of Cajamarca.[65] (They were not alone as there were ongoing attempts in the 1650s to revive the mita to Potosí.)[66] From the perspective of regional landholders on Peru's northern coast, Indians serving mita could solve the labor crisis created by the precipitous decline in the importation of black captives. In response to the same problem, the crown argued the opposite and suggested in 1650 that colonial authorities replace the required Indian mita with what it presumed were large numbers of blacks and mulatos from the valleys surrounding the viceregal capital of Lima.[67]

The communication delay between Peru and Spain, in part, explained the crown's mistaken understanding that enslaved men and women were still being sold as captives from the transatlantic and Pacific slave trade into Lima and its surrounding environs. As regional authorities corrected the crown's misinformation, the assumption that Africans and their descendants could replace Indians serving mita—or vice versa—underlines both a metropolitan and a viceregal perception that regardless of origin or casta, blacks and Indians had the same labor abilities.

When colonial authorities or colonizers differentiated between blacks and Indians as laborers, they did so for strategic reasons. A Cartagena councilman (*regidor*) in 1643 stressed the physical superiority of blacks in comparison to the nature of "miserable" Indians. Cartagena and what is today the Colombian Caribbean coast along with the Panamanian isthmus served as a conduit of information, merchandise, and people between the viceroyalty of Peru, including its capital of Lima, and the Atlantic world including Spain. His comparison had a context. The Cartagena councilman was attempting to persuade the Consejo de Indias to allow transatlantic merchants (such as the Portuguese) to resume their trade in captives. Therefore, the regional official argued that African slaves were necessary to the prosperity of the Spanish colonies because they were "naturally so robust and strong."[68] Another Cartagena official likewise suggested that "Indians were not capable of so much work" in comparison to blacks.[69] As beneficiaries of the slave trade, these representatives of an official Spanish American slave port brought attention to alleged physical differences as part of a strategy to reinvigorate the profitable commerce in black captives. Like slave merchants, they were highly invested in emphasizing the value of imported captives as another claimed that one black was worth three Indians.[70] These ideas, including the value of blacks versus Indians, could be animated at particular moments such as in the interest of resuming the official slave trade when Cartagena officials constructed black men as stronger than indigenous men.

Regional authorities as well as local landholders and mine owners during this period tactically constructed stark differences between blacks and Indians. In 1647 the magistrate in the silver mining town of Potosí explained that blacks were required for agrarian work because Indians were needed for mining.[71] Rather than articulating a fixed distinction, the regional authority named this differentiation as part of a petition to restart the official slave trade into the Peruvian viceroyalty. According to the magistrate, for years landholders had demanded more black slaves. Without the importation of captives sold from transatlantic merchants to agents and others in Río de la Plata, both landholders and mine owners were turning to an increasingly unwilling and diminishing indigenous population.

Landholders, mine owners, and other colonial property holders were also coming into competition with each other. It is also possible that enslaved men equaled more laboring hours, since indigenous men could return to their communities or seek out wage labor opportunities that were more lucrative than the colonial mita.[72] Suggesting the value of enslaved laborers, an anonymous chronicler of Peru declared that "blacks [were] stronger than Spaniards" and always performed the heavy work.[73] In contrast, the seventeenth-century observer claimed that Spanish men were always idle, indicating that rather than physical strength, the distinction was between enslaved men who were forced to work hard and lower-status Spanish migrants who avoided manual labor. Those who were dependent on enslaved labor presented enslaved men as stronger and more necessary because blacks were increasingly conceptualized as the desired laborers.[74] Thus when faced with a reluctant indigenous labor force, whoever required workers emphasized the strong, robust labor of an African slave to argue for who should be made more available to Spanish colonizers.

Indians occupied a more distinct legal designation than blacks. Some scholars have argued these differences were sociopolitical while others have elaborated on a Spanish understanding of blood and lineage.[75] The evocations of distinctions and similarities between black and Indian regardless illustrate the malleability of colonial casta constructions, even at an official level. Colonial authorities could evoke, exaggerate, or ignore differences of Africans and Andeans according to particular economic realities or political situations. In the mid-seventeenth century, when a decline in required indigenous labor coincided with a decline in the official slave trade, viceregal authorities challenged the differentiation of black and Indian labor promoted by crown officials. When necessary, regional authorities promoted their need for black labor then changed to demand Indian labor. At the same time, the perceived contrast between the categories of black and Indian was central to colonial decisions regarding enslavement and labor exploitation. The labor system did not affix perceptions of distinctions between black and Indian. Instead, the shifting deployment of these casta characteristics illuminates how economic profit underlay their cultural constructions. Labor demands dictated how casta distinctions were articulated, especially in periods when colonizers perceived a labor crisis. Equally intriguing, the multiple contrasts of Indian versus black labor illustrate the contradictory and changing nature of casta construction—even among authorities.

Dissolving Distinctions

In the later seventeenth century, the Spanish crown adjusted to a shifting labor landscape in the Peruvian viceroyalty. By the 1660s it renegotiated official slave trade licenses, increasing the number of captives sold into Peruvian markets. Also, royal authorities at this time were at least addressing the fact that indigenous people were not staying in assigned Indian towns but exchanging their labor for wages, land, and other resources throughout the Andes. Without as many Andeans following the regulations of the colonial reducciones, it became more difficult for the crown to claim that

it protected Indians. Unable to construct Indians according to official specifications, royal authorities were less likely to construct a binary between
so-called fragile Indians and hypothetically dangerous blacks. As a result of
the changing availability of laborers and the explicit nature of wage labor
arrangements in the viceroyalty, the crown shifted its discourse regarding
casta categorization.

In the 1680s Viceroy Duque de Palata addressed the causes of what he
(and other officials) perceived as Indian misery as well as reasons for the
disastrous fiscal state of the viceroyalty. He identified the onerous mita as
one reason for indigenous migration from colonial Indian towns. Rather
than eliminate the labor draft, though, he attempted to expand its scope
to include indigenous members living apart from their assigned communities.[76] As part of these changes, intent on protecting a necessary labor force,
the viceroy accused clerics of usurping property from their indigenous parishioners.[77] The viceroy's reforms failed, but he was not alone as others repeated these official concerns with the "wretched" and "miserable" Indians
who fled from any form of work.[78] Viceregal reformist attempts point to
an ongoing royal characterization of "Indians" as subjects to be pitied and
protected, characteristics that Andeans could continue to call on throughout
the seventeenth century.

Indigenous communities changed ahead of colonial regulations. After
the 1690s the crown and viceregal authorities understood that protection
of Indians within their colonial towns was no longer viable. Some officials
continued to explain that the disappearance of Indians was because of their
bad treatment by mestizos, blacks, and mulatos or other external attacks on
the Republic of the Indians.[79] Colonial demands, however, had pushed indigenous people from the Indian towns—settlements that had not contained
Andean populations even in the sixteenth century.[80] Andeans migrated away
from their assigned reducciones, found work in cities and landed estates,
created vibrant local and regional markets, and otherwise survived the impositions of colonial demands.[81] To some extent, royal mandates recognized
these Andean actions. New regulations involving migrants (forasteros) with
or without land, laborers (yanaconas) on Spanish estates, and tribute-payers
living in urban neighborhoods became more explicit in the late seventeenth
and early eighteenth centuries.[82]

In some senses the crown had absorbed the implications that Indians
could no longer be defined as those attached to their assigned towns. Nonetheless, the crown and the church continued to construct and reconstruct
Indians as weak and miserable. In other words, historical interpretations of
the wealth produced by Indian labor—as well as the ability of Andeans to

find alternative markets for their labor and to take advantage of the colonial markets—did not change the crown's depiction of Indians as incompetent and susceptible. Royal mandates, then, perpetuated a representation of Indians that held up the crown's vision of its native subjects necessary to its own definitions of what constituted just and paternalistic rule.[83]

By the later decades of the seventeenth century, crown and viceregal officials associated a demise of Indian protection with the rising intervention of non-Indians. The king noted that indigenous towns were vulnerable to some Spaniards who lived among Indians and stole from them, causing indigenous people to flee from their colonial settlements.[84] Royal inspectors also observed that blacks, mulatos, and mestizos were allowed by those Spaniards to steal from indigenous villagers.[85] The royal mandates reflected trade and exchange among Andeans and Spaniards (and probably others) that in some senses was profitable for all sides.[86] The crown also correctly perceived that landholders who usurped communal land, ranchers who allowed their cattle to destroy irrigation canals, and magistrates who sold wine at high prices or in exchange for formidable debt, harmed Indians.[87] Unable (and perhaps more unwilling) to address the detrimental economic effects of colonization, the crown focused its condemnation on the infiltration of outsiders to the Republic of Indians.[88] While the crown did or did not address the causes for the erosion of the idealized Republic of the Indians, indigenous people were, in fact, in the process of constructing and deconstructing the boundaries of their assigned casta of "Indian."

During the seventeenth century, when some Andeans refused to meet the official requirements expected of Indians, other viceregal representatives attempted to fit Africans and their descendants within a model of the republics. The crown instituted tribute collection from free blacks and mulatos that recognized how urban people of color had an obligation to their rulers much like that of indigenous people who were unattached or separated from their assigned colonial towns.[89] In another rendition, in exchange for their service as subjects, Viceroy Conde de Chinchón suggested that the crown provide a *protector* (an appointed legal advocate) for enslaved blacks "similar to the one of the Indians."[90] According to him, if treated well, blacks like Indians had the potential to be humble and pious. Later, in 1681, the crown equated the free status of Indians with those of *pardos* (free blacks) and *cuarterones* (men of hypothetically one-quarter African descent). The crown cited an earlier order that prohibited the personal service of Indians and equated their situation to that of enslaved pardos and cuarterones who, as vassals, deserved "good treatment" rather than the "wretchedness" that faced "poor people."[91] Thus all the destitute deserved mercy regardless of their casta categorization. According to the ideal vision of the realm, the crown (with the church) communicated that in particular cases African descendants could successfully serve as loyal vassals to protective lords. As the fiction of Indians as a protected group dissipated, the need to define blacks in one particular manner—the one that constructed them as dangerous to vulnerable Indians—also dissolved.

Clerics, likewise, continued to collapse the constructed differences between Indians and blacks. The 1677 archdiocese meeting condemned Spaniards and many mestizos who did not allow blacks, slaves, and Indians on their haciendas to attend Mass on Sundays and holidays or to learn Christian doctrine.[92] Rather than distinguish between blacks and Indians, clerics saw all of these laborers as equally suffering from a lack of access to Catholic practice. Ecclesiastical authorities also defended the ability of both blacks and Indians to be married in the Catholic church.[93] Throughout the seventeenth century, clerics continued to promote Indians and blacks as deserving evangelization. In their annual letter from the late 1670s, the Jesuit provincial in Peru described Indians and blacks as neophytes and "humble people" who presumably deserved their missionizing efforts.[94] The Jesuits arranged religious instruction around the time of laborers' availability, conducting doctrinal classes for both Indians and blacks at night.[95] From the clerical perspective, blacks and Indians were equally deserving of evangelization and the means to meet their Catholic obligations.

In early eighteenth-century Peru, colonial officials focused on containing, not comparing, Indians and blacks (as well as their descendants). The crown required in 1725 that all blacks, mulatos, Indians, and mestizos wear more moderate clothing. Clothing had the potential to create chaos. According to the royal mandate, inhabitants of colonial Lima were driven to rob to maintain their "scandalous excess of clothing."[96] Increased thefts at public fiestas may have been troublesome, but the inappropriate dress of the people of the "lower sphere" implied a greater public disorder. Clothing, hats, facial hair, and other public indicators marked the status of colonial inhabitants, with officials and landholders wearing imported silks and buckled shoes as opposed to the coarse cloth and open-toed sandals of indigenous laborers or the bare feet of slaves.[97] More than the question of labor, the crown was more likely to agree with colonial authorities that those who disrupted social hierarchies should be punished.

As crown and viceregal authorities issued fewer stark comparisons of Indians and blacks, they articulated more concerns with control of all people of color. In 1661, Lima's Real Audiencia prohibited mulatos, free blacks, slaves, zambos (men of indigenous and African descent), and Indians from carrying weapons.[98] The decree (and others) really exposes rivalries among governing officials who armed their servants and slaves in displays of power and prestige.[99] At the same time, the attempted ban also suggests how colonial authorities flattened distinctions among indigenous and African people. In this scenario, just as Indians like blacks could be laborers in any location, all could contribute to colonial disorder. Nonetheless, viceregal authorities focused on blacks as a more likely cause for disorder. The Peruvian viceroy complained that nightlong mourning gatherings of blacks quickly became drunken gatherings "against the laws of these kingdoms."[100]

The distinctions between Indians and blacks in official colonial discourse, however, did not disappear at the end of the seventeenth century. Crown and viceregal authorities as well as clerics continued to call attention to the protections afforded to Indians, wherever their locations and the dangers were constructed as posed by blacks, enslaved or free. Nonetheless, the colonial construction of fragile Indians to be defended against supposedly predatory blacks was not as effective if Andeans refused to be contained by their assigned locations. Royal and viceregal expectations of Indians as miserable people who required protection still circulated and could be employed by Andeans. At the same time, shifts in the seventeenth-century labor market changed how royal and viceregal officials constructed the castas of Indian and black. If all laborers were in demand, then divisions between them dissolved.

The meanings of casta were constructed on an unstable axis between the categories of Indian and black throughout the seventeenth century. In one instance Indians could be a protected group against what colonial authorities constructed as dangerous blacks, while in another they were called upon as able-bodied laborers designated to work with anyone. Crown and viceregal officials highlighted, juxtaposed, interchanged, and ignored distinctions between blacks and Indians depending on specific material realities, including the rise and fall of the transatlantic slave trade. The constructions of casta were therefore not solely cultural but material. Economic and political circumstances did not fix the meanings of Indian and black, however. Instead, the effects of slave markets, crown interests in Indians as revenue, and colonial labor demands served to destabilize casta construction, in addition to ideological expectations throughout the seventeenth century.

According to royal mandates, indigenous people were free subjects who could claim subjecthood within their assigned colonial towns. Colonizers could not enslave Indians who were vassals of the crown.[101] In contrast, the crown attempted to shield enslaved blacks from excessive abuse but did not include them in the majority of laws regarding royal subjecthood. Clearly, Africans and their descendants asserted their status as Catholic vassals to claim protections from abusive slave owners as well as insert themselves into a colonial body politic.[102] Free men of color would also claim their rights to collect commissions, wear officer uniforms, court immunity, and other privileges within militias to articulate as a "republic."[103] Moreover, royal mandates continued to change and sometimes contradict clerical intentions into the early eighteenth century. Previous orders to control blacks overlapped with new, ambiguous instructions regarding their vassalage to make crown rulings full of authority but fragmentary. Enslaved and free agency, however, did not significantly alter how royal and viceregal authorities constructed Africans and their descendants as critical laborers or contributors to colonial disorder. Rarely were blacks constructed as corporate vassals.

Casta categorization, as articulated through overlapping and in some cases clashing orders, reflected and constructed colonial expectations of colonial peoples. Royal mandates regarding African and indigenous people articulated casta as a series of projected characterizations. The Spanish crown and its representatives reproduced discourses that divided colonial inhabitants into protected versus predatory status as well as dictated possibilities of permanent or temporary incorporation into colonial society. Royal jurists, ecclesiastical authorities, and colonial officials justified crown rule by comparing Indians—who supposedly required protection—with blacks who were deemed dangerous to colonial order. When employed by royal and viceregal authorities, casta mandates expressed anxieties about colonial rule and assessments of the profitability of the viceroyalties of the Americas but not necessarily the identities or the categories employed by enslaved and indigenous people in everyday exchanges. For these questions, chapters 2 and 3 turn to the ways in which Andeans and Africans on the northern Peruvian coast engaged with official mandates to construct their own differences.

2. Working Slavery's Value, Making Diaspora Kinships

THE APPLICATION OF ROYAL MANDATES varied according to economic and political circumstances. As mentioned previously, however, enslaved Africans and their descendants could claim limited protections from abusive owners, were able to be married and baptized as Catholics, and participated in a customary practice of purchasing their freedom.[1] Africans who had been sold into the transatlantic slave trade, however, mostly were unaware of these colonial laws but had widely been exposed to an alternative logic. By subjecting men and women to inadequate shelter, food, and water as well as imprisonment in dark and stifling jails of the slave castles or the barren and filthy enclosures of the slave pens, merchants and traders along the West and West Central African coasts had communicated that enslaved Africans were anonymous prisoners.[2] Shackled and confined on slave ships, captives may have understood that they had been cursed, fallen victim to warfare and greedy rulers who had sold them to the Americas (or Europe) to work for white people or their assistants.[3]

The violence of the crew, the severe displacement, the tight quarters, the high mortality rates, and the inability of captives to respond with appropriate funerary rites for their dead conveyed clearly that captive Africans had left one status for another.[4] Whichever port the survivors entered, a market rationale was evident. In the case of colonial Peru, the stark nature of the royal agents' records from the Caribbean port of Cartagena reflected commodification of captive men and women. By the 1660s the term "piece" had come to mean a unified standard of an adult male between the age of twenty and twenty-five with the height of "a yard [plus] three quarters high."[5] Recently arrived captives and rural or provincial enslaved people struggled to claim legal protections afforded to blacks in the Spanish Americas and were left with the forces of the market.

Scholars of slavery in Latin America have grappled with locating captive and enslaved Africans and their descendants as both objects of property and subjects of a Catholic crown. For the historian Herman Bennett, although "civil law sanctioned the master's dominion over chattel," an emphasis on enslaved private lives—especially as expressed through their positions as Catholic persons under canon law—revealed that Africans were not merely property, workers, and objects but lovers, family, and friends.[6] Unquestionably, enslaved and free people relied on Catholic family structures to create and re-create networks and communities in the Americas. Enslaved men and women also employed their value within the market to protect themselves and develop new kinships in the Americas. Galvanized by the research of historians Ariela Gross and Walter Johnson, I suggest that captive and enslaved Africans (with their descendants) engaged in the acts that made them into property—in the courtroom and in the market place. By performing their commodification at the moments of sale, enslaved people took on the paradox of their locations and in some cases gained a chance to subvert the outcome.[7] Undoubtedly, the laws of nineteenth-century United States fixed African Americans in racial locations unlike the multiple castas that circulated in seventeenth-century Spanish America. The slave markets in the nineteenth-century United States did not include the large numbers of West Central Africans and West Africans who were sold (legally and illegally) into the viceroyalty of Peru of the seventeenth century.[8] Nonetheless, in both contexts merchants and agents purchased and sold captives. In both circumstances, enslaved men and women developed a keen sense of how slave traders marketed them and learned to leverage their value.

Little to no access to secular courts combined with the deadening forces of the market demanded that that Africans and their descendants immediately develop and sustain kinships. Indubitably, men and women sold to the northern Peruvian coast chose partners from the same African origins and established African Diaspora religious communities with firm roots in West Central African or Yoruba practices.[9] Detecting transfers of specific religious beliefs or social practices, however, has proven difficult in the Trujillo region, where ecclesiastical documentation such as marriage petitions for the seventeenth century is scarce and Africans from certain broad regions such as the Gold Coast (called mina) or Angola rarely constituted more than 25 percent of the total enslaved population for more than a few generations.[10] Even those from such regions as the Bight of Benin (including people who were called and called themselves arara) and Kongo with substantial percentages over a number of decades would develop forms of kinships that did not entail choosing marriage partners or godparents from the same African region of their origin.[11]

Rather than separate the experiences of the market from those of kinship, this chapter attempts to understand how one created the other. The multiple market transactions or sales of captives that occurred from the Atlantic to the Pacific coast allowed multiple opportunities for enslaved men and women to develop new kinship connections. Many Africans did not express "coherent cultural groupings that shared much in common—language, kinship, religion"—given the multiple passages that captives were forced to traverse from the Atlantic African coast to the Peruvian Pacific coast.[12] Kinship, in other words, was not a given, but had to be created in the diasporic setting, as this chapter complicates an assumption that common origins predisposed communities of Africans from particular culture zones.[13] It appears more likely that captive and enslaved Africans articulated multiple identities that shifted according to context and even challenged the colonial or slave trade assignations of casta or nación.[14] Adaptation would prove critical. Newly arrived Africans had to quickly form affinities in order to feed themselves, find shelter and clothing, as well as secure better work assignments on sugar estates, wheat farms, and cattle ranches of the northern Peruvian valleys. Men and women called arara (the Bight of Benin) or mina (the Gold Coast) built on their shared languages to create immediate shipmate kinships and to act on compañero ("comrade" or "companion") affinities with particular individuals.[15] In the longer term, enslaved Africans developed new types of relationships or continued old kinships in novel forms within the diasporic environment of people coming together from multiple origins.

Even with protective legislation in Spanish America, captive and enslaved people could be dismissed from a colonial body politic that was based on membership in corporate entities. In addition, according to Spanish official discourse, "blackness" communicated a lack of innate allegiance that was a requirement for vassalage and subjecthood in Spanish America.[16] Enslaved men and women, especially recently arrived Africans, may have correctly read that there was very little privilege for them to claim within Spanish American law. At the same time, the protection of slaveholders' claims to slaves communicated that enslaved people had value as property, allowing a few captive and enslaved people to employ their unique locations against the flattening tendency of the slave trade's commodification. In a more sustainable adaptation, captive and enslaved people expressed kinships that emerged from their experiences within the slave trade.[17] Apart from legal protections or their market values, affinities built from the violence of multiple market transactions, multiple sales, and multiple slave trades and labor demands would prove critical to how enslaved men and women expressed their collectivities. These affinities would prove all the more valuable if newly arrived rural captives had limited access to judicial mechanisms. Furthermore, in both realms—market and kinship—the lived experiences illustrate how men and women of the African Diaspora created collectivities according to their own standards and at the margins of secular and ecclesiastical imperatives of colonizers.

Market Value in Multiple Passages

Men, women, and children who were enslaved in colonial Peru during the seventeenth century had experienced an exceptionally prolonged journey to their final destinations. Unquestionably, the distance between the Atlantic African coast and Peru, the rough passage between the Caribbean and the Pacific, and the time the voyages took increased the mortality rates of captives. Some, however, also employed their value during multiple points of sale or commercial transactions to survive these many passages. The lengthy and violent journey, in some cases taking years, allowed survivors to develop more abilities to communicate with each other and even their captors.[18] Witnessing repeated market transactions could have also exposed captives to currencies and values of the slave trade.[19] In all cases the repeated transactions, distinct configurations of companions, and numerous voyages shaped how enslaved people could assess and in some cases employ their worth as propertied persons.

The lengthy journey began even before captives left the Atlantic African coast. If they were sold from Guinea-Bissau (those called *bran, balanta,* or *folupa,* for example) in the early seventeenth century, then they most likely had been raided or taken in warfare, traded to Luso-African intermediaries, and sold to Cape Verdean traders and eventually Portuguese merchants.[20] If they were sold from Luanda, the Portuguese trading port of Angola, their captivity had also been produced by raiding of interior local communities (defined by descent) or through warfare campaigns mounted by powerful lords with small minorities of armed Portuguese.[21] Those sold from the Gold Coast beginning in the mid-seventeenth century had been captured, traded, or sold during more extensive wars of territorial and commercial expansion and held in jails of European fortresses along the coast (such as São Jorge de Mina) until their sale to any number of English, Dutch, French, and Portuguese transatlantic traders.[22]

Likewise, men and women who would be called and called themselves *arara* in the Americas in the later part of the seventeenth century were sold into the slave trade for transgressions against rulers, failure to pay debts, or as captives from warfare of the states inland from the Bight of Benin.[23] The violent disruption of the interior West African and West Central African slave trading would be complemented by the long waits in the coastal pens or forts, where food and water would be often in short supply and diseases were legion.[24] European traders began the process of commodification in these barracks by describing all captives regardless of sex, age, or health "as equally suitable for exchange on the Atlantic market."[25] The transfer from the land to the ships signified the destruction of social and kinship ties that reduced people into standardized, tradable goods.

Men, women, and children enslaved in Peru experienced a lengthy transatlantic journey. Similar to many others, they survived a Middle Passage bound together for months in cramped quarters with poor food and water supplies as well as the effects of rampant diseases.[26] Enslaved people traded into Cartagena testified that they were kept below deck chained by the neck in groups of six and bound together by shackles on their feet.[27] Those from Angola explained that during the crossing they were fed only a small amount of maize or raw millet and water.[28] The official destinations for slave traders into the Spanish Americas during the seventeenth century were supposedly Cartagena or Veracruz, and the voyage from the African coast could take anywhere from one to two months, with mortality rates ranging from 10 to 40 percent.[29] Slave ships, however, did not take direct routes and certainly made port throughout the Caribbean and the Atlantic. Because of bad weather or attracted by profitable markets, captains would land in the Brazilian ports of Pernambuco, Jamaica, or along what would become the Venezuelan or Colombian coasts.[30] Captives could be sold (illegally) or be kept to recuperate before another forced journey to another port. A transatlantic passage thus extended into the Caribbean for those men, women, and children who would be enslaved in Peru.

Arrival in the teeming port of Cartagena meant another step in the process of commodification. There, royal authorities counted captives to assess the customs and entry taxes owed to the crown as well as the local tax due to city officials.[31] Captives were also measured according to an emerging standard of a *pieza*, or piece.[32] In official rosters the value of women, children, and the disabled were discounted according to this male adult normative.[33] Captives could also be further differentiated according to their skills, languages, origins, personal qualities, and religious beliefs, which would add or subtract value to them during exchanges within the colonial slave market. In Cartagena, however, the purpose was to transform a range of diverse characteristics into a taxable form. At the very least, captives experienced these acts of objectification in two ways. First, in addition to the sign of the *asientista*, or licensed slave trader, women and men were branded with the mark of the crown to indicate their official entry.[34] Second, following inspections by royal officials, transatlantic ship captains disembarked captives to barracks, cells, or rooms in particular merchant warehouses.[35]

People who had been sold from the same communities and those who had survived the Middle Passage together may have been separated as men were divided from women.[36] In some cases agents held captives between two to six months as they recovered from dehydration and disease inflicted by the unsanitary, cramped, and deadly conditions of the slave ships.[37] The slave-holding barracks, nonetheless, were places where people often died as merchants did not invest in rudimentary medical care or provide water, food, and shelter to those who appeared ill.[38] Cartagena (and other Caribbean ports) must have been another site of painful marking and dispiriting dispersal for men, women, and children. At least in the early part of the seventeenth century, captives were sold several times either privately or at public auction before being transported to Peru, the Panamanian isthmus, Central America, or the interior of what is today Colombia and Ecuador.[39]

The forced journey from the Caribbean to the Pacific could prove fatal or liberating for captives. Captives embarked on smaller sailing vessels for the nine- to ten-day voyage between Cartagena and Portobelo, the official Caribbean port of the Spanish convoy and transatlantic market *feria* (market meeting).[40] From the Caribbean, captives crossed mountainous passes and skirted deep ravines until the Chagre River, where they continued by canoe.[41] Poisonous snakes, tropical downpours, and fevers (with other recurrent illnesses) made the journey difficult and dangerous, as traversing the isthmus could take days or weeks.[42] For instance, three free men of color trafficked a *partida* (parcel) of newly arrived Africans from Portobelo to Panama for agents of licensed slave traders. They declared that four of their charges had died during the trip—one because of a caiman attack a few days before arriving in the Pacific port of Panama.[43] The geography of the isthmus also provided opportunities to captives. Because many traveled at night, the crossing provided a chance for captives to escape to the numerous fugitive slave settlements that would become recognized towns of free people.[44] As described by Spanish travelers, fugitive slaves attacked travelers but also approached them to exchange food, offer their services as guides, or perhaps communicate with accompanying captives.[45] Deathly and difficult, the slave trade across the Panamanian isthmus provided captives with the possibility to exchange their status for that of free agents on the littoral of the colonial markets.

The slave trade from the Caribbean to the Pacific continued the process of commodifying Africans and their descendants. Slave merchants often sold captives to owners in Panama, a busy port on the Pacific of merchants, traders, treasury officials, and clerics, where Peruvian silver, Central American gold, and Castilian textiles were traded.[46] In this commercial crossroads, captives succumbed to the physical strains of crossing the isthmus as well as the notorious fevers and other illnesses that particularly afflicted newcomers unaccustomed to the regular and torrential afternoon rains in the tropical city.[47] Held in merchants' compounds, captive men, women, and children in Panama regularly contracted dysentery and still appeared like survivors of the transatlantic crossing: thin, pallid, and near death. Here, agents for the licensed slave merchants would often sell captives to traders who plied the Pacific coastal routes between Panama, Guayaquil (Ecuador), the northern Peruvian port of Paita (for the town of Piura), and the northern valleys surrounding Trujillo as well as Lima.[48] For captives, arriving in Panama often meant another encounter with the marketplace and this time with regional traders, smaller vessels, and interior routes into the Andean coast and highlands away from newly established friends, kin, and enemies.

Panama was a site of new collectivities as well as despair. During the height of the Portuguese-dominated trade, enslaved people such as Vitoria of *casta angola* gave birth to her son who in Trujillo was known as Francisco Criollo of Panama.[49] Both mother and son were sold from Panama to a Trujillo landholder who traded wheat as well as people along the Pacific commercial routes. Likewise, Ventura, a criollo of Panama, and Elena, a criolla of Panama, were sold from the isthmus to the northern Peruvian coast.[50] Africans were among the majority of captives sold from Panama to Peru, but they joined other enslaved people sold from their families and neighborhoods along the Caribbean coast and Mexico.[51]

These captives carried skills of their acculturated status, such as Clara Criolla, a "ladina of the city of Panama" who was sold for three hundred pesos and then for a higher price to work on the landed estates of the northern Peruvian valleys.[52] Marcos, for another example, was identified as a criollo of Tierra Firme who had been sold to Mexico, sold back to Panama and then to Trujillo, and again to Panama.[53] The multiple passages therefore served to add value to the enslaved man. Other captives employed their knowledge of the Pacific trade routes to escape, like Juan criollo of Panama, whose Trujillo owner empowered a third party to search for him in the Pacific port.[54] An acculturated Catholic, the criolla Barbola de Cáceres argued against and physically resisted being sold away from her husband in the San Lorenzo mines on the Pacific coast of Nicaragua.[55] Her owners ordered her to be chained and locked in a room until she was shipped southward to Panama (and eventually to Lima), as other enslaved criollas and criollos found themselves caught in the southward pull of the Pacific slave trade.

In the years that followed the Portuguese withdrawal from the official slave trade to Spanish America, captives experienced possibilities brought about by a reduced number of slaves in the markets of Panama. A Trujillo slaveholder complained that he had purchased "a black, García casta *congo*" from a Panamanian resident for five hundred pesos under the assumption that the slave was a *bozal*, newly arrived from Africa. On the northern Peruvian coast, García had worked as a muleteer and his continuing respiratory illness, accompanied by gastrointestinal disease, was not because he had recently survived the transatlantic slave trade.[56] The consequence of García's disclosure of his illness (either strategic or unavoidable) was a return to Panama, where the enslaved man rejoined previous acquaintances and perhaps kin but also presumably an irate former owner.

Francisco Balanta and his *compañero* (or companion) Manual Congo were also able to affect a similar reversal of their sale. In 1650 the ladino Francisco Balanta explained that a man who he assumed was his owner, a Mercedarian cleric, had brought him and his compañero Manual Congo from Panama to Trujillo. The two men were hardly from the same region, with Manual Congo indicating his origins in West Central Africa and Francisco Balanta's surname suggesting that he had been sold from Guinea-Bissau. Nonetheless, they became "fellows" in Panama or during their passage to Trujillo. There, Francisco Balanta disclosed to the inquiring civil judge that the man passing as his owner had hired out the two men in Trujillo to work loading flour. By providing evidence that a defrocked cleric had absconded with slaves from his monastery, the enslaved man facilitated his return along with his workmate to the Panamanian monastery where they had been "serving as slaves."[57] Perhaps the two men preferred their status as slaves of the monastery, working for the clerics rather than as contracted laborers in the

northern Peruvian city that was new to them.[58] They may have also left behind kin and community in Panama.[59] Regardless, with his workmate, Francisco Balanta revealed that a fraud had been committed and, subsequently,
caused a reversal of their fate. More desperate for enslaved laborers once the
Portuguese had withdrawn from the slave trade, Pacific traders and Trujillo
owners may have felt forced to capitulate to pressures and insinuations from
enslaved men and women.

Most Africans and their descendants, however, could not change the direction of the trade as they were forced to board ships sailing from Panama
to Peru. Still weakened by the Middle Passage and the Panamanian crossing, captives experienced recurrent or new illnesses on overcrowded ships
that sailed in hot, damp conditions.[60] Dutch and English pirates attacked
the small ships of Pacific traders and then abandoned crews, passengers,
and captives on coastal islands or tropical coasts.[61] If the ships sank, people
would be pulled into the sea by their chains, as were eighty captives on the
ship carrying cleric Francisco Solano from Panama to Lima.[62] During the
voyage that could take about a month, however, the smaller groups of captives would have been able to build a shipboard community.[63]

For example, in 1658 eleven men, two women, and one boy were supposed to be transported from Perico (Panama's port) to Huanchaco, the port
of Trujillo, on the frigate *Our Lady of the Angels*. The ship's captain identified his
human cargo as "bozales of the Rivers of all different castas," suggesting that
the captives had survived the transatlantic slave trade from Guinea-Bissau to
the Americas. Within the small group were two men both called Antonio.
One was identified as Antonio, a ladino, and the other as "the Captain of
them," suggesting that the group included a translator as well as a leader recognized by slave traders.[64] The captives may have relied on the two men to
ensure that the ship's crew administered their "food and good treatment" as
outlined in the commercial agreement.[65] Before reaching the northern Peruvian coast, the ship entered Guayaquil's port, where the ship's captain sold or
purchased one or two more enslaved people to join the captive community
from Panama.[66] With a core group from a similar West African region plus a
Spanish-speaking member, survivors of this forced ocean journey were capable of sharing accumulated information regarding slaveholding along the
Pacific coast as well as developing relationships among themselves.

The extensive journey may have supplied some captives with cultural
tools to challenge their new owners. After a journey of about two weeks,
ships often landed at Paita, the northern coastal port of the town of Piura, then captives were forced to walk south toward Trujillo and eventually
Lima.[67] The land route brought captives near the estates and indigenous com-

munities that for many would be their final destination. María of *bañol* land escaped from a slave ship traveling from Panama to Lima at the port of Chérrepe (near Saña). Described as "between bozal and ladino," the woman from Guinea-Bissau knew her owner, a Portuguese man named Diego Mendes, and also knew that slaves could protest abusive physical punishment.[68] Once captured, she employed this information to claim that she fled from him because of an excessive lashing.[69] Initially, María was able to survive in the uncultivated lands of the Jequetepeque valley for about a year. She met Juanillo, another fugitive, who knew how to acquire maize from the residents of the nearby indigenous village of Guadalupe.

The rural guard eventually captured María, but her successful escape suggests that by the time captives who had been sold from West or West Central African ports such as Cacheo or Luanda into the transatlantic slave trade reached the Peruvian northern coastal valleys, they had been exposed for months, if not years, to Portuguese crews, ladinos, or acculturated blacks of Caribbean and Pacific trade routes. The transit was arduous, lengthy, and deadly, but the extended slave trade to Peru also produced opportunities for captives to exchange information and learn more about slavery conditions and market standards.[70] With this knowledge enslaved people like María claimed customary protections, extralegal alliances, and even lodged a formal protest that was rooted in Spanish American mandates regarding slavery.

Disembarkation in Peru offered additional dangers as well as opportunities for enslaved people to negotiate their enslaved status. In addition to the more northernly ports, traders also disembarked captives at Malabrigo close to the landed estates of the Chicama valley and Huanchaco, the port for the coastal city of Trujillo and notorious for their inadequate and dangerous anchorage.[71] Indigenous mariners ferried goods and people on small skiffs through the crashing surf, often capsizing in the process. In one instance indigenous swimmers with small balsa boats (*caballitos*) attempted to rescue captives and a ship's crew from their skiff that had been tossed by the rough seas of Trujillo's port, Huanchaco.[72] For men and women who knew someone or had maritime skills, the port could also be another opportunity for escape. Juan, a native of Seville and slave of a Lima merchant, had traveled from Guayaquil to Huanchaco on board a trading ship. Upon arrival at the port, Juan supposedly stole a box of knives from the chief petty officer, swam ashore, and made his way inland to Trujillo. Captured by the urban night watch, Juan declared his intention to be "sold in this city."[73] The well-traveled and knowledgeable Juan activated his customary right to seek an alternative owner.[74] He seized the chance presented by the harbor's calm seas and the city's state officials to negotiate a new arrangement of his propertied status.

Dangerous and deadly, the prolonged nature of the slave trade also allowed captives to learn more about their new environs and provided instances (in the long term) for them to established networks. After receiving captives at Piura's port of Paita on the northern Peruvian coast and traveling for days, drivers would have sought out the inn (tambo) in the northern Chicama valley. There, captives would have encountered María Angola, for instance—a free woman who worked in the field and house of her patron.[75] Other men and women labeled as angola constituted significant numbers of the enslaved populations on the rural estates.[76] Thus from the late sixteenth century into the seventeenth century, captives traveled through a land filled with strangers, but among these strangers were some who could speak to them. Captives caught within the northern Peruvian slave trade also would have been left to their own devices. In 1686 a Spanish farmer complained that a "lot of black bozales" had destroyed his maize field and threatened him with knives. Although the yeoman described this event to seek restitution from a defensive slave trader, his depiction of captives as "insulting him in actions and words" undercuts a singular vision of newly arrived Africans as ill and disoriented.[77] The accounts that we have come from slave traders who simply described the transportation of human commodities through the northern Peruvian coast to eager buyers in colonial Trujillo. At the same time, reading particular events in context reveals a slave trade in which captives improved their Spanish, learned the terrain, and at least got to know the people accompanying them on the forced journey. With these skills and experiences some captive men and women could begin to influence their treatment as slaves in the city of Trujillo and surrounding valleys.

Contrary Property

The value of captives increased along the arduous routes between the Atlantic African coast and the Pacific valleys. In the early seventeenth century an adult male captive would have cost about 270 pesos in Cartagena but would have been sold in Trujillo for roughly twice the amount.[78] Place and time also changed the characteristics of captives that were esteemed by merchants and slaveholders. By the later part of the seventeenth century, officials and traders infused castas with market qualities so that minas were worth more than angolas. Like others in the Americas, infusing casta terms with particular characteristics allowed slave traders to reject captives sold to them by transatlantic merchants as well as create traits desirable to potential buyers in the Spanish American markets.[79] Market demand in the Atlantic and Caribbean as well as the distance from the transatlantic trade handicapped northern Peruvian slaveholders and lessened their ability to extensively utilize the differences of these casta characteristics. One enslaved woman, discussed below, traveled with these discourses that allowed her to claim a value according to circulating notions of her casta's worth.

In the first half of the seventeenth century—even while clerics, slave traders, and enslaved people named distinctions among Africans—secular and ecclesiastical authorities attempted to collapse their differences. In the 1630s an anonymous colonial chronicler warned against arming enslaved men yet suggested that because Africans were of so "many nations and castas," it followed that "almost all of them were enemies of each other" and thus would never agree.[80] A decade or more later, in arguing for a renewal of the official slave trade licenses, a petitioner to the Consejo de Indias described how Africans "were of different castas that they rarely se hermanan" (or "make brotherhood") among themselves—a quality that was assumed among people of a shared casta.[81] By acknowledging but then declaring that differences among Africans were inconsequential, both the chronicler and the petitioner engaged in a fantastic construction of reality.[82] In describing the clear distinctions between people from Guinea-Bissau, Angola, and other regions who dominated the black population in Peru in the midcolonial period as canceling out a potential for solidarity as enslaved people, they attempted to justify the continuation of a legal slave trade into the Spanish Americas.

Slaveholders imagined the lack of uniformity among Africans as further proof of the lower social development of enslaved people and as reassurance that rebellion was not imminent. In the 1640s, when Peruvian officials attempted to encourage and then plead for a continuation of the official slave trade after its abrupt interruption, they also had to explain how they would control potentially large numbers of enslaved people. An official from Lima described the looming threat of eighty thousand black slaves "oppressed, vexed, and desirous of freedom." To dissuade this specter of rebellion, he declared that if the population of diverse nations, castas, and languages were "people of more rationality, they would have risen up" and seized the weapons of their owners against their imposed servitude.[83] There was no mention that diverse enslaved populations often found many affinities regardless of their differences.

Like colonial jurists, Lima slaveholders (often one and the same) wrote to the crown that large numbers of enslaved blacks were not a threat to public order because the diverse nations were incapable of communicating with each other.[84] For slaveholders and colonial authorities the multiplicity of enslaved Africans was both a practical deterrent to organized resistance as well as proof of their subservient location as slaves in the colonial order. Flattening distinctions among Africans also served slaveholders' desires to create enslaved men and women—or at least their representation—as docile, complacent, and obedient.[85] By brushing aside the wide variety of cultural distinctions such as language, religion, cultural practices, kinship relations, and other facets of distinct Diaspora cultures, slaveholders made room for their own constructions of enslaved characteristics.

Reflecting how slaveholders labeled captive Africans, Jesuit missionary Alonso Sandoval simultaneously recognized and condensed the diversity of captive Africans into particular categories. In Cartagena he communicated through male interpreters with people from distinct regions of the Atlantic African coast, but he did not honor their self-identifications. Sandoval reported that he would ask "which casta are you?" to choose the necessary interpreter to baptize the newly arrived captive. He recounted that those from Guinea-Bissau would declare such "names" as Cacheo, Basserral, Bojola Papel, or Pessis in response to his question.[86] In these exchanges, captive people identified themselves according to places of origin, such as the region in or near the trading town of Cacheu ("cacheo") or the Pecixe ("pesis") island, one of the coastal islands of the Mansoa River in Guinea-Bissau.[87] Sandoval listed other "names" that captives gave themselves and explained to his reader that these terms were the same as saying "I am of *casta bran*."[88] In this way Sandoval collapsed the multiplicity of diasporic identity and transatlantic allegiances from the "rivers of Guinea" into the casta category of *bran*. Recognizable among missionaries and slaveholders throughout Spanish America, *bran* was one of the many casta terms of slave trading and would become an identity for Africans and their descendants in the Americas. Notably, rather than recording the affinities of those from Guinea-Bissau, Sandoval created a new singularity or a casta even as captives articulated the multiplicities of their identities.

By the later part of the seventeenth century, distinctions among captives were not a priority for slave traders or slaveholders in Cartagena or the Peruvian northern coast. After the temporary cessation of the legal slave trade during midcentury, Cartagena residents called for ships to depart for any part of the Atlantic coast, including "Arda" on the Bight of Benin, "Calabar" on the Bight of Biafra, the Kingdom of Kongo or Angola in southern West Central Africa.[89] Northern coastal Peruvian slaveholders, especially owners of large sugar estates, sent relatives and clients to sell sugar or wheat in Panama and, with the profits, purchase slaves. While enslaved men and women from the Caribbean islands such as Jamaica and even those born in Nicaragua and Cartagena were also among the captives in the Panamanian slave market, Peruvian slaveholders preferred newly arrived Africans.[90] In comparison to Spanish-speaking criollos and criollas, slaveholders imagined that captives directly from the transatlantic slave trade would be more easily controlled.[91] The transatlantic slave trade into the southern Spanish Americas either reflected or created these preferences. By the time that the crown reinstated the official slave trade, the agreement listed that blacks of any nation could be imported.[92] To illustrate the constructed nature of slaveholder desires, market demand for labor in the midcentury muted a larger discussion of inclinations toward particular castas.

Slaveholders' preferences were clearly tied to market availability. In the early part of the century, Sandoval reported from Cartagena that slaveholders preferred those called mandingas (from northern Senegal) or brans or balantas from Guinea-Bissau because they were "much more loyal than all the others, of great reason and capacity, more handsome and disposed; blacks of [solid] bones, healthy, and [made] for much work."[93] Captives from these regions, however, dominated the numbers sold into Peru during this period.[94] Traders based in Cartagena, and probably elsewhere, articulated a desire for a type of captive already supplied by the market.[95] Likewise, in the early eighteenth century, Cartagena's municipal council and some Panamanian merchants declared that mina and cabo verde captives were healthy, robust, and easy to sustain.[96] The crown and the merchant consulate in Seville disagreed, proclaiming that minas were fierce and that cabo verdes were susceptible to illness and prohibiting the French company (with the legal slave-trading license) from importing captives of these castas.[97] The disagreement appears to emerge from the crown's interest in discouraging the illegal slave trade from the nearby Caribbean island of Curaçao held by the Dutch, who easily sold captives from their Gold Coast forts (called "minas") into Spanish America.[98] The radically distinct characterizations suggests that traders and owners were aware that enslaved people differed in terms of color, size, facial markings, and languages but created the value that corresponded to the casta of slaves according to who the market made available.

The circulating discourses regarding the qualities of transatlantic castas such as cabo verde and mina were also available to enslaved men and women. By invoking her market value in a legal dispute among slaveholders over her status as property, one woman who identified herself as María was able to articulate an alternative worth. Indicative of the resurgent slave trade into Spanish America in the later part of the seventeenth century, María, a ladina black woman of mina casta, testified in Trujillo that a Spanish woman had purchased her in Cartagena when she had first arrived from Guinea (Africa). María testified that her new owner sent her to sell bananas in the streets, as marketeering or vending was a common occupation among enslaved and free women of color in the Spanish Americas.[99] After returning without the exact amount of her goods, her new owner whipped and hit her. María experienced a reoccurring infection, but in Cartagena she was able to cure herself with herbs that resembled, as she explained, the ones she had used in "Guinea." With a chronic illness and enslaved to a cruel owner, María explained to Trujillo's investigating civil authorities that she had tried to slit her throat, leaving a large scar on her neck.[100] The owner sold her to traders who transported her to Panama, where she was purchased by another Spanish woman, but upon suffering the same infection, she was sold to a Pacific slave trader. Recognizing her "defects," the experienced merchant purchased her with a sale recorded on unofficial "simple paper," signifying an informal transaction in which a notary did not guarantee her good health.[101] María's illness combined with her response to a demanding owner had in effect pushed her into the Pacific slave trade.

Slave traders and slaveholders attempted to fit enslaved people like María into the commodity categories that they created. Once in Trujillo, on the northern Peruvian coast, the slave trader advertised her qualities and "lent out" María to three potential buyers in order for them to evaluate her within their own households. Juan Dávila, a wealthy merchant and free man of color, brought María home so that his wife could examine her.[102] On the way, he would later explain, he encountered a surgeon who pronounced her "a very good black woman slave." All who saw her reported that they were interested in María because of "her good face, young age, and good looks." Among other qualities, these physical features appear to have supported slaveholder expectations that María would be of a "good disposition" and have a willingness to serve. By changing the location of the sale, the Pacific slave trader attempted to erase María's previous reputation as a sick and "worthless" slave in Panama. In effect, he transformed a slave whose owner had found her so "defective" that she sold her as a coveted commodity in the new market of the northern Peruvian coast.

Without the cooperation of María, however, the market performance did not work. During a trial period of two hours in his home, the slaveholder Juan Dávila found that María had "not wanted to serve" and thus returned to bargain (unsuccessfully) with the Pacific slave trader for a reduction of one hundred pesos in price.[103] Martín Ximenez (a local carpenter) paid eight hundred pesos for María and then, after finding that she did not meet his expectations of service, sold her within two days. Apparently, both men did not see (or wish to acknowledge the meaning of) the scar on her neck from her previous suicide attempt and did not inquire as to her previous illness—both customary inspections of purchasing a slave.[104] They had also not anticipated that she would refuse to do as they demanded. It is plausible that Trujillo's slaveholders projected a quality of obedience that included sexual or domestic service.[105] Based on the buyers' extreme interest in María combined with their descriptions of her physical appearance, Trujillo's slaveholders imagined that she would offer services that distinguished her from other women whose constructed characteristics made them into mere laborers. In any case, she refused.

The testimonies recorded in the civil suit illuminate how María was able to seize on the acts or events of commodification to advocate for her own interests. Working in the markets and streets of Cartagena allowed her to exchange information with other enslaved and free people regarding not only the fruit markets but the slave markets.[106] María did not choose her sale to Panama but may have been able to activate her knowledge to succeed in being purchased by a Spanish woman rather than a lower-status individual. In Trujillo the civil case illuminates how she clearly understood the value of her commodified status. She discouraged a sale to a man of color (Juan Dávila) and refused to serve the artisan, Martín Ximenes. Then, after these two failed transactions, María arranged her own sale to Captain don Gerónimo de González, a landholder who had been Trujillo's alcalde ordinario.[107] More than seizing on the opportunities for change provided by the slave market, María manipulated the slaveholders' projections to move herself into a better position albeit as a slave.

Even when slaveholders discovered that the characteristics that they had imagined were not real, María continued to employ the limited values of the market at her disposal. Following his purchase, Captain don Gerónimo de González also expressed disappointment when María did not meet his expectation of a commodity. María refused to "serve" her new owner and proved to be what he complained was "proud and arrogant and very much the owner of her own will." She had, in effect, manipulated her own commodification.[108] González's witnesses explained that he felt "deceived" that her exorbitant price was not matched by the promise of her "personal attributes."[109] The seller, Martín Ximenes (the artisan), still defended his sale. He declared, what did González expect, as it was common knowledge that "the nation of the casta mina was more haughty" than others?[110] Certainly there were multiple and contradictory characteristics of minas circulating in the Spanish Americas, but in Trujillo even the traits that should have troubled slaveholders added to María's unique value. Underlining the constructed nature of slave-trading casta categories, as a mina María was desired by slave-holders but refused their demands. In effect, María proved the expectations of her casta in that she did not and would not agree to whatever González and other Trujillo slaveholders had attempted to exact.

María continued to refuse to comply with the expectations of her price and category. In addition to refusing to serve, she threatened to kill herself when pressed by her new owner. Slaveholders such as González were aware that mortally inflicted wounds were costly to cure and that suicide was a mortal sin. Slaves were conscious of slaveholders' fears and would attempt suicide in protest of gruesomely abusive treatment or to escape their enslaved status.[111] Incarcerated during the civil investigation, María demanded a knife so that she could cut her throat, becoming "furious" when she was unable to complete the deed. Her actions disrupted the sale. By exposing that she had a wish to disfigure her "good appearance," María devalued her propertied status from an expensive domestic servant to a slave woman whose scar carried a story of disobedience—now known throughout Trujillo. Unable to secure the owner of her choosing, María may have destroyed many parts of herself including the presentation of a mina woman with special market value.

María of casta mina did not employ the colonial courts to call on protections from an abusive owner or to gain recognition of her Catholic and pious status. Her actions are available for analysis because of her exceptional value as a propertied person. Unlike most captives of the multiple passages between Cartagena and Peru, the combination of her gender and her casta brought María unusual attention from a variety of Trujillo's male slaveholders. In this scenario she acted, violently, within one of the few venues available to her, the market to undo what it had sought to produce.[112] Hardly resistant, María's repeated actions of self-mutilation could be read as proof of the slave trade's physical and psychological violence.[113] The acts of suicide could also be read through a diaspora lens as an attempt to return home across the multiple Pacific, Caribbean, and Atlantic waters.[114]

Regardless, acting within the categories of commodity and property, as the example María of casta mina illustrates, was limited. She employed her commodity status by playing on her unique characteristics, yet she moved from being one man's property to another's. By acting within the category of "slave," enslaved men and women had to deal with qualities of their enslavement as defined by slaveholders. As the historian Alex Bontemps has suggested, enslaved people were capable of making themselves "sensible" or understandable to slaveholders.[115] This sensibility in some cases was untenable or destructive, since by selling, punishing, belittling, maiming, and even killing, slaveholders continued to treat enslaved men and women as objects. Also, enslaved people would employ their locations to become fugitives or rebels and to manumit themselves and thus define their persons as free from enslavement. To move beyond the limitations of the assigned category of "black slave," men, women, and children would have to insist on their kinship, collectivities, and family connections beyond slavery's boundaries. In a counterintuitive approach, those who survived longer passages to their final destinations as slaves were often able to amass more information and resources not just about their market value but about how to go about building kinships as persons.

Creating Kin, Creating Diaspora

The slave trade and market exchanges often stripped captive and enslaved men and women of their social and cultural connections. In response, Africans created kinships in the context of the multiple passages or their enslaved experiences and with the people who shared their experiences.[116] Creating kinships allowed captive and enslaved Africans to articulate diaspora communities or identities in the Americas. In some cases enslaved men and women employed the same transatlantic casta categories familiar to slave traders and slaveholders to name their communities and seized on the provisions of the Catholic church to create kinships through baptism and marriage.[117] Most newly arrived rural laborers, however, did not have access to priests, ecclesiastical courts, and the funds necessary to pay for these services. Outside of the institutional structures of Catholic marriages or religious brotherhoods, enslaved men and women also made use of terms for each other such as *pariente*, or relative, to suggest a much more dynamic experience that "challenged the coherence of slaveholding categories such as 'Mina.'"[118] Certainly in response to the labor demands of the rural estates, enslaved men invoked diasporic kinships that superseded their positions as mere slaves.

Some enslaved and free Africans recalled in judicial documents or notary entries their most recent experiences of sale into the Trujillo region. In a rare civil case a slaveholder called on the testimonies of enslaved laborers to establish his ownership of a slave in 1656. The son of a Pacific slave trader declared that Anton Mozanga had escaped or been stolen during his initial journey of captivity to Trujillo. The young slaveholder asked elderly men and women to remember who had been in a partida or coffle traveling to Trujillo more than thirty years ago. Francisco Angola recalled that he had arrived in the northern coastal valleys following the "big earthquake."[119] The sixty-year-old man probably referred to the lasting effects of the violent 1619 temblor when hundreds of coastal residents perished.[120] If Francisco Angola was brought as a captive into the northern coastal valleys in the late 1620s, he would have witnessed the crop sterility and general poverty that many residents continued to blame on the earthquake as late as 1634.[121] The enslaved West Central African also recounted that he had been brought with other "compañeros" (companions), including the younger slave whose ownership was in question. Meeting again, after thirty years, Francisco Angola spoke to Anton Mozanga and verified that they had endured the journey together by ship from Panama to Paita, and then, on foot, south toward the Chicama valley.[122] Three other captives also supported Francisco Angola's account and remembered, in their judicial testimony, that the boy who was their shipmate kin was now a fugitive seeking a new owner.

In recalling their passage to the northern valleys, the enslaved men and women wove their past forced journeys into their present relationships. Their testimonies were prompted by the Trujillo slaveholder because each enslaved witness supplied similar information probably in response to the list of questions provided by the owner's legal representative. Despite the uniformity of their answers, their responses reflected a shared past.[123] Along with Francisco Angola, María Lucumí and Agustín Arara also explained that they had first been brought from Brazil with Anton Mozanga by a "Portuguese" whose name no one remembered. Portuguese traders were active on the West Central African coast, where captives called *angola* were sold from Luanda. The Portuguese were also trading along the Bight of Benin, where they purchased men and women called *arara* and *lucumí*. In the first half of the seventeenth century, Portuguese merchants held the official license from the Spanish crown to trade from the Caribbean port of Cartagena into the South American interior.[124] Then, with the Dutch invasion of Brazil in the 1620s, the Brazilian economy experienced a collapse in sugar prices because of a period of depression in Europe coupled with the fighting among colonial powers.[125]

In response to the Dutch invasion, slave traders would have rerouted captives from Brazil to more lucrative markets in the Spanish Americas. Thus the four enslaved people reunited in the Chicama valley on the northern Peruvian coast in 1656 had probably been captives together from a northern Brazilian port. If they had traveled from Brazil, they would have endured passage through the Caribbean, across the Panamanian isthmus, and southward along the Pacific coast. Their "shipmate" kinship was therefore based on multiple journeys, suggesting a deep bond that in some cases would be the basis of establishing new lineages in the Americas.[126] Furthermore, by arriving in a new place together as a group, Francisco Angola, María Lucumí, and Agustín Arara with Anton Mozanga (though of radically distinct origins) constituted a community or even a family, especially in relation to the strangers they would meet on the estate where they were sold.[127] Their strong ties were reflected in Francisco Angola's ability and willingness to remember and recognize Anton Mozanga. Apart from the judicial strategy of the slaveholder to recover the young man as his property, the testimonies of the enslaved elderly man (and the others from the same shared passages) suggest that Anton Mozanga may have been seen as a junior kinsman who had returned to share his experiences and renew his obligations.

Shipmate kinships provided enslaved men and women with the means to begin lineages and families in the Americas. When enslaved man Miguel de Ocampo of casta chala married María Rosa de Saavedra of casta chala in the northern coastal town of Lambayeque, the couple called on other enslaved men from the same West African region to serve as their witnesses. Antonio de Chuburría named himself as a chala and testified that he knew both bride and groom since they had been sold to northern Peru. The threesome called themselves by the same casta—chala—suggesting their origins in the interior of eastern Ghana and western Togo.[128] Their usage also underscores how they employed the terminology of slave traders in their marriage petition. The couple's first witness, Fermin de Escurra of casta mina, declared more information about the groom, suggesting a much stronger bond with him. The enslaved ladino declared that "they brought him from his land; that he came in company with Miguel de Ocampo."[129]

Fermin de Escurra's testimony suggests that he had survived first the transatlantic crossing with Miguel de Ocampo as well as the second Pacific slave trade to the northern Peruvian coast. According to him, the groom was single and free to marry, a requirement for Catholic marriage. Fermin de Escurra matched his strong endorsement of the groom with his testimony of the bride by declaring that he and the bride were of the same casta. While Fermin de Escurra identified as mina and the bride was identified as a chala, his declaration points to the general nature of slave trade categories but also the ability of enslaved and free people to shape their meaning.[130] Fermin de Escurra laid claim to the bride as kin united through their casta. In doing so, the enslaved man invested in an expansion of kinship for himself as well as an endorsement that the engaged couple begin a new lineage in the Americas—a critical means to economic success but also the formation of a collective identity.[131] Enslaved men and women thus employed shipmate relationships (as well as the Catholic institution of marriage) to continue expanding their kinships but also the way that affinities would be defined in the Americas.

Enslaved people appeared to be creating multigenerational alliances with their marriages. Cayetano de Escuría was fifty years old and most likely older than the marrying couple. Likewise, when Simon Arara married María Camacho, their other witness, Joseph Arara who agreed that the younger couple were free to marry, was over fifty.[132] This marriage petition also reveals that in a diasporic setting, the categories of casta had meaning but even at their invention "they strained at the seams."[133] Though labeled a mina, the witness Cayetano de Escuría clearly saw himself as kin to an arara. Indeed, in the late seventeenth century, Bahia merchants purchased slaves they called Mina from the ports of Grand Popo and Ouidah on the Leeward Coast of present-day Togo and Benin.[134] Since an international band of slave traders, legally and extra legally, provided the Spanish Americas with captives during this period, people the Bahians called Mina may have easily been from the same regions as those called Araras.[135] If Cayetano de Escuría, a mina, could present himself as stand-in kin for Antonio de la Banda, an arara, then the slave trade terms had less meaning among enslaved people than their declared kinships. People of the African Diaspora were creating new meanings from the slave-trading terminologies.

Enslaved Africans and their descendants took the initiative to make their unions legitimate by using the institutions of the Catholic Church. In the rural valleys a slaveholder could pay the marriage fees for enslaved men and women who were part of their households, such as the case of Lucha, a samba cook on the rural estate of Nuestra Señora de la Concepción.[136] Recently arrived Africans, however, rarely had this type of patronage relationship with their owners, and most enslaved people could not afford the fees.[137] In the rare recording of thirty-two rural enslaved matrimonies on the estates of Ascope and Facala (and their surroundings) in the Chicama valley between 1678 and 1737, enslaved men and women employed their choice of marital partnership to create kinship from their regional affiliations or perhaps shipmate affinities.[138] Mina men and women almost always married each other, or a mina man wed a criolla or African descendant born in the Americas. In this small sample, minas never married araras. Those called or calling themselves araras married other araras, and arara men married local women who were identified by the recording cleric as mulata, criolla, or mestiza.[139] Congo men married other conga women but were also likely to marry criolla women or those called popo (from the Bight of Benin) and even indigenous women. Since the transatlantic and Pacific slave trades included more people from the Bight of Benin and the Gold Coast in this period, it is perhaps not surprising that those who were called arara and mina were more likely to find spouses from their same region than men and women from West Central Africa.[140]

The limited records suggest that African men, regardless if they originated on the Gold Coast or the Bight of Benin, also sought to make official their relationships with criolla women and therefore establish local kinship networks. In urban areas enslaved Africans were much more likely to marry or at least leave records of their official Catholic matrimonies. Of the surviving records for Trujillo's Cathedral parish, in the seventeenth century, thirteen of the matrimonies involving Africans were between men and women of the same general regions.[141] Eight marriages were between men and women of radically distinct origins, and in the case of two matrimonies criollo men married women from West Central Africa.[142] The contrast with the rural marriage records suggests that more women of color, either criolla or African, were demographically present in the urban areas versus the rural environs.[143] The limited marriage records of Africans also suggest that men and women in urban areas developed matrimonial relations based on other criteria than what can be read as within the assigned slave trader categories.

Enslaved men and women employed the baptism of their children to extend their kin networks. The record of a Catholic baptism was particularly significant to rural enslaved people in part because child mortality was high on the coastal estates.[144] Rural slaveholders rarely sponsored the baptism of an enslaved child, leaving parents to secure the funds to pay an itinerant cleric to perform the rite. With these odds, the ten baptisms of enslaved children with African parents recorded on the estates of Ascope and Facala (and their surroundings) in the Chicama valley between 1675 and 1737 provide a rare glimpse into a very important event in the lives of enslaved families.[145] Only two baptisms indicate an arara network, suggesting that enslaved people adapted their identities in particular contexts.[146] More commonly, parents chose godparents who expanded their kinship networks. In 1724, when María Josefa of casta arara (perhaps sold from the Bight of Benin coast) and her husband Nicolas Requena of casta chala (suggesting an origin in the Volta interior) baptized their five-month-old son, Rafael, they chose Catalina of casta arara who shared a general cultural origin with the mother but was enslaved to a different owner. More interestingly, for the godfather, the legitimately married couple chose Cristobal Joseph Alegre, an indigenous highlander and migrant to the coastal valleys.[147] Likewise, María of casta arara and Manuel Arara chose Diego Nicolás, an indigenous migrant and resident laborer on the estate where they were enslaved, as the godfather of their child.[148] These couples had married within their general cultural zone as perhaps they shared a language or knew others who were shipmate kin. Upon the birth (and survival) of a son, they sought to cement relationships with their coworkers and neighbors who were not even of African descent, employing the shared cultural idiom of Catholic baptism.

In this context of kinship, enslaved men and women sold from the Bight of Benin had more in common with Andean migrants. Because local Andean villages did not always fully accept indigenous migrants, indigenous laborers would have welcomed the chance to develop new relationships with enslaved Africans who were similarly disconnected from their home communities and kinship networks. Enslaved people would have appreciated a connection with indigenous migrants whose wages may have allowed them to pay marriage and baptismal fees. The reverse was possible as well. In 1690, María Juliana and Salvador Asvedo, of an indigenous fishing community in the Chicama valley, chose Antonio Arara as the godfather for their eight-month-old son. Sold from the coastal lagoons along the Bight of Benin, Antonio Arara may have been a fisherman himself, a welcomed alliance for the shrinking numbers of indigenous coastal natives.[149] The act of baptism was a mechanism for enslaved Africans to continue old practices of creating kinship with new partners. In 1680 either the same man or a different Antonio Arara served as the godfather for an infant identified only as a four-month-old black of unidentified parents.[150] Among Spaniards and their descendants his actions would have indicated his dubious association with an unclaimed and illegitimate child.[151] Yet he also acted with a Catholic sensibility of charity and from a West African perspective, Antonio Arara engaged in a common practice of fostering the less fortunate. The outcome could be only favorable, as both he and the young boy would gain kin.[152] Antonio Arara was joined by doña Francisca, an indigenous woman of significant status in the coastal Andean town of Santiago de Cao, who served as the baby's godmother. In addition to a junior kinsman, Antonio Arara also may have solidified a peer relationship or performed recognition of the indigenous elite woman as a patron through participation in the Catholic practice of godparentage. Catholic institutions played a key role in African adaptations to local contexts that included indigenous people.

Religious brotherhoods (confraternities) also provided a central location for Africans to publicly articulate more extended communities. In Lima and in Trujillo the Jesuits sponsored confraternities, and in Lima the Dominicans helped to establish a confraternity specifically for *congos*.[153] In Trujillo there were numerous brotherhoods for blacks, mulatos, and free people of color.[154] Reflecting the adaptations of men and women from Guinea-Bissau in the first half of the seventeenth century to colonial Catholic society, in 1637, a notary in Trujillo recorded the sale of a property belonging to the

San Nicolás de Tolentino confraternity, conducted by two officers of that lay religious institution. The two representatives were Pedro Bran and Anton Folupo, who were not identified as either enslaved or free.[155] Unsurprisingly, the two men from the Guinea-Bissau region headed a confraternity that was known in Mexico and Peru as a common avocation for Africans and their descendants.[156] It is also plausible that Pedro Bran and Anton Folupo shared certain understandings of Catholicism. Pedro Bran could have been a Brâme from the Casamance River, where Anton, as a Falupo, also originated. Pedro Bran and Anton Folupo would have been traded through the West African ports of Cacheo and Cape Verde as well as the northern Pacific entry points of Cartagena and Panama, and in each location they would have been exposed to Catholic practices and beliefs.[157] Thus their Catholic identity was not merely an opportunistic strategy employed in Peru but an expression of an ongoing cultural adaptation across the Atlantic and southward along the Pacific coast, as they combined diasporic expressions with the possibilities offered by Catholic institutions.

Outside of the prospects offered by Catholic organizations and in response to enslavement, enslaved people acted together to infuse the general terms of the regional slave trade with choices suggesting their mutual bonds. In 1737, as more men and women were sold to Peruvian slaveholders from the Gold Coast, three men identified as casta mina had become fugitives in the uncultivated lands of the Trujillo valley. Once captured by the city's alcalde (the leading municipal official), the men explained that they had survived by stealing yucca, yams, hens, maize, and sheep from their owners' fields as well as the farms of coastal Andeans. As ladino or acculturated men ranging in age from twenty-four to thirty-four, they were familiar with the regulations of the court. To avoid a more severe charge of battery, they denied the allegations that they had worked together to assault the indigenous highlanders who pastured their cattle on the knolls near the ocean.

The men called mina were joined by others. Josepha, a ladina mina, explained that she had fled from her owner to join Joseph Antonio, whom "she slept with," and the man she named as Juanillo was also accompanied by his common-law wife.[158] The three mina fugitives traded sheep for salt and chicha with their contact in the city, Antonio of casta mina. In turn, the enslaved woodcutter testified that he was in the process of locating new owners for the fugitives, a legal procedure that often shifted people from the category of escaped slaves to ones merely in transition to a new master.[159] As an ally, Antonio provided proof that the mina threesome were attempting to rectify their fugitive status and return to slavery. Also, Antonio provided useful information on how to gain access to the legal protections afforded to enslaved men and women as communicated through an apparent mina network.

The mina men also acted within more complicated hierarchies. Juanillo identified himself as Juan Negro ("John Black") of casta mina or chala. In his testimony the enslaved fugitive agreed with the notary that he could be called mina, suggesting that he fit with those who had been sold from the coast named for the slave-trading fort of São Jorge da Mina (Elmina). Juan Negro also categorized himself as of casta chala, suggesting his affiliation with an interior people who had moved southward and westward into the Volta region near the Ghana-Togo border by the twentieth century.[160] In addition, the enslaved fugitive claimed Black as a surname, indicating a choice of a Spanish colonial term over a slave trade category. Adding yet another layer to his identity, Juan Negro acted with other minas. Each of the three men described how one afternoon they had encountered an enslaved ox driver of casta mina who was missing an arm. He asked them to steal some clothing from the highland Andeans (serranos) he had seen on the beach. In the criminal investigation the three men of the fugitive group declared that they refused the offer or the demand from a fellow mina. Juan Negro, however, suggested that they would have executed the robbery except they had only an old lance. To distance himself from the criminal charge, he then suggested that the armless black man must have committed the crime with other enslaved men, or his compañeros, from the same estate. Understanding that Juan Negro provided his account in the context of a criminal case involving charges of theft, escaping, and assault, it is hardly surprising that he sought to protect himself (and his fellows) from further prosecution.

In addition to his judicial strategy, Juan Negro may have also been engaging in kin negotiations with his fellow mina. The armless mina man also made a request of his kinsmen by explaining that he "needed" the cape and the poncho, items that would be crucial in the wet, winter months to come.[161] Slaveholders did not usually supply these critical pieces of clothing, so enslaved laborers had to acquire blankets of low-quality felt or pieces of woven cloth called mantas to warm themselves.[162] In contrast, a cape, cut to fit, or a poncho woven from wool or alpaca could be warmer and communicated a superior status to enslaved and free, African and indigenous, inhabitants.[163] The mina ox driver therefore was asking for a signifier of status from armed, adult men who claimed to have denied his request. Even though most of the exchange is not recorded, through the language of prosecution in the criminal trial, mina men articulated hints of a junior age-set speaking to their senior kinsman.

Judicial cases are difficult texts to locate kinship relations as judicial prosecution targeted enslaved men as criminals. Nonetheless, enslaved men articulated hierarchies indicative of junior and senior kinsmen as well as regional animosities within relationships that Spanish colonial scribes listed as mere workmates. In 1717 a slaveholder filed a criminal case against four enslaved arara men accusing them of murdering another arara man. The testimony of the foursome suggests potent conflicts as well as lasting bonds. By the end of four months following their sale to a sugar estate in the Chicama valley, the four arara men grew increasingly desperate. The overseer had refused to advance their rations, indicating that their allocations were not sufficient or that their provision grounds had not yet produced.[164] Although it is probable that the four arara men had the skills to grow their own food, as new arrivals they may have not been able to claim water resources or not been assigned work tasks that allowed time to cultivate their assigned plots.[165]

After hearing their plans to kill the overseer, their elderly arara foreman counseled the men not to retaliate but to serve their owner and grow old as he had.[166] Especially since his words come to us from the testimony of the younger enslaved men, it is possible to understand the elderly arara man's position as a loyal agent of the slave owner; he may have simply wished to stifle rebellion.[167] Since the older supervisor spoke in a shared language, the younger arara man who provided this information may have also described a position of a senior kinsman since the elder also reminded them of their lower rank.[168] Whether it was advice for survival or a command to cease their resistance, the elderly arara man and the younger arara men exchanged more than words.

The four arara men did not follow the elderly man's counsel or directive. Concerned that he would reveal their plot to the overseer, the slaveholder pursuing the judicial case accused the arara foursome of beheading the arara foreman, each holding a limb. It is possible that the four men committed this act. They had been sold into the transatlantic slave trade during a period of intensifying armed conflict among the polities of the Bight of Benin, so their actions could be understood as those of soldiers, decapitating a competitor or a defeated enemy.[169] Nonetheless, through the act of beheading, the four arara men marked the elderly arara as a superior in terms of age as well as position.[170] Able to speak to one another, in their actions those called arara illustrated categorical differences among people who carried a similar name, arara, that perhaps was not of their choosing.[171] Their conflicts also suggest that just as enslaved men could construct their kinships in the Americas around transatlantic terms such as arara, they could also break ties that were no longer beneficial.

The act against the elderly arara supervisor can be understood as part of a larger plan to gain relief from the work regime on the rural estate. Once they killed their supervisor, the four arara men set out for the provincial capital of Trujillo. They attempted to retrace their captive journey. Before their sale to the Chicama estate, another fugitive arara man ensconced in the Franciscan monastery had warned the foursome to avoid being purchased by their owner, who was known to be cruel. If they were in fact sold, the refuged arara explained, they should kill a compañero or a workmate and then come to the Franciscan monastery presumably to seek temporary immunity and asylum. The refuged arara had provided valuable advice given the local context, as colonial religious orders had recently defended their legal ability to shelter accused criminals against the impatient demands of colonial secular officials.[172] The description of the four arara men makes sense in the context of the northern Peruvian coast. Trujillo slave traders often did not or could not maintain strict surveillance of their *partida*, or parcel, of captives who banded together to forage for food or information while awaiting sale outside of Trujillo.[173] The actions of the four arara men suggest that they acted based on reliable information. Together, but among strangers, they trusted their arara informant enough to act on his counsel once sold to the rural estate.

The enslaved men who had become fugitives were no longer unfamiliar to each other. They had gained access to an arara network on the northern Peruvian coast that provided resistance strategies in a shared language even if, in some cases, there were disagreements among its affiliates. The ones bonded most tightly were the four arara men who had been sold together to the Chicama estate and therefore acted in concert based on an affinity that preceded, and yet transformed, their mutual experiences as slaves. During the criminal investigation, one of the arara slaves, Ubaldo, testified that he and his three companions had agreed to tell the same story to the investigating officials "because they were relatives."[174] In fact, the bonds of kinship probably strengthened the resolve of the four men who suffered seven months of interrogation that, unlike other secular criminal trials of the period, included torture. According to their confessions, the four men had arrived together to Trujillo presumably after surviving the Pacific slave trade from Panama if not other Caribbean or transatlantic ports. Their refusal to blame each other for the murder of the elderly arara foreman during the criminal trial that dragged on for months, provides evidence of their strength and utility of their affiliations that they articulated as kinship.

The slave trade shaped how men and women would be able to claim kinships with each other, but as their claims to Catholic affiliations and kinship commitments illustrate, the market dynamics of the slave trade would not dominate all aspects of their lives. Africans created kinships in the diaspora as a strategy for survival but also as a means to express allegiances, hierarchies, and relations that could not be fully registered in Spanish colonial institutions. The majority of kinships among enslaved people remained unrecorded or only casually acknowledged by slaveholders requiring an examination of judicial cases to locate enslaved families and friends. African testimony also suggests that kinships carried additional functions. Among Africans in the Americas, maintaining kinships meant performing origins as well as articulating their survival of multiple slave trades. Kinships were not merely familial or strategic but articulations of identities and collectivities only superficially detected in civil and criminal cases, property sales, and personal wills. When read in the context of colonial exclusions, African articulations of kinships demonstrate how enslaved men and women intertwined but did not define their affinities with Spanish institutions.

———

As the Pacific trade of Africans primarily from Senegambia and Central Africa in the early seventeenth century shifted to sales of men and women from the Gold Coast and the Bight of Benin in the later part of the century, slave traders and agents constructed captives as commodities and located recently arrived Africans on the periphery of an already marginal status in the Spanish Americas. In multiple commercial transactions across the Atlantic, throughout the Caribbean, crossing the Panamanian peninsula, and in Pacific ports, slave traders expanded their terminology as they marketed men, women, and children to potential buyers. Employing transatlantic casta categories such as bran, mina, or angola in an effort to designate distinct (if mistaken) origins, traders and owners attempted to translate particular qualities of labor or character. In turn, enslaved people employed knowledge of their value to defend themselves within slavery. For their own benefit, enslaved people thought like both slaves and people or property and personhood.[175] By understanding the categories and characteristics assigned to them, enslaved men attempted to claim a limited mobility, and at least one enslaved woman called on the constructed value of her assigned casta in an effort to choose her owner. By acting as persons within processes intent on making them into objects, captive men and women claimed the value of their own status as property.

Rural slaves, with limited access to primarily urban courts or clerics whose visits to estates were rare, looked for other means to articulate kinships in addition to Catholic institutions. Regardless of gaining official Catholic recognition, kinship would prove critical to survive enslavement and even gain manumission since other forms of corporate identities and collective affinities were denied to Africans and their descendants or made difficult for rural and provincial enslaved men and women to claim. In addition, the ways that Africans articulated their kinships illustrate how in the Spanish Americas they inhabited an ambiguous legal and religious position. Colonial jurists located Africans and their descendants within the juridical Republic of the Spaniards but without the obligations and the rights afforded to subjects of the crown. The crown instructed slaveholders to limit physical punishment of enslaved people and to allow slaves to purchase themselves.[176] Africans and free people, however, still were definitively not vassals—a position offered to indigenous people who claimed the colonial category of "Indian" that included rights to govern their own Republic apart from so-called corrupting Spaniards.

In conjunction with and apart from the market, enslaved people created kinships from their experiences as captives and the possibilities offered by the Catholic Church. Ecclesiastical provisions mandated that owners must allow enslaved people to be baptized, to marry and receive final sacraments, while religious orders promoted specific African congregations that allowed for the expression of public diaspora communities.[177] Clerics in Peru reaffirmed the right for enslaved people to marry, and African-descent people as Catholics were included in canon law—one of the many legal realms of Spanish colonial judiciary.[178] Catholicism offered a location within the colonial body politic as Africans and their descendants were able to claim to be fellow Christians, a status they could share with Spanish subjects. At the same time, colonial Spaniards believed that enslaved and free Africans with their descendants carried a rejection of Christianity (including latent Muslim affinities) that made their identities as Catholics suspect.[179] In the case of recently arrived Africans, the customary practices of the market may have been more accessible than the colonial courts or ecclesiastical institutions. In this way, similar to developing a black legal consciousness, captives developed a market consciousness, and some were able to take advantage of their value.[180]

3. Acting as a Legal Indian

Natural Vassals and Worrisome Natives

SECULAR LEGAL DISCOURSE COMMUNICATED AN exclusion of Africans and their descendants from colonial society and extended more rhetorical inclusions to Andeans as Indians. Africans, especially those who recently survived multiple slave trades to Peru, invested in kinship connections and employed their market value to build new relationships within enslavement. Understanding how Andeans responded to colonial demands in relation to the agency of Africans reveals how the Spanish crown offered to protect indigenous people from colonizers' labor exploitation and land usurpation as long as they submitted to tribute and work obligations. Enslaved, rural Africans did not have a similar corporate location even though they claimed redress in colonial courts. As other scholars have explored, Andeans seized on opportunities to invoke juridical rulings, viceregal orders, and royal mandates that, although erratically respected, allowed some to protect communal land holdings or shield communities from the colonial labor draft (mita).[1] To take advantage of these legal possibilities, Andeans rhetorically assumed the role of the "poor Indian" and positioned themselves as "wretched" subordinates requiring paternal protection.[2] Andeans acted as Indians in legal forums that strategically eliminated Africans from juridical narratives. "Acting like an Indian" also had a price, however. In the 1640s the crown engaged in a massive process of land privatization that in effect dismantled the limited judicial power of the indigenous *reducciones* (assigned colonial towns). The Indian act, as tied to the crown-appointed reducciones, no longer functioned as effectively and required coastal Andeans to seek new ways to employ their Indian identities.

Coastal Andeans employed the legal category of "Indian" before and immediately following their de facto judicial disenfranchisement. To review, "Indian" was not an inherent communal identity. On the northern Peruvian coast (as elsewhere), indigenous communities did not call themselves "Indian" before Spanish colonization, and they continued to name themselves according to particular local nomenclatures following the establishment of colonial reducciones. In the centuries preceding 1532, coastal Andeans organized themselves into "infinitely sub divisible" moieties, or *parcialidades*, whose members created and maintained the water canals that irrigated their fields that had sustained advanced coastal civilizations.[3] In the latter part of the sixteenth century, colonial officials condensed these distinct moieties into reducciones or Indian towns where indigenous people continued their affiliations but also came to employ the possibilities of their new colonial communities. Colonial indigenous leaders (called caciques, *segunda personas*, and *principales* in colonial documentation) headed the moieties and towns based on reciprocal relations between commoners and elites.[4]

In response to the demands of colonial authorities, communities contributed tribute and sent laborers to local estates. Nobles, leaders, and other elites were exempt from labor requirements. Coastal Andeans identified themselves as farmers and fishing folk, weavers and potters, and other occupations—as they had before the Spanish arrival.[5] The diversity of coastal Andean communities was also reflected in the reported languages. Fishing people spoke a difficult language (according to the Spanish) compared with the inland valley inhabitants, who spoke *yunga* or *mochica*.[6] In addition, indigenous leaders sometimes spoke Quechua, reflecting the coastal Chimu's recent subordination (in the fifteenth century) to the highland Inca.[7] In the seventeenth century coastal Andeans continued to speak local languages and recognize the authority of their moiety (sometimes over that of the colonial reducción), suggesting that indigenous identities paralleled colonial assignations.

With a foot in both Andean and Spanish worlds, by the seventeenth century colonial indigenous people comprehended that the colonial categories assigned to them were both a means of exploitation and an opportunity for appeal. As "Indians," Andeans produced silver or the necessary goods (textiles, foodstuffs, alcohol, coca leaves) for the mining economies that provided the Spanish crown with significant revenue, at least initially.[8] On the northern Peruvian coast in the first half of the seventeenth century, the work of coastal Andeans complemented enslaved labor on regional estates that contributed flour, alcohol, and other products to regional economies that supported mining operations. Colonial mandates, in turn, translated their economic roles into legal locations such as a mitayo (an indigenous man who served mita), a tribute-payer (tributario), or a colonial messenger (chasqui).

Andeans who were known as mitayos, tributarios, or chasquis carried other identities, categories, affiliations, and associations but used these "Indian" locations in Spanish colonial courts. Reading judicial records "along the grain," I argue that Andeans assumed their roles as Indians in legal arenas as performative acts, which suggests that indigenous people were not simply or essentially made into Indians during the colonial period.[9] When possible, Andeans attempted to pick laws and categories that most bolstered their case in a plural legal order where the colonized were capable of engaging with multiple, however repressive, legal systems.[10] Indigenous legal activism therefore occurred within a discursive context of Catholic admonishments to protect the newly evangelized, crown orders to recognize native vassalage, and viceregal discussions of labor allocations. When taken in the context of Andean judicial agency, the casta term of "Indian" was used as an act rather than a fixed identity, indicating that coastal Andeans understood how "Indian" was an externally imposed category applicable in colonial judicial situations.

In the early decades of the seventeenth century, Andeans employed crown mandates to limited success in defending their communal lands against expanding sugar estates, wheat farms, and cattle ranches. Coastal reducciones, did not contend with the massive pull of the mita requirements to the silver mines in the southern Andes or the textile mills of the northern Andes, but still negotiated the labor demanded by local agrarian enterprises. Coastal Andeans were itinerant laborers alongside enslaved men and women on the estates. In these capacities they did not mention their interactions with Africans in judicial presentations in order to conform to crown expectations of separate spheres between blacks and Indians. During the composición de tierras in the 1640s the crown ordered viceregal representatives to sell off so-called vacant lands of indigenous communities throughout the Andes.[11] On the northern Peruvian coast this series of land sales reduced indigenous land holdings and pushed coastal Andeans away from their colonial towns due to a lack of arable land and reduced access to irrigation water.[12] Coastal Andean communities immediately responded to the material crisis of the land privatization but also to the change in crown policy. The royal mandates to sell off communal Andean lands communicated a judicial and discursive betrayal of a colonial agreement between the crown and indigenous communities. In response, Andeans presented themselves as Indians on new stages and, in some cases, against prescribed colonial expectations.

Acting Like an Official Indian

In the early seventeenth century, Andean communities appealed to crown representatives to protect their laborers and communal lands from usurpation by local colonizers. In some cases indigenous individuals were able to negotiate new landownership that fit with the general trend of privatization.[13] In other instances Andean communities capitalized on local demands for labor to avoid delivering laborers for a mita quota to far-off mines and estates.[14] Overall, indigenous communities faced difficulties employing crown orders for their own benefit because royal mandates were not uniformly enforced.[15] In addition, on the northern Peruvian coast, private Spanish landholders had steadily encroached on indigenous fields and irrigation canals since the sixteenth century.[16] In the early part of the seventeenth century, owners of coastal estates continued to demand that local reducciones supply more laborers to the required mita, even as communities were documenting to colonial officials that their populations were declining.[17] Nonetheless, coastal Andeans employed multiple (and overlapping statuses) and performed their legally expected roles to claim what the Spanish crown had decreed, including fair wages, reduced tribute obligations, and land allocations.

Coastal Andeans, like their counterparts throughout the Americas, were legally astute. Through legal assistants appointed to represent Indians in colonial courts (*protectores de naturales*), they called on relevant mandates and employed judicial language to describe their official characteristics.[18] Indigenous people probably manipulated the intentions as well as the mechanics of colonial judicial cases. Many of their assigned legal representatives were informally trained and interested in pursuing more lucrative appointments. It is also likely that these protectores were inclined to favor Spanish landholders, or had merely paid for their position to exact fees.[19] Indigenous leaders maintained control of legal actions by retaining community notaries who kept copies of royal orders, viceregal announcements, and other compilations of legislation to help with the composition of legal writs.[20] Indigenous legal representation was further facilitated by cultural adaptation. By the seventeenth century most coastal indigenous leaders spoke Spanish, rode horses, owned private land, and some maintained houses in Trujillo.[21]

With these skills and resources, for example, leaders of the indigenous reducción of Mansiche bestowed don Antonio Chaybac with the legal permission to petition the viceroy in Lima for a recount of their population. A new census would allow them to reassess the amount of tribute and the number of mitayos owed by their community.[22] With this petition Mansiche leaders hoped to lower the amount of tribute and the number of mitayos owed by their reducción. In all likelihood the Mansiche representatives included the biannual registers in the notarized "power of attorney" to prove the actual population of their reducción in their certification of Chayguac. The notary of the agreement certified with the marginal notation "my eyes," indicating that he agreed that their documents were correct and further suggesting that the information was not from his archives.[23] By calling for (and agreeing to pay for) a reinspection of their population (a specific legal action afforded to Indian reducciones), the Mansiche delegation presented themselves as vassals or subjects of the king who deserved an audience with his highest representative.[24] In doing so, the Mansiche leadership (like other indigenous communities) demonstrated their ability to "act like Indians" to affect an outcome that they planned and desired.

Indigenous people understood that they had to present themselves within specific roles assigned to Indians to employ the colonial courts. In 1639 the couriers of the reducción of San Pedro de Mórrope complained that they had not been paid in years. Because they provided such a critical service, they drew on a well-established body of viceregal mandates, including a Toledan order from the sixteenth century that local magistrates needed to properly care for indigenous couriers or chasquis. They also invoked a reiteration from 1601 of viceroy don Luis de Velasco, who had warned provincial magistrates to pay indigenous couriers in a timely fashion for their service of carrying messages throughout the Andes.[25] Spanish colonial orders contributed to the idea that only indigenous men, serving as chasquis, carried letters, copies of lawsuits, merchant accounts, and other important documents between the colonial cities. In fact, mestizo muleteers, Spanish ship captains, and even enslaved men conveyed official and unofficial documentation along coastal routes.[26] Nonetheless, in the judicial case the indigenous men of Mórrope emphasized the "Indian" nature of their work.[27]

Their Spanish and Spanish-speaking indigenous witnesses testified that the Mórrope chasquis had one of the worse routes in the viceroyalty that included crossing the Sechura desert between the fertile Lambayeque valley and the Spanish city of Piura, more than thirty leagues to the north. Only they—"Indians" with native knowledge and local networks—could service this desert route.[28] The case was contentious because colonial officials had not paid the Mórrope men for years even as the Andean men had repeatedly sought compensation.[29] For the indigenous couriers the solution was clear. They presented a receipt from 1630 to verify that they had previously been paid thirty pesos for their work as "*chasqueros.*" Presenting themselves within their valued and recognized Indian status (regardless of who else worked as couriers), the coastal Andean laborers sought to reconcile an ongoing debt between their community, themselves, and the colonial state.

Likewise, in the early seventeenth century, coastal Andeans took advantage of landholders' need for laborers and employed their status as mitayos to argue for better working conditions. In 1630 indigenous men from the Chicama valley reducción of Magdalena de Cao utilized an assigned representative to present a civil suit against a local landholder. Salvador Guaman, Gaspar Tupí, Lorenço Cecoram, and Pedro Guaman claimed that Bartolomé Miranda and other owners had assigned more cattle than the herders could control. The coastal Andeans pointed out how two mitayos were necessary to guard the allotted cattle rather than one.[30] With the assistance of their legal representative, they explained that without sufficient herders, the cattle escaped and the resulting damage to local fields was charged to the assigned men serving mita. To control the large herds, the men were forced to hire helpers, at their own cost. The coastal Andeans framed their argument within crown expectations of "poor" Indians and suggested that their loyal service caused them to become more impoverished.[31] Since the cattle owners did not respond to their request, the Magdalena de Cao men appeared before Trujillo's magistrate, to ask that "owners of cattle hire two men" for the task.[32] Requiring the workforce to double during a period when local landholders could barely fill their current allocation was a bold move for the rural herders.

Further illustrating the intrepid move of the lawsuit from the indigenous reducción of Magdalena de Cao, while legally accused of misconduct, Bartolomé Miranda and other landholders were not breaking the law. According to the indigenous testimonies, Miranda and other Chicama valley landholders appear to have been following a set of ordinances from 1591 that required mitayos to pay for lost cattle and obliged laborers to hire an assistant.[33] Because of the "multiple legal systems" of colonial orders, there was also a regulation that an owner whose cattle damaged fields and crops would be forced to compensate the farmer.[34] Ignoring the second regulation and passing on the cost of their cattle's damage to the assigned mitayos, Chicama valley landholders were not committing a crime, since Spanish colonial law was not a set of codes to be uniformly enforced.[35] More important, because justice was "not about obedience to laws or abstract moral criteria," the landholders relied on being treated according to their status.[36] Even as indigenous people called on an alternative set of mandates, Bartolomé Miranda, like other landholders, employed regulations that served his superior position as a cattle owner who enjoyed royally appointed mita allocations.

To argue against the landholders' position, the legal representative of the four indigenous men from Magdalena de Cao emphasized the crown protections afforded to the Indians as mitayos. The representative invoked orders issued by viceroy Francisco de Toledo from the late sixteenth century outlining the types of labor to be performed as mita service. The former viceroy had distinguished between easier tasks (such as guarding sheep, goats, and pigs) and the harder work that cattle required (herding by horseback).[37] Toledan orders also differentiated between "large" cattle that required more skill and the apparently less significant labor required to herd smaller animals that the indigenous laborers emphasized in their testimony.[38] Interestingly, the legal representative working for the men from Magdalena de Cao did not mention skill. Instead, he hinged his argument on "the types of cattle" (with a nod to legal mandates) and argued that the local landholders should employ one mitayo for oxen and another for horses. Like their legal representative (and most likely following his directives), indigenous witnesses called attention to the distinct categories of cattle by specifically listing cows, horses, oxen, and mules as those guarded by the Magdalena de Cao mitayos.

Quantity also mattered as two "native Indians" of the reducción claimed that one mitayo assigned to Bartolomé Miranda's ranch was not sufficient for his ninety-two mules and oxen.[39] Again, the assigned representative and his witnesses called on specific ordinances that allotted eighty cattle for each "Indian herder."[40] Astutely, the legal representative described the complaints of the men from Magadalena de Cao to fit into viceregal and royal mandates intended to protect native vassals. The community of Magadalena de Cao had many other reasons to complain about the landholder Bartolomé Miranda, who had usurped their communal land and allowed his cattle to destroy their irrigation canals.[41] Regardless, the men from the reducción specifically acted like Indians—insofar as mitayo indexed a position of native vassalage, not just a labor category—in the judicial narrative to mount a spirited legal attack.

In addition to royal protections afforded to Andean men serving crown-mandated mita labor, coastal indigenous laborers also employed legal discourses to emphasize an overall injustice or an imbalance in the Chicama valley.[42] If the excessive number of cattle made their jobs impossible, the men from Magdalena de Cao also complained that the cattle were inquieto, or restless. According to the coastal Andeans who served mita as herders, cattle of this nature were expensive. If they were to guard "restless cattle," then the owners should pay for two laborers and the cost of the damaged fields. It is possible that the legal assistant composed this aspect of the accusation, but the invocation of "restless" suggests an ironic usage. When employed in a legal sense, "restless" implied a person who enjoyed aggressive conflict versus a hardworking, peaceful, and deserving person of a tranquil nature.[43] More specifically, magistrates, notaries, and other legal representatives in colonial Peruvian courts often used the word "restless" to describe indigenous people. For example, a "restless Indian" was a rebellious troublemaker who did not work and caused damage that hinted at violence (the opposite of a humble, hard-working Indian vassal who did not draw attention to himself).[44] The Magdalena de Cao men who served mita, bound within legal protocols and customary practice, could not directly insult a Spanish landholder who they worked for and who increasingly exercised control over their communities' water supply and land holdings. By implying that Miranda's cattle were rebellious and not the landholder himself, the petitioners reversed accusations that could be leveled at indigenous men such as themselves who filed legal complaints against their social superiors. By acting within their humble role of mita-serving Indians who guarded cattle, coastal Andeans pointed out the lawless actions of their opponent.

In judicial narratives, indigenous laborers were constructed as law-abiding in an effort to fit within the protections afforded by royal mandates. Whether influenced by their legal assistants or operating under their own understanding of legal procedures, the men who serve mita from Magdalena de Cao repeatedly referred to official edicts or that which was "ordered."[45] In addition, they offered an alternative to their assigned legal representative's solution of one mitayo for each type of cattle that was lifted directly from royal mandates. They suggested the landholder Miranda should employ two mitayos to guard his oxen, horses, and mules. Two men could control the "restless" cattle and keep them from wandering into fields that could even belong to the mitayos or members of their community.[46] In this way indigenous men attempted to address a labor problem within their treatment as "Indians." As coastal Andeans, they manipulated the colonial legislation that protected them in their capacities as Indians serving mita—as mitayos—but they also asserted themselves as neighbors to an abusive landholder. By employing their positions as Indians within their expected location as mitayos, the men from Magdalena de Cao redefined the nature of the required work.

Indigenous men from the assigned reducciones who employed colonial mandates did not abide by all royal expectations of subservient Indians. In 1640 two brothers paid a notary in the provincial city of Trujillo to draw up a rental contract. They had inherited lands from their father, the leader of Santiago de Cao, a colonial reducción in the neighboring Chicama valley. Perhaps the two brothers were not considered to be the reducción's leaders and therefore could not legally rent out lands that their father held for the community.[47] Usually rental agreements were direct and formulaic, but the document indicates that the two brothers, don Jacinto and don Pablo Paypaymamo, were practiced operators in the colonial judicial terrain as they paid and directed the notary to complete the record according to their specifications.[48] Unlike most notarized land sales, they included an order from the viceroy to the Trujillo magistrate allowing indigenous landholders to rent communal lands.[49]

The Paypaymamo brothers employed the viceregal order to overrule the local magistrate's denial of their petition. They invoked the viceroy's permission granted to the leaders of Paiján in the nearby Jequetepeque valley. The recopied document was useful. The Paiján leaders employed language that would be familiar to colonial authorities. They called themselves "poor people" and "implored" officials to grant their petition by pointing out that without the income from the rented fields, they would be unable to pay their tribute.[50] In these sentences the Paiján leaders employed the characteristics of Indians as wretched people that commonly circulated in colonial orders and mandates. As did other Andean communities, the Paiján leaders as well as the Paypaymamo brothers pitted local colonial authorities against viceregal and crown officials.[51] Moreover, both suggested that local colonial authorities inhibited them from fulfilling their duty as tributarios, or tribute-paying vassals of the crown.

Did either the Santiago de Cao brothers or the Paiján leaders believe that they were impoverished or wretched? Possibly.[52] The Paypaymamo brothers' relatively wealthy status also indicates that they employed the official location assigned to Indians—the reducción—for their own purposes. In the case of Paiján, they petitioned to rent their landed property as an alternative to exchanging or selling their acreage.[53] In other words, the coastal indigenous community attempted to permanently retain control of their lands rather than renting them for short-term gain. The Paiján leaders argued that more income, in the form of tribute, would be generated for the crown if they were allowed to keep their lands. As for the Paypaymamo brothers, they transferred the judicial narrative of lowly reducción Indians into the notary records (a transaction that they paid for), but attempted to capitalize as private landholders.

At the same time that leaders of indigenous rural communities and certain coastal Andean men employed their positions as loyal mita-serving, tribute-paying vassals, they (with their legal representatives) erased their labor experiences with enslaved men. When indigenous men provided mita to rural estates, whether to guard cattle or to work in fields, they labored alongside or in close proximity to enslaved Africans and their descendants.[54] Members of indigenous reducciones who served as mitayos formed close, if itinerant, relations with enslaved laborers. For example, Cristina, "of Angola land," confessed when she was caught that she had escaped from her owner's ranch with an "Indian mitayo."[55] Together, they had managed to travel undetected from the Jequetepeque valley into the adjoining Chicama valley. It is plausible that the indigenous man who had been serving mita knew local people and proved to be a useful ally for Cristina.[56] Contact with enslaved men and women, however, was not useful in judicial narratives, where legal mandates constructed Indians as devoted native vassals who served the crown in separate capacities from blacks.

More commonly, indigenous communities included Africans and their descendants into their judicial narratives as enemies. Depicting Africans as predators of Andeans fit with legal expectations and colonial predictions of indigenous-black relations.[57] For example, coastal Andean communities repeatedly complained that fugitive men stole from their fields, robbed their members, and (in some cases) sexually assaulted indigenous women.[58] Describing blacks as preying on indigenous communities served to bolster the depiction of Indians as helpless victims, even if in many cases coastal Andeans and fugitive Africans also traded and knew each other as fellow laborers.[59] In 1626, Juana Quispi, the wife of Juan Cipirán (a member of the Ulchop parcialidad in the reducción of Magdalena de Cao), registered a criminal complaint against Mateo, a black congo slave from the Farias estate in the Chicama valley. According to her, Mateo accused Juan Cipirán of stealing a horse and then murdered her husband on the road to Trujillo.[60]

Juana Quispi (or her legal representative) suggested that Mateo was angry with her husband and had sought retribution from his owner for the death of her spouse. One tactic was to depict the enslaved man as an aggressive black preying on an innocent Indian, a common circulating trope in clerical texts and colonial judicial language.[61] Details from the case, however, suggest ongoing relations between enslaved laborers (such as Mateo) and the members of the local indigenous reducción. Diego de Poses, a native of

Magdalena de Cao, testified that he was in a field of a local landholder "eating with the rest of the mitayos" when Mateo, the enslaved black congo man, arrived on horseback and said to an enslaved mulato (who apparently was also taking a break from working with the mitayos) "that he did something really bad."[62] Also, Salvador Cumozan, a native of the Ulchop parcialidad, had offered Mateo congo some chicha when he passed on the road.[63] Mateo therefore was not a stranger to the indigenous residents of Magdalena de Cao. In addition, Mateo of casta congo and Juan Cipirán appear to have disagreed over a trade agreement; witnesses declared the two men had argued earlier about the cost of a mare.[64] The incident suggests that in daily relations coastal Andeans had amicable and ongoing contact with enslaved men. When constructing themselves as vulnerable Indians in judicial narratives, however, coastal Andeans reshaped their contact with enslaved Africans into evidence of antagonism.

Before the land privatization of the 1640s, indigenous communities in the Chicama valley may have maintained an upper hand in their relations with enslaved laborers. In 1617 indigenous leaders and commoners (as well as other Andean laborers) gathered to drink but also to meet and discuss community issues at a ranch in the Chicama valley. According to multiple witnesses, Francisco Mandinga (an enslaved man) came across the group while on an errand for his owner and joined them. Francisco knew members of the Santiago de Cao reducción well enough to greet them. According to indigenous witnesses, however, Francisco Mandinga either failed to take off his hat when he entered the gathering or sat in the spot that had been occupied by the indigenous alcalde.[65] It is possible that some of those gathered associated Francisco with a local landholder, Bartolomé Miranda, who was engaged in a protracted struggle over land and water rights with local indigenous communities including the Santiago de Cao reducción.[66] According to indigenous witnesses, Francisco Mandinga had also deeply offended the coastal Andeans who by all accounts had invited the enslaved man to drink, a clear sign of companionship among laborers, and then presumably insulted them.[67]

Whatever the cause, the indigenous men seized Francisco Mandinga, knifed him, and left him for dead. In the ensuing criminal case, the assigned representative of the indigenous community attempted, weakly, to construct a judicial narrative of helpless Indians as the slaveholder pursued monetary damages for the cost of his wounded slave. Members of the Santiago de Cao reducción claimed that Francisco Mandinga had begun the fight and tried to take their food. Witnesses, however, declared that the official from the Santiago de Cao reducción had ordered twenty of the gathered indigenous men to kill Francisco Mandinga before he killed them, because "blacks are real dogs."[68] The overwhelming evidence of indigenous aggression against a single enslaved man (regardless of his cultural infractions) served to bolster the refutation by a slaveholder's legal representative.

As coastal Andeans named themselves as Indians to be protected, they produced their own sense of justice that could exclude Africans and their descendants. When the magistrate's assistant came to Santiago de Cao to pay the chasquis in 1626, don Diego Mache, the head of Santiago de Cao and an indigenous leader in the Chicama valley, seized on the opportunity to denounce a Spanish overseer for beating his son. Accompanied by another community member, Mache's son had attempted to open an obstructed irrigation canal. Upon finding the indigenous men interfering with the water supply to the estate, a slave and a mitayo along with the overseer of the estate beat Mache's son and his companion. In addition, the overseer directed the enslaved laborer with the mitayo to close off the water supply to the indigenous reducción of Santiago de Cao. In retaliation, before the magistrate's representative, the leader of Santiago de Cao claimed that the Spanish overseer was stealing water. According to don Diego Mache, the indigenous reducción of Santiago de Cao held customary rights to the "irrigation ditch of the Indians of the parcialidad of Ulchop, reduced to Magdalena de Cao."[69]

Mache claimed that the owners of the estate had unlawfully diverted the water to their fields. He also referred to customary, coastal Andean allocations of water that colonial officials had initially recognized when they reduced indigenous communities to colonial villages and allocated communal landholdings.[70] His indignation suggests that he still understood that indigenous leaders, not landholders, decided the water allocations in the valleys.[71] Furthermore, Mache declared, his son had merely been carrying out the orders of the colonial officer who governed water distribution in the valley. Mache therefore fit his complaint into the laws governing indigenous communities. In doing so, he represented himself and his community as Indians who appealed to the crown's promise to protect corporate allocations (including water rights) of their native vassals that clearly distinguished them from enslaved laborers and Spanish or Spanish-descent landholders.

Don Diego Mache's court case ends with an anonymous document that suggests a deft usage of colonial judicial discourse from an indigenous perspective. The writer claimed that the "Spaniards who have fields and estates and ranches" are "totally our enemies because they take our lands and water."[72] When thinking about who composed the anonymous document, it is useful to recall that indigenous adjudicators borrowed from official mandates.[73] The document included in don Diego Mache's case recalls the words of a viceroy who declared that the "enemies" of the "poor Indians" were "their magistrates, their priests, and their caciques."[74] Echoing contemporaneous language regarding Indians, the author (or authors) condemned all Spanish landholders in the Chicama valley and drew on a common rhetoric of royal officials who bemoaned the "bad treatment" of Indians who were "such miserable people" that they were taken advantage of by their "worst enemies," the magistrates, as well as by their leaders.[75]

Indicating how coastal Andeans employed this judicial language and changed its meaning, the author in the 1626 document from the Chicama valley did not blame indigenous leaders or appointed officials, who in this case could have been the authors or patrons of the document. Instead, the writer or writers charged Spanish estate owners with mistreating indigenous laborers and not paying "Indian mitayos." Again, the author alluded to early seventeenth-century royal and viceregal assessments that bad treatment and the lack of just wages caused impoverishment and destruction of the Indians.[76] The authors employed colonial mandates to serve as a rousing defense of indigenous communities at a local level but in the process contributed to a legal discourse where only Indians suffered injustices.

Even though the document is not signed, it is highly plausible that don Diego Mache influenced its message.[77] According to his will, Mache kept "many sworn statements and documents" that may have included copies of sermons, short tracts, or clerical *relaciones*. Furthermore, buried in Trujillo's surviving notarial records, is evidence that Mache paid the salary of his community's legal representative.[78] He therefore had access to the discursive means and could influence, if not control, the legal spokesmen to communicate his message. In addition, don Diego Mache came from a family who had quickly risen to leadership positions in the sixteenth century.[79] He was Catholic, fluent in Spanish, and (based on his will) owned lands and houses as well as two horses with a saddle.[80] In addition, the core of Mache's complaints, if we can take his patronage as authorship, was the overexploitation of Indians as laborers. According to the document, the "blood and sweat" of the "poor Indians" was uncompensated, as "the Spaniards owed the Indians more than two thousand pesos" in wages.[81]

At a local level Mache's fortunes were at stake. Without their wages, indigenous people would not contribute to their community's biannual tribute payments, leaving Mache and other indigenous leaders to pay the hundreds of pesos owed to the local magistrate.[82] The writer employed colonial language regarding indigenous laborers and their need for royal protection to argue for just compensation based on circulating attributes of Indians to claim money owed to the laborers of Santiago de Cao and to their leaders.

At the same time, the author or authors clearly erased any affinities with enslaved Africans and their descendants, who sweated and worked on the same tasks as indigenous mitayos—and even suffered similar abuses at the hands of coastal landholders.

A wide cross section of indigenous people on the northern coast of Peru had access to judicial language describing Indians. Crown representatives presumably announced royal edicts in public locations during commercial hours.[83] In the first half of the seventeenth century, indigenous communities maintained their own notary or scribe who recorded and safeguarded the pertinent land titles, tribute counts, and water rights rulings for his community or took advantage of urban notaries who traveled to rural environs.[84] Rural parish priests were supposed to read from doctrinal guides influenced by an ecclesiastical interpretation of Indians as oppressed minors who deserved protection.[85] Coastal Andeans did not merely imitate these examples of a colonial discourse that was flatly derogatory and that denied them the status and capacities of adults.[86] Instead, privileged indigenous people who were rooted in functioning reducciones employed legal assistants to use the colonial legal terms and royal rulings to their advantage. They utilized the colonial courts to insert their demands into colonial rhetoric and claimed membership as Indians within the Spanish colonial sphere. As long as the reducción remained intact, indigenous people would employ the judicial category of Indian for their own benefit. The judicial narrative, however, required that legal representatives and indigenous people remove Africans who were undoubtedly a part of everyday relations, even for Andeans of the reducciones.

A Broken Pact: Land Sales of the 1640s

Spanish usurpation of indigenous land and water intensified in the 1640s. Driven by the crown's need to fill its empty coffers, the viceroy mandated a *composición de tierras*, or an inspection and reallocation of land holdings in the viceroyalty.[87] Although some communities won their appeals against this abrupt usurpation of communal holdings, the 1640s mark a radical shift in indigenous land tenure as well as reducción membership on the northern coast. In the northern coastal valleys indigenous communities lost significant portions of communal and individually owned property to private Spanish buyers. Without sufficient land and water, indigenous people increasingly abandoned their assigned reducciones, leaving indigenous leaders with fewer resources to submit tribute payments and supply mitayos. Claiming protections as Indians from reducciones, then, became no longer viable as indigenous officials who were appointed by local colonial authorities increasingly challenged indebted Andean leaders. By the end of the 1640s coastal Andean communities understood that the crown and its representatives were no longer interested in their appeals and therefore they would turn to other strategies, collectively and individually.

Colonial officials had rearranged indigenous land allotments before, but in 1642 a viceregal appointee, don Pedro de Meneses, began a reallocation of supposed "vacant" lands that would result in a monumental usurpation of indigenous holdings by Spanish estates.[88] By 1643 the Meneses inspection had moved from north to south through the Lambayeque valley to Jequetepeque and by 1644 into the Chicama and Trujillo valleys.[89] Initially, indigenous leaders attempted to comply with Meneses's inspection of land titles on the northern coast but eventually were unable to halt the illegal usurpation of their landholdings. According to the king's orders, the inspector was supposed to review the existing land titles and legalize untitled lands by selling them to the highest bidder.[90] Unlike previous land inspections, Meneses strictly interpreted his orders and allocated indigenous communities only the amount of land that corresponded to their official rolls (that were not always accurate) of residing tribute members.[91] In some cases indigenous communities had underestimated their resident members in an effort to reduce their required tribute payments.[92] Many indigenous leaders who had successfully employed their legal status and their communities' enactments as Indians experienced Meneses's inspection as a drastic reversal of colonial relations.

Leaders of indigenous reducciones attempted to resist the new colonial order by employing previous methods including utilizing crown orders against local demands. In 1643 the leader of the Ulchop parcialidad of Magdalena de Cao in the Chicama valley flatly declared that he did not have enough Indian men to supply required numbers of mitayos to guard cattle. With his legal representative he invoked Toledan orders specifying that the number of mitayos be proportionate to the resident population and then pointed out how the parcialidad had experienced a severe demographic decline since their last population assessment during the late sixteenth century.[93] The indigenous leader emphatically declared that the parcialidad therefore "did not have the obligation to supply mita."[94] The Ulchop representative enacted Indian claims as had other Andean communities before the land inspections but this time suffered radically different consequences. Months after his spirited defense, and as the land inspections began in the Chicama valley, the colonial judge of the treasury imprisoned the indigenous leader from Magdalena de Cao. The earlier means of petitioning for royal justice was beginning to dissipate on the northern Peruvian coast.

Petitioning royal representatives to follow crown regulations was contingent on the active involvement of reducción leaders. Indigenous leaders continued to defend their communities and their positions, but faced mounting pressures.[95] In addition to his refusal to supply mitayos, in 1643 the Ulchop leader discussed earlier declined to reveal more information to local colonial authorities regarding the numbers of reportedly dead or absent reducción members.[96] As was the common practice of colonial caciques, he was reluctant to disclose the actual population of the Chicama communities.[97] A reported increase would mean he was responsible for increased tribute payments and supplying more mitayos.[98] The Ulchop leader's refusal to follow colonial mandates indicated a growing suspicion of their perceived efficacy. It appears likely that given the disrespect that reducción leaders (caciques, principales, segunda personas) experienced during the land inspection, many understood that the rules of the game were changing.[99] Indicating how the land inspection impacted coastal Andeans, for decades before the 1640s there were no records of communities in arrears for tribute payments in the notary records that I reviewed in the Trujillo archives. By 1649 at least two indigenous leaders from Santiago de Cao and Paiján were in debt to Spanish officials for tribute payments owed by their communities.[100] Indigenous leaders appeared to be less likely to negotiate with local colonial authorities who had become more exacting.

The land sales also coincided with the emerging power of appointed indigenous officials over those who came from elite or noble indigenous families. In late October 1643 the elected alcalde of the Ulchop parcialidad in Magdalena de Cao, Alonso Jaratán, directed deputies to burn thatched homes found in the surrounding fields. According to Jaratán, he was carrying out "provisions dispatched by the royal government" to force reducción members to leave their temporary residences and to inhabit houses in their assigned town. He claimed the order had been announced in the central square and streets of Magdalena de Cao in September suggesting that reducción members should have had time to move into town.[101] In one sense Jaratán was following long-standing royal orders repeated in multiple viceregal mandates that indigenous people return to their assigned reducciones to pay tribute and to serve mita that perhaps had taken on new urgency with the royal land inspection. In his capacity as a representative of Ulchop, Jaratán invoked old colonial mandates to burn down the field home of don Juan Chumbi Guaman, Magdalena de Cao's principal, or one of its hereditary leaders.[102]

According to Chumbi Guaman, Jaratán also destroyed important papers and allowed a notebook that included imperative documents to be taken. As the impending Meneses's inspection required indigenous leaders to produce land titles or tribute rolls, Jaratán might have ensured that Chumbi Guaman would be unable to defend his or his community's land ownership.[103] Jaratán's actions can be explained due to the increasing tensions between his parcialidad and the main leadership of the reducción (as represented by Chumbi Guaman) over land allotment. Trujillo's magistrate had reallocated lands to Ulchop that had once belonged to "the Indians of Magdalena de Cao."[104] The threats of the land inspection might have also encouraged members of the Ulchop parcialidad to revisit grievances that began when the Indian towns had been created in order to challenge the dominant leadership of Magdalena de Cao.

Jaratán's behavior underlines the rise of indigenous officials who had been appointed by colonial authorities. By labeling Chumbi Guaman as an Indian who "rebelled" against publicly declared royal mandates, Jaratán enforced his own position as an obedient Indian. The Ulchop leaders, however, did not follow the previous tactics of acting like official Indians and were not necessarily interested in following all royal mandates. For instance, in 1643 the Ulchop leadership employed a legal representative to counter crown orders that charged indigenous leaders with locating and bringing back missing members.[105] The newly appointed leaders did not follow local protocol. In 1647 one of the appointed Ulchop leaders took the cape of the reducción's hereditary leaders and sold it to an overseer from a local estate.[106] In addition to usurping the value of the clothing, the new official humiliated the established leader by retailing a symbol of his authority.[107] In both cases the aggressive behavior of appointed indigenous authorities heralded the dismantling of the indigenous reducciones just as the land inspections had undermined the positions of hereditary leaders who could no longer protect their communities.

The effects of the land inspections were immediate and long-lasting. On the northern Peruvian coast, indigenous communities lost lands that appeared to lie fallow or were deemed too extensive for their population; they also lost lands that were fertile and in use.[108] The royal inspector favored Spanish and Spanish-descent landholders by notifying them (and not indigenous people) of the public auctions, and conducting land sales when indigenous elites could not attend.[109] In other cases colonial officials appropriated inventories and land deeds from indigenous people and refused to return them to inhibit indigenous appeals.[110] Consequently, indigenous leaders in Lambayeque complained that the new lands allocated to their communities were small, distant, barren, and lacked sufficient water.[111] Most notably, Meneses sold significant portions of the communal holdings of Paiján, Santiago de Cao, Magdalena de Cao, and other reducciones to "Spaniards" in the Chicama valley.[112] Without sufficient land or water, then, members abandoned their assigned reducciones and migrated to work on local estates or in regional cities, or even as far as the mines in the southern Andes.[113] With more land and water as well as an increase in laborers, the private estates in turn expanded on the northern Peruvian coast.

Coastal Andeans understood that they were losing their claim to the protections of their assigned Republic that depended on populating the reducciones. The transformations in this period were not unique to the northern Peruvian coast.[114] In Cochabamba, in the southern part of the Peruvian viceroyalty, the number of adult males who claimed or were assigned the category of tributary shrunk dramatically, while in the northern Andes the majority of indigenous people migrated to work away from their assigned reducciones.[115] In response, the viceroy attempted to collect tribute from indigenous people even if they had left their assigned reducciones, further discouraging connections to Indian towns.[116] Whether from the demands of the local mita or the push from land privatization, by the 1640s coastal Andeans were less likely to locate themselves or their judicial narratives according to the ideal of an Indian paying tribute and serving mita while living on an assigned reducción. In the northern Peruvian valleys coastal Andeans would redefine their claims to the category of Indian in and off their original and adopted reducciones.

Restless Indians

Leaders from reducciones in the Lambayeque and Chicama valleys attempted to sue Meneses, the royal appointee who redistributed lands, in viceregal and eventually Spanish courts. In return, the colonial official mounted a vigorous defense and argued that the charges of abuse against him were false because Indians by nature were unstable and restless people who easily lied.[117] Particular coastal Andean communities maintained a longstanding feud with Meneses. In their 1648 appeal, hereditary indigenous leaders of the Chicama valley charged that the recent Dutch attacks on the Peruvian coasts had done less damage to His Majesty "and his vassals" as Meneses had committed in his offenses against the "natural Indians of these jurisdictions."[118] The only harm of pirate attacks was the loss of silver, while the royal inspector had cut at the heart of the kingdom.[119] With these words the Chicama leadership included Indians in a well-known portrayal of Spain and its colonies.[120] Even if native vassals were the workers, forming what the Franciscan Juan de Silva called "the clay feet, the arms and the main body" (and not the head), they were still part of the colonial society.[121] In this vision of colonial Spanish America, Spaniards and Indians formed together "a congregation and council of Christians, vassals of his Majesty" as members of the same "republic" (that pointedly did not include blacks).[122] In these petitions coastal Andeans continued to remind the crown of their earned location in this version of colonial hierarchy.

The appeals cases regarding the 1640s land privatization communicated how the process and the outcome of the land inspections challenged Andeans. Why would they continue to act according to colonial expectations? Indigenous landholders from Lambayeque repeatedly stated that Meneses, the colonial land inspector, had seized inherited lands even though they repeatedly had shown their written titles.[123] Their arguments were based on ancestral land claims as well as their dependence on written documentation, both of which they understood had ensured their land ownership.[124] In their judicial presentation the Lambayeque men expressed their dismay that this arrangement apparently had been shattered without explanation or warning. Chicama indigenous leaders also described how even their assigned legal representative in addition to other provincial officials had closed the door to justice.[125]

In both appeals cases indigenous people argued not only for a reversal of past legal decisions and the punishment of the offenders—solutions that recalled previous approaches. In the late 1640s coastal Andeans implored the crown to restore balance in the valleys by returning the lands that would conserve the "natives."[126] Without justice, what the historian Tamar Herzog has described as social harmony would be ruptured.[127] Andeans on reducciones had understood that they had a legitimate place in colonial hierarchies that they paid for with their loyal service, and they asked that the crown force its representatives to respect their location. For indigenous petitioners what was at question in the late 1640s was not only the violation of royal mandates or colonial laws but a larger issue that acting like an Indian had been devalued.

Coastal Andeans who were not from the inherited class of indigenous leadership, had not been appointed by colonial authorities, and had questionable membership in assigned reducciones discarded previous judicial narratives and seek out new ways to act like Indians. Provoked by a viceroy who "had not executed justice," the Lambayeque indigenous communities overstepped the usual channels and sent their own Andean representative directly to "ask for justice" from the king.[128] In the late 1640s don Andrés de Ortega presented himself to the viceregal court in Lima and then to the royal court in Madrid. According to royal mandates, "noble Indians" could travel to the *Audiencia* court in their district (in this case, Lima) to "present their complaint [or] ask for satisfaction of an offense."[129] By continuing to Spain, don Andrés overstepped provincial colonial authorities. In disregard of royal orders he reached the place where he could appeal to the king.[130] There, he described how the Indians of Lambayeque had experienced nuisances, imprisonment, and "bad treatments" from the previous and current magistrates.[131]

Don Andrés employed legal assistants to file charges against the Peruvian viceroy who had executed the royal order that set in motion the 1640s land inspections as well as the official who carried out the mandate.[132] The suit described how "miserable Indians" (from Lambayeque) demanded an impartial judge to investigate the multiple abuses that had caused the rapid diminishment of indigenous populations threatening crown revenue.[133] In doing so, don Andrés claimed that local magistrates were not fulfilling their royally mandated role of protecting Indian communities entrusted to their care.[134] More interestingly and a rare strategy, by appealing directly to the king, the indigenous representative from Lambayeque disrupted the normal chain of command. Discarding the part of a humble Indian and seizing on the role of an honorable cacique, don Andrés's presence in the Spanish court provided evidence of an assertive native vassal.

Colonial officials dismissed the denunciations, but in particular they discredited don Andrés de Ortega by attacking his status. In the courts of Madrid and Lima, he had presented himself as a cacique and *pachaca principal* (a leader of a particular parcialidad).[135] A don Andrés de Ortega was not recorded in the lineages of Lambayeque hereditary leadership, but it is plausible that he considered himself to be a member of the interim faction in the 1640s, when the reducción's leadership was under dispute.[136] Regardless, the ex-magistrate presented indigenous witnesses who claimed that don Andrés had falsely presented himself as a noble and a leader. As the case wound its way back to the Peruvian northern coast, Lambayeque residents claimed that don Andrés was a "base and lowly man, subjected to serving mita and [paying] tribute." Reducción members charged that as an "ordinary Indian," Andrés de Ortega owed "back" tribute payments for the time he was in Spain petitioning redress for Lambayeque.[137]

The testimonies against don Andrés de Ortega could have been part of a strategy to discredit him (or his faction) from their claim to Lambayeque's leadership. During his absence don Andrés Achache seized the position of cacique with the help of the ex-magistrate's supporters and then testified against don Andrés Ortega.[138] It still is possible that don Andrés Ortega was a leader from Lambayeque even though witnesses from the opposition described him as an Indian who did not belong in the role that he claimed. For some members of the Lambayeque reducción, don Andrés was a commoner who had falsely claimed to be a noble. For Spanish officials, don Andrés had not employed the tactic of presenting himself as a "poor Indian" but presumptuously as an indigenous leader. In either case his strategy stepped far outside the realm of acting as an Indian who kept within the boundaries of the assigned colonial reducción.

Don Carlos Chimu also traveled to Lima and Madrid to file an appeal against the notorious colonial official don Pedro de Meneses in 1646. Despite his fortitude, however, the royal court recast don Carlos according to the role he was supposed to play. In Spain don Carlos presented himself as "the cacique principal of the Indian Town of Lambayeque in Peru." The court refused to hear his petition in its entirety. Royal representatives claimed that without more verification than don Carlos's testimony, they could not make a ruling. According to the court's logic, an indigenous leader could be a representative of the king's vassals, but only from Peru could he petition for justice. They dispatched him back to the Americas, ordering that as an Indian, don Carlos Chimu deserved charity so that he could "embark, to go to his natural place where justice would be executed."[139] While the judiciary agreed with don Carlos's petition to "conserve" indigenous populations, the royal court found that "the nature of this Indian is worrisome."[140] Pushed by the perception that local colonial authorities were unable or unwilling to execute justice, don Carlos's petition in Spain illustrates how far coastal Andeans were willing to go beyond their assigned reducción. Simultaneously, the Spanish court's responses illustrate the royal discomfort with the transformations of indigenous subjects who were no longer (or had never been) merely humble, loyal native vassals.

Don Carlos Chimu, like don Andrés de Ortega, employed the colonial judiciary and even invoked colonial protections reserved for "miserable Indians" similar to other indigenous leaders before the 1640s. After the betrayal of the land inspections, however, they (or their patrons) chose a more aggressive route of appealing directly to the king in a form that belied the assigned role of the obedient vassal supplicating before colonial authorities. Instead, the appearance of a Spanish-speaking indigenous man, knowledgeable of courts and laws, disturbed the crown. While officially recognized as a rightful vassal, the coastal Andean was dispatched from the royal court as a sign of a world out of order. Spain's judges found don Carlos Chimu to be "restless," or *inquieto*—a term associated with the assumed worrisome and violent nature of migrants or strangers.[141] By naming don Carlos Chumu as "restless" in a legal setting, the court disassociated him from expected characteristics of compliant reducción Indians who stayed in their place. To provoke the Spanish courts in this manner, don Carlos and don Andrés undoubtedly were manifestations of an emerging colonial Andean outlook.[142] The repeated and egregious disregard for promised crown protections by colonial inspectors throughout the region marked a deterioration of royal authority throughout the viceroyalty.[143] In Spain the crown attempted to contained threats to an old colonial order—Andeans who demanded compensation and appeared beyond the official boundaries of the colonial reducción—by dismissing charges against their officials.

In the viceregal courts the land inspector Meneses continued to defame don Carlos Chimu. To discredit the Lambayeque representative, Meneses found a reputable witness (the former priest of Trujillo's Indian parish) who testified that Carlos Chimu was given two hundred lashes for stealing church vestments to make a skirt for his lover.[144] The rumor or actual event meant that don Carlos had been publicly humiliated. That would have been impossible for an indigenous leader.[145] Further investigation into the surviving local judicial cases reveals that Carlos Chimu was a wealthy and knowledgeable indigenous embroiderer and silk worker who kept a shop on Trujillo's main plaza.[146] He also identified himself as "major sergeant of the Indians of Saña."[147] In many ways don Carlos was no longer a reducción Indian man who could claim the protections assigned to its members. Still, he and don Andrés de Ortega were embroiled in defenses of the reducciones. It is plausible that as the indigenous reducciones changed during the 1640s, don Carlos Chimu, in the urban setting of Trujillo, could have acted as an indigenous leader of migrants from the northern valley of Lambayeque.[148] Likewise, Ortega may have connected urban indigenous migrants with rural reducciones. Ortega did not hold a formal position in Lambayeque, but as a parcialidad foreman who assisted the cacique by collecting the tribute payments of absent reducción members, he still was connected to the rural Indian town even as he lived in Trujillo and Lima to oversee the court cases.[149]

While not recognized with a formal title by colonial officials, don Andrés de Ortega played a crucial role of maintaining contact with migrant men and their families, as did other Andean intermediaries.[150] Reducción men worked in Trujillo, on the surrounding Spanish estates, or married into other indigenous communities. Regardless of contradictory colonial mandates and the fact that Andeans removed themselves from their designated towns, indigenous leaders often hoped to collect tribute from their migrant members.[151] In the wake of the 1640s land privatization, indigenous populations were separate from but still bound to their reducciones. In this context of transformations, together don Andrés de Ortega and don Carlos Chimu represented a vanguard of coastal Andeans who moved claims to "Indian" identities beyond the colonial reducciones.

—

Undoubtedly the term "Indian" was part of colonial discourse that constructed an indigenous population "as the object of empire and as colonial subject."[152] But the nature of the colonial casta, Indian, worked in multiple directions. Spanish colonial categories including tributario and natural defined indigenous people as inferior while legal codes enacted symbolic violence intent on "transforming Indians into able bodies and obedient subjects" by "demanding that Indians surrender their sovereignty to the Crown."[153] At the same time, the terms provided some Andeans who acted within their assigned locations of the colonial reducción the ability to claim particular protections. Indigenous people would not be summarily dismissed from membership in the "body" of the Spanish colonial kingdoms. Coastal Andeans used the tools of colonialism, such as the courts, to defend land and water rights. They constructed themselves as "natural vassals" of the crown and performed their legal location within the category of "Indian." In this way, coastal Andeans asserted their positions as vassals. They claimed to be part of the "republic" as hardworking laborers and diligent vassals, deserving harmonious and just treatment.

In addition, the multiple terms and the adaptability of coastal Andeans illustrate that rather than totalizing, categories of "Indian" were fragmented, reflecting the fractured project of colonialism itself.[154] In the first part of the seventeenth century, indigenous people understood that if they acted like Indians—in many distinct ways—they could gain access to a bundle of allowances and obligations, duties and requirements, mandated by royal orders and customary judiciary practice. Even as a basis for labor and resource exploitation, the multiple means to claim the terms that constituted the casta of Indian provided more opportunities for indigenous people to secure particular protections and to underline their distinctions from Africans and their descendants.

The fracturing of the 1640s land privatization lessened the legal power of the reducciones on the northern coast and revealed the unwillingness of the crown to favor its native vassals over its Spanish subjects. The terms, the language, and the concepts of what constituted an Indian were not, however, articulated solely according to crown mandates. Dismayed at the destructive effects of land privatization and conversant in court strategies, coastal Andeans (especially as exemplified by don Andrés de Ortega and don Carlos Chimu) adapted to the transformations of the reducciones and petitioned for "Indian" protections under new circumstances. By the mid-seventeenth century coastal Andeans presented themselves as Indians in places that they were not supposed to be and, in doing so, would create new Indian acts for the decades to come.

4. Market Exchanges and Meeting the Indians Elsewhere

IN THE 1640s CAPTAIN GABRIEL, his lieutenant Domingo, and those who inhabited their *palenque*—or community of escaped slaves—relied on their market relations with coastal Andeans to survive in their hillside settlement. Though accused of attacking Indians, Gabriel and his companions traded with local indigenous communities, contracted laborers on Spanish estates, and indigenous men working on the communal lands in the nearby valley.[1] While participating in these profitable exchanges, indigenous leaders of *reducciones* called on local officials to protect them and eventually joined the military assault against Gabriel's fugitive settlement.[2] Coastal Andeans who had removed themselves from the reducciones to take advantage of the local labor market also joined the accusations against the palenque. Alonso Loxa, an indigenous laborer working on the Facala estate in the neighboring Chicama valley, accused other fugitives who (mistakenly) were associated with Gabriel and Domingo's palenque of attacking the women of his nearby *reducción* and robbing the men.[3]

Loxa called on customary stereotypes of Africans to level charges against the fugitives, but analysis of the criminal cases involving the palenque reveals long-standing and beneficial relations among Africans and Andeans on the estates.[4] For example, an indigenous laborer on Facala took the risk to hide a fugitive rather than notify the rural guard.[5] Indigenous men who moved from the reducción to the estate in the midcentury continued to assert their status as native vassals deserving protection, but they also seized the opportunities of the growing labor market, which included ongoing relations with Africans and their descendants who could include members of Gabriel and Domingo's palenque.

Pulled into colonial labor markets and engaging in cash economies, coastal Andeans challenged and reconstituted what it meant to be Indian— elsewhere—away from their landed location as natural colonial vassals. Colonial laws dictated a separation of Indians from blacks, and indeed colonial authorities could be forced to recognize coastal Andeans as natural vassals of the crown; blacks were expected to act as humble property or were criminalized as fugitives. Nonetheless, indigenous people and Africans (and their descendants) exchanged goods and labor within an informal economy regardless of royal mandates. Through these and other practices, Indians ended up in what the historian Philip Deloria has called "unexpected places."[6] Admittedly, Deloria focuses not on colonial Peru but writes about places where inhabitants of the modern United States expected to find Native people, such as in primitive hinterlands, engaged in barter or gift economies, rather than in urban settings participating in cash exchanges for goods.[7] Deloria is still very useful because he calls on scholars to recognize not only the imposed stereotypes but also how to see economic situations and cultural events from a native perspective to ask from whose expectations is a (historical) narrative constructed.

Deloria's ideas can challenge how colonial Latin American scholars, as well as colonial Spanish authorities, struggled with how to name Indians who we and they found in "unexpected places." Indians who did not live on reducciones, pay tribute, and serve mita altered what the casta of "Indian" meant according to crown law. Many historians have documented the large numbers of Andeans who lived and worked outside of the official reducción (or the urban Indian parish).[8] This chapter explores how migrants, laborers, muleteers, and urban Indians continued to employ the legal category of "Indian" even when they could no longer claim to inhabit the assigned colonial locations. Again, Deloria's point is methodically or theoretically useful. Analyzing how late nineteenth- and early twentieth-century American Indians were placed and claimed their place inside of modernity, Deloria poses an invigorating challenge for Andean historians. He explains that in the United States, by expecting Indians to be in certain places (on reservations) rather than where they actually were (sitting under hair dryers in beauty shops, for example), people in the United States created and reinforced a host of expectations and categories.[9] The same could be true for historiographical expectations of Andeans. In the seventeenth century, indigenous communities continued to experience land usurpation, recurrent epidemics, and labor exploitation that pushed and pulled them into the colonial market economy. Still, Indians did not stop Andean practices or cease to make claims to Indian categories. Rather, coastal Andeans created other versions of "Indian."

This movement of coastal Andeans away from their assigned colonial reducciones has led other scholars to suggest that indigenous people disappeared from the northern coastal valleys entirely.[10] Although the numbers of official residents on reducciones dramatically declined in the seventeenth century (in some cases losing half the registered population), many coastal Andeans moved into, in some cases, more lucrative positions on the neighboring expanding estates, while not leaving kinship and village networks behind.[11] Indigenous migration and participation in colonial markets therefore could be a regenerative process. If Andean communities lost members, they gained in new populations.[12] For this reason, indigenous reducciones welcomed migrants who contributed labor and brought goods with them; eventually these migrants paid a reduced amount of tribute and apparently severed official ties to their place of origin.[13] Similarly, in the northern coastal valleys of Peru, indigenous people distanced themselves from their reducciones to escape tribute and mita demands especially after the drastic loss of land and water during the 1640s *composiciones de tierras*. But, contrary to what other scholars have argued, migration did not destroy kin relations, nor did it solely create new kinships.[14] As the historians Thierry Saignes and Ann Zulawski have suggested for Alto Peru (today's Bolivia), the colonial markets provided the means for indigenous communities to survive as Andeans who strategically changed their identities but did not dissolve their ethnic solidarities.[15]

Demanding mitayos and then expanding into communal indigenous lands, private landholders gradually required the labor of Andeans from reducciones that they ironically helped to destroy by purchasing and expanding onto communal indigenous lands. In other words, coastal estates generated the need for indigenous people to abandon the colonial reducción by taking away their arable fields and adequate water supply. Simultaneously, coastal estates provided alternative labor opportunities for coastal Andeans to work as laborers and muleteers. Likewise, Andeans in the southern highlands seized on similar opportunities afforded by mining and agricultural enterprises to sell their labor, but they also transformed their identities. *Ya-naconas* pretended not to know their village, changed their dress or names, and blended into populations of mestizo and *mulato* peons to in some cases become an "incipient petite bourgeoisie" in certain regions.[16]

Asking again whether colonial markets destroyed or reinvigorated Andean communities, one response has been that indigenous people unfixed the meaning of *forastero* or *yanacona* during this period of intense social and economic mobility.[17] By manipulating their appearance, their affiliation, and their categorization, indigenous migrants were able to fully seize on the possibilities offered by the dynamic labor and commercial markets of the seventeenth century.[18] The northern Peruvian coast provided a similar dynamic labor market, especially in the 1650s, when the transatlantic slave traders were no longer legally supplying captives to Spanish landholders. By employing the possibilities of the colonial marketplace, including contact with Africans and their descendants (as well as Spaniards), Andeans contributed to the perpetuation of their assigned colonial category by employing it in places not officially designated as "Indian."

In the northern coastal valleys these "Indians elsewhere" were made by the local markets to which in turn they contributed. Coastal Andeans worked on Spanish estates, but they did not always sever their ties with nearby or regional home reducciones—where their status as a wage-earner, muleteer, artisan, or other skilled laborer was a valued asset. Through their market activity, coastal Andeans did not cut ties with their place of origin and did not necessarily rebuild the same relationships in new places. In fact, indigenous laborers made new claims on the persistent category of "Indian" even while entering the vibrant coastal markets of foodstuffs and labor. Their relocation challenged a colonial expectation to fix Andeans to the reducciones. Simultaneously, coastal Andeans continued to claim and to identify (when useful) according to the colonial category of Indian—elsewhere.

Opportunities of a Mixed Economy

Coastal Andeans seized on market opportunities as well as their role in the production and export of wheat and sugar. By the mid-seventeenth century, landholders were increasingly dependent on indigenous labor because of the abrupt end of the official slave trade into Spanish colonial Latin America. Landholders could no longer (if they ever could) rely on mita labor supplied by the reducciones, since the land privatization initiated in the 1640s had encouraged indigenous people to leave their assigned towns. In this economic climate local and migrant Andeans could leverage landholder need for mobile laborers against the crown demands for sedentary tribute-payers. Some coastal Andeans became indebted to regional authorities or local landholders due to their continued tribute payments. But participation in the colonial market did not automatically fix indigenous men and women into new fiscal categories that portended debt peonage.[19]

By the end of the 1640s the land privatization had produced coastal land-holders who were land rich but labor poor. As a result of the implementation of the composición de tierras, private estates had expanded their holdings and claims to water supplies.[20] Still, coastal landholders did not immediately profit from their cooptation of indigenous lands because they lacked laborers—enslaved or Indian. By the early 1640s royal authorities in Lima reported that the official importation of African captives had ceased into the Peruvian Pacific.[21] Even when the Spanish crown renegotiated slave-trading licenses with new transatlantic merchants in the 1660s, northern coastal landholders still demanded labor as they paid increasingly higher prices for African and African-descent captives.[22] By 1670, Trujillo slaveholders paid on the average of 650 pesos for an able-bodied enslaved man or woman, the highest mean price in my sample of slave sales from 1640 to 1730.[23] The characteristics of captives did not matter to slaveholders. Northern coastal slaveholders appear to have paid any price demanded by the renewed trans-atlantic slave trade partially because of their inability to obtain indigenous laborers through the previous means of mita service.[24]

In this period landholders in the northern coastal valleys, to their cha-grin, relied more heavily on contracted indigenous laborers. In a sample of yanacona and other indigenous labor contracts from the Trujillo notarial archive, only one was recorded for 1640, when the transatlantic slave trade was still official, as indicated in table 4.1. In contrast, labor contracts be-tween landholders and indigenous laborers increased dramatically in the sampled years of 1645, 1650, and 1655, when the official slave trade was dis-rupted.[25] Local landholders hired mostly local and coastal indigenous men to plant, cut, and sell alfalfa, clean irrigation canals, and drive mule trains.[26] In the 1650s more of the labor contracts included agreements that employers would pay debts or tribute payments owed by yanaconas. The increase of these debt clauses suggests that indigenous laborers did not freely contract their labor, but needed to sell their labor to meet their obligations in their re-ducciones. Most notably during this period, landholders paid a higher price for indigenous labor than they had earlier in the century.[27]

In 1645 employers paid indigenous men an average of twenty-one pe-sos per year; by 1650 that number had risen to thirty-six pesos. The wage for yanaconas in the coastal valleys would remain high for the rest of the

Table 4.1 Sampled Contracts for Yanaconas, 1640–1695

Year	Number of contracts	Average period of service (years)	Annual payment (pesos)	Number that includes a debt or tribute agreement
1640	1	1	6	—
1645	9	1.2	21	1
1650	9	1.14	36	5
1655	14	1.4	29.6	5
1660	3	2.5	31.7	2
1665	1	1	25	0
1670	1	1	40	0
1675	2	1	50	0
1680	0	—	—	—
1685	3	1.33	42.7	0
1690	0	—	—	—
1695	1	1	60	1

Notes: ADLL, Protocolos. Escobar. Leg. 143 (1640), 470; ADLL, Protocolos. Escobar. Leg. 146 (1645), 644; ADLL, Protocolos. Paz. Leg. 205 (1645), 275, 375v; ADLL, Protocolos. Viera Gutiérrez. Leg. 253 (1645), 260v, 360v, 407v, 421, 431, 465, 468v; ADLL, Protocolos. Moto. Leg. 182 (1650), 108, 136v, 238, 405v, 477, 490, 520; ADLL, Protocolos. Viera Gutiérrez. Leg. 257 (1650), 82, 82v; ADLL, Protocolos. Cortez. Leg. 97 (1655), 62; ADLL, Protocolos. Viera Gutiérrez. Leg. 258 (1655), 205, 251, 252, 274, 293v, 365v, 421, 422, 520, 603v, 655, 687v, 726, 732; ADLL, Protocolos. García. Leg. 166 (1660), 62v, 98, 526v; ADLL, Protocolos. Ortiz de Peralta. Leg. 189 (1665), 68; ADLL, Protocolos. Ortiz. Leg. 194 (1670), 161; ADLL, Protocolos. Verde. Leg. 250 (1670), 136v; ADLL, Protocolos. Salinas. Leg. 234 (1675), 406, 586; ADLL, Protocolos. Cortijo Quero. Leg. 100 (1680), 211; ADLL, Protocolos. Salinas. Leg. 237 (1685), 195, 209, 247; ADLL, Protocolos. Espino y Alvarado. Leg. 151 (1690), 206; and ADLL, Protocolos. Espino y Alvarado. Leg. 156 (1695), 139v.

century. The higher wages suggest that indigenous laborers were fewer in number or reluctant to work for landholders. The rise in wages also suggests that local estates appear to have been dependent on indigenous laborers especially since many communities gradually sent fewer and fewer mitayos. Instead, "rented Indians" (indios alquilos) who lived in their assigned reducciones worked on the estates for cash.[28] In the case of a Lambayeque valley estate, "rented" Indians supplied alfalfa for the oxen and butchered cattle as well as cleaned irrigation canals.[29] With the decrease of arable land following the 1640s composición de tierras, there were fewer indigenous men available (or willing) to serve mita from the local reducciones. Some indigenous laborers were also pulled into employment on estates for a monetary advance or to pay their tribute, but apparently not enough for the demands of landholders.[30] Ironically, the landholders had gained land but lost their previous access to labor.

Coastal landholders, however, were able to pay these higher wages to indigenous laborers partially because in the 1650s the Trujillo and Chicama valleys prospered from a regional demand for wheat and flour. In the 1650s prices for wheat and flour doubled in Panama, a constant market for foodstuffs from the northern Peruvian coast.[31] Owners of smaller estates continued to profit from the sale of wheat, flour, and other foodstuffs to Lima as well throughout the 1660s.[32] With regional and local markets landholders prospered from their expansion onto indigenous lands and could therefore pay for the necessary workers despite the rising costs of labor. Eventually the slave trade into coastal Peru began to expand in the 1660s, and with it sugar production reignited in the northern coastal valleys. Landholders replaced wheat with cane to take advantage of the rising prices for sugar.[33] Nonetheless, landholders did not completely switch to sugar in this period.[34] Local and regional markets for flour, meat, soap, and hides were still lucrative so estates still produced wheat and cattle.[35]

Taking advantage of this diverse economy, the comparably fewer indigenous residents of the colonial reducciones provided specialized labor by the mid-seventeenth century. As an example, in 1660 don Francisco Azabeche, the cacique of the reducción of Moche, obtained a viceregal order prohibiting Trujillo's magistrate from obligating his community to supply two mitayos to the city's butchers. Since the inhabitants of Moche served as guides between the community's tambo and the one located farther south in Casma, Azabeche argued that the community was already fulfilling its labor obligations through this specialized service. In the 1670s the cacique of the tintomines reminded Trujillo's magistrate that the community was not to be assigned regular fieldwork for its mita service. As an indigenous community of mitimaes, who claimed to have been resettled in Guamán by a sixteenth-century crown official, the group still asserted their origin as a service contingent of the Inca.[36]

A few years earlier, their leader, don Gregorio Asmat, argued that the tintomines served the colonial state as fishermen and chasquis, not as regular field laborers or pastors.[37] Asmat constructed an astute argument based on a claim to a particular category of Indians, mitimaes, who performed specialized labor before and after Spanish colonization.[38] These arguments and others could be effective as the municipal council excused the fishermen of Guamán as well as the coastal reducciones of Moche and Huanchaco from supplying fish to the city when the surf was particularly rough.[39] By asserting that his group of tintomines continued to fulfill their colonial obligations, don Gregorio Asmat was still able to appeal for protection of his Indian community but based on their special identity and unique labor, not necessarily their faithful residency on a reducción.

Landholders and local authorities relied on indigenous laborers (contracted or serving mita) to trade foodstuffs in the local subsistence market, but they also remained dependent on reducción members for access to water. The coast received seasonal rains but relied on a managed system of irrigation canals, ditches, and sluices whose outputs were carefully measured and often disputed. In particular, sugar estates required more water than wheat farms and owners were continually attempting to secure reliable sources.[40] As a wealthy landholder remarked, the sugar mill of Facala was a prosperous enterprise because it was situated inside the valley, closest to the highland ascent, where it had "independent water"—an intake controlled by the owner that flowed directly from the river to the fields.[41] The need for water, especially in sugar production, meant that landholders carefully documented the multiple sources that were allocated to their estates.[42] Documenting the coastal water supply also meant recording its maintenance because the infrastructure also required at least a yearly cleaning of debris as well as the repair of stone-lined canals, earthen walls, and wooden sluices.[43]

Water maintenance implied indigenous labor. As throughout the Andes, indigenous leaders helped their communities maintain irrigation systems by organizing regular communal work parties that, supplied with chicha (corn beer) and food, combined celebration with necessary labor.[44] In the Chicama and Trujillo valleys these practices continued in a modified form in the mid-seventeenth century. As noted by Domingo Payco in 1655, a ladino Indian and native of the Chiquitoy parcialidad of Santiago de Cao, when the indigenous community benefited from the Sacope canal, they regularly cleaned it.[45] Those of Chiquitoy followed the customary practices of water allocation so that the beneficiaries of water canals participated in its cleaning.[46] By maintaining the irrigation systems—even those that flowed to Spanish lands—indigenous communities asserted a limited claim to the valley water supply.

By the later part of the seventeenth century, indigenous labor had become synonymous with irrigation maintenance. Spanish landholders preferred Andean labor since indigenous villagers were highly motivated to clear the canals efficiently and thoroughly, so the water supply would continue to their fields.[47] Andeans also understood the cycle of the water system maintenance. Indigenous leaders recalled the timetable required for cleaning the local canals as the cacique of Paiján, don Pedro Rafael Chayguac, declared that early March (around Easter or immediately following the seasonal rains) was the correct period to clean the main canal.[48] Andeans who worked together (presumably under local leadership and according to regional custom) appeared to have been in demand. The Spanish priest in a Lambayeque water dispute, for example, declared that without natives to perform a mita, or any indigenous tribute-payers, elderly community laborers, *cholos*, or migrants, the irrigation canal had run dry.[49] Indeed, coastal landholders associated local Andean labor with the irrigation systems as a Chicama farmer, Bartolomé Gonzalez, created a contract with the Chiquitoy Indians to clean the Sacope canal.[50] Local, communal, and knowledgeable, coastal Andeans supplied a type of labor—irrigation maintenance—to the valley agriculture that fueled both export economies and local subsistence even as indigenous reducciones were losing their populations.

By the 1680s, landholders in the Chicama valley enjoyed very few allocated mitayos. Mita had come to mean the communal work necessary to clean the irrigation canals and readjust the allocation of water rather than the labor allocation to particular Spanish and Spanish-descent landholders. In addition, rather than Spanish landholders demanding a number of mitayos, indigenous communities themselves could call for a "mita." For example, when water ceased to flow in 1681, the leaders of Magdalena de Cao claimed that a mita had not occurred for more than twenty years, or since the early 1660s.[51] Indigenous communities continued to maintain particular sections of the irrigation canals; inhabitants of Magdalena de Cao sent members to work for six days a year to clear their assigned part.[52] As late as 1694, landholders in the Trujillo valley recognized that both Spaniards and Indians benefited from the Mochica canal and therefore were equally obligated to participate in its "mita."[53] As indigenous lands had been reduced, coastal Andeans still were assigned to support, in many respects, landholders' profits.

Seizing the Market: Caciques to *Labradores*

Colonial indigenous leaders on the northern Peruvian coast were adversely affected by the ongoing demands on indigenous communities. As membership decreased on the reducciones, caciques found it harder to collect tribute from their absent (or dead) members.[54] By the 1640s northern coastal indigenous leaders went into debt to local magistrates or to contracted collectors of tribute payments.[55] By the 1660s biannual payments had accumulated, and some caciques owed hundreds of pesos to private parties and colonial authorities.[56] Indigenous leaders were held personally responsible for the debts of their communities. The magistrate in Chiclayo, for example, embargoed and auctioned the goods of don Pedro Quepse, the appointed indigenous official of Lambayeque, to collect the amount owed in tribute payments.[57] The principal pachaca of Mansiche mortgaged lands to pay tribute while the Chicama cacique sold lands for the same reason.[58] Others stated simply that they could not pay.[59] The notarial documents recording the debts of indigenous leaders, either hereditary or those appointed by colonial officials, indicate that the reducción had become (or had been) a liability.

To pay their obligations indigenous leaders tried new strategies. For instance, Capitan don Carlos Coronado, the indigenous leader of Mórrope, traveled to the court in the regional capital of Trujillo in 1678. He intended to pay the tribute assigned to his community that supposedly he had collected from the "Indians who lived in the alto [neighborhood] outside of this city."[60] Coronado, like other indigenous leaders, often knew where to find "absent" members who had migrated to work in cities or on estates.[61] The leader may have employed the same tactic as indigenous leaders elsewhere who falsely reported the deaths or absence of their members to reduce their community's tribute obligations.[62] Listed as absent from their reducciones, indigenous men migrated from their home communities or worked locally sometimes with their cacique's knowledge but "hidden" from colonial authorities.[63] His tactic, as opposed to employing the crown protections of the reducción, was to recuperate funds from his migrant members to pay his community's debt.

Indigenous elites also attempted to resecure their positions by transitioning to the market economy. In some cases indigenous leaders acquired lands rather than losing them during the 1640s land privatization and its 1650s appeals. Don Diego Bernardino, an indigenous leader of Lambayeque, purchased about 143 acres during the 1643 auction of so-called vacant communal lands, while don Geronimo Puyconssoli, the cacique of Jayanca, purchased about 372 acres.[64] Don Antonio Chaybac, the cacique of Mansiche and Huanchaco, employed the composición de tierras inspection to confirm his ownership of lands called Sopala in the Chicama valley.[65] In addition, some indigenous leaders were able to acquire property that was more lucrative or convenient. Don Joan de Mora y Ulloa, the head cacique of the Chicama valley, exchanged hereditary lands (Tulape) in the adjoining valley of Saña for the ranch (and its water) called Uchpon near the town of Paiján (closer to his residence in Chocope) during the land inspections.[66]

Acquiring privately owned land was a common strategy among indigenous leaders who had to deal with the pressing need to come up with tribute payments in many parts of the Andes and may not have been entirely voluntary.[67] But rather than understanding indigenous leaders as accommodating the trend toward privatization, their engagement in the market also provided a solution to their obligations to the state. Some rented the communal lands assigned to their communities to Spanish inhabitants to pay debts, as did don Pedro Asavache, the indigenous leader of Moche.[68] Indigenous leaders also rented their own lands. Don Luis Guaman, who named himself as the principal and gobernador of Santiago de Guaman (outside of Trujillo), rented a site called Chuchipe in the interior Conache valley to an Indian *vecino* ("municipal citizen") of the city. He explained that the lands belonged to him "as the cacique principal of Guaman."[69] Thus indigenous leaders acquired and employed lands that they owed or controlled (some left vacant by their absent members) to fulfill the colonial obligations still required of their reducciones.

With the size and the quality of the lands acquired, some indigenous leaders became private landholders in their own right. Communal landholding (while rooted in precolonial practices) was central to the compact between the colonial state and Indians of the reducción. Moving away from these obligations—much like migrant indigenous commoners—indigenous leaders developed landholdings for profit. Don Pedro Azavache, the cacique of Moche, rented out San Ysidro de Conache, a small farm with rights to eight days of water from an irrigation canal, farm tools, an oxen team, and a substantial orchard.[70] Indeed, in their positions as caciques, these indigenous landholders could claim rights to water that increased the value of their property.[71] Don Luis Guaman, the cacique of Guaman, guaranteed that the lands he rented out in the Conache valley were allotted four days of water from the neighboring irrigation canal.[72] The caciques of the northern coastal valleys were similar to the indigenous leaders in other market-driven agricultural regions in the Andes. For instance, as indigenous people abandoned their assigned communities, caciques acquired not only lands but estates in coca-growing regions near La Paz and Cochabamba.[73] With the lucrative markets in cattle and wheat, the lands left vacant by other indigenous inhabitants on the northern coast could be made profitable as commercial ventures headed by coastal Andeans.[74]

Some indigenous leaders became known as *labradores* (farmers) who rented land for their own benefit. In 1649 don Gonsalo Cichaguaman, a principal of Magdalena de Cao, rented a site near his town that was owned by a cacique from the neighboring valley.[75] Don Antonio Chaybac, an indigenous leader of Mansiche and Huanchaco, rented a farm called Santa Catalinia from Trujillo's Mercedarian monastery.[76] This group of indigenous men may have worked the fields or orchards themselves. In the case of don Gonzalo Cichaguaman, witnesses claimed that his father and uncle had planted the lands that in 1669 were under dispute.[77] Others retained relatives to perform the necessary manual labor. In the case of don Joan de Mora y Ulloa, the cacique of the Chicama valley, some kin—including his marriage witness—cleared, farmed, and occupied his ranch called Uchpon.[78] Some indigenous leaders were wealthy enough to own slaves.[79] Don Diego Timón, the gobernador of the Chicama valley owned three West Central African enslaved men with one enslaved woman and her children who worked on his cattle ranch.[80] Timón was similar in his wealth and status to the "new" caciques of the southern Andes or those who were appointed after hereditary leaders were removed for not fulfilling their tribute obligations. As on the northern coast, these caciques became landholders who traded in wine and coca.[81] We could understand these indigenous leaders as taking advantage of the local markets to acquire another public position located between the reducciones and the estates.

As landholders who still were entrusted with tribute collection, indigenous leaders were positioned to engage in local trading foodstuffs—especially between the countryside and the city. The cacique principal of Santiago de Guaman sold a Spanish municipal citizen of Trujillo seven pesos and four *reales* of maize. In addition, don Joan de Mora y Ulloa, the indigenous leader of Chicama, listed a number of small debts with other indigenous people generated from the business of his small farm.[82] Mirroring the success of some indigenous leaders in landholding, others became relatively prosperous through their trading. Don Antonio Salvador Chaybac traded a hundred pesos in meat with a city official in Trujillo.[83] Indigenous men who claimed positions of leadership gained from their market exchanges with Spanish officials and landholders with whom they came into contact.[84] For instance, don Diego Isla Guaman, an indigenous leader of Magdalena de Cao, traded maize and wheat with indigenous as well as Spanish-descent men and an enslaved man of a neighboring estate.[85]

The market empowered many of the indigenous elites who mobilized themselves to seize the leadership positions from the hereditary or previous cacique.[86] For example, don Diego Isla Guaman noted in his will that among his ongoing judicial suits, the magistrate still owed him for revealing where Indians were hidden—"as directed by His Majesty."[87] The appointed indigenous leader appeared to be responding to a recent royal order to locate Indians who owed tribute yet removed themselves from authorities' purview.[88] By "finding" absent Indians (and not quietly collecting tribute from them), don Diego Isla Guaman sided with colonial officials and probably exposed the tactics of a local cacique or another indigenous leader.[89] This political maneuver coincided with don Diego Isla Guaman's economic strategies. Just as he exchanged foodstuffs, the indigenous leader also traded in missing (and mobile) tribute-paying Indians. Regional marketeering—in goods and people—was part of how emerging indigenous elite promoted themselves.

In some cases indigenous leaders helped each other sustain their positions within their reducción as the Magdalena de Cao families of Sichaguaman and Isla Guaman intermarried.[90] Still, most alliances among this small group appear to strategically link the indigenous elite across the boundaries of the reducciones for political ends. Don Alonso de Vergara, a slaveholding cacique of Viru, testified in favor of the rising new leader don Diego Timón, who would eventually name himself as the leader of the Chicama valley.[91] Don Diego Timón in turn defended don Gonzalo Sichaguaman's claim to land.[92] Unsurprisingly, the most prosperous attempted to develop their wealth by intertwining kin and commerce. Don Diego Isla Guaman sold a horse to his brother-in-law and purchased wine and cattle from his son-in-law, who were both strategically connected to other local families— Spanish and indigenous.[93]

In addition to gaining trusted agents, indigenous elites solidified connections with families of other communities. Don Juan Perez Timón of Magdalena de Cao (the son of don Diego Timón) and don Antonio Chaybac, the cacique of Mansiche and Huanchaco, attempted an ambitious alliance of new and old elite indigenous families. In 1655, in front of the magistrate and their assigned protector, Timón signed a dowry agreement of five hundred pesos for his nine-year-old daughter to eventually wed Chaybac's fourteen-year-old son.[94] Whether they achieved their status from claiming leadership or from the profits of local commerce, particular indigenous families sought to solidify their positions through acts of loyalty and eventually strengthening the ties of kinship.

Whether from hereditary families or from new, rising elites, seventeenth-century caciques combined Andean and colonial markers to lay claim to their leadership positions that were rooted in market success as much as in indigenous and official recognition. Many of them employed local courts to further their commercial interests, such as don Diego Isla Guaman who hired notaries in Trujillo and Magdalena de Cao as well as legal assistants.[95] Like their counterparts in the sixteenth century, indigenous leaders wore Spanish clothing, rode horses, and furnished their house much like their Spanish peers.[96] By the midcolonial period many indigenous elite had adopted the material objects of Spanish colonial culture.[97] The use of "Spanish" clothing or the adoption of Catholic rituals did not necessarily mean uniformity of acculturation.[98]

Hardly assimilating, the indigenous elite from the northern coastal reducciones invested in particular institutions that instead expressed their elite colonial Indian identities. Don Joan de Mora y Ulloa, a cacique principal in the Chicama valley, asked to be buried at the altar of a particular confraternity in the Chocope church, the Souls of Purgatory. He had founded the confraternity but also belonged to the Mother of God of Consolation, presumably in the same rural Indian parish.[99] With less religious devotion, don Diego Isla Guaman noted his membership in the Santa Barbola confraternity in the church of Magdalena de Cao.[100] Their activity underlines the Catholic convictions, at least publicly, of many indigenous people in the seventeenth century. For indigenous leaders, control of confraternities in rural areas signified their prestige but also provided a location to organize fiestas, a critical means of political organizing and community building among colonial indigenous populations.[101] The religious organizations were one way that indigenous elites invested in the institutions of their "home" communities (whether hereditary or recently acquired). Rather than moving to the urban centers, the Timón, Chayhac, and Isla Guaman families remained located in rural communities to remake their leadership positions.

Even as their commercial success in local markets helped some claim new positions or renew old ones, Spanish landholders and colonial officials continued to remind other caciques of their Indian identities. Unlike those who had prospered, don Joan de Mora y Ulloa had suffered under the land privatizations of the midcentury. After exchanging his hereditary land for a privately owned ranch, Mora y Ulloa was unable to pay for the titles to be registered in his name.[102] Without documentation his ownership would remain more reputational than official. In another instance don Gonzalo Sicha Guaman supplied his titles and papers to the assigned surveyor who worked for the land inspector. Like others, such as don Diego Isla Guaman, the Magdalena de Cao principal never had his documents returned.[103] Lacking written proof of ownership, Sicha Guaman faced usurpation from a Spanish or Spanish-descent landholder who appealed the case for years, claiming that he had purchased the lands from the "Indians of Paiján."[104] Whether it was private or hereditary property, indigenous elites also lost their land through the same expansionist tactics that affected Andean commoners.

In addition to their liability as those responsible for tribute collection, indigenous elites were still susceptible to the discriminatory acts committed against Indians by colonial officials. Don Manuel Fernandez Asmat suffered from being labeled as an Indian when he attempted to collect a debt from

Captain Juan Antonio Jirón for a small amount of maize. Rather than pay his debt, Jirón charged that as a "tributary Indian," Fernandez Asmat actually owed him for missing payments.[105] Allies of Fernandez Asmat argued that in the reducción of Guaman, where male heirs were lacking, the *cacigazgo's* female leaders traditionally passed the title to their husbands.[106] Fernández Asmat's wife was recognized as the *casica* of Guaman and thus her husband was understood as the cacique because men were "more capable since the Indians obey and respect" them more than female leaders.[107]

Installed by the magistrate and accepted by a number of indigenous inhabitants of Guaman, Fernandez Asmat continued his suit to claim his small debt as an indigenous leader. His case suggests that Spanish-descent competitors in the local market attempted to displace the rising indigenous elite by questioning their privileges as caciques, principales, and other leadership positions—the very ones put in place by colonial authorities and employed by colonial Andean elites. By affirming that indigenous leaders were still Indians, nonindigenous traders reasserted previous colonial boundaries regardless of the opportunities claimed by emerging indigenous landholders and marketeers.

The crown-sponsored land inspections furthered the process of land privatization already under way in the colonial Andes and, unsurprisingly, some indigenous leaders even profited.[108] Their ability to exploit or their ability to succeed no longer was dependent on the manipulation of colonial mandates. On the northern Peruvian coast particular individuals and their families were able to take advantage of a mixed economy to seize the opportunities of local commerce. Undoubtedly the criteria required on the northern coast for indigenous men (and in some cases, women) to ascend to the hereditary rank of cacique and other leadership positions of the reducción was fast eroding. Nonetheless, indigenous elites defined new ways of presenting themselves as Indian to their communities and beyond that included material prosperity as well as kin loyalty and Catholic obligations. Even as indigenous elites transformed what it meant to be a leader within their communities, nonindigenous competitors reimposed the restrictive category of "Indian" onto these landed elite. In other words, men like don Diego Isla Guaman claimed indigenous practices in part because it implied their elite status within their communities. At the same time, their casta of Indian would be reemployed to limit their ability to rise in the colonial market economy.

Working the Reducción, Working the Estate

If indigenous elites established themselves in the marketplace, coastal Andeans employed the reducción for new purposes. By the mid-seventeenth century, indigenous migrants from the coast and the highlands moved away from their assigned colonial towns to seek work on the estates and even join other, underpopulated reducciones. The expanding estates required specialized labor and exchanges in goods or currency and engaged indigenous people who moved into the market current. In these places—outside of the reducciones—coastal Andeans still identified themselves and were identified as Indians. In addition, indigenous people brought their kinship connections, ties to communities of origin, and claims to colonial regulations to their new residences and workplaces. By migrating out of the reducciones, they moved claims to the category of Indian as well as Andean identities with them.

The obligations of the reducciones followed indigenous migrants. On the one hand, colonial authorities recognized that those who moved away from their assigned communities were exempt from mita or should pay a lower tribute fee.[109] Officials distinguished migrants from residents of assigned reducciones with the label of *forastero*, or Indians who moved around, and were disconnected from a reducción or a parish.[110] On the other hand, the colonial terminology also reinscribed obligations for Indians. By the later part of the seventeenth century, colonial officials attempted to extract labor and revenue from indigenous migrants. Rural priests required tithes from forasteros, and the Trujillo municipal council attempted to collect tribute from those who had settled in the Santa Ana parish and other indigenous neighborhoods in the city.[111] By categorizing indigenous migrants, colonial authorities sought to extract revenue from them.

Indigenous communities were also concerned with the revenue that migrants could provide, but were more concerned with incorporating forasteros. In many cases indigenous communities who had drastically lost their membership provided land to migrants.[112] As other scholars have suggested, indigenous communities were eager to gain men who would contribute tribute obligations and mita requirements.[113] In some cases migrants named their place of origin—such as Piura, San Pedro de Lloc, Cascas, Lambayeque, or Guaman—but many were listed as only forasteros, suggesting their attempts to create a clear distance from the obligations that they had left behind or a conscious decision to officially erase their origins. In the 1675 parish records from the indigenous reducción of Santiago de Cao, more than half the recorded marriages were between migrants and local inhabitants.[114]

In most cases migrant men married local women, such as Pedro Gonçalo who married Lucia de Assumpción, a native of the town. Coastal Andeans employed migrants to build deeper kinship connections. Local residents of Santiago de Cao asked migrants to be the godparents to their children, such as Juan de Morales, who served as the godfather for the young son of a couple from the parcialidad of local fishing people.[115] In addition, migrants created kinship networks among themselves by marrying each other and becoming godparents for each other's expanding families to defy the official discourse that portrayed them as vagabonds.[116] By assigning themselves to reducciones, indigenous migrants made a previous colonial imposition into an opportunity for a new place of belonging. By adopting migrants and adapting market strategies, individuals and communities transformed indigenous identities but also what colonial authorities and local landholders could expect from Indians.

Though forbidden by colonial authorities, even rural indigenous reducciones incorporated mixed-descent people into their communities. Since their inception, the crown had designated the reducciones as strictly for Indians and prohibited Spaniards and non-Indians from spending more than a night.[117] Local magistrates attempted (or so they claimed) to expel Spaniards, Africans, and their descendants from the reducciones but appeared to have a limited impact. Witnesses claimed that "in the town of Virú . . . there lived among the Indians some mestizos and mulatos" who remained even though the magistrate and his lieutenants attempted to remove them.[118] In a review of another magistrate's tenure, witnesses testified that he had allowed mestizos and Spaniards to "mix" in the Indian towns.[119] These testimonies could have been attempts to discredit the magistrates. At the same time, given the active trade on the northern coast, indigenous communities perhaps did not actively discourage non-Indians from taking up residency in their towns. Furthermore, indigenous communities were not solely composed of "Indians" because mestizo and other mixed-descent children had been part of colonial populations since the sixteenth century.[120] Indeed, in some cases indigenous people actively encouraged non-Indians to live with them, as Elvira, a widow from Santiago de Cao, lived openly in the indigenous town of Magdalena de Cao with Juan de Aguirre, a Spaniard.[121] Thus, regardless of the royal mandates intended to keep "pure" indigenous reducciones, Andeans appear to have welcomed or at least allowed non-Indians to live among them.

Indigenous residents, however, employed royal prohibitions against mixed residency when they were useful. In the case of Elvira (the widow from Santiago de Cao), natives of Magdalena de Cao notified the magistrate that the unmarried couple "lived and slept" together and scandalized the Indians in the nearby farms.[122] The indigenous men who testified presented themselves as protecting Elvira, who, they claimed, had been taken by the Spaniard to Santiago de Cao, where "she could be more at his command."[123]

In this way the indigenous men enforced an official purity of the reducción when they sought to eliminate a Spaniard in their midst. The indigenous men may have also been intent on ejecting Elvira, who was not a native of their reducción. Likewise, natives of Catacaos (near the northern city of Piura) testified against their assigned priest in 1660 by strategically relying on royal prohibitions against mixture with non-Indians.[124] They claimed that the cleric ministered to Spaniards, mestizos, mulatos, and black people even though he was charged (and paid) to attend to the Indians.[125]

Although it is plausible that the inhabitants of Catacaos wished to expel unwanted residents, their accusation appears more about ridding themselves of the priest. Indeed, indigenous communities may have capitalized on the circulating mandates that warned against Indian contact with "mestizos, mulatos, loose people, and [those] of bad intentions," but it is unclear if they believed that the mandated segregation was in their best interest.[126] Intent on "preserving the Republics," the viceroys lamented that those outside of the reducciones such as mestizos and migrants were growing in number and in resistance against colonial authorities.[127] While colonial authorities attempted to shore up a shrinking labor and revenue base, indigenous individuals and communities on the northern coast invoked legal mandates, but in the later part of the seventeenth century and early eighteenth century, they did not necessarily expel targeted individuals, including people of mixed or African descent.

In addition to incorporating new members, private landholding also offered a way for indigenous individuals, aside from caciques and other Andean elites, to shield themselves from the overwhelming demands of tribute and mita. As opposed to communal landholding, "individual title to land, recognized by Spanish law, protected the owner from legal confiscations" to which communal reducción land was subjected.[128] Undoubtedly, privatization was a part of the dissolution of communal landholding, a key component of Andean society.[129] At the same time, coastal Andean communities appear to have employed the commercial exchange of land for cash as a mechanism to sustain communal holdings. In 1671 the "community and Indians of Chimo" (of the Trujillo valley) with their appointed protector purchased the farm of San Gerónimo in the Chicama valley. The lands required irrigation and were mostly intended for herding roughly a thousand goats and sheep that were included in the purchase. The Chimo community also became slaveholders and beneficiaries of the ongoing mita allocations. The land included the "right" to six Indian mitayos supplied by the neighboring Paiján reducción as well as three enslaved men; Miguel of casta *angola*, Gaspar Melemba, and Diego, a criollo.[130] With the profits from this private holding, ideally the Chimo community could submit its required tribute allocations and pay other indigenous men to serve its mita obligation. Indigenous communities retained their positions as legally recognized entities in Spanish colonial law by employing mita and slaveholding. Discarding the onerous obligations of Indian status, the Chimo community secured corporate privileges as native vassals through a commercial exchange.

Outside of communal strategies or elite connections, however, most indigenous people had to find other ways to take advantage of the market conditions. A native and a resident of the indigenous reducción of Santiago de Cao in the Chicama valley, Pedro Esteban Peñarán was apparently a prosperous wheat farmer, but he did not own land. Instead, he worked his rented fields "in company," or according to a business contract of dividing the harvest and the risk with a partner who supplied the seeds.[131] Based on information from his probate case, those who collected from his estate were Spanish landholders, a local cleric, and the cacique of Santiago de Cao with other indigenous elites.[132] Even with these debts, Pedro Esteban Peñarán was not like the absent or missing northern coastal Indians who had lost their fields during the seventeenth century described by historians.[133] Instead, Peñarán was an example of indigenous farmers who had been adversely affected by the expansion of the estates but had transformed themselves into critical members of the local economy.

Engagement in local markets was a way to make new meanings of indigenous identities. Indigenous authorities probably collected tribute from Pedro Esteban Peñarán since he was a native of the reducción of Santiago de Cao, but he was wealthy enough that he could pay another man to serve his mita requirement.[134] He owned a house, oxen, mules, and more than sixty goats that may have grazed on lands that he owned with his brothers.[135] He remained under the jurisdiction of indigenous authorities including an *alcalde ordinario* who oversaw the payment of debts and allocation of property following his death. Indeed, Peñarán was even subject to the municipal guard in Santiago de Cao, who had seized two of his guitars during one of their nightly rounds.[136] Still, he was a man of a certain social standing who owned a horse, stirrups, and a sword, which located him among other men—regardless of casta—who claimed public honor through these insignia of colonial masculine honor.[137]

Far from a "poor Indian," Peñarán also owned shoes, a handkerchief embroidered with blue and red wool, two hats (one of black vicuña and the other of white leather), as well as two capes—one for every day and the other of black woolen cloth "for mourning."[138] His clothing suggests that although he may have labored in his fields and did not carry an honorific title of *don*, he had purchased or obtained clothing that was not for work but appropriately reflected his prestige in the indigenous town of Santiago de Cao.[139]

Pedro Esteban Peñarán's participation in local markets and purchase of colonial goods did not make him any less an Indian. At the time of his death, he held additional fields "in company" with five men who were all coastal Andeans, including Juan Siccha, the *alguacil mayor* of Santiago de Cao, and Diego Matias Mache, possibly related to the secondary cacique family of the Chicama valley.[140] In other words, he shared the risk of whether the fields would produce a good harvest with other coastal Andeans who owned small plots planted with maize, wheat, and beans.[141] Indeed, Peñarán found a way to work communally with indigenous men, albeit with a contract and a division of profit—still reflecting previous reciprocal practices in the northern coastal valleys.[142] In addition, Peñarán had not migrated from Santiago de Cao but maintained his family within the reducción by marrying his daughter to another member.[143] Lastly, he kept what appears to have been the account book of the Santo Cristo confraternity, which along with a golden cross, an image of Santa Rosa, and a print of the Virgin of Guadalupe testified to his religious devotions.[144]

These objects suggest that Peñarán was a leader of the Catholic confraternity that on the northern coast was associated with agriculturalists.[145] In this capacity Peñarán would have organized annual religious festivals with other confraternity members that allowed indigenous communities to express local beliefs.[146] Pedro Esteban Peñarán's example suggests how coastal Andeans employed Spanish institutions to profit from a market economy but also to sustain connections with those they considered a native community. Coastal Andean communities found the regulations regarding their location useful and continued to perpetuate the meaning of Indian even when many had become Indians elsewhere. Identified by Trujillo's magistrate as an Indian, Peñarán did not define himself according to crown protections and obligations. Instead, he expressed a native ("*natural*") identity through his business, kin, and religious connections rooted in a revised relationship with his reducción and defined by current colonial circumstances.

Muleteers as Indians Elsewhere

The reducción and the maintenance of a colonial "Indian" category demanded a set of claims and performances to protection that were not as necessary for Andeans who took themselves elsewhere—economically and juridically. Their place of origin, however, remained critical. As muleteers, indigenous men retained connections with their home communities, especially those on the main transportation routes. Melchor de los Reyes was named as an "Indian muleteer" and a native of Sechura.[147] Pedro Bernabe identified himself in a notarized agreement as an "Indian native of Mochumí, muleteer on this route, and resident of Trujillo."[148] Origin complemented the Indian identity claimed by these coastal muleteers. Furthermore, their origins helped explain their occupations. Men from these coastal towns were known for managing mule trains that carried goods and passengers along the main road connecting Lima with the northern port of Piura.[149]

Along the northern routes that passed through deserts, scrub forests, and unpopulated regions between the irrigated valleys, kin and neighbors were more likely to supply water to those they knew.[150] Muleteers could quickly get into debt or not turn a substantial profit if they paid the market prices to feed their pack animals. Indeed, Miguel Rafael de Mendosa, who was identified as an Indian and native of Trujillo, had to contract himself as a yanacona for three years to an owner of a mule train to pay his debts throughout the coastal settlements of Lambayeque, Saña, and Trujillo.[151] Without the economic assistance provided by strong ties to indigenous communities along the trade route, Mendosa was forced to sell his labor. Thus the mule drivers retained their ties to home communities as part of their market strategy.

Muleteers also re-created their communities of origin in the new places that they migrated. By the second half of the seventeenth century, muleteers from Mochumí congregated in Trujillo's Santa Ana parish in a neighborhood called "the alto of the huaca," or the high area near an ancient sacred site. Located on the outer edges of the city near the slaughterhouses, the neighborhood must have had corrals that allowed muleteers to tend their pack animals.[152] Asserting themselves as residents (if not official vecinos, or municipal citizens), Mochumí muleteers Gaspar Guachin and Juan Pablo charged Trujillo's colonial authorities with overstepping their authority.[153] In a petition to the viceroy they protested against municipal officials who had demanded that the migrants perform mita and personal service. The muleteers explained that without allotted lands, they were unable to pay tribute to their indigenous leaders.[154] Astutely, they employed colonial mandates that correlated tribute demands with the royal allocation of land and water.[155]

In doing so, they defended themselves as Indians—people who paid tribute while avoiding the undesirable mita. At the same time, the muleteers reinforced their market value and justifiable removal from their assigned reducciones. They reminded (and perhaps threatened) Trujillo's authorities that if they were returned to agriculture on the reducciones, there would be a lack of available muleteers, resulting in a "big loss."[156] Indeed, landholders (who were also local officials or beholden to them) contracted muleteers to move sugar from their estates to the ports and paid hundreds of pesos to transport their valuable commodity from Trujillo to Lima.[157] Capitalizing on the high value of their service, Mochumí muleteers sustained a community identity but attempted to separate themselves from the obligations of the official status of Indian.

With their strong economic position, muleteers developed an independent leadership structure. In 1660, Francisco Siba named himself as a vecino of Trujillo, a ladino Indian, and alcalde of the muleteers.[158] In doing so, he claimed titles that were not assigned to indigenous people, such as "municipal citizen," and reappropriated the colonial title of alcalde to name his community. Siba exemplified an urban indigenous community that acquired new cultural markers of its identities.[159] Fluent in Spanish, knowledgeable of colonial laws, and dexterous in the marketplace, urban Indians such as Francisco Siba created a legal space for themselves by adopting the offices of colonial society. The Mochumí men who challenged the magistrate's claim to their labor defied Trujillo's appointed indigenous authorities. Gaspar Guachin and Juan Pablo complained that the bailiffs and native alcaldes conducted nightly watches that disrupted the Indians of the neighborhood.[160]

Indeed, indigenous officials (like their counterparts in the Republic of the Spaniards) were empowered to monitor urban Indians for adultery or drunkenness as well as boisterous gatherings or parties that could lead to these sins.[161] In this case the Mochumí men claimed that by entering their homes at night, the appointed Indian male officials opened the honor of their wives and daughters to question. In other words, the Mochumí muleteers defended the patriarchal oversight of their homes as they attempted to unseat the locally appointed Indian officials. In addition, Gaspar Guachin and Juan Pablo invoked a sixteenth-century Toledan order against the nepotism of the same indigenous authorities.[162] By challenging Indian authorities in Trujillo, these migrant muleteers asserted jurisdiction over their own communities, which they defined within established urban Indian neighborhoods.

Migrant men who lived in Trujillo articulated identities to remove themselves from the purview of assigned indigenous authorities. Juan Pisanquiliche, an Indian native of Otuzco and resident of Trujillo, argued against the Indian alcaldes in Trujillo. He claimed that because he married a mestiza, a daughter of a Spaniard, he should not be forced to perform mita or personal service.[163] Utilizing a mandate of the Real Audiencia and a royal order, Pisanquiliche convinced Trujillo's magistrate to remove him from this labor service. The married man employed the casta of his wife to separate himself from the obligations of his casta while still naming himself as an Indian.

Juan Pisanquiliche was not alone in resisting the authority of urban Indian officials. Lázaro Ramos, a native of the highland town of Aismango and a resident of Trujillo had become the official of the water allocation for the urban indigenous population. One day in 1677 he attempted to stop Domingo de Guaman, an indigenous resident, from stealing water from the main irrigation canal (the Mochica). Ramos, with his official staff in his hand, attempted to detain Guaman, who had "mistreated him much" with words. Pedro Bran, a native of Cajamarca and a free criollo with another ladino highland migrant broke up the fight, but not before Guaman had ripped the hair and clothing of Ramos. Charged with assault by the magistrate, Ramos complained that Domingo de Guaman considered himself a "free Indian who on other occasions had lost respect" of him and the other alcaldes of the nearby Mansiche reducción.[164] Without a testimony from Domingo de Guaman, it is difficult to tell how he identified himself or why he claimed the water of the Mochica canal. Still, the indigenous official insulted Domingo de Guaman as an Indian who did not respect Indian authority or the colonial rules of water allocation. It appears that a "free Indian" was a term for Andeans who operated outside of community standards that highland and coastal, migrant and local, indigenous officials understood as definitive.

Regarding the most ubiquitously mobile indigenous laborers, muleteers moved in a sphere that set them apart from Indians bound to the reducción. First, muleteers handled large amounts of cash or credit in their negotiations with landholders and merchants. Coastal elites also depended on indigenous muleteers as their sole means to transport valuable commodities to ports and cities. Undoubtedly, losing precious cargo could cause a muleteer to go into debt.[165] Still, as the estates expanded and indigenous people on reducciones became more dependent on landholders for access to irrigation canals and employment, muleteers could take advantage of the necessity of their position. Pedro Bernabe, a Mochumí native and muleteer owed one of Trujillo's most prominent landholders, Captain don García de Bracamonte Dávila, over twelve hundred pesos. The amount constituted a loan that Pedro Bernabe promised to pay in eight months—a short period of time, indicating the muleteer's confidence in his market abilities.[166]

Second, in their mobile capacity, indigenous muleteers also had frequent contact with fugitive and enslaved men. In 1666 an enslaved mulato was being taken to Lima to be sold. Along the way, in the Guañape *tambo* (outside of Trujillo), a muleteer accused the enslaved man of stealing some silk stockings and other merchandise. Quickly, a free criolla black woman defended the accused, and her son, and the goods were returned. Still, the record of conflict provides evidence of everyday contact that must have been common in the inns and other way stations along the coastal routes.[167] Muleteers were among the few indigenous commoners who owned enslaved people. For example, Diego Bartolo, an Indian muleteer and resident in the Santiago de Cao town, sold a colonial official an elderly enslaved man, Lorenso Cano.[168] Enslaved men carted produce and goods between landed estates; they also ran errands to the urban areas, so they often crossed paths with indigenous muleteers.[169] Negotiating with colonial Spaniards and working with African descendants, indigenous muleteers stretched the boundaries of what defined the casta of Indian in everyday practice.

Indeed, indigenous muleteers could be allies of fugitive or errant enslaved men. In Lima, Juan de la Cruz approached an indigenous man named only as Cobo who worked on a coastal mule train. A fugitive, de la Cruz asked if he could be taken along in exchange for a stolen ring.[170] In his testimony to the magistrate Cobo reported that he refused, perhaps fearing both the punishment of the rural guard as well as the disapproval of his employer.[171] Determined to return to his home in Quito, Juan de la Cruz followed the muleteers and caught up with them at the swollen Paramonga river (north of Lima), where they were detained for a few days. After his inability to negotiate with a worker on the mule train, Juan de la Cruz spoke to the driver, mestizo Juan de Palacios. He convinced the driver that he was free and that he would pay to be taken to Trujillo, where his mother lived. Later, muleteer Antonio Guaman, a ladino Indian from Santiago de Cao, testified that they feared Juan de la Cruz was a fugitive. The characteristics that distinguished a fugitive and a free person were often hard to discern, but the shifting testimonies also indicate discrepancies between what happened during the trip north to Trujillo and what was then reported to the investigating magistrate. Nonetheless, the muleteers transported him from Lima to Trujillo and appear to have notified colonial authorities only when the native of Quito did not pay. Moving goods and people along the coastal routes, indigenous muleteers acted from their sense of profit, not necessarily the official boundaries of casta.

Market Exchanges across Castas

Whatever their relation with the reducción, indigenous people also exchanged goods and services with Africans and their descendants on and around the expanding estates. In turn, Africans and their descendants who stepped into the market circumvented the impositions of slavery, if in a limited and temporary manner, or simply employed trading possibilities for their survival. Enslaved men and women may have experienced hunger because renters, administrators, and overseers were notorious for reducing food supplies to lessen their overhead costs.[172] Thus it is possible that enslaved people relied on trading with their indigenous neighbors or others to supplement their weekly rations of beans, garbanzos, maize, and occasionally meat.[173] Most of the exchanges in the rural areas were not recorded since laborers did not hire a notary for small sales and local barter. Nonetheless, regular markets and improvised trading were common throughout the northern coastal cities and valleys, as was the case in Lima and Quito.[174]

Certainly urban as well as rural enslaved people attended weekly markets in Trujillo and in the surrounding area, especially on Sundays, when supposedly they were free from work.[175] Also, indigenous and enslaved inhabitants in the rural areas relied on each other for certain goods. Enslaved laborers sought out indigenous vendors to purchase chicha (corn beer).[176] Indigenous villagers knew that enslaved laborers sold pigs and chickens that they had raised on the estates.[177] In an example revealing the informal exchanges, indigenous migrants living in and around Trujillo's Santa Ana parish in 1693 sought out enslaved men, such as their "friend" Juan Agustín, who traded sugarcane syrup.[178] Pedro Mina, an enslaved man who worked grinding cane in a sugar mill, had been warned to not sell the sugar by-product as ordered by the magistrate and viceroy.[179] Still, indigenous men knew that enslaved workers in the sugar mills were the primary source for this type of alcohol. Trade, then, could draw indigenous and enslaved laborers together.

If enslaved people could acquire lucrative goods, then indigenous men and women helped them to exchange them in the market. In 1697, Antonio Mina stole wheat from his owner and took it to the household of Gregorio Espejo and María Josepha. The mestizo and indigenous woman guarded the wheat and even had it ground into flour at a nearby mill.[180] Like the enslaved men who trafficked in sugarcane syrup, Antonio Mina had access to large quantities of wheat because he transported the grain from the estates to the mill. In turn, the mestizo and indigenous pair served as trusted intermediaries who increased the wheat's value by having it ground. Then they presumably hid the flour until it could be sold in a lucrative market where coastal landholders still complained of a wheat blight.[181] Indigenous people and those with indigenous networks provided a means for enslaved laborers to transform stolen goods into marketable products. When Francisco Arara stole a kettle from his owner, he entrusted it to Agustina Rodríguez, a mestiza tavern keeper.[182] Drinking establishments attracted local clientele, but also drew peddlers and travelers.[183]

In a matter of days, Rodríguez had sent the kettle to the highlands, where presumably it could be sold without being recognized and reclaimed by the owner.[184] In both the case of the usurped wheat and that of the pilfered kettle, Gregorio Espejo and Antonia Rodríguez astutely declared in the judicial trial that they had not known the goods were stolen. Regardless of what was true, on estates and in slaveholders' households, enslaved laborers worked in close proximity to valuable goods. They transformed their enslaved position into profit by strategically tapping into the networks of their free, Andean acquaintances.

Indigenous people also provided clothing to enslaved Africans and their descendants who were often allotted the bare minimum by slaveholders.[185] On the northern Peruvian coast, owners or administrators annually purchased a set of clothing for enslaved workers that usually included only a simple shirt and a pair of trousers or a skirt made from cordellate, a coarse wool fabric favored for its durability.[186] Rural estate holders were known to purchase roughly made blankets and ponchos for enslaved men and women.[187] Given this scarcity, enslaved people sought clothing and bedding from indigenous people who often traded in textiles.[188] For instance, García of casta congo attempted to purchase a blanket from an Andean woman living in Miraflores, an indigenous neighborhood on the outskirts of Trujillo.[189] Indigenous producers may have welcomed the opportunity to trade; Anton Congo also claimed that an Indian had given him the trousers he was found wearing.[190] Perhaps rarely recorded, Andeans, Africans, and others must have exchanged clothing regardless of where they lived or worked.

As a portable and liquid asset, clothing functioned as a form of durable currency among northern coastal inhabitants. Francisco Cabero, an enslaved mulato, bet his money in a Trujillo gambling house one Sunday against some items of clothing, including a shirt, white trousers, a pair of silk socks, and two pillows.[191] In this instance clothing was equal in value to cash. For enslaved people, clothing was a more valuable commodity than foodstuffs that could spoil or livestock that were easily stolen or procured by slaveholders. Instead, clothing could be hidden and sold discreetly, and some pieces could be exchanged for high prices to those who had access to markets and consumers.[192]

In fact, the fugitive community headed by Gabriel and Domingo (the example that began this chapter) appear to have sustained themselves partially from the theft of clothing. Indigenous traders along the road descending from the highlands as well as the indigenous laborers in the upper Trujillo valley complained that the fugitives stole their ponchos and shirts—as Blas Angola and Anton Angola confessed during the trial of some palenque members.[193] It is also possible that in addition to theft, palenque members traded with indigenous people. Regardless, while members of the settlement may have worn the stolen clothing, they also stored the ponchos, shirts, and pieces of cloth, suggesting that these items were intended for sale.[194]

A few years later a fugitive named Pedro Angola was able to sustain himself by stealing clothing, bedding, and other textiles from local and migrant indigenous laborers in the Trujillo valley. The enslaved man sold the stolen goods to clients throughout the valleys including "some *serranos*" or highlander Andeans, indicating his wise choice to move clothing from where it would be recognized by previous owners into a new market.[195] Like the members of Gabriel and Domingo's settlement, fugitive Pedro Angola was integrated into the indigenous society and served a key role in the local economy. With his mobility he served as a middleman between enslaved suppliers and Andean highland consumers such as Barbola, an enslaved elderly woman who may have supplied Pedro Angola with a Castilian white blanket, a cape of Quito green cloth, and underwear that went missing from the Spanish owner on the farm where she labored.[196] Fugitives, especially those in established communities, were even more able to capitalize on their intermediary status. Those who lived in the dry hillsides between the coastal valleys and the mountain roads moved between the coastal and highland populations. Like their enslaved counterparts, fugitives acquired clothing and bedding that, because of their mobility, they were able to sell to their multiple contacts throughout the valleys and beyond.

Enslaved and fugitive people valued indigenous clothing and textiles as well as Andean trade networks. Juan Grande, an enslaved man, was accused of stealing shirts, underwear, trousers, handkerchiefs, hats, and a fishing net as well as a cotton poncho from the lodgings of indigenous mitayos from Chiclayo who were working in or near Trujillo.[197] Indigenous laborers from these regions would have been likely sources for cotton shirts and ponchos because indigenous women in the Jequetepeque and Lambayeque valleys produced these common items of trade and export.[198] Juan Grande was knowledgeable about both the goods and the current market. He stole clothing that was common, in demand, and thus could be easily sold, as proven by Miguel Alonso, a Spanish-speaking shoemaker and indigenous native of Trujillo, who attempted to buy the cotton poncho from Juan Grande only days following the theft. Enslaved men tried to make use of indigenous trading networks. Enslaved men Diego and Juan Criollo were accused of taking seven "pieces" of new clothing from an indigenous woman who formed part of a household of hired yanaconas. Easily preserved, the clothing would have been highly valuable. Then they attempted to sell the ponchos and shirts to Gabriel, an urban enslaved man who allegedly refused to act as a middleman for the two thieves.[199]

Probably to avoid criminal charges, Gabriel claimed that "he did not know anyone who could buy" the pieces. Instead, an indigenous herder named Pedro agreed to keep the stolen clothing. Cognizant that the evidence comes from criminal proceedings initiated by Trujillo's magistrate, Gabriel and Pedro's association with Diego and Juan Criollo reveals a plausible network of enslaved and indigenous middlemen (legitimate and illicit). The items of exchange—clothing produced and possessed by indigenous men and women who traveled southward from the northern, cotton-producing valleys to labor on the Spanish estates in the Chicama and Trujillo valleys—pointedly suggest African and African-descent adaptations of local, indigenous and colonial, standards of value.

Enslaved and fugitive men also employed indigenous and Spanish clothing to express relationships and hierarchies within a diasporic community. Significant clothing items could adorn, serve as gifts, and signify patronage or cement kinship.[200] In this sense Nicolas of casta *malamba* gave a cape made of green Quito cloth to his fellow fugitive and *compañero* Pasqual of casta angola and marked internal relations among members of the fugitive settlement headed by Gabriel and Domingo in the upper Trujillo valley. Like Nicolas, the "lieutenant" of the palenque community Domingo wore a blue cape that he took from a Spaniard on a local estate, allowing him to communicate his title in a constant, material sense.[201] The captain of the settlement, Gabriel, wore a seamed, ruffled shirt of black taffeta taken from the same raid.[202] Indicating Gabriel's acute understanding of his clothing's power, a member of the rural guard who attacked the palenque noted that the captain of the fugitives wore this garment.[203] Gabriel probably understood the expensive shirt reminded members of his community that he was their leader. The shirt also visually declared his status to outsiders.[204]

Enslaved and fugitive people chose types of colonial indigenous clothing to express a prestigious status also recognizable by other coastal inhabitants. Reflecting an understanding of what constituted valuable clothing on the northern coast, an enslaved man named Pedro with another compañero stole a new, lined hooded cloak and a dyed purple cape from an indigenous man in the Chicama valley.[205] Given their selection of these items from others that they left behind, the clothing was not solely based on a market value but also suggests a cultural adaptation as enslaved Africans and their descendants came to recognize the value of particular indigenous products.[206] Enslaved and fugitive men may have sold or worn these items of clothing also to communicate their status to and through Andean means, as Nicolas of casta malamba (a fugitive in Gabriel and Domingo's palenque) wore a blue cape that he took from an indigenous man.[207] As Nicolas may have known, indigenous leaders or men of a high social standing wore capes, such as the indigenous alcalde in Trujillo, who donned a black cloak and carried a staff that signified his position.[208] Far from indicating mere crimes, these judicial accusations of theft reveal how enslaved and fugitive men shared, adapted, or at least understood the tastes and hierarchies of Spanish and Spanish-descent slaveholders, but also those of indigenous neighbors and fellow traders.

Mixing across Casta

Urban environments left more evidence of market exchanges that perhaps went undocumented in the rural areas and indicate social mixing among Africans and Andeans that superseded strategic usage. In Trujillo shop owner Juan Dávila, a free *moreno*, native of the city, and slaveholder, kept accounts with enslaved and indigenous people alike. Coastal Andeans from Moche, Huanchaco, and Santiago de Cao as well as a Paiján cacique owed the store keeper for mules and wine, suggesting integration into the coastal trading routes.[209] Indeed, as petitions against colonial magistrates suggest, northern coastal indigenous communities were heavily involved in the trade as well as consumption of these goods.[210] Indigenous caciques and muleteers were not the only traders in and out of the city.

Suggestive of how active enslaved men and women were in the local markets, shop owner Juan Dávila owed an enslaved black woman named Antonia and an enslaved man, Agustín.[211] Because the shop owner was in debt to Antonia and Agustín, he probably purchased goods (or services) from them as opposed to selling items to enslaved consumers. He may also have paid the enslaved couple in cash or goods, like other slaveholders.[212] Indicating their market activity, in Trujillo enslaved men and women earned daily wages and sold goods for their owners in the city as well as throughout the valleys.[213] In turn, enslaved people purchased goods, especially chicha, from indigenous venders. For example, enslaved and free men and women frequented Lorenza de la Cruz's house, where she sold gourds filled with chicha worth a half real or a peso late on Saturday nights.[214] In another example enslaved African men, such as Juanillo Malemba and Diego of casta angola, stopped by the *chichería* of Juan Criollo, an Indian, to have a gourd of the alcoholic drink before going on to work at the nearby flour mill.[215] Socializing must have accompanied drinking. Through everyday exchanges in the city (as suggested for the countryside) enslaved and free people of color mixed easily with indigenous migrants and locals—especially if their exchanges were profitable.

During festivals and holidays indigenous men and women joined with their enslaved and free neighbors to honor saints and celebrate public devotions. In Trujillo the municipal council ordered local Indians to dance and process in the Corpus Christi celebrations. For the birth of Prince Felipe those from the nearby reducciones of Mansiche, Huanchaco, and Moche conducted bull runs and bull fights in the city.[216] As they did in Lima, enslaved and free people must have also joined in these public celebrations.[217] At least in Saña, "black girls" danced in Carnival processions, while the Jesuits reported how drunken Indians joined Spaniards in the same festivities.[218] In addition to public celebrations, indigenous people were attuned to the gatherings of Africans and their descendants. Pedro Lucas, who was identified as a ladino Indian, explained that passing by a cleric's house he heard "a lot of murmuring and weeping of black men and women" during a gathering (perhaps a funeral).[219] Other indigenous people provided testimonies in the resulting criminal case regarding the conflict between a criollo black named Pasqual and an African man Anton Folupo who had been compañeros, or fellow slaves, in the cleric's house. Chance encounters such as these combined with the reports from public celebrations suggest that indigenous people were not estranged from Africans and their descendants but aware and engaged in each other's lives.

Urban Indians left more records than their rural counterparts regarding their contacts with enslaved and free people. Juan Barta, who identified himself in his will as a ladino Indian, a barber, and migrant from highland Simbal, left his household goods to his family and his tools to his apprentice.[220] His debts indicated that he traded goods and services primarily with other indigenous men and women, thus reproducing the bonds of casta. Juan Barta also resembled indigenous people who reproduced their familial ties with kinships that extended into their trading networks.[221] Still, Juan Barta requested that the confraternity of Nuestra Señora del Rosario—which he (or the notary) noted was "of the natives and the morenos" (a term that was preferred by free people of color rather than "negro" or "black")—accompany his funeral procession.[222] The indigenous migrant also left funds for San Nicolás de Tolentino, a confraternity "of the morenos."[223] Juan Barta's choice of these religious confraternities indicate that he considered them to be potent spiritual interlocutors or carefully chosen status symbols.[224] Juan Barta may or may not have been a member of these religious lay institutions, but his choices indicate that urban indigenous men and women inhabited and valued the same social spaces as Africans and their descendants.

Africans and Andeans, enslaved and free people, intermingled in Trujillo perhaps as they did on estates and crossroad settlements in rural areas. The city was not segregated but included mixed residencies and neighborhoods where enslaved and free people lived among indigenous locals and migrants. Although Indian neighborhoods were located outside of the city or distant from the main plaza in some colonial cities, indigenous caciques and commoners lived in the center of Trujillo with non-Indians as well as in indigenous parishes.[225] Enslaved people and their owners and free people of color could be found living throughout the city as in Lima and in Mexico City.[226] Contact translated into relationships as indigenous people married non-Indians. The clerics of Santa Ana and San Sebastian, two indigenous parishes of Trujillo, defended their right to marry indigenous men and women with mestizos, black women, and "people of mixture."[227]

Apart from official unions, indigenous and African-descent people had long-term relationships outside of marriage. Without the marriage records of the indigenous parishes, it is difficult to gauge who Andeans married in Trujillo. Still, the Cathedral records of Trujillo list, for example, the baptism of a samba, the daughter of a "native" and a man of African descent, as well as the baptism of a one-year-old son of a *pardo* and an Indian woman.[228] As many scholars have noted, indigenous and African-descent men and women were having children together.[229] In 1678 the indigenous nighttime watch of Santa Ana arrested Cristobal Valencia and Melchora because they had caused a scandal in the neighborhood by living and eating together "as if they were married."[230] Cristobal Valencia identified himself as a *quarterón* of mulato, a shoemaker, single, and a native of Lima, while Melchora named herself as an Indian, single, and a native of Cajamarca. While punished for their cohabitation, Cristobal Valencia and Melchora of Cajamarca were undaunted by the differences of their casta and perhaps tied by their shared identity as migrants. The question remains: what did the distinctions of casta matter to them?

Most tellingly, single women shared households with each other that blurred the lines between the colonial "republics." Juana Xofre identified herself in a civil case as a free mulata and a vecina of Trujillo. She lived with another elderly woman, María Magdalena de Alvarado, who she described as a "good woman."[231] Other witnesses maligned Alvarado, describing how she would become drunk and then shortchange customers in the store where she worked. Labeled as a mestiza, Alvarado was often seen eating with the shop owner—a sign of domestic intimacy.[232] Undoubtedly, single women, especially those of mixed descent who worked in public, were easily criticized as dishonorable and dangerous.[233] Still, Juana Xofre shared her house with María Magdalena de Alvarado and defended her boarder (or friend) in the face of expected but harmful testimonies. The civil case from Trujillo illuminates that when casta differences were not useful or profitable, lower-status people appeared to disregard them.

In fact, close proximity led to a blurring of casta boundaries. In the rural areas colonial authorities lamented that indigenous men passed as mestizos in an attempt to avoid paying tribute or serving mita.[234] By changing clothes or occupations, indigenous men transformed their identity into a more useful category, just as mestizos presented themselves as Indian when strategic.[235] Demonstrating the fallibility of casta categorizations more than their flexibility, mixed residencies challenged the representativeness of the colonial labels in their daily experience. For instance, Juana Escobar lived with Antonia Martínez near the water reservoir in Trujillo. One evening, Antonia Martínez called out to a young apprentice who was passing in the street. She asked him to go to the store and purchase a half real of candles. The exchange was interrupted by the apprentice's master, who objected to the young man's absence from work as well as his conviviality with the young women. Interestingly, the resulting criminal case illuminates the fact that indigenous people were less easily categorized when they were found in unexpected places or at least outside of indigenous reducciones or Indian parishes.

Juana Escobar named herself as a ladina Indian and native of Trujillo, but another witness identified her as a young woman but first named her as a mestiza and then an Indian woman. Her living companion, Antonia Martínez, may have been prompted by the notary or corrected herself, but she also described Juana as a "mestiza young woman I mean Indian woman."[236] Either by her clothes, her manner of speaking Spanish, or her affinities, Juana Escobar was taken as both mestiza and Indian. Indeed, mestiza identity had to be performed or acted out to be understood. Juana Escobar's intimacy with Antonia Martínez (who was unquestionably named as Spanish) as well as the mestizo apprentice may have confused her identity to the notary and the municipal official and even her friends and associates. As an Indian found elsewhere than her assigned reducción, Juana Escobar defied colonial categorization and made a new Indian identity for herself.

Colonial regulations dictated the differences between the castas of Indian and black. In practice, indigenous and African people with their descendants traded and celebrated with each other. They shared religious organizations and neighborhoods. They lived together, had children together, and shared households. Indigenous people who became detached from their assigned reducciones and established communities in the provincial urban areas mixed with enslaved and free people of African descent. Critically, the mixture among indigenous as well as African peoples and their descendants did not end the usage of casta. Even though casta categories could not encompass their experiences or relations, they used the colonial terms to their advantage when necessary or possible. Some discarded the terms especially in urban areas where alternative residencies and occupations allowed indigenous men and women to promote other networks and affinities.

Indigenous people increasingly turned up in unexpected places during the seventeenth century and into the eighteenth century following the privatization of land in the 1640s.[237] In the mid-seventeenth century, as a result of the land inspections, the coastal estates successfully pushed indigenous communities to the margins of the arable land in the valleys. Indigenous people, however, did not disappear. Persisting as farmers and laborers in the rural areas and moving into the urban environs to join others as artisans, shopkeepers, and muleteers, indigenous people continued to identify themselves according to their reducción origin. Still relying on their colonial location as Indian, coastal Andeans claimed protections from abusive indigenous officials or Spanish priests. Indian protections did not isolate coastal Andeans from their neighbors and coworkers. Indeed, Indians who were elsewhere (not on the reducción) also lived and worked with enslaved and free people. Whether rural or urban, the ties of family, origin, and kin were still strong for Andeans who transferred or re-created intimate relations with other indigenous people even while developing ties with Africans, Spaniards, and their descendants.

Tracing how Andeans expanded a colonial Indian identity outside of the reducción or seeing Indians elsewhere underlines both the use and the weakness of casta categories in colonial Spanish America. On the northern Peruvian coast the privatization of land accelerated a shift away from indigenous people's claims to official categories and protections of the Indian casta. Their case, however, illustrates the constructed nature of colonial casta categories overall. Indigenous people could use their casta location under particular legal circumstances, but the term "Indian" did not work at all times. In fact, Indians were not always correctly identified, such as when Juana Escobar named herself as an Indian but was known as a mestiza in her neighborhood. The constructed nature of casta is also illustrated when indigenous people carried the casta of Indian from the reducción to the city and also employed it there. Still, no longer bound to the reducción, coastal Andeans mixed and mingled with black people, mestizos, and whoever else they encountered in the markets that pulled them out of the reducciones onto estates, rural crossroads, urban neighborhoods, and beyond. In other words, coastal Andeans made the casta Indian work for them, illustrating its unfixed but definitive nature.

Indigenous people employed informal markets in labor and land in ways that worked contrary to the boundaries of casta. At midcentury the transatlantic slave trade declined. Coastal landholders had to rely more on migrant indigenous laborers. In the labor-scarce economy coastal muleteers and valley marketers seized on landholders' demands to fuel a dynamic movement of goods and labor between Trujillo and the rural estates. There—in the neighborhoods of Trujillo, along coastal trade routes, and inside weekly markets—enslaved and free, indigenous and African, people continually traded and drank together to expand the categories of casta that separated them in law. By the 1670s the Spanish crown had reassigned the slave-trading license so that merchants again (legally) sold Africans who had survived the transatlantic passage into the Pacific and eventually colonial Trujillo.

Given the exuberant possibilities of the colonial market, casta continued to create and to mark binding distinctions. Even when their landholdings were usurped, indigenous people could still claim limited protections as Indians under colonial law, which was not the same for people of African descent. Furthermore, indigenous people generally found themselves unable to compete with Spaniards and their descendants in the export economy that required immense capital investment simply beyond the means of caciques or commoners who were still charged with fulfilling tribute payments and even mita obligations. Without land and now with less demand for their labor, coastal Andeans found themselves fully thrust into the colonial marketplace. Exchanges of goods and labor loosened the strict demands of mita or tribute and brought Andeans closer to enslaved people but would not undo the bonds of slavery.

5. Justice within Slavery

IF ANDEANS NEGOTIATED WITH THE impositions of tribute and the *reducción*, the enslaved contended with how slavery functioned, especially as sugar estates expanded in the northern coastal valleys during the late seventeenth century and early eighteenth century. To understand possibilities encapsulated in the casta "black," this chapter examines the mechanics of slaveholding from the perspective of enslaved men, the predominant enslaved population on northern Peruvian estates. According to a sample of estate inventories, men were roughly 80 percent of the enslaved population of northern coastal estates, with women at 20 percent.[1] In addition, colonial officials and the rural guard who prosecuted the criminal trials that constitute the source base for this chapter targeted men over women. As other scholars have suggested, colonial authorities consistently criminalized enslaved men's acts of resistance, while women's were repeatedly ignored, downplayed, or underreported.[2] Analysis of these criminal trials reveals how enslaved men countered slaveholders' claims on their time, overt supervision of their labor, and control of their rest time by invoking customary practices. Enslaved men also employed colonial laws that curtailed abuse to protest the punishments inflicted by their owners, but official mandates did not extend to labor practices—one of the central activities of rural slavery.

The civil and criminal cases examined here reveal enslaved men's tenuous connections to official local legal practices (including hearings before a magistrate, investigations conducted by an alcalde, or petitions filed in court) as well as tensions among enslaved men on rural estates. Colonial courts and local judicial authorities were charged with providing justice to petitioners and mediating conflict.[3] Enslaved people, especially those from rural environs, often did not participate in legal venues under their own volition. In the following judicial cases, enslaved men often testified as witnesses to crimes that had resulted in a loss of or damage to "property"—enslaved people —for slaveholders. Enslaved people were not alone in the law's dismissal. Colonial laws (ecclesiastic or civil) were not intended to cover all aspects of colonial life, as "local usage and long-standing practice" were critical to determining the outcome of judicial cases as well as settling local disputes.[4]

Certainly enslaved men and women influenced legal precedents by engaging in legal petitions, by becoming fugitives, or by engaging in manumission practices.[5] Nonetheless, colonial courts and local officials were intent on restoring harmony for slaveholders but not necessarily for or among enslaved people, including those who participated in judicial proceedings. Regardless, Africans employed local courts, they worked to find justice according to their own standards and in doing so stretched the possibilities of colonial law. Enslaved agency revealed within legal records, in many ways, foregrounds corporate inclusions in other circumstances. Simultaneously, slaveholders in some cases "contracted out" the everyday mechanisms of surveillance, order, and control to proxies who sometimes included indigenous officials from neighboring reducciones. Furthermore, indigenous policing benefited coastal Andean communities but because they were superseded by Spanish and Spanish-descent colonial officials, the hierarchy created distance from the crown or its representatives that further challenged and deterred the ability for slaves to employ colonial legal mechanisms.

As a result, though advocating within their legal jurisdiction, enslaved men also moved their contestations of injustice to realms outside the courts. To protest the rapid pace, the onerous tasks of their daily work, and the disruption of their work hierarchies, enslaved men defended their skills and customary rights to rest against the demands of overseers, foremen, and owners who constituted the authorities in their everyday lives. In doing so, enslaved men contested the bodily harm and the incessant demand for their work, as well as the irregular surveillance that was central to northern Peruvian slaveholding. Their confrontations were not limited to slaveholders but included conflicts with other enslaved men over disagreements regarding the tasks and the order of work on rural estates. Since colonial authorities and local courts focused on settling the cost of a wounded or deceased enslaved laborer and were not concerned with rectifying unjust situations that affected enslaved rural men, enslaved laborers worked out separate standards of labor, food allocation, and rest time, further underlining their extralegal locations. The documentation highlights violent incidences but also affirms the severe physical conditions of slavery on the rural estates and emphasizes the hard-won nature of political alliances among enslaved men.

Historians of colonial Latin America have demonstrated how enslaved men and women utilized the protections of the Catholic Church to defend themselves against abuse and to argue for freedom.[6] In these circumstances enslaved people developed a legal consciousness by defending their ecclesiastical rights against the demands of slaveholders.[7] Unquestionably, enslaved and free people employed ecclesiastical and secular courts as well as notaries and patrons to claim their Catholic prerogatives as Christian vassals but also to contest brutal punishments, to demand rest time on Sundays, and to argue for manumission.[8] In comparison to indigenous laborers enslaved people on the northern Peruvian coast had more finite contact with the authorities who could oversee their legal petitions, such as the clergy, colonial officials, and even their actual owners.[9] This book's dual focus on both Andeans and Africans underscores how enslaved people were afforded fewer regulations governing their rights within slavery in comparison to the copious mandates regarding indigenous labor and Indian governance. In the countryside, slaveholders and their proxies constantly and violently demanded that enslaved men complete their work, discard their senses of community, and discount their masculine pride. Enslaved men and women established kinships and seized on Catholic institutions to organize themselves into new communities whose religious, cultural, and political manifestations were vibrant and effective. The point here is to explore how, rather than the law, slaveholders ruled, providing an additional barrier to organizing legal advocacy in colonial courts.

As discussed in previous chapters, the Spanish crown did not offer the kinds of protections to enslaved laborers as it did to indigenous people. Even as coastal Andeans removed themselves from their assigned colonial villages—the sites where they were supposed to enact their vassalage—indigenous men and women still named themselves as Indians to claim a location in colonial jurisprudence. In the meantime, secular laws regarding slavery in the sixteenth and seventeenth century did not offer enslaved men and women a similar location in the public sphere.[10] Colonial laws primarily forbade extreme abuse or acute neglect of enslaved men and women, but was ambiguous about providing enslaved people with a republic or another corporate location from which to make claims. The limitation of colonial legal practice is further illuminated by enslaved protests.[11] Judging from their actions, enslaved people on the northern coast employed legal avenues to argue with how, when, and with whom overseers and foremen demanded work, an aspect of slavery unregulated by colonial law.[12] In addition, if colonial legal practice was largely negotiated locally, enslaved people were further disenfranchised since slaveholding local officials largely issued legal rulings. To emphasize the pivotal comparison, enslaved men and women often found themselves outside the bounds of law while indigenous people contested usurpation of their labor within the more expansive legal parameters they were allowed. Nonetheless, these enslaved people called for justice by contesting the personal authority of northern coastal slaveholders and also by articulating their demands within legal discourse.

Contesting Labor, Claiming Time

On the northern Peruvian coast slaveholders attempted to extract labor from enslaved laborers who in turn contested the surveillance of their time and the attempt to dominate their order of work. Slaveholders imposed work schedules, assigned labor tasks, and regulated rest periods to force enslaved laborers to produce sugar, harvest wheat, or complete other designated tasks. These demands only heightened in the later part of the seventeenth century and early eighteenth century as the official transatlantic slave trade into Spanish America stabilized, allowing sugar estates on the northern coast to expand production.[13] Northern coastal estates also harnessed water power and expanded the fields under cultivation during this period.[14] Sugar processing on a larger scale increased the tempo of enslaved labor.[15] When slaveholders demanded that enslaved men work around the clock to process sugar or otherwise exceeded previous labor demands, as other scholars have discussed, enslaved men rebelled, escaped, or refused to work.[16]

In addition, when ordered by slaveholders, overseers, or foremen to complete a task, enslaved men attempted to assert how, when, and with whom they would perform their assigned jobs. These enslaved standards of work functioned in some cases because slaveholders depended on skilled laborers who knew how to process cane into sugar or to irrigate but not flood wheat fields. As a result, slaveholders were dependent on the skills and knowledge of enslaved laborers and therefore had to concede to customary practices such as working by task or taking regular rest periods. To some degree, slavery on the northern Peruvian coast was negotiated but not only between enslaved people and slaveholders.[17] Enslaved laborers also monitored and penalized each other for violating what they had agreed on would be rest time or the order of work tasks. These conflicts illustrate that in addition to pushing back against slaveholders, enslaved men developed fair work standards among themselves.

If slave trading was based on the value of an enslaved person as property, the value within slaveholding rested on the control of enslaved people's time. On the northern Peruvian coast, slaveholders did not attempt to assert control over enslaved people's bodies by locking men and women overnight into barracks, as was done in nineteenth-century Cuba.[18] The rural guard did not check passes of enslaved people traveling between estates or into the city, as was practiced in the antebellum southern United States.[19] Movement was not monitored on the northern Peruvian coast. Enslaved men owned, borrowed, or stole mules and horses to travel between the estates and settlements, and into such provincial cities as Trujillo.[20] Likewise, enslaved women moved throughout rural settlements to sell bread or other goods.[21] Slaveholders did not constantly check on the location of enslaved laborers, but they expected obedience to their work schedule. If slaves were not present Monday mornings (the beginning of the work week) on the estates, slaveholders punished them.[22] If enslaved men tarried or were late when executing an assigned errand, slaveholders castigated them.[23] The daily practices of slaveholding controlled the laboring time of enslaved people and, in doing so, slaveholders attempted to dominate their persons in intimate and public ways.

In 1702, for example, Juan Hurtado, a criollo from Panama, was accused by the head of the rural guard of killing his owner's nephew.[24] Although it is possible that Juan Hurtado was forced to confess to the crime, he explained that the act was premeditated.[25] He suggested that throughout the late summer afternoon of working on an irrigation canal, he had thought about taking revenge against his owner's nephew. He was not alone. Juan Hurtado claimed that the other men who were working with him also had indicated a willingness to kill their supervisor. Their agreement may have stemmed from the work that the owner's nephew demanded from them. Together, the enslaved men cleaned an irrigation canal that may have become silted or damaged during the season's rains or was in danger of flooding when the next deluge occurred.[26] It was probably hard work because usually the lowliest laborers performed this task.[27] Juan Hurtado's accused crime therefore can be understood as acting against the excessive impositions of a man who was not even his owner but a stand-in. As an enslaved man born in the Americas and one who carried a surname, Juan Hurtado may have considered himself to be too high in the estate hierarchy for this work assignment.[28] In addition to the onerous nature of the work, his honor was at stake.

Juan Hurtado and his workmates may have also objected to the pace of labor. Enslaved laborers were accustomed to taking breaks from work to eat, drink, smoke, and rest.[29] The enslaved men may have expected that they would work on the irrigation canal alone or with the supervision of an enslaved foreman rather than the owner's nephew. Their sense of injustice, however, was not shared by the prosecuting authority. The head of the rural guard conducted the investigation swiftly and in a matter of days issued his intention to execute Juan Hurtado and then display his head on the royal road for one month and his hand on the estate where he supposedly committed the murder.[30] The local official was clearly interested in restoring a sense of order in the valley for slaveholders who would have expected him to look after their interests.[31] Without the testimonies of witnesses for the defense or an independent plaintiff, however, it is difficult to know who among the enslaved laborers favored taking the life of the owner's nephew.[32]

Examining the actions outside of the court case that was controlled by slaveholders and their agents, however, provides some clues. One hint is that enslaved laborers who witnessed the event did not chase after Hurtado after he committed the accused murder. Their lack of action stands in contrast to other instances in which enslaved laborers pursued a workmate who they believed committed an egregious crime, such as usurping another man's lover.[33] Instead of capturing Hurtado, another nephew of the estate's owner notified the rural guard, who seized him on a neighboring estate.[34] It is possible that other enslaved laborers agreed with Juan Hurtado when he objected to the pace of the work. In his confession Hurtado explained that the nephew would not let him (and presumably others) rest.[35] When the nephew would not listen to Hurtado's requests, perhaps he or another enslaved laborer punished the owner's proxy for a violation of what they considered to be an appropriate work rhythm. Hurtado's actions suggest that he protested the slaveholder's betrayal of the customary agreement regarding how and when enslaved men worked.

Enslaved laborers also objected to interference in the pace of their work and even opposed disruptions regarding how they conducted an assigned task. According to enslaved witnesses, early in the morning an enslaved man called Sebastian of casta *arara* (from the Bight of Benin) roused laborers on a Chicama valley estate to make adobe bricks. After they had been working, the Andalucian overseer appeared and reprimanded Sebastian for starting so late. By many accounts, Sebastian was insulted. According to the young slaveholder who had been left to manage the estate in his father's absence (who heard from a "mulato who goes to the highlands," the son of the enslaved mulata cook), Sebastian answered that "if he was not doing a good job of foreman, then [the overseer should] name another."[36] Offended by Sebastian's resistance, the overseer had demanded that the enslaved laborers seize the foreman. They did not, strongly suggesting their disagreement with the overseer's intrusion. For the benefit of the investigating magistrate, the young slaveholder called attention to the arrogance of the enslaved foreman, a quality that was not tolerated by local slaveholders.[37] Enslaved witnesses also corroborated the statement—as did Sebastian himself—but instead suggested that they shared a positive evaluation of the enslaved foreman's work and his response to the Spanish overseer.[38] The later start time may have been more amenable to the enslaved community on the estate or may have been how Sebastian intended to encourage the group to complete the assigned task. In any case enslaved witnesses favored Sebastian over the accusations of the overseer or the young slaveholder.

It is difficult to tell if Sebastian's statement reflected his perspective, especially since he evaded capture for two months and had to be transported from the estate by its owner to the public jail in Trujillo for his confession. Nonetheless, the enslaved foreman added to the account of the incident. He explained that he had insulted the overseer by calling him a "cuckold" and continued to positively evaluate the choices he had made regarding the day's labor tasks and schedule, boldly calling on his superior to prove his case otherwise.[39] After all, enslaved foremen regularly delegated workloads to enslaved laborers, assigned daily tasks, and managed workers.[40] The confrontation, it seems, conflated work order with a sense of masculine honor.[41] During the altercation when Sebastian was still refusing to submit, a number of witnesses explained that he ordered those working to move aside as he leapt from the adobe mud trough and with his free hand grabbed a dagger from his waist to mortally wound the overseer. Then, clearly aware that he would be punished, Sebastian mounted a horse, fled into the canyons in the upper valley, and eventually sought refuge in Trujillo. Like other enslaved laborers who witnessed this exchange, Sebastian defended his prerogative to decide on the task and the timing of work on the estate. Boldly, Sebastian refused the surveillance of his time, the control of the people working under his purview, and the attempt to usurp his dominance that would have undercut his role as the public leader (chosen or appointed) of the estate's enslaved community.

As enslaved men resisted slaveholders' attempts to manage work time and assert control over their internal hierarchies, they also guarded their free time. An enslaved man on a northern valley estate, Domingo Arara, understood that Sunday was supposed to be a day when he was not required to work. He protested the orders of his owner and overseer to collect firewood, an imposition of working on a "day of fiesta."[42] He echoed what ecclesiastical authorities had ordered for centuries: that enslaved laborers be free from labor on Sundays and holidays.[43] In this case clerics did not confront slaveholders; instead, most of the other enslaved laborers had left the estate to visit others or to entertain themselves elsewhere.[44] This was not unusual. Throughout the Americas enslaved people spent holidays working in their own fields, gambling, visiting, or marketeering.[45] Many seized on the opportunity of Sundays and fiesta days to attend Mass but also to meet with friends and relatives, expanding the intention of the ordered day of rest.[46] For example, on a holiday in 1662 enslaved men and women from neighboring estates gathered on the Chicama estate of Santísima Trinidad. There, enslaved men described their activity as *holgando*, "hanging out" while women cooked.[47] Sundays and fiesta days therefore were the usual time for recreation on the estates. Even as enslaved women continued to work, they did so for their families and communities but not for their owners. More than pushing against the imposition of working on a rest day, Domingo Arara pointed to what was considered fair and just by enslaved (and other) laborers that local officials generally respected.

Enslaved men and women also claimed their time away from work through the collective act of drinking. In the urban setting, their actions were noted as disruptions of colonial order. Trujillo's municipal authorities bemoaned the usual occurrence of "*borracheras*" of lower-status people, but in particular the drunken gatherings in the city's *chicha* (corn beer) taverns that could include indigenous people as well as other laborers.[48] To curtail these drunken gatherings, officials ordered enslaved and free people of color to stay in their houses after religious services rather than allow them to assemble in the streets or bars. According to colonial officials on the northern coast and elsewhere, public drinking could lead to fighting, illicit sexual activity, and other dangerous behaviors.[49] Trujillo's authorities therefore objected to the congregation of enslaved people in public spaces during rest days and opposed drinking altogether. It appears that city officials (who were also slaveholders) were made uncomfortable by how consumption of alcohol facilitated contact among enslaved people.[50] As enslaved people claimed unsupervised free time or drinking regardless of mandates to the contrary, colonial authorities sought to reinstate control over the possibility of enslaved solidarity as well as their time.

On the rural estates enslaved laborers claimed drinking time that signi-

fied moments of rest. Valentín of casta arara explained that he took a break
from his work task to consume sugarcane alcohol with a workmate on the
Facala estate in the Chicama valley. The enslaved man explained that the
chala (most likely from the Bight of Benin) black man was his compañero, or
workmate, on the estate, but he did not know his name.[51] (Valentín may have
not provided his workmate's name to save him from punishment or he may
not have known his Christian name or the one employed by his owner that
would have been demanded in the colonial court.) Alcohol consumption
was a common activity among men who worked together.[52] In this context,
the two men understood that by ducking into a rustic house to drink, they
made a similar claim to what historian Philip Morgan has called the "slave's
time," or the assertion of individual choice while enslaved.[53] Drinking collectively, whether in a boisterous tavern in Trujillo or in a rural lean-to,
meant taking periods of time away from a slaveholder but also removing
one's self from the control of the owner in favor of contact with other laborers—intimate or anonymous.

Enslaved laborers correctly understood that time rather than alcohol
consumption was at stake for slaveholders. Slaveholders did not prohibit enslaved men and women from consuming alcohol as Jesuit administrators
supplied low-quality rum to enslaved laborers on fiesta days.[54] In addition,
because they produced their own alcohol, enslaved laborers on sugar estates did not limit their consumption to holidays. Indicating the ease and
normalcy of alcohol production, Pedro Angola, an enslaved ladino man,
sold sugarcane alcohol that he had just made to the inhabitants of the Nuestra Señora del Rosario mill.[55] If drinking interfered with work, however,
slaveholders objected. Some slaveholders believed that enslaved laborers became ill by drinking too much on Sundays, making them unable to work on
Mondays.[56] Other slaveholders complained that enslaved laborers died from
the consumption of "strong" sugarcane alcohol made from the sugar syrup
produced from the first stage of boiling.[57] Slaveholders, however, did not attempt to ban the public consumption of alcohol like city officials in Trujillo.
Illustrating the power, perhaps, of enslaved claims to the social space provided by drinking as well as profits (however small) of alcohol sales, slaveholders objected only when enslaved drinking interfered with work time.

Time also mattered to enslaved men. If slaveholders complained when
enslaved laborers "stole" work time, then enslaved men objected when their
peers took away their free time. In other words, enslaved laborers expected
other enslaved people to respect their claims to Sunday or holiday time.[58] In
1702, Trujillo's magistrate accused Domingo Arara of murdering Francisco
Mina on a Chicama valley estate. According to enslaved witnesses, Fran-

cisco Mina had been preparing some yucca to eat when the older enslaved man killed him with a hatchet. After the magistrate's rapid investigation, the owner declared that he would not defend his enslaved laborer and suggested that he be punished as an example to others.[59] According to the slaveholder's expectations, the magistrate condemned Domingo Arara to death. From the enslaved laborer's perspective, however, the murder was not unwarranted. The owner of the estate had assigned Domingo Arara to work with Francisco Mina, a notorious fugitive.

When Francisco Mina fled again from the estate, the slaveholder blamed Domingo Arara for allowing the escape. As a result, the woodcutter was shackled like a fugitive himself and made to work on Sundays until four or five in the evening. In his confession, he explained that the owner and over-seer punished him for not stopping Francisco Mina from fleeing the estate.[60] Domingo Arara understood his punishment as more than a mere change in work schedule. The slaveholder had violated customary labor practices on the northern coast that usually distinguished "time belonging to the master and time belonging to the slaves."[61] Previously, as a woodcutter, Domingo Arara probably worked at a daily task or collected a quota of firewood, leaving him able to engage in other endeavors.[62] Domingo Arara did not act on his sense of injustice toward a foreman, overseer, or another representative of a slaveholder as did other enslaved laborers. For reasons that are difficult to ascertain due to the charged nature of the criminal trial, he targeted Francisco Mina, his errant workmate, who had caused the additional labor time.

Yet in this instance other enslaved men on the estate disagreed with Domingo Arara, indicating an independent sense of justice and injustice from the community. Only enslaved men were present when Domingo Arara brought an ax down on Francisco Mina's head. According to their testimonies, they rushed to capture Domingo and then secured him in the stocks before notifying anyone else.[63] It is possible that the enslaved witnesses were coerced or provided this testimony to the magistrate to distance themselves from the event. The details that they provided, however, indicate that apart from the magistrate's investigation, they also judged the actions of Domingo Arara. First, the enslaved laborers noted that Domingo Arara had taken advantage of Francisco Mina's inattention and attacked when the enslaved man was frying yucca. The enslaved laborers emphasized that Domingo Arara had approached Francisco Mina from behind, perhaps a cowardly choice among men.[64]

Second, the enslaved men who witnessed the event emphasized that Domingo Arara had assaulted a coworker during a period of rest when all enslaved people, no matter their positions or actions, merited respite. It appears that Domingo Arara may have agreed. According to their testimonies, he repeatedly declared to his coworkers after killing Francisco Mina: "I killed him, here I am. I will pay for it."[65] He did not resist capture by his workmates. By admitting that he had committed the murder, Domingo Arara condemned himself to punishment and facilitated the magistrate's sentence. It is also possible that he or his workmates explained that he had confessed to his community his violations of agreements that protected rest time among the enslaved.

Just as enslaved laborers monitored their days off from labor, they also considered daily rest time to be sacrosanct and enforced its regulation. On the northern coast slaveholders charged overseers, renters, and administrators with producing specific quotas of sugar, wheat, soap, and other products, but they did not specify how the work would be performed.[66] In turn, slaveholders' proxies delegated the distribution of labor tasks and the enforcement of work schedules to enslaved foremen. Owners of estates therefore were not necessarily in charge (and they appear to not have wanted to be) of the hour-to-hour or day-to-day labor of their slaves. As a result, enslaved communities developed standards of behavior as well as equivalencies of job assignments that were separate from the overall demands of slaveholders themselves.[67] Violation or evidence of labor codes among enslaved men, however, are difficult to document because their existence was inconsequential to slaveholders who filed judicial suits, or paid the notaries for inventories that form the document base for understanding rural enslaved communities on the northern Peruvian coast.

Nevertheless, it appears that enslaved laborers developed their own work culture on the estates. For example, Pasqual, the enslaved foreman of a Chicama valley estate, arrived at the house of the local indigenous official to report that Baltasar Mina had murdered an enslaved arara man known as the "Singer."[68] The indigenous authorities testified that Pasqual was in a great fright, suggesting that he was surprised or caught off guard by Baltasar Mina's actions. It is possible that the indigenous authorities misrepresented Pasqual's emotional state or he presented himself as fearful to distance himself from culpability of the accused crime. The judicial proceedings unfortunately do not illuminate more about the conflict except that the murder took place while the "Singer" was asleep and that the estate was in the middle of its sugar harvest, when enslaved laborers usually worked around the clock in the mill.[69] On the northern Peruvian coast enslaved men who fed the cane into the grinders or who stirred the boiling sugar very rarely got more than a few hours sleep during the harvest.[70] Enslaved laborers therefore would have protected their allocated rest time during these periods. What the indigenous authorities reported as fright may have been Pasqual's shock from

Baltasar Mina's disobedience, or fear that he could also be murdered while resting. As suggested by the enslaved foreman's punctuated declaration, enslaved laborers held each other to standards of work time versus rest time that were distinct from the demands of slaveholders. If slaveholders focused on the relationship between time and production, enslaved laborers understood how time shaped their lives.

As slaveholders or their proxies pushed enslaved men to work, enslaved men defended how they labored as well as the time they needed to rest. Similarly, as slaveholders monitored the work, enslaved men defended their own schedules and defended the internal hierarchies among the enslaved. Enslaved protests shifted along with slaveholder demands. If work time was under surveillance, enslaved laborers demanded time free from labor. Slaveholders in turn disciplined enslaved men who questioned their authority and punished any who resisted the imposed schedule of work and rest. In the case of the enslaved foreman Sebastian, who insisted that the overseer find a new supervisor if he did not like his work, he was publicly hanged and his head mounted on the estate as "an example to the blacks who should respect the Spanish."[71] By pushing men to work and then punishing them for claiming customary free time, slaveholders enacted the laws of slavery at the everyday level. Time was critical, and consequently enslaved men scrutinized each other to keep internal practices of enslaved labor. Undetected by slaveholders or their proxies, enslaved men claimed their time even if it meant conflict with their workmates or death. Simultaneously, enslaved laborers defended community standards of rest and dignity, which indicated a wider sense of justice and injustice among rural slave populations than the slaveholders' imposition of order.

Claims within Slavery

Enslaved people developed alternative means of protesting and avoiding abusive or intolerable treatment by making customary practices normative. Francisco of casta mina fled from his owner out of fear that he would be whipped after what he considered to be a false accusation of a robbery.[72] By becoming a fugitive, Francisco joined many other enslaved men and women on the northern coast who became fugitives and sought out permanent fugitive communities in the hillsides surrounding the valleys.[73] Fugitive communities and groups of fugitives deeply troubled northern coastal authorities, including indigenous officials who complained of their bold attacks on farms and travelers.[74] In addition to the independence of long-term fugitives, truancy, or the practice of short-term absenteeism, however, functioned as a means to renegotiate certain terms of enslavement.[75]

Like other enslaved men, Francisco of casta mina employed the practice of truancy to change aspects of his enslaved position. When accused of physically and violently resisting his owner and then fleeing, Francisco explained that he had escaped in the hopes of finding a friend of his current owner who would serve him as a padrino, or "godfather."[76] By the seventeenth century, enslaved men and women on the Peruvian northern coast engaged in the practice of "looking for a patron," or a replacement for their current owner.[77] Staying legally enslaved but actively soliciting a new owner allowed enslaved people to maneuver within slaveholding and also provided a way to transition from the more dangerous fugitive position back to slave status. Josepha de Horra, an enslaved mulata, was a fugitive, but her lover Pasqual Vallejo explained that she was looking for a padrino during the time of her absence.[78] In this way Horra was not presented as a defiant fugitive acting in resistance to slaveholding but merely as a slave moving within slavery. By inserting oneself in the practice of looking for a padrino, enslaved people could provide a narrative for their perhaps illegal actions. Gonçalo, an enslaved black man, explained that he met two other presumably escaped blacks in the uncultivated and uninhabited area above the valleys, and together they looked for a patron.[79] Whether fugitives or not, enslaved people solicited alternative slaveholders who would purchase them.[80] In this way enslaved men and women attempted to exchange abusive owners for more tolerable situations.

The custom of securing a new owner was not promoted by royal jurists or colonial authorities but was publicly practiced. Royal mandates stated that slaves could purchase themselves and their families but did not necessarily allow that they could exchange one owner for another.[81] Doing so would undercut a central premise of slaveholding: owners were to decide the fate of enslaved men and women. As the historian Alejandro de la Fuente has explained for Cuba, enslaved people on the northern Peruvian coast employed their only right—to protest abuse—in order to change owners.[82] The local courts adapted to local practice.[83] By the late seventeenth century, Trujillo's courts had accepted the custom which, for example, Andrés de Arroyo, an enslaved criollo, presented to Trujillo's magistrate. Andrés de Arroyo argued that he required a new owner because he was "being killed with bad treatment" by his current master.[84]

In addition, well aware that enslaved people absented themselves from their current owner to secure a new one, colonial authorities did not prosecute the ongoing practice. Rather, they explained that enslaved fugitives who fled usually returned with the promise of a patron, as was "the custom of blacks and slaves who flee."[85] Clearly there was a difference between this practice and another of refusing to return to slavery.[86] Colonial authorities appear to have gone along with the practice of enslaved laborers who returned to slavery and therefore were understood as not challenging the principles of slaveholding.[87] As opposed to what was understood as fugitives (cimarronaje) that was prosecuted, local courts on the northern coast of Peru sometimes did not discourage the practice of "looking for a padrino."

Enslaved men could gain the upper hand in these negotiations. In 1692 the rural guard investigated the accusations that a mulato named Blas de Lureño was hiding fugitive slaves on lands he was farming. According to Lureño, a suspected fugitive slave was working on his farm because his owner had encouraged him to look for a new master.[88] In this situation there was clear slippage between the practice of hiring out and that of looking for a new owner.[89] Whether the accusations were true or not, Lureño offered the customary practice of "looking for a padrino" to excuse himself from the charge of hiding a fugitive slave.[90] Regardless of whether Lureño considered himself to be harboring a fugitive or hiring itinerant labor, other free laborers and farmers looked to capitalize on fugitives who operated as "free agents," independent from the demands of their owner in the late seventeenth century and early eighteenth century on the Peruvian northern coast.

When minor cleric Antonio Vanegas encountered Andrés of casta arara in an alfalfa field outside of Trujillo, he asked if he was a fugitive. Rather than turning him into the rural guard, Vanegas offered to serve as Andrés's padrino.[91] Retaining the upper hand, Andrés refused the cleric and robbed him. It would seem that the expanding sugar estates and the contracting indigenous reducciones coincided with an increased demand for laborers on the smaller estates and labor opportunities for enslaved men.[92] Adding to the indications that there was a market for itinerant workers, fugitive laborers later testified against Blas de Lureño, who they claimed had refused to pay them a daily wage.[93] Whether or not Lureño had cheated fugitive or truant men from their compensation, once caught by the rural guard, the enslaved men invoked customary practices to explain their actions. As one man explained, when he became a fugitive, his intention was to apadrinar, or to look for wage work hypothetically that would also benefit his owner.[94] By attempting to deal with fugitive or truant men, Lureño, as a free man of color, and the minor cleric who attempted to make a deal with Andrés of casta arara may have threatened the powerful landholders who financially supported the investigating rural guard.[95] Consequently, Lureño and the cleric were in weak negotiating positions. Regardless, enslaved men were able to take advantage of the apparent market for itinerant laborers by employing the customary practice of seeking a new owner to achieve a limited mobility in the northern valleys.

As enslaved men employed customary practices and seized on market possibilities, they appeared to articulate a different understanding than slaveholders or colonial authorities of what it meant to look for a new "patron." Some fugitives suggested that to *apadrinarse* meant not just to find another owner but to secure one who would pay them a wage for their work.[96] They appear intent to achieve the status of a slave who is hired out for wages that are paid to the owner.[97] Although the practice was common for urban slaves, the same may not have been true for those working on estates, farms, and ranches in the northern valleys.[98] In the case of rural enslaved men, the desired effect appears to have been to secure more independence and mobility from their task work. Recognized as a customary practice but not firmly situated within the regulatory powers of the law, some enslaved men and women employed "looking for a patron" to gain wage-earning capabilities within slavery.

In rare moments when enslaved men directly petitioned the provincial courts, they asserted their interpretation of slaveholding's parameters. In the magistrate's court Andrés de Arroyo accused his owner of gross mistreatment, including withholding food, refusing to allow a search for another owner, and threatening severe physical abuse while he was being held in prison as security for his owner's debt.[99] In doing so, Arroyo pointed to specific colonial laws that mandated colonial authorities protect enslaved laborers from severe abuse.[100] Technically the owner had not broken the law (since a threat of violence was not the same as physical abuse) but appeared to have violated expected relations between owners and enslaved.[101] Arroyo argued that he was not a criminal but that he was merely in prison because his owner was in debt. Boldly, the enslaved man invoked customary practices to publicly attack his owner, one of the most powerful men in colonial Trujillo, Capitán don García de Bracamonte Dávila. As the head of the rural guard in the later part of the seventeenth century, Bracamonte Dávila was notorious for conducting a reign of terror in the northern coastal valleys.[102]

Local slaveholders had previously accused Bracamonte Dávila of forcing their fugitive slaves to work on his Chicama valley estate. In one case Bracamonte Dávila compelled an enslaved man to work in shackles until his leg and foot putrefied, necessitating amputation.[103] Most important, according to Arroyo, enslaved men and women knew Bracamonte Dávila was a torturer.[104] Arroyo explained that the slaveholder had ordered enslaved men held at his estate to be brutally hung and even cut the ear off of an enslaved woman who had been captured as a fugitive.[105] Arroyo's witnesses added to his testimony. The other imprisoned men recalled the intimidation suffered by Arroyo. They testified that Bracamonte Dávila threatened to punish Arroyo for asking to work for wages (a practice that many enslaved people expected) and warned that he would remove Arroyo to his rural estate, where he could punish him with impunity.[106]

As opposed to other judicial cases in which enslaved men employed accusations regarding property to articulate their grievances, Arroyo utilized colonial courts, royal directives, and customary practices to mount a personal defense but also to voice collective objections against the brutal practices of his owner and perhaps other slaveholders who supported the head of the rural guard. As Bracamonte Dávila defended his actions, Arroyo attempted to appeal to the Real Audiencia in Lima, but the case is inconclusive and Arroyo disappears from the judicial record in Trujillo. Still, it is significant that the magistrate heard his petition perhaps due to an animosity with Bracamonte Dávila or the severity of the crimes. Like fugitives who sought wage-earning opportunities, in the official venues of the colonial court Arroyo advocated for relief from an abusive slaveholder within the spirit of royal protection.[107] The unique nature of Arroyo's case suggests that legal avenues—especially when the courts could be controlled by slaveholders—may not have consistently been the avenue chosen by enslaved people.

In addition to working within the limitations of slavery's laws, enslaved laborers reached for alternative legal practices to bolster their cases against slaveholders. In 1692, Trujillo's magistrate accused Miguel Gamarra Zaseretta y Ortis, an enslaved cook, of killing an indigenous man. In his confession Gamarra explained that he escaped from his owner to live among the indigenous inhabitants near the reducción of Mansiche. According to Gamarra, his owner had treated him so poorly that he had repeatedly asked to be sold. Gamarra called on customary practices on the northern Peruvian coast (and elsewhere in the Americas) to replace his owner with another, but he also called on laws that transcended Spanish colonial boundaries. He identified himself as a native of Goa, suggesting that he measured the possibilities of Spanish American slavery against his previous experiences in Portuguese India. There he would have known other laws of slavery that meshed Muslim and Hindu beliefs with indenture and other labor practices followed by the Turkish, Persian, Arab, Chinese, and Ethiopian merchants and sailors who frequented the Indian Ocean port.[108]

While being accused of murder, Gamarra emphasized the acts that he considered to be criminal. In his confession to Trujillo's magistrate, Gamarra complained that "in this land even though slaves ask their owners [to be sold], they [the slaveholders] and the justices refuse."[109] In effect, Gamarra compared exchanging his owner for another with what had been possible in Goa, where manumission could be negotiated with dying owners, in

exchange for work, or by converting to religions of the surrounding ter-
ritories.[110] Remarkably, when the practices of the northern Peruvian coast
did not work in his favor, Gamarra expressed alternative solutions based on
his past experiences in the Indian Ocean. He had attempted to apply these
practices to the circumstances of the northern Peruvian coast. Perhaps understanding that he was seeking refuge in an alternative territory, he had fled
on horseback from his owner, and then sought refuge with indigenous communities. Unfortunately his strategy did not succeed, and he was later condemned to death by Trujillo's magistrate, most likely because his owner did
not come to his defense. Regardless, Gamarra proposed an alternative system
to demonstrate that not all enslaved men considered themselves bound by
royal mandates or even local practices.

Enslaved laborers understood local applications of colonial mandates
while asserting their own interpretation of how these regulations should be
enforced. Juan de Dios, who identified himself as an acculturated ladino of
casta arara, testified to the investigating magistrate that when he saw that his
compadre (friend or companion) Custodio was armed, he exclaimed: "How,
being a black, can you go around with these two knives?"[111] Colonial mandates prohibited enslaved men from carrying weapons and Juan de Dios's
question suggests that he knew (or wished to perform that he knew) about
these royal orders.[112] He appeared to protect himself during the magistrate's
investigation. By explaining to the investigating official that he had warned
Custodio how he would be punished, in many ways Juan de Dios distanced
himself from the accused man. Juan de Dios reported that the enslaved
"Portuguese" black man replied: "Compadre, what I have to do with these
[knives] is because of the circumstances." This was a reference to the excessive whippings inflicted by his slaveholder.[113] According to Juan de Dios's
account, Custodio also knew the prohibitions but discarded them to kill his
owner for inflicting such brutal punishments. Whether Juan de Dios's testimony represents his own or Custodio's perspective, the recounting of events
indicates that one or both of them employed a keen reading of colonial laws
against slaveholder abuse to their own initiative to execute justice.

Like Custodio or Juan de Dios, other enslaved men reinterpreted the laws
and practices of slaveholding.[114] One night in 1688, Trujillo's justice of the
peace claimed to have encountered Gregorio de la Cruz Biafra urinating in
front of the Franciscan monastery. According to his report, the local official
reprimanded de la Cruz Biafra and then arrested him for illicit relations
with a black woman who accompanied him, refusing to remove his hat,
and insulting the justice of the peace.[115] In his confession de la Cruz Biafra
pointedly disagreed with the colonial official. He understood that he needed

to remove his hat to the justice of the peace, but because "it was a holiday" he testified that he had drank more than usual. Therefore he argued that he was not acting rationally and was not conscious of what he had done.[116] The enslaved man presented a common defense of inebriation to contest the charges.[117] He also drew on a shared understanding that restrictions were relaxed during periods of celebration, when enslaved men and women attended markets, dances, and processions.[118]

De la Cruz Biafra's perspective is hard to discern since his testimony was wrapped into his defense strategy within a secular court case. Nonetheless, "fiesta time" notoriously featured subordinates engaging in parodies of authority figures or reversals of gendered or racial hierarchies; it was also the time for enslaved and free people to engage in African Diasporic religious practices.[119] De la Cruz Biafra had been drinking in an orchard with his friends the night he encountered Trujillo's justice of the peace. He also claimed a diaspora identity—Biafra—as part of his last name, even though he was a nineteen-year-old man who also identified as a "criollo black of Guadalupe town."[120] Biafra therefore did not signal where he had been born; interestingly, he claimed a rare casta term on the northern Peruvian coast. Most slaveholders referred to enslaved men and women sold from today's eastern Nigeria along the Bight of Biafra as *carabalí*, a corruption of a name for the inland region (and origin for captives) Calabar, employed by transatlantic slave traders.[121] By claiming Biafra as his surname, the enslaved man separated himself from the labels usually applied to slaves and suggested a diaspora identity that may have been recognized by his companions. In addition, de la Cruz Biafra did not elaborate on what he and his fellows were doing in the orchard, but his actions suggest that enslaved men and women understood that holiday or fiesta nights were their time or designated for their own use and desires. With only his confession to interpret, de la Cruz Biafra employed his knowledge of how slaveholding worked in Trujillo to seize on the customs that allowed limited mobility to defy official attempts to control his movements.

Collective actions against slaveholding were more rare, but in 1679 enslaved men employed a magistrate's investigation of an enslaved death on a Chicama valley estate to accuse their administrator of forcing them to work on holidays and not allowing them to attend Mass.[122] In many ways the enslaved witnesses were assisted by their owner who wished to recover the cost of his dead slave. The enslaved men from the rural estate called on specific royal orders commanding that slaveholders could not force enslaved laborers to work on Sundays and holidays.[123] Sticking closely to the colonial mandates, one witness, enslaved mulato Juan Gonzales de Careaga, explained that the administrator made them work on holidays and, as a result, he and his fellows did not hear Mass and therefore could not live as Christians.[124] Enslaved petitioners appropriated the language of claims (if not rights) provided by Christianity in the ecclesiastical courts.[125] The men on this rural estate were not alone in asserting their Catholic identities as a way to claim protection within slaveholding. In the case of Andrés de Arroyo discussed earlier, the enslaved man defended the quality of his witnesses by explaining that as Christians they would not lie under oath.[126] Catholicism therefore helped enslaved men in legal activity by asserting that as Christians they deserved trust in their testimonies before the court.

In addition to the slaveholders' interests, the enslaved laborers from the Chicama estate appear to have been disturbed by the administrator's abuse of their coworker. According to them and the investigating indigenous officials, the administrator, Phelipe de los Reyes, angered that a wheat field had not been sufficiently watered, beat Sebastian of casta congo, an elderly slave, until he was unable to walk and left him to die. Later, when Sebastian of casta congo did not recover, the administrator then attempted to secretly bury the body to avoid suspicion.[127] Instead of the murder, some of the enslaved laborers on the estate accused de los Reyes of starving them. In notarized contracts, administrators, renters, or overseers were required to provide adequate food, clothing, and medical attention to enslaved laborers and were supposed to compensate slaveholders if enslaved laborers died or escaped.[128] According to the binding contract between the administrator and the owner of the estate, de los Reyes should have had to pay a fine for killing one of his enslaved charges. Therefore de los Reyes committed a crime against the owner of the estate. Some of the enslaved men on the estate employed the language drawn from these contractual arrangements between slaveholders and overseers or administrators to assert their grievance.[129] In effect, the collective of enslaved men used a legal civil agreement between a slaveholder and his proxy to call attention to what they considered to be an egregious crime: the murder of their coworker.

In the initial testimony Bartolomé Mandinga, who many of the enslaved laborers noted was their leader, stated that when confronted by de los Reyes, the murdered slave, Sebastian, explained that it had been too dark to see the dry plot of wheat the night before and he would water it immediately. According to Mandinga, de los Reyes was not satisfied, became enraged, and insulted Sebastian as he beat him without respite, even while the enslaved laborer called on God's mercy. Later, enslaved coworker Juan Gonzales de Careaga testified that in the rustic home he shared with Sebastian, the injured man called de los Reyes a "bad Christian who would make me die unjustly" and cursed him by saying: "If the justice of this world does not punish him, that of Heaven will for such a grave and atrocious crime."[130] With or without Sebastian's testimony, it is difficult to verify whether he uttered these words. Nonetheless, in their initial accounts Mandinga and Gonzales de Careaga suggested that enslaved laborers deserved to be protected from such extreme abuse. Perhaps these enslaved laborers recalled royal mandates that repeatedly ordered slaveholders to provide "good treatment" to slaves and not to punish them cruelly.[131] They may have been prompted by the legal representative of the estate's owner. Beyond the slaveholder's interests or the legal mandates, the two enslaved men emphasized that de los Reyes used a staff to beat Sebastian, who had only offered to fix his mistake. Their objections appear to have lain in the excessive nature of the beating and de los Reyes's merciless pursuit of Sebastian.

The magistrate's investigation initially appeared to have substantial evidence. Indigenous men from the neighboring reducción of Santiago de Cao (including a healer and another who worked for the priest) testified that Sebastian of casta congo had died from blows inflicted by de los Reyes, a point of view that they asserted was shared by all of the estate's slaves and most of the members of their reducción.[132] Enslaved men from the estate provided correlating accounts that de los Reyes had beaten Sebastian and treated them poorly.[133] As a result, the magistrate imprisoned de los Reyes. From Trujillo's jail the administrator of the estate defended his actions. He claimed that after he had reprimanded Sebastian, the enslaved man fled from the estate and the next day returned cold, wet, and sick. De los Reyes attempted to cure him of what he diagnosed as lockjaw but failed. The administrator explained that although he required enslaved laborers to perform minor tasks on holidays, he provided them with plenty of bread and meat and ensured that Mass was performed on the estate.[134] The testimony by the married, fifty-year-old native of Trujillo radically altered the trajectory of the judicial case. Perhaps Trujillo's magistrate was reluctant to hold a presumably white man for allegations only supported by slaves and Indians. Perhaps the enslaved witnesses had been threatened or tortured to change their testimonies to fit with the magistrate's revised understanding of justice.[135]

In any case, following de los Reyes's confession, enslaved laborers redacted their testimony. Lucas de Castro, an enslaved criollo, declared that the slaves had lied and when Sebastian returned to the estate, he had contracted lockjaw from falling in an irrigation ditch.[136] Bartolomé Mandinga explained that he had been angry during his testimony and organized his coworkers to provide identical accounts to the magistrate.[137] The indigenous witnesses also withdrew their testimony by explaining that they had heard the slaves had complained against de los Reyes in revenge for the beatings, and some enslaved laborers agreed.[138] The magistrate declared that testimony from enslaved laborers on a rented estate was worthless "because slaves hate their owners."[139] With the support of other overseers and administrators, de los Reyes was released from jail with all charges dropped. In all likelihood the administrator and the owner had come to an agreement about their settlement and the magistrate had discontinued the case because justice, defined in this instance as harmony among elites, had been reached.[140] As a result, the enslaved laborers' petition for justice ended in the colonial courts.

Enslaved laborers may have been forced to retract their testimony, but they continued their defiance. After the case turned in favor of the administrator de los Reyes, enslaved laborers supplied additional testimony that did not necessarily support the new direction of the magistrate's investigation. Manuel Congo from Lima and Francisco Ariju of casta arara agreed that they had lied as instructed by Bartolomé Mandinga, while others noted Juan Gonzales de Careaga had prompted them.[141] Perhaps the enslaved laborer Salvador de Toledo Congo followed the notary's cues and repeated de los Reyes's explanation that the administrator only required the men to cut grass for the cattle and supply four pieces of firewood on Sundays—otherwise unavoidable maintenance that even the Jesuits allowed on their estates.[142] Enslaved laborers continued to express their discontent, though, suggesting that the impetus for testifying against the administrator emerged from the moral economy among the enslaved men on this Chicama valley estate.[143] Even as he withdrew his complaint in Trujillo's court by explaining that de los Reyes treated the enslaved laborers "like a father," enslaved criollo Valentin de la Madris declared that on some days the administrator whipped them because they did not work well.[144] Juan Gonzales de Careaga agreed that he gave false testimony because de los Reyes beat him but also stated that he had waited a long time for the opportunity to take revenge.[145] It is possible that enslaved laborers understood that they were required to agree with the magistrate, the notary, and other judicial officials.[146] Nonetheless, they managed to continue documenting their protest against how Phelipe de los Reyes had poorly treated them as a group on the estate.

In addition to objecting to de los Reyes's actions, enslaved laborers also appear to have regretted their inaction while Sebastian was first being beaten and then, later, was dying. In addition to blaming the administrator, the enslaved men also appear to have contemplated their own role in the unjust end to Sebastian's life. Bartolomé Mandinga, Manuel Congo, and Pedro Cobec of casta lucumí watched the administrator whip Sebastian until he could not stand but did not intervene (according to any of the testimonies including the administrator's). According to their initial statement, after de los Reyes beat Sebastian, only one man, "the little black from the Mimita estate" helped the older slave get up.[147] In one sense the enslaved witnesses astutely avoided the expected physical violence as they explained de los Reyes readily employed the whip and the stocks to force their compliance.[148]

In another sense the enslaved men may have been left with uncertainties about the series of events that resulted in Sebastian's death. Enslaved laborers testified in both versions of their statements that Sebastian had died without confession, but it seems unclear who they blamed. In the first versions enslaved laborers faulted de los Reyes for his violence and his negligence.[149] In the second versions enslaved laborers declared that de los Reyes was not to blame, a strategic move given that the investigating magistrate had begun to favor the administrator over the enslaved laborers. It is also possible that the men from the estate regretted how Sebastian had died. Following Sebastian's death, Lucas de Castro criollo and Manuel Congo of Lima had brought his body from the estate's chapel to the church in the neighboring reducción. There, Sebastian was buried but without the presence of other enslaved laborers from the estate. Phelipe de los Reyes may have killed Sebastian, but his coworkers had buried him without a funeral perhaps in violation of their own understandings of what death required.

While judicial cases were one location to secure justice, they were not the only venue. The testimonies of the enslaved men suggest that they considered how Sebastian of casta congo died without the rituals that he probably shared with other enslaved laborers on the estate, including those from West Central Africa. In their second testimonies Lucas de Castro, a criollo, and Bartolomé Mandinga recalled that Sebastian had returned to the estate (after fleeing from Phelipe de los Reyes) wet and freezing from falling in an irrigation ditch.[150] Salvador de Toledo of casta congo explained in his first testimony that de los Reyes had left Sebastian for dead in the water after beating him.[151] Even in his second testimony Toledo emphasized that Sebastian had gotten wet.[152] The testimonies are confusing about exactly when Sebastian became soaked but, regardless, cold and dampness were among the dangers of working as an irrigator on the northern Peruvian coast.

At the same time, water was highly significant for West Central Africans, who made offerings to the associated spirits when approaching streams, lakes, or other bodies.[153] Sebastian, like the other West Central Africans on the Chicama estate, may have feared not just the health effects of the winter cold, but the spiritual consequences associated with falling into water. He may have contracted tetanus (lockjaw), as suggested by de los Reyes, but the agony that he suffered before he died may have reflected fears from his contact with the water and its malignant powers. In their first and second testimonies enslaved laborers worried that Sebastian had died without proper Catholic rituals as denied by de los Reyes, but also perhaps because they had been unable to inter him in the correct manner.[154] For enslaved Africans and their descendants throughout the Americas, burials provided a means to honor ancestors and to ensure that the living would not be visited by the discontented spirits of the dead.[155] Without a proper funeral, enslaved West Central Africans could have believed that Sebastian would return as an evil spirit to cause sickness and death among the community on the estate.[156] Within their testimonies to the magistrate enslaved laborers appear to worry how Sebastian's untimely death would affect their community. Regardless of the investigation's outcome, the enslaved men of the Chicama estate may have objected to a cruel administrator who had also denied them the opportunity to transition a community member from this life to the next.

Slaves' protests were easily altered and quickly dismissed by slaveholders. Nonetheless, enslaved laborers invoked royal orders, colonial mandates, and local customs when possible to protect their claims. Enslaved men and women had their own standards of justice that demonstrated how they marked the limits of physical punishment, the dangers of denying proper burial, and the necessity of changing owners. Because of the limited nature of colonial laws, enslaved men and women did not rely on colonial authorities—who were often slaveholders themselves—to protect them from owners or administrators.[157] The Spanish crown and the Catholic Church may have offered official protections of enslaved laborers, but in practice these state entities had few agents to enforce colonial mandates in the provincial cities or rural estates independently from the interests of local slaveholders. The cases above indicate that enslaved laborers invoked laws and argued in court, but moved beyond what was protected by colonial laws. In some cases, as in the enslaved man from Goa, their legal consciousness superseded the limited offering of colonial judicial discourse and local practice.

The Coercion of Slaveholding

In Trujillo slaveholders appear to have held the upper hand in the late seventeenth and early eighteenth centuries so while a discourse of royal justice circulated, it was subsumed to slaveholders' demands. In 1681 the king ordered the viceroy and Lima's *audiencia* to liberate four enslaved men from a hat factory where their owner repeatedly inflicted excessive physical punishments and refused to allow them to see their wives. Both charges violated royal mandates that forbade abusive beatings of enslaved people and commanded that slaves be allowed to practice Christianity. The order echoed commands to protect indigenous people, making a surprising connection between shielding indigenous and enslaved workers. The crown referred to a 1609 mandate that prohibited forced personal service of indigenous laborers. By invoking the "enslavement" of indigenous people, the royal mandate equated the suffering of Indians with blacks and suggested that colonial authorities be concerned with the exploitation of enslaved men as they were with the exploitation of indigenous people.[158] The royal orders from 1681, however, did not emphasize or seek to strengthen previous prohibitions against physical punishment of enslaved laborers. In fact, the crown targeted one slaveholder who had disrupted societal harmony.[159] The crown ordered the protection of enslaved people from abuse but did not indicate that it would challenge the collective prerogatives of slaveholders.

Occasionally Trujillo's authorities prosecuted individuals for extremely abusive treatment of enslaved laborers and upheld the standard of benevolent slaveholding. In 1698, Trujillo's justice of the peace investigated the murder of Ana Criolla of Panama, who had been brutally whipped and scorched from her back to her calves.[160] An anonymous woman (probably a neighbor) alerted the colonial official who was made more suspicious by Ana Criolla's immediate burial. Witnesses explained that the slaveholder, Nicolas Sanz de la Vega, shackled, whipped, and eventually burned Ana Criolla because she refused to follow orders. Ana Criolla's perspective is lost but based on witness testimony, she had repeatedly escaped after previous beatings. She was courageous to have defied her slaveholder, who was widely feared. Even Spanish neighbors who were not under the purview of Sanz de la Vega did not challenge the slaveholder's authority. Only when prompted by the justice of the peace, an indigenous woman and a young man explained that they had been disturbed by the cries coming from the household. In response to the local authority's questions, the witnesses explained that both María of casta conga and Ana Criolla called out in pain when beaten by their owner, who treated his slaves with "much impropriety."[161] Witnesses suggested that the slaveholder violated local practices, or a moral code, rather than crown regulations, and only complained after Ana Criolla's disturbing death.[162] As illustrated by her repeated escapes, however, Ana Criolla had articulated her own attempts to resist the slaveholder's violence since local colonial authorities could not be counted on to intervene.

Ana Criolla was not the only enslaved woman or man on the northern Peruvian coast to refuse the lash, but Nicolas Sanz de la Vega was rare among slaveholders to be charged specifically for his violence against a slave. Trujillo's local justice of the peace questioned witnesses regarding how the slaveholder had burned Ana Criolla repeatedly and extensively.[163] He found the local merchant guilty of killing Ana Criolla with extreme cruelty and fined him and collected two hundred pesos.[164] The colonial authority enforced a crown regulation against excessive punishment, resulting in the death of a slave most likely because the event had caused a public scandal. In a similar case Trujillo's magistrate had initiated a criminal investigation against owners who had whipped their slaves, Juan de Arara and Garcia Congo, to death.[165] The brief accusation, however, focused on the attempt of the slaveholders to hide their crime from colonial authorities rather than the severe violence against the enslaved men.

Other slaveholders committed equally heinous acts against enslaved people and were not punished. In addition to pouring hot fat or wax onto the bare skin of enslaved laborers, slaveholders and overseers hung slaves by their arms or cut off their ears or feet for punishment.[166] Regional slave traders left captives without food or shelter for days in fields outside of Trujillo.[167] On the large, rural estates, slaveholders or overseers imprisoned enslaved men and women and shackled them until their limbs contracted gangrene.[168] Only the level of extreme violence against Ana Criolla, the concerns of the neighbors, and perhaps the low status of the mestizo slaveholding couple may have resulted in the verdict against Sanz de la Vega.

Trujillo's authorities punished residents such as this merchant who caused disruptions in societal harmony but did not prevent slaveholders as a whole from inflicting violent punishments on a corporate group of enslaved laborers. Slaveholders inflicted physical punishments on enslaved people as a matter of course. Under viceregal orders Trujillo's magistrate investigated accusations that two slaveholders (a mother and son) had killed one of their slaves, Juan (also named as Melchor) Arara, by whipping him to death.[169] Rather than murder, the court officials accused the owners of attempting to deceive authorities by covering up the death. In other words, slaveholders were reprimanded for lying to investigating authorities. Exceptional physical violence was perceived by regional authorities as a means of maintaining peace for elites and suggests that the law may not have mediated slavery's practices.

Once sold into the rural areas, slaveholders actuated the positions of enslaved men and women through physical punishment. Whether producing wheat or sugar, the inventories of coastal estates usually listed chains, shackles, and stocks. Designed to punish and to degrade enslaved men and women through a physical enactment of their lowly position, slaveholders considered these expensive metal items as necessary "tools" of enslavement. Northern coastal estates kept between one to nine pairs of small or thick chains "for the security of the blacks."[170] Owners and renters also maintained a number of iron shackles that in one case were designated "to serve for the fugitive slaves of this estate."[171] Larger estates kept one or two stocks made of local carob wood complete with iron pins, bolts, and padlocks to punish resistant laborers.[172] Illustrating the investment of slaveholders in punishing enslaved laborers, estates such as the sugar mill La Santíssima Trinidad had two rooms with doors and keys that contained stocks and served as prisons.[173] Located next to the slave quarters of rustic houses made of adobe or clay with cane roofs, the small jail served as a constant reminder to enslaved inhabitants of possible punishments.[174] Given the careful maintenance of these items, slaveholders appear to have understood that inflicting or threatening physical punishment was the standard way to treat enslaved men and women.

Slaveholders pursued legal action against other slaveholders only when enslaved men and women, their property, had been incapacitated to the point that they could not work. The owner of a sugar mill called San Francisco del Valle specified that his renter was required to treat the slaves well and "if any should die because of poor treatment," he would not reduce the rental price.[175] In this equation slaveholders defined physical abuse in monetary terms. According to the common phrase in a notary contract, slave owners perceived that renters, administrators, overseers, and others were more likely to abuse slaves who were not their own. In 1679 the notorious head of the rural guard, Captain don García de Bracamonte Dávila, brought a fugitive man named Juan Romero to his estate. Assessed as a "good piece," the slaveholder understood that Juan Romero had a recognizable market value but did not safeguard him as his own slave.[176] Bracamonte Dávila's overseer had Romero placed in shackles to deter him from fleeing. In the following months, Romero was forced to work in the mill and the forge until his shackled ankles and legs were gangrenous (as discussed earlier). When his owner claimed him, Juan Romero was so incapacitated that he could not work. For Romero's owner abuse had resulted in a loss of property. For the enslaved man, his attempt to find a new owner left him disabled. These events reveal how enslaved people were ruled through violence as their violated bodies marked their difference.[177] The power of slaveholders, especially in their capacity as landholders of the expanding sugar estates, heightened how enslaved people were violated in a way that separated them from indigenous and Spanish people.

Official tolerance of violence against enslaved men and women was also practiced on the northern Peruvian coast because slaveholders increasingly served as the colonial authorities who facilitated judicial proceedings in the northern coastal valleys. In the 1670s a new magistrate fined don García de Bracamonte Dávila for not attending municipal council meetings. The recently appointed colonial official accused the head of the rural guard (and infamous abuser of enslaved people) of attending to his slaveholding estate in the Chicama valley rather than the affairs of his position.[178] In a similar investigation the public notary of the municipal council (Antonio Verde) was accused of not keeping his offices open while he was attending to his estate as a slaveholder.[179] In both cases the Consejo de Indias in Spain dismissed or reduced the charges, indicating that the crown could not enforce attendance or attention to colonial offices or did not wish to punish powerful landholders.[180]

In the same period Trujillo's bishop complained that local estate owners were allowing their slaves to deposit waste (ashes, canes, leaves) from sugar production into the city's main irrigation canal. As a result, the city was without sufficient water—a constant problem on the northern Peruvian coast.[181] Furthermore, the ecclesiastical leader continued, the expansion of the sugar estates meant that inhabitants had to go at least three leagues (approximately nine miles) to gather firewood.[182] The bishop's complaints indicate that the power of slaveholders was growing on the northern Peruvian coast.[183] By the early eighteenth century, city officials accused local estate owners of contaminating the city's water supply with the waste from sugar grinding as well as the lye used to process the cane.[184] The owners of the large sugar estates and other slaveholders were either serving as colonial authorities or were able to successfully defy local officials.

Direct protests by enslaved people against extreme abuse were not supported by local authorities, who in many cases were slaveholders themselves. In 1682 the viceroy ordered Trujillo's magistrate to investigate the murders of two enslaved men, Josef and Melchor Arara, who were probably whipped to death by their owners.[185] There is no evidence, however, that the local authority complied with the order from his superior. In addition, colonial authorities and slaveholders avoided even the most explicit charges of abuse against enslaved laborers. In 1696, Trujillo's local magistrate proceeded with a criminal case against an enslaved man, Phelipe Lucumí, for the crime of killing an enslaved overseer. The colonial official had ordered indigenous assistants to torture Lucumí who proceeded to destroy the tendons in Lucumí's arms and otherwise render him unable to speak or eat.[186] In response, Phelipe Lucumí's owner sought compensation for the loss of his property.[187]

Rather than denounce the abuse of the enslaved man, Lucumí's owner called on a royal order that prohibited capital punishment without approval of the pertinent royal office. The torture of the enslaved man, Phelipe Lucumí, was not in question. Instead, the Trujillo slaveholder employed a legal technicality to gain monetary compensation. Trujillo's medical authority, the *protomedicato*, certified the cruelty but there is no record that the magistrate investigated or the slaveholder was punished. By seeking a superior authority, the slaveholder overstepped local, colonial authorities, suggesting that royal protections of enslaved laborers did not have currency among officials in Trujillo or were not considered enforceable. More pointedly, on the northern Peruvian coast, crown mandates were superseded by the demands of slaveholders who, if they were not serving as colonial authorities, were often more powerful.

Indigenous Defenses and Policing Slavery

By the later part of the seventeenth century, coastal Andeans adapted to the expansion of the northern coastal estates by serving the interests of landholders and slaveholders. Indigenous people worked seasonally and permanently on ranches, farms, and estates as field hands, muleteers, artisans, and domestic workers. The boundaries of indigenous jurisdiction, however, became more porous as coastal Andeans moved outside of their assigned reducciones to live and work on the private property that surrounded them. There, according to law as well as local practice, indigenous laborers were still treated distinctly from enslaved men and women. At the same time, indigenous people found new ways to articulate an Indian location that continued to be in distinct from enslaved Africans. By policing enslaved laborers on neighboring estates, indigenous authorities maintained their status as Indians and in the process sustained slavery.

At the end of the seventeenth century, the contract between the crown and indigenous people had ruptured. Many coastal Andeans no longer paid tribute and few served mita while living in their assigned reducciones. Furthermore, landholders had gained the upper hand in the northern coastal valleys and did not follow colonial mandates designed to protect Indians, including respecting communal indigenous petitions for their share of water.[188] Consequently, indigenous leaders shifted their strategies away from the defense of communal holdings. In fact, coupled with the migration of coastal Andeans away from reducciones, indigenous leaders, such as those from Mansiche and Huanchaco, sold land with the condition that community members would continue to clean its water canal.[189] Coastal Andeans were increasingly becoming dependent laborers because their reducciones no longer could claim Indian protections that still had been possible earlier in the century. Indigenous claims to rights as colonial vassals who worked their communal lands—a tactic that had limited success—had worn thin by the end of the seventeenth century.

Coastal Andeans shifted to a defense based on claims to new types of

Indian status. In 1699 the indigenous inhabitants of Guañape, the port south of Trujillo near the Indian reducción of Virú, filed an objection against the regional magistrate. The local colonial official had refused to recognize the elections of the port's justice of the peace and instead appointed an indigenous contracted laborer from a neighboring estate. The "Indians and vecinos" of Guañape made an impassioned argument that blended legislated protections of indigenous reducciones with service to the crown.[190] They referred to the "custom" of indigenous communities to elect their own justices with only a confirmation of the local magistrate that in fact was colonial law.[191] Indigenous towns were guaranteed their autonomy, but in practice colonial officials were known to influence the outcome of elections.[192]

For example, one year later, Trujillo's magistrate chose the justices of the city's indigenous parishes of San Sebastian and Santa Ana, provoking the objection of the migrant residents. On Sunday at the door of the San Sebastian church in Trujillo, the magistrate reported that Indians "with much anger" broke the staff of one appointed official.[193] Objections to unwanted indigenous officials were not entirely unusual as indigenous communities defended their autonomy.[194] According to the crown, male members of indigenous towns were supposed to elect justices of the peace, bailiffs, and other officials to govern their communities.[195] In addition to administrating communal lands, indigenous officials adjudicated disagreements and conflicts, providing oversight against criminal behavior in the region.[196] Even as the land base and population of reducciones shrunk, coastal Andeans made demands to elect their own officials with minimal interference from colonial authorities, as was their due according to colonial law.

Indigenous communities claimed their status as royal vassals while seeking to prove their loyalty to the crown through means that simultaneously benefited local landholders. Returning to the case of Guañape, the indigenous leaders declared that the viceregal government had named the port as a "free Town." The *avecinado* Indians, or those who claimed municipal "citizenship" in Guañape, explained that they served His Majesty by working as lookouts and provisioning those who disembarked from the port.[197] Like the *chasquis* of earlier decades, the indigenous port workers of Guañape defended their community based on their critical service to the king. In place of providing communication among the coastal cities, the Indian citizens of Guañape ensured Pacific commerce since without their services, they warned, navigation into the port would be compromised. Furthermore, as soldiers and sentinels, indigenous men contributed to the defense of the region's ports because pirates continued to inhibit trade along the northern coast.[198] Unlike the message-carrying chasquis, the inhabitants of Guañape did not claim back pay or denounce the abusive overuse of their services. Instead, they merely petitioned for the right to govern themselves. As local communities diminished under the expansion of the private estates, indigenous leaders of Guañape claimed their independence by proving their loyalty to the king and by asserting their necessity to the success of regional commerce.

Indigenous claims to autonomous governance, though, also included a rhetoric of exclusion. The representatives of Guañape objected to the magistrate's intervention but also to the leadership appointment of an indigenous laborer whom they considered to be an outsider. In some senses their tactics were consistent with those of other indigenous communities who expelled newcomers when economic conditions were dire.[199] The leadership also attempted to defend the port of Guañape that was not as important as they claimed. With its distance from the trading center of Trujillo combined with a lack of water supply, mostly local landholders, such as the owners of nearby San Ildefonso estate, only shipped an inexpensive product, charcoal, from Guañape rather than the lucrative products of sugar or wheat.[200] Furthermore, at the turn of the century Guañape could have been experiencing a decline in trade, and therefore income, based on the regional agrarian crises.[201]

Given these circumstances, the spokesmen of Guañape may have been defending personal incomes or at least their prerogative to control the small revenues of the port. Still, the Guañape leaders did not make an economic argument but claimed Indian vassalage in colonial courts. Even though they were not an official Indian reducción, they chose elements of this colonial institution to articulate their defense. In addition to their autonomous governance, the four petitioners asked permission to establish a church or chapel in the port (rather than attending Mass in the neighboring Santa Elena estate) that would further transform Guañape into a reducción.[202] Avoiding the worst impositions of Indian vassalage, however, they did not insist on paying tribute or serving mita. Instead, they created their own version as they named themselves like a reducción, including expelling indigenous non-natives to distinguish themselves more clearly from the nearby settlement, the Santa Elena estate.

In the late seventeenth century coastal Andeans also transformed their colonial prerogative to self-governance by expanding the purview of official leadership positions. For example, indigenous muleteers elected or agreed upon a justice of the peace who governed not only their community but also intervened in other affairs.[203] In 1708, Lorenzo Martínez identified himself as the muleteer justice of the peace and the son-in-law of an indigenous woman living in a settlement bordering a Chicama valley estate. In this capacity as an indigenous authority, Martínez located a fugitive enslaved woman in his kinwoman's house and reported to her owner.[204] Even though his action indicates that a family member may have been providing refuge to a fugitive or truant slave, Lorenzo Martínez may have hoped to be rewarded by the slaveholder. His actions indicated that he could employ his position to intervene in situations that involved other indigenous people and also served the interests of local landholders.

As indigenous authorities emerged where coastal Andeans congregated (even outside of official reducciones), they increasingly participated in the control over enslaved men and women. On the large sugar estate of Facala in the Chicama valley, a man identified as the Indian justice of the peace of the estate accompanied the colonial bailiff and the estate overseer to rouse indigenous residents in the middle of the night in 1691. The colonial official delegated the indigenous justice to lead coastal Andeans in a confrontation against the enslaved laborers who refused to allow the rural guard to apprehend a fugitive.[205] In this case indigenous authorities attended to slaveholders' goals, and security became a lucrative niche for coastal Andeans. By filling jobs of surveillance and control over enslaved laborers, indigenous men maintained a position within the colonial state but increasingly to the benefit of local landholders and slaveholders.

Even as mita labor faded on the northern Peruvian coast, indigenous officials were often the only legally recognized authorities in remote, rural areas. When Sebastian de la Cruz, a free *sambo* and a peon on a mule train, needed to leave his cargo of sugar to track down a missing mule, he left the goods with the justices of the peace and bailiffs in Supe, an Indian town on the coastal highway.[206] Undeniably there was a clear distinction between the authorities of the Spanish Republic and those provided by the Indian Republic. Indigenous authorities could not assume the roles of magistrates, judges, or the colonial justices of the peace. Nonetheless, indigenous authorities, like other rural justices, served as witnesses, dealt with immediate threats to social order, and then reported to higher authorities.[207] In doing so, representatives of reducciones and other Indian settlements were critical to the colonial judiciary if only at the lowest level. By serving as justices, coastal Andean communities also demonstrated their loyalty to the crown. Even as the local economy changed, the legal basis for the claims of Indian reducciones to their status remained the same: in exchange for protection, indigenous people provided service.

By working for the powerful estate owners, indigenous men gained employment but continued to articulate a corporate identity as Indians. Slaveholders relied on indigenous authorities to investigate local crimes. In 1702 an estate owner asked the indigenous justices of the peace from Santiago de Cao to investigate a body found in the Chicama valley's Fonolipe woods.[208] According to what indigenous officials learned from the enslaved people on the estate, all suspected that the dead man was Joseph of casta arara, an enslaved man who had become a fugitive, resisted capture, and then took refuge in Trujillo's Franciscan monastery. The slaveholder may not have trusted Trujillo's magistrate to investigate this death. Owners often employed monasteries to shelter their accused slaves from secular authorities, and the magistrate had violated the sanctuary of ecclesiastical refuge by removing Joseph of casta arara from the monastery.[209] Illustrating the colonial judicial hierarchy, the magistrate was the highest colonial secular authority in the region and may have not considered the case of a dead, enslaved African to be worthy of investigation.

It fell, then, to indigenous officials to transport the body of Joseph of casta arara to their parish church. In addition to collecting testimony from the enslaved witnesses, the indigenous authorities assessed the mortal wounds and reported their findings to Trujillo's magistrate. In performing their legal services, however, indigenous authorities functioned as intermediaries between Spanish officials and enslaved laborers. In addition to learning the identity of the dead body from the enslaved inhabitants of the estate, the indigenous justices of the peace from Santiago de Cao ascertained a possible motive. Their investigation suggested that Joseph of casta arara had left the refuge of the monastery, possibly returned to the estate to exact revenge, and the enslaved foreman may have killed him.[210] By following a similar legal procedure as colonial officials, indigenous officials underlined their distinction from enslaved Africans and their descendants; they proved themselves necessary to the enforcement of slaveholders' order in the rural areas.

In another case from 1702 the enslaved foreman from a Chicama valley sugar mill sought out the indigenous bailiff in a neighboring settlement. He reported that an enslaved man, Marcelo of casta arara, had found an elderly slave named Baltasar Mina inside his rustic house sleeping in his bed, and killed him with an ax.[211] The overseer of the estate had been unaware of the murder until Marcelo was absent from the morning role call after having found refuge in the Franciscan church in Trujillo. As suggested by the overseer's indifference, Spanish slaveholders were concerned with the ability of enslaved laborers to perform their work and rarely took note of other aspects of their lives. Indigenous authorities, on the other hand, interviewed enslaved laborers such as Pasqual, the enslaved foreman, and Jacinto, a ladino enslaved laborer.

As a result, indigenous authorities provided the main testimony in the official criminal court case filed in Trujillo and in fact relayed enslaved accounts to Spanish officials. In one sense, indigenous authorities conveyed enslaved perspectives in colonial courts—but for the purpose of a slaveholder gaining compensation for a slave. Through their investigation of crimes on rural estates, indigenous men could also contrast themselves with African and African-descent men who, colonizers suspected, were categorically violent and dangerous. In policing enslaved Africans (and their descendants) through official colonial judicial processes, indigenous people promoted themselves as performing a role necessary to slaveholding.

Indigenous officials were also motivated to police rural environs to collect the monetary rewards offered for apprehending fugitive slaves. As in other parts of the Americas, indigenous men captured fugitives in exchange for a set price often paid by the slaveholder.[212] For instance, the Jesuit administrator of the Tumán estate awarded the justices of the peace from the reducción of San Pedro de Lloc twenty-five pesos for catching a fugitive slave.[213] Arrangements in the northern coastal valleys were made between indigenous communities and colonial officials. The head of the rural guard in Trujillo reminded coastal Andeans from Moche who captured fugitive Domingo de Castro that they were obligated to capture fugitive slaves.[214] Indigenous communities therefore fulfilled the expectation that they would patrol the countryside and deliver enslaved fugitives (and other accused criminals) to Spanish colonial officials.

Hardly bound by their municipal jurisdictions, indigenous authorities competed with the rural guard for these benefits of policing the countryside. In 1697 indigenous men from Santiago de Cao challenged the members of the rural guard and some herdsmen for the capture of four enslaved fugitives. For months the fugitives had lived in the uncultivated lands near the indigenous reducción by stealing from the fields and corrals of both indigenous and Spanish landholders, but perhaps they also participated in trading activities.[215] Two herdsmen with others from the rural guard tracked the fugitives to their encampment only to have the three men and one woman escape. In the morning the group followed the fugitives' tracks into Santiago de Cao, where they learned that the reducción members had taken up the chase. Given that the fugitives lived close by, it is plausible that indigenous residents were well aware of their location. According to the rural guard, with the indigenous men they captured Bernaldo Criollo, Francisco Folupo, Silvestre Angola, and Catalina and deposited them in Santiago de Cao's jail.

The Andeans appeared to be very versed in the legalities of capturing fugitive slaves. When the rural guard demanded that the fugitives be released, the Andeans claimed to have (but did not produce) a commission allowing them to retain the enslaved laborers.[216] The reducción enjoyed a limited sovereignty that the members of the rural guard, operating on the edge of colonial policing often as contracted and improvised authorities themselves, were forced to respect.[217] The patrol complained to the head of the rural guard that the Andeans attempted to "make themselves masters" of the captured fugitives.[218] In turn, the men from Santiago de Cao leveraged their positions as Indians to compete in the market of captured fugitives and independently sought out slaveholders to successfully bargain for a price to return their enslaved laborers.

As indigenous officials from the reducciones and as independent agents, coastal Andean officials also captured and returned enslaved men and women to slaveholders. While indigenous villagers continued to trade and to establish long-term relations with their enslaved or free neighbors, they seized on the opportunities to inform colonial authorities where fugitives were hiding and provided prison facilities for the rural guard.[219] In one case coastal Andeans served as torturers for Trujillo's magistrate in a criminal case against an enslaved man accused of killing his overseer. According to the accusations of the slaveholder, eight Indians severed the tendons of Phelipe Canegue, leaving the enslaved man disabled in both arms.[220] By the mid-eighteenth century coastal Andeans serving in official reducción capacities were established authorities who responded regularly to slave revolts and other rebellions.[221] Their service was not coincidental. Mutual labor exchanges and ongoing connections with enslaved and free laborers were useful but by policing enslaved laborers, some indigenous men justified their communities and profited financially. In the process coastal Andeans played a role in maintaining and producing slavery on the northern coast.

⚊

Africans and their descendants struggled to renegotiate the hold of slavery in the late seventeenth and early eighteenth centuries against the often violent restraints practiced by slaveholders and their assistants. The mechanics of enslavement, however, did not always encourage solidarity as some enslaved people participated in the capture of fugitives and the punishment of resisters. Nonetheless, by engaging in the practices of truancy and searching for new owners as well as continually protesting work regimes, enslaved people sought to remove themselves from abusive owners. In some instances the demand for justice, even if unsuccessful, allowed Africans and their descendants to provide legal testimony and in rare cases to directly petition for legal redress. Enslaved men were sometimes able to capitalize on particular royal legislation that provided them with a "juridical personality" or an entry into litigation.[222]

The discussion in this chapter strongly supports the notion that enslaved men and women, especially those in rural areas or in provincial cities, clearly understood that colonial mandates regarding enslavement were not meant to protect or to defend their communities. Their engagement should be read as one of many enslaved strategies. Legal practices, instead, were intended to enforce social norms for local elites. Aware of their marginalization within colonial law and its local practice, enslaved men articulated juridical notions and moral agency that reflected the implications (if not the impact) of crown orders.[223] By illustrating their knowledge of colonial legal protections, enslaved men pushed against the limits of colonial law while deploying standards developed within their own communities. From the margins of legality, rural enslaved men demanded justice that usually was not forthcoming. More important, enslaved men and women developed alternative ideals of justice that circulated within their communities, which in the instances discussed here revolved around labor such as standards of rest, their bodily safety, or work rhythms. Enslaved men were troubled by death, relations with their peers, and recognition of their positions within complex hierarchies.[224] Enslaved articulations of these demands, worries, and conflicts point to more discussions outside of a juridical framework.

Indigenous men provided essential services to northern coastal slaveholding, and their experiences offer a corrective to previous interpretations of how Andean people fit within colonialism. Slavery was a critical part of some Andean regional economies. Slavery on the northern coast, however, did not mean that Andeans were no longer required by landholders. Coastal Andeans in fact adapted to the expansion of landed estates in late seventeenth and early eighteenth centuries, demonstrating how Indians remained critical to the economic success of Spanish colonialism even where landholders relied on enslaved African and African-descent labor. As other historians have suggested, Andeans were not merely victims of the market changes brought about by Spanish investments in mining or agriculture.[225] On the northern Peruvian coast Andeans adapted to regional markets and inserted themselves as muleteers, artisans, and laborers, as discussed in chapter 4. In addition to contributing labor to the expanding estates, Andeans also assisted the expansion of Spanish colonialism by controlling enslaved laborers.

CONCLUSION

THE LAWS OF CASTA, THE MAKING OF RACE

IN THE EARLY SEVENTEENTH CENTURY, the Andean chronicler don Felipe Guaman Poma de Ayala composed a lengthy, illustrated letter to the king describing, among other themes, how the Spanish had disrupted indigenous society. Writing as a native vassal, Guaman Poma petitioned the crown to punish magistrates for exacting excessive tribute from Andean communities and to correct clerics for demanding too much labor from their indigenous parishes. To support his argument that Spanish colonizers were to blame for the deterioration of Andean communities, Guaman Poma provided specific examples of the exploitation inflicted by Spaniards. Africans and their descendants played a critical role in his protest of the Spanish presence in the Andes. In some passages the Andean writer represented the benefits of Spanish colonialism including images of successful evangelization of indigenous people as well as Africans portrayed as good and humble Catholics.[1]

In others—keeping with his rejection of cultural and racial mixture—Guaman Poma portrayed acculturated blacks as part of the foreign intrusion

Figure C.1. Drawing 202. The royal administrator orders an African slave to flog
an Indian magistrate for collecting a tribute that falls two eggs short. Source:
Guaman Poma de Ayala, *El primer nueva corónica y buen gobierno* (1615–1616).

faced by Andeans.[2] Within his pantheon of Spanish abuses, Guaman Poma
twice depicted an African-descent man punishing an Andean under the orders of a Spaniard. Figures C.1 and C.2 illustrate a violent beating of a na-

Figure C.2. Drawing 300. The royal administrator orders an African slave to flog an Indian magistrate for collecting a tribute that falls two eggs short. Source: Guaman Poma de Ayala, *El primer nueva corónica y buen gobierno* (1615–1616).

ked and partially naked indigenous man.[3] Pointedly, Guaman Poma showed the African-descent man as the executioner of colonial injustice and as an intermediary between the Andean and the Spaniard. This depiction of a black punishing an Indian as directed by a Spaniard encapsulates a common stereotype of racial hierarchies in Peru's colonial past—one that this book works to correct.

The visual and written language of Guaman Poma's appeals can be read in much the same way as the legal discourses of colonial criminal and civil trials from the northern Peruvian coast. Guaman Poma positioned himself as an Indian pleading for the mercy of a benevolent crown. He characterized Andeans as suffering vassals much like coastal Andeans presented themselves in court as dutiful Indians who deserved the protections afforded by the Spanish crown. Through his images and his language, Guaman Poma produced Andeans according to an expected location of "poor Indians" of Spanish colonial judicial language. In the instances of legal petitioning on the northern coast, Andeans employed their *casta* category of Indian to make claims to royal authority and also located themselves within Spanish colonial legal and cultural expectations.

Unlike what Guaman Poma described, blacks were not merely intermediaries of the Spanish. Occasionally, colonial Spaniards employed enslaved Africans to dominate Andeans.[4] At the same time, Andeans defended their land or labor (based on the *reducción* or elsewhere) by presenting themselves as Indians and invoking Africans as dangerous blacks, regardless of their everyday amicable relations, in colonial courts. Indigenous officials also profited from policing enslaved men and women on the northern Peruvian coast. Andeans were therefore not merely victims of Africans. As a result, this book works to undo Guaman Poma's message—one that was adopted by influential historians of Peru.[5] The position of a royal subject (below that of Spaniards) embedded Andeans into a racist hierarchy that offered clear advantages for indigenous people who were willing to perform their Indian identities in the judicial sphere according to crown expectations. Further complicating the imagery of Guaman Poma, enslaved men on rural estates on the northern coast employed the limited possibilities of their legal locations and expansive extralegal negotiations to push against the demands of slaveholders. In other words, black men did not merely serve their white owners. By examining how enslaved men and women employed their market value, kinship connections, and labor negotiations in extralegal realms, the book has illustrated their varied agencies within slavery. Hardly intermediaries, Africans defended themselves against the impositions of slavery while Andeans employed their legal locations to defend against the demands of colonialism.

This book has placed the relations between Africans and Andeans at the center in order to explore how colonialism and slavery, together, contributed to the history of the Andes and Latin America. By understanding how two mechanisms of labor exploitation were embedded in colonial mandates and customary practice as well as how enslaved and indigenous laborers struggled against and within these impositions, the book developed three points. First, the African Diaspora, slavery, and colonial discourses of blackness were influential to Andean history. Second, while hardly systematic, casta categories such as "black" and "Indian" did the work of race. Third, casta categories and their hierarchies were powerful because lower-status people employed them.

A Black Andes

Whether enslaved or free, Africans and their descendants were central to the making of the colonial Andes. Regardless of the geographical location, black laborers were present or were discussed. Crown officials and viceregal authorities weighed the options of sending enslaved, black laborers to the highland mines rather than further tax indigenous populations. The metaphors of "slave" that circulated in secular and ecclesiastical texts were based on experiences in Europe and the Americas of racial slavery of Africans and their descendants. Highland populations of black people in such urban areas as Cuzco, La Paz, and Quito provided a critical labor source to the households, domestic economies, and religious institutions that lay at the core of colonial Latin American financial networks.[6]

Africans and their descendants did not merely inhabit marginal or particular regions such as the Pacific coast or the lowlands regions like Popoyán and near Mizqué (around Cochabamba in Alto Peru). These areas were not separate from the Andes but were integrated into Andean kinship networks and connected through trade routes. Andean institutions of leadership or *cacigazgo*, communal labor, and kinship structures were shared between the highlands and the coast just as fugitives and free people moved between the valleys and mountains indiscriminately. In short, black labor was critical to how colonial officials constructed the Andes just as Africans and their descendants were integral to colonial Andean society.

Afro-Andeans, however, have been erased from colonial history partially because of a disavowal of race in Andean studies. For Andeanists the word "race" can trigger an association with processes of nationalism, imperialism, and modernity, ushering in a particular form of racism that targeted indigenous majorities and people of African descent.[7] Liberals and conservatives—as well as reformers and nationalists—ascribed fixed physical characteristics, imagined moral failings, and a lack of intellectual capacities to exclude indigenous people from citizenship.[8] Creole elites also erased Afro-

Peruvians, Afro-Ecuadorians, and Afro-Colombians from national narratives by describing them as uncivilized and unable to integrate themselves into the market economy as dutiful laborers.[9] Modern racism also was rooted in categorizations and divisions that, in particular ways, continue when scholars construct Andeans as an ethnicity and blacks as a race, regardless of how cultural and physical factors informed discrimination against both groups.[10] The components of race certainly changed from the seventeenth to the nineteenth century, and Andeans were constructed as Indians in a distinct manner than Africans were represented as blacks. Nonetheless, both Africans and Andeans were racialized in ways that demand a continuing interrogation of race in the Andes.

This book includes the construction of race and the agency of Africans in an Andean history by exploring how slavery shaped everyday casta construction. In the seventeenth century the crown defined limited protections for enslaved people. Enslaved challenges to slavery also occurred within the market sphere and in relation to slaveholders, who would come to serve as authorities in provincial regions such as the Peruvian northern coast. In addition to their interpretations of the few useful royal mandates, enslaved people employed their value as property and laborers to seize on opportunities to purchase, to sell, and to barter their labor and goods. Itinerant and small-scale, yet regular and necessary, the market constituted an exchange of goods between mutually dependent enslaved laborers and indigenous farmers who fueled the local circulation of foodstuffs and clothing.

Whether bound to the estates as slaves or tied to the *reducciones* as Indians, coastal inhabitants crossed paths in the marketplace and when they participated in shared religious holidays. Their interactions provide evidence that enslaved and indigenous people relied on each other for the necessities of daily living. Their intermingling, however, did not change the legal and labor distinctions between the casta designations of black and Indian. More important, when laborers and marketeers enacted their differences on the farms or sugar fields, or in the households or taverns of the northern coastal valleys, they did not necessarily call attention to origin, parentage, or specific physical appearances that have previously been defined as the principal components of casta.[11] This is not to say that Andeans or Africans did not know the difference between an Indian and a black. Their attention more often focused on whether a person was available to work or had something to trade. In the context of a rural economy, one's casta and subsequent legal privileges distinguished who would be forced to work and under which set of conditions, as well as who moved freely without suspicion.

Clearly casta was not inconsequential. While Africans and Andeans met in the marketplace, they still maintained their distinctions. Enslaved men, especially those who had recently arrived, tended to rely on each other for support and guidance. Africans from particular regions called on diasporic collectivities—sometimes through their transatlantic castas such as *arara*. In turn, coastal Andeans appealed to their families, leaders, and communities to protect communal land and water. Given the costs of staying in their assigned reducciones, indigenous people renegotiated their status by migrating or working for wages nearby. Off the reducciones, the crown still offered official protection to indigenous agricultural workers by regulating their yearly wages, ensuring a "letter of contract," and prohibiting their patrons from employing them in the sugar mill.[12] Colonial authorities were supposed to ensure that indigenous laborers were promptly paid on estates and punish slaves who stole from Indian workers.[13]

Andeans, however, were not protected by solely their casta location. Coastal Andeans did not choose but worked on neighboring estates because they had been pushed from their colonial reducciones by the reduction of available land and water. Nonetheless, coastal Andeans sold their labor and even supplied their own work animals and tools to earn a daily wage on the estates.[14] In contrast, the crown only attempted to protect enslaved men and women from extreme physical abuse and mandated that owners provide food, clothing, and treatment for illnesses.[15] Mostly, enslaved people created their own standards of justice and work routines against slaveholders' demands. The point here has been to contrast the two legal locations: Indians and blacks. Distinct from Africans, Andeans could call on colonial officials or indigenous leaders or assigned, crown-appointed lawyers and pay for legal representation. In contrast to enslaved laborers who worked with them, indigenous people claimed a level of autonomy that slaves could not claim within a colonial legal context, but enslaved people nevertheless used extralegal spheres to gain a measure of justice.

In the Andes, indigenous and enslaved laborers were bound together in contrasting and sometimes overlapping strategies that opposed colonialism and slavery. To understand these everyday relations, I have juxtaposed legal discourse with material circumstances. Andeans and Africans were not part of a fixed or systematic hierarchy as depicted by Guaman Poma. To gain access to legal protections or to utilize their market value, Andeans and Africans employed the imposed terms and characteristics of casta categories to varying degrees. Just because they used the legal terms, however, does not mean that indigenous or enslaved men and women saw themselves exclusively through official casta classifications. Hardly fixed or hegemonic, Andean and African use of casta categories allowed them to use the limited powers of the law or the market for their own ends. In doing so, Andeans acted based on historical circumstances that included the African Diaspora.

Casta: To Do the Work of Race

Casta did the work of race. Casta articulated a colonial construction of difference and differential power relations. In this way, casta worked like race when Spanish colonial officials and slaveholders constructed and re-constructed categories to separate Andeans and Africans from each other and from Spaniards.[16] The work that casta did, overall, was to name and to distinguish one group from another to the benefit of Spanish colonizers and slaveholders. Surely race does similar work in the present, although a simple equation of race to casta ignores the particular legal and lived experiences of Andeans and Africans on the northern Peruvian coast in the seventeenth century—and throughout Latin America.

By examining "Indian" in relation to "black," though, the book has sug-gested that not all casta categories did the same type of work. The category of "Indian" discursively allowed more successful entries into the colonial legal sphere. That "Indian" carried more official legal heft than "black" (apart from the meanings infused and advocated by Africans) points to how race was made in the seventeenth century: unevenly. Spanish colonial authorities relied on the construction of Indians to justify their presence in the Americas and did not require the same of the construction of blacks. African and Afri-can descendants were highly legally active and deftly judicially aware, but the term "Indian" carried more legal weight than the term "black." In fact, the comparison between the two signified a colonial construction of inequality at the highest level. Furthermore, casta categories worked and constructed these colonial distinctions based on elites' reliance on the enslavement of African people and their descendants. In this sense, casta (like race) served elite interests of creating differences to serve Spanish and Spanish-descent demands. Andeans participated in this racial construction within the conceit of Spanish colonialism while enslaved men pushed against the limitations of their legal positions to create new locations of articulation (recognized or not by colonial officials or slaveholders) to claim justice and to name com-munity. The very power of casta in the colonial period points to its work of race. At the same time, the caution is for colonial Latin American historians to not treat casta categories as if they accurately describe different "types" of people who were intended to inhabit the same social plane.

The use of casta categories in the seventeenth century was not the same as modern race and racism. Casta categorization elided the standardization of physical characteristics, the imposition of uniform expectations of behavior, and the obsessive definitions of phenotype that were central to nineteenth- and twentieth-century institutionalized racism.[17] Markedly, the shifting terrain of how Andeans claimed their Indian locations and the proliferation of terms employed (even by slaveholders) to name Africans speaks to a distinct form of racial ideology specifically rooted in the seventeenth century. The early modern or the colonial period relied on a variety of definitions and contradictory mandates that shaped official actions and elite imaginaries as well as the possibilities for subaltern actions. Casta did the work of race but did not articulate a fixed racial hierarchy that would emerge as modern race and racial categories.

While casta categories were a means to gain or to exercise power, they were hardly systematic but they were also not fluid.[18] In other words, in everyday experience casta was not a fixed location within a rigid hierarchy. At the same time, a person could not simply perform a category that was radically inconsistent with his or her location within colonialism and slavery. The stark differences between colonialism and slavery meant that indigenous and African-descent people acted according to divergent strategies, even when they were in close contact with each other. For example, in 1672, Diego Nicolas, an indigenous laborer on a Chicama valley estate, filed a civil complaint against Pedro de Cuebas, a *mulato* tailor. Diego Nicolas claimed that Cuebas had stolen a mule; the accused retorted he had purchased the animal.[19] Cuebas won the case partly because the testimony of his witnesses—including a landowner and other artisans—was considered to be more reliable in the urban court than that of an indigenous laborer.[20]

In contrast, Diego Nicolas's witnesses included a rural cleric and the overseer of the estate where he worked, but mostly he relied on Andeans of the nearby reducción of Santiago de Cao and other migrants from his home of Jequetepeque. The witnesses called by each man reflected their distinct urban versus rural networks as well as their different occupations. The possibility of trade brought Diego Nicolas and Pedro de Cuebas together, but their disparate professions and different associations with slavery separated them. Labor and patronage therefore were integral to their enacted casta distinctions and were the elements that could separate people within the colonial sphere.

Certain indigenous people could gain positions of power. In 1725, when enslaved laborers reported that the bridge between the Conache valley and the city of Trujillo was burning, the estate owner sent his servant, Miguel Beltrán, to investigate. In response to his patron (the slaveholder of the estate), the native of Mansiche rounded up the "blacks and Indians of Conache" to follow the tracks of three *congo* woodcutters who had been seen smoking near the bridge.[21] In this case the Spanish landholder employed an indigenous dependent to retaliate against enslaved Africans. In turn, the Andean resident laborer called on his relationships with indigenous neighbors and other enslaved laborers to implement his patron's orders. The trail led to the field of another Andean man who greeted the estate owner's servant and told him where to find the enslaved men of casta congo. Under the direction of Miguel Beltrán, the people of the valley tied up the accused and returned to the estate, where the owner ordered the three enslaved woodcutters to be locked in the stocks.

Miguel Beltrán drew his authority from his relationship with the estate owner but also from his status as an Indian from a reducción that maintained communal land and private fields in the Conache valley.[22] In comparison, men from the indigenous reducción of Moche who worked on the estate served as mitayos and seasonal workers. They could not remain on their reducción because they needed to earn funds to pay tribute owed by their community.[23] These witnesses and "others of their quality" testified for the estate owner that the bridge had been a critical component of their economic survival. Without it, they could neither get to their parishes and their wives in Trujillo, nor bring vegetables, maize, and other foodstuffs to sell.[24] Their testimony illustrates the widening gap between Andeans who defended their reducciones versus indigenous laborers who worked elsewhere. Still rooted on the reducción, Moche Indians were dependent on the patronage of the Spanish landholder as well as the estate resident, Miguel Beltrán, who had secured a position of dependence but also authority over Andean and African laborers.[25] Lastly, indicating the clear divisions between Andeans and Africans, none of the indigenous laborers or servants stepped up to defend the enslaved African laborers.

The examples of the stolen mule and the burned bridge demonstrate that casta ascriptions were extremely consequential but circumstantial. Throughout the Spanish colonies, landholding elites and colonial officials invoked descent, residency, and origins to delegate obligations according to values assigned in the market, colonial legislation, or conjectured characteristics. This process defined the categories of differences, or the castas of Indian and black. Casta categories also contained a shifting vocabulary of contracts regarding labor, land, and relations. For example, indigenous communities in Mexico's Tierra Caliente region welcomed Afromestizos when their population declined but rejected these "outsiders" after land resources became scarce.[26] Depending on the state of local economies, whether a region was an empire frontier, or what the settlement patterns were, indigenous and African-descent people engaged in hostile or harmonious relations or somewhere in between.[27] Focusing on the economic and social circumstances of a particular region illuminates the cultural logic of both casta and race as practiced by enslaved and indigenous laborers. In addition to revealing how these communities saw themselves and others, this approach demonstrates that the elements that constituted race depended on the composition of the local populations, the opportunities available in the local economy, and the possibilities for exchange among laborers.

Casta Constructed from Below

This book has demonstrated how casta was constructed by enslaved and indigenous laborers. Indigenous people who gained access to colonial courts, hired notaries, or paid legal representatives presented themselves within the legal definitions of colonial Indians.[28] Enslaved men and women who were able-bodied and had valuable skills were able to activate—and perpetuate— slaveholders' ideals of slaves, and they were also able to defend themselves in court if they had access.[29] I understand these actions, however, as occurring within the official definitions of "Indian" and "black." When enslaved or colonized people employed a casta term for themselves, they did not believe that they became the colonial image in some essential way. Rather, Andeans and Africans employed the characteristics of the casta terminology to argue for their preferred outcome.

Approaching casta from Andean and African perspectives illustrates how casta, and race by extension, was contextually constructed. The scholar Laura Lewis has described blacks as intermediaries between Indians and Spaniards to detail the liminal positions of African-descent people against the suspected sinfulness of indigenous Mexicans.[30] Lewis complicated racial triangulation by including gender distinctions while invoking state impositions. Her approach, however, located subjects out of historical and cultural contexts that could explain their animosities or strategies. In this book I have taken advantage of the available evidence that demonstrates how casta was culturally produced based on the economic and social relations in a rural region. Other studies along these lines have explored imperial policies or colonizers' perspectives rather than relations between lower-status people.[31] Rather than using these top-down approaches, this book has built on work that locates black-Indian conflict in specific historical situations.

At the same time, enslaved and indigenous laborers did not change the motivations of slaveholders and local estate owners. By understanding how slavery and colonialism functioned from below, however, we can see that enslaved Africans and coastal Andeans engaged in the imposed terminologies with surprising results. Slaves seized on their value in the marketplace while Indians called on the power of their reducción assignment. By doing so, enslaved people affected the outcome of their sale, or indigenous inhabitants defended their labor time. Casta categories were vessels that the majority of inhabitants of Spanish America shaped according to their own boundaries or obligations, and they were not static terms that were infinitely interchangeable. If casta did the work of race, then race mattered to Andean and African people along the colonial Peruvian coast, but not because they were always concerned with ascending to whiteness or assuring the legitimate descent of their progeny.[32]

Coastal Andeans and enslaved Africans tactically negotiated the structures and categories imposed by colonialism and slavery. Other scholars have explored how indigenous people passed as mestizos to challenge colonial rule or enslaved people resisted slaveholders by becoming fugitives.[33] Rather than studying how indigenous or enslaved people removed themselves from colonial categorization, I have focused on Andeans and Africans who employed casta terms; they changed their meanings, though, in a way limited by the constraints of legal systems and landholder demands. Furthermore, engagement with casta terms as juridical categories was a means to access the rare protections embedded in colonial law. In this way I move away from defining colonial casta terms as mixtures of race, class, and other components previously named in the infamous caste-class debates.[34] As a legal term, "casta" was like other mandates, orders, and rulings within Hapsburg colonialism: it could bind and it could be manipulated, but it rarely emanated from one central location. By understanding "casta" as a legal term or a means to gain access to colonial laws, we can see that enslaved and indigenous laborers used casta categories to optimize their situations, but in the process they contributed to the continuous production that sustained the colonial state.

This understanding of how enslaved and indigenous people claimed and discarded casta categories suggests an alternative vision of the colonial state as a web or a net, and not a totalizing instrument of surveillance. Recently, histories of race in colonial Latin America have been rooted in a modern conception not only of race as phenotype but also the state as uniformly powerful.[35] Andean and African engagement with casta categories suggests that the Hapsburg colonial state could not afford to enforce its laws or monitor its subjects in a totalizing manner. Unlike its modern counterpart, this version of the colonial state did not intend to pursue a coordinated program of surveillance of its subjects, much less those not considered capable of vassalage—such as people of African descent.

Colonial regulations in the seventeenth century were disparate, diffused, and contradictory.[36] Viceroys, magistrates, and estate owners debated the use and efficacy of mita as well as when, how, and under which circumstances to collect tribute. Colonial mandates and royal orders were repeatedly reversed.[37] Lima's slaveholders feared slave revolts and extensive numbers of fugitives while simultaneously demanding an increase of the slave trade to the viceroyalty of Peru.[38] In distinct regional economies, local authorities employed casta terminology to produce and reproduce multiple layers of colonial order. Some mandates emphasized indigenous tribute as a critical form of crown revenue, while other laws named the beneficiaries of colonial hierarchies by reserving clerical and governing appointments for Spaniards.[39] Regulations were sporadically enforced as local officials invoked or ignored rules regarding casta distinctions according to the given occasion. In addition, colonial officials on the northern Peruvian coast deferred to the powerful landholders, who became the de facto state during the long seventeenth century. The estate owners encouraged indigenous people to separate from the reducciones and tolerated enslaved mobility in an effort to foster à robust labor market. Far from uniform, the state on the northern Peruvian coast was comprised of independent landholders and itinerant officials, suggesting an instability within casta that may not have been intended within modern definitions of race.

Further complicating the assumption of a uniform colonial or slaveholding rule, in legal cases slaveholders depicted blacks as property but simultaneously recognized Africans as men. Enslavement illustrates the continual creation and maintenance of casta—a social production that was also true for race. The legal representatives of slaveholders seeking to protect enslaved men (their human "property") from execution or exile (in punishment for accused crimes) would posit an image of the accused men as humble and obedient slaves to undermine the prosecution's emphasis on their violent or brutal actions.[40] Both representations were possible. Multiple rather than singular, contradictory rather than comprehensive, articulations of legalized casta characteristics circulated in the colonial Andes making race multivalent.

Hardly unique to the northern Peruvian coast, the meaning of caste could be changed or at least adjusted. Colonial authorities attempted to create categories such as Indian (and others) to name indigenous people as laboring, subordinate, and colonized. In turn, coastal Andeans did not just fulfill their assigned colonial roles as laborers and tribute payers. Indigenous people migrated to estates, worked for their own gain, and transferred communal land to private holdings. Likewise, notaries employed transatlantic terms such as *congo* or *lucumí* but would be corrected by the enslaved men and women who employed these terms to create new, diaspora communities.[41] By developing meanings within colonial terminologies, indigenous and African people with their descendants expanded the terms employed by colonial authorities and private slaveholders to describe their identities and communities. By extension, indigenous and African people would continue to construct the meaning of casta and thereby destabilize race's official definitions in many other places and periods.

Most important, by demonstrating the process of making race, this book disrupts a common assumption that contemporary racism originated in an unbroken line from the colonial past. Undoubtedly, colonial Latin American society was rooted in a racial hierarchy that privileged those of Spanish descent. Clearly, positing that race was constructed does not mean that race and racism was not real—in the past or the present.[42] But how laboring people engaged in the construction of colonial terms reveals how colonial laborers did not perform casta in ways that would later determine the biological "fixity" of nineteenth-century scientific racism.[43] Instead, casta categories provided important points of leverage but did not inexorably freeze one's status. Subaltern articulations of casta had little to do with descent or heritage but were more centered on changing cultural practices and labor expectations. By using the colonial categories that bound them and others, Andeans and Africans engaged in remaking colonialism and slavery and in the process helped make what we would come to know as race.

Origin of Slaves Sold in Trujillo over Time by Percentage (1640–1730)

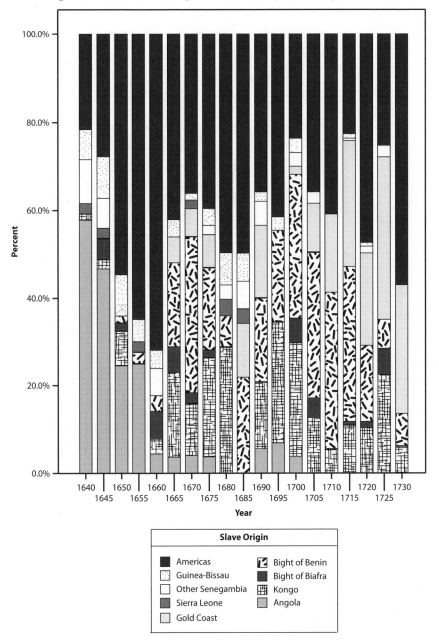

Price Trends of Slaves Sold in Trujillo (1640–1730)

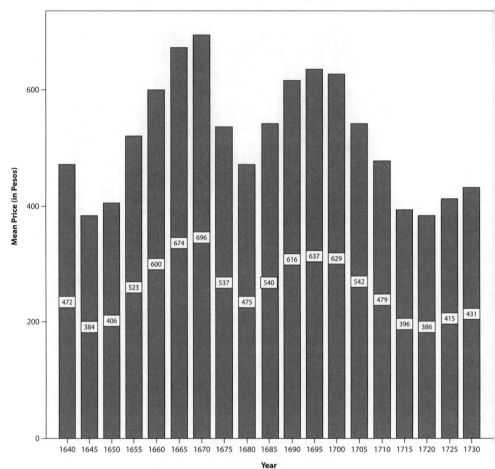

EXPLANATION OF APPENDIX DATA

THE TWO APPENDIXES—Appendix 1, "Origin of Slaves Sold in Trujillo over Time by Percentage (1640–1730)," and Appendix 2, "Price Trends of Slaves Sold in Trujillo (1640–1730)"—were created from a three-step process.

First, I collected every slave sale in the existing notary books in the Archivo Regional de La Libertad (ARLL) and the Archivo Regional de Lambayeque (ARL) for every five-year period between 1640 and 1730. The notaries that I consulted at the ARLL included: for 1640: Escobar Legajo (Leg.) 143; for 1645: Antolinez de Valdez Leg. 93, Escobar Leg. 146, Paz Leg. 205, Viera Gutiérrez Leg. 253; for 1650: Viera Gutiérrez Leg. 257, Moto Leg. 182, Valdez Leg. 93; for 1655: Cortez Leg. 97, Rosales Hoyos Leg. 210, Viera Gutiérrez Leg. 258; for 1660: García Leg. 166, Ortiz Leg. 187, Viera Gutiérrez Leg. 260, García Leg. 166; for 1665: López Bigne Leg. 168, Ortiz de Peralta Leg. 189, Pacheco de Guevara Leg. 197; for 1670: Verde Leg. 250, Álvarez Leg. 87, Ortiz Leg. 194; for 1675: Álvarez Leg. 90, Nuñez de Valcera Leg. 184, Salinas Leg. 233, Salinas Leg. 234; for 1680: Álvarez Leg. 92, Cortijo Quero Leg. 100, Nuñez de Valcera Leg. 186; for 1685: Álvarez Leg. 92, Cortijo Quero Leg. 102, Espino y Alvarado Leg. 149, Nuñez de Valcera Leg. 186, San Román Leg. 211, Salinas Leg. 237;

for 1690: Espino y Alvarado Leg. 151, Cortijo Leg. 104, Cortijo Leg. 105, Salinas Leg. 240: for 1695: Espino y Alvarado Leg. 155, Espino y Alvarado Leg. 156, Nuñez de Valcera Leg. 186, San Román Leg. 211, Salinas Leg. 241; for 1700: San Román Leg. 214, Cortijo Quero Leg. 110, Espino y Alvarado Leg. 159, Espino y Alvarado Leg. 158; for 1705: Cortijo Quero Leg. 114, Cortijo Quero Leg. 115, Chumbi Guaman Leg. 82, Espino y Alvarado Leg. 161, Nuñez de Valcera Leg. 186, San Román Leg. 215; for 1710: Cortijo Quero Leg. 120, San Román Leg. 218; for 1715: Cortijo Quero Leg. 125, Cortijo Quero Leg. 126, San Román Leg. 220, San Román Leg. 221, Aguilar Leg. 262; for 1720: Espino de Alvarado Leg. 329, San Román Leg. 225, Cortijo Quero Leg. 129; for 1725: San Román Leg. 228, Espino de Alvarado Leg. 332, Espino de Alvarado Leg. 333, Lopez Collado y Daza Leg. 372, Lopez Collado y Daza Leg. 373; and for 1730: San Román Leg. 230, Espino de Alvarado Leg. 338, San Román Leg. 230, Aguilar Leg. 264.

The notaries that I consulted at the ARL included: for 1670: Renteros Leg. 1; for 1700: Rivera Leg. 4; for 1720: Rivera Leg. 4, Lino de Herrera Leg. 3; and for 1730: Cossio Leg. 1, Lino de Herrera Leg. 11.

Second, after its initial collection, I coded and entered this data into a Statistical Package for the Social Sciences (SPSS) database. The variables included slave *casta* (both African and criollo categories), age, gender, any skill (which was rarely recorded), the origins or locations of the actual and previous seller and the buyer in an attempt to gauge the flow of the trade from Panama. I also entered the price of the slave(s) and whether they had been sold with others, including children or other family members, as well as other compelling information. There were seventy-three distinct castas including colonial terms and transatlantic or diaspora terms that I condensed into the general regions employing multiple sources but following John Thornton's model in *Africa and Africans in the Making of the Atlantic World* (xiv).

With the assistance of Ms. Shabnam Moobed (in the Math Department at the University of California, Irvine), I analyzed this evidence employing SPSS. I was able to document distinct shifts in the origins of the African Diaspora from first Senegambia to those from the Bight of Benin with a consistent presence of West Central Africans as well as the price fluctuations indicated in the two appendixes.

I eliminated the large number of unknowns within the data to emphasize the available evidence. For example, in an entry, although I could decipher that a slave was a woman and casta *angola*, her age was not recorded or I was unable to read it because of the deteriorated nature of the paper record. Therefore, for a variety of reasons, it was not always possible to enter all the categories for each entry. In other entries perhaps the notary entered a slave's casta but not his or her age. To compensate for the unevenness of the entries, I have not treated this database as offering definitive quantitative data. Instead, I have employed the information from the database to suggest general trends.

NOTES

Introduction: Constructing Casta on Peru's Northern Coast

1. Kenneth Mills named the period between the 1640s and the 1750s as "midcolonial." Mills, *Idolatry and Its Enemies*, 3. Kenneth J. Andrien discussed abuses of governmental offices between the 1630s and the 1740s, declining or migrating indigenous populations faced by colonial authorities between the 1630s and 1720s, and the economic shocks between 1687 and 1730 that suggest how events of the seventeenth century spilled into the eighteenth century. Andrien, *Andean Worlds*, 59–60, 64–65, 94. Ann Zulawski documented transformations in colonial Andean labor systems that emerged between the seventeenth and eighteenth centuries. Zulawski, *They Eat*, 199.

2. For a discussion of Africans as part of the Christian body, see Bennett, *Africans in Colonial Mexico*, 38, 41, 43.

3. For a discussion of the marginal position of African descendants, see Lutz and Restall, "Wolves and Sheep?" 194; and Martínez, *Genealogical Fictions*, 221.

4. Mörner, *Race Mixture*, 7, 53. One side of this exchange has argued that increased

commercial development gradually replaced racial identities with class categories. See Chance and Taylor, "Estate and Class in a Colonial City," 454–87; Chance and Taylor, "Estate and Class: A Reply," 434–42; and Seed and Rust, "Estate and Class in Colonial Oaxaca Revisited," 703–24. Other scholars have agreed that although class mobility may have increased, social stratification was still largely based on race—a construct in which "political, economic, and bureaucratic privileges and prohibitions conferred by racial origin confirm the caste-like basis" of colonial ideology; see McCaa, Schwartz, and Grusbessich, "Race and Class in Colonial Latin America," 433.

5. For definitions of the *sistema de castas*, see Cope, *Limits of Racial Domination*, 24–25; and Martínez, *Genealogical Fictions*, 162, 166.

6. Burga, *De la encomienda*; Cushner, *Lords of the Land*; Davies, *Landowners in Colonial Peru*; Keith, *Conquest and Agrarian Change*; Ramírez, *Provincial Patriarchs*; and Vegas de Cáceres, *Economía rural*.

7. Aguirre, *Agentes de su propia libertad*; Blanchard, *Slavery and Abolition*; Espinosa Descalzo, *Cimarronaje y palenques*; Hünefeldt, *Paying the Price of Freedom*; and Walker, "Ladies and Gentlemen."

8. Brockington, *Blacks, Indians, and Spaniards*, 115, 140, 161, 196; and Tardieu, *El negro en el cusco*, 127–38.

9. In her study of the mining and hacienda zones in rural Bolivia, Ann Zulawski opened the door for more research by suggesting how *yanaconas* (indigenous laborers detached from their villages) adapted to regions under Spanish influences that included Africans and other mixed descendants. See Zulawski, *They Eat from Their Labor*, 170.

10. Other Peruvian scholars had previously pointed out this neglected aspect of Andean colonial history. See Harth-Terré, *Negros e indios*, 11, 23; and Millones Santagadeo, "Población negra en el Peru," 41–42.

11. Bowser, *African Slave in Colonial Peru*, 151, 153.

12. For contributions to the history of conflict between blacks and Indians, see Flores Galindo, *Aristocracia y plebe*, 233.

13. Karen Graubart and Juan Castañeda Murga have also documented trade relations and cohabitation in the provincial city of Trujillo among Africans, Andeans, and their descendants during the sixteenth and seventeenth centuries. See Graubart, *With Our Labor and Sweat*, 86, 91; and Castañeda Murga, "Notas para una historia," 165, 166.

14. Lane, *Quito 1599*, 28, 102, 106, 142; Tardieu, *El negro en el Cusco*, 127–34; Bridikhina, *Mujer negra en Bolivia*, 23, 24, 30; and Hünefeldt, *Paying the Price of Freedom*, 37–96.

15. Bowser, *African Slave in Colonial Peru*, 7.

16. Restall, *Black Middle*, xi, 4; and Sharp, *Slavery on the Spanish*, 129, 146.

17. Lewis, *Hall of Mirrors*, 69; and Silverblatt, *Modern Inquisitions*, 171, 183.

18. For both Tiya Miles and James Brooks, nation building and abolition were

also critical factors. See Miles, *Ties That Bind*, 108, 111, 173; and Brooks, *Captives and Cousins*, 308, 364.

19. Burga, *De la encomienda*, 59, 64–65; Cook, *Demographic Collapse*, 133–34; and Ramírez, *World Upside Down*, 26–29.

20. Zulawski, *They Eat from Their Labor*, 73, 127, 177, 198; Powers, *Andean Journeys*, 39, 54, 89, 121, 156; Larson, *Cochabamba, 1550–1900*, 97; and Wightman, *Indigenous Migration and Social Change*, 62, 88, 89.

21. For discussion of how Andeans reshaped colonial identities, see Saignes, "Indian Migration and Social Change," 189–90. For discussions of how Inca symbolism articulated with specific regional identities, see Dean, *Inka Bodies and the Body of Christ*, 80, 111, 145; and Lowry, "Forging an Indian Nation," 51, 271.

22. Mangan, *Trading Roles*, 83, 101; Cosamalón Aguilar, *Indios detrás de la muralla*, 155, 196; and Garofalo, "Conjuring with Coca and the Inca," 66, 70, 74.

23. The description "between cold mountains and a turbulent sea" comes from Calancha, *Crónica moralizada*, vol. 5, 1225.

24. Ocaña, *Viaje fascinante*, 53.

25. Vázquez de Espinosa, *Compendium and Description*, 395. Coastal people fished the rivers as well. See Calancha, *Crónica moralizada*, vol. 5, 1228.

26. Cieza de León, *Travels of Pedro de Cieza de León*, 234; and Modesto Rubiños y Andrade, "Noticia previa," 320.

27. Lizárraga, *Descripción breve del Peru*, 73; and Calancha, *Crónica moralizada*, 1230.

28. Disembarking from ships in Paita, travelers rented mules and engaged muleteers and guides from such indigenous towns as Olmos and Motupe. Ramírez, "Descripción del Reyno," 28.

29. Anómino, "Fragmento de una historia de Trujillo," 97, 98; Ramírez, "Descripción del Reyno," 29; and Vázquez de Espinosa, *Compendium and Description*, 390, 393, 394.

30. For slaves purchased in Panama for the northern coast, see Archivo Regional de La Libertad (ARLL), Ca. Ords. Leg. 36. Exp. 698 (1716); and Busto Duthurburu, *Historia marítima*, 543. For purchase of Castilian products in Panama, see Aldana, *Empresas coloniales*, 59.

31. Ramírez, *Provincial Patriarchs*, 156.

32. Archivo General de Indias (AGI), Lima Cartas y expedientes: Virreys del Perú. Leg. 407 (1700), 1v; and Pablo E. Pérez-Mallaína, "La fabricación de un mito," 75, 81.

33. Glave Testino, *Trajinantes*, 193.

34. For the Chicama valley, see ARLL, Protocolos. Paz. Leg. 205 (1645), 191v; and ARLL, Protocolos. Viera Gutiérrez. Leg. 253 (1644), 12v. For the Trujillo valley, see AGI, Lima. Leg. 101 (1654). For Jequetepeque, see Burga, *De la encomienda*, 123–25. For Lambayeque, see Ramírez, *Provincial Patriarchs*, 147, 151.

35. AGI, Lima. Leg. 100 (1648), 2; AGI, Escribanía. Leg. 511A (1648), 11; Burga, *De la encomienda*, 100; and Ramírez, *Provincial Patriarchs*, 148.

36. During his *visita* (inspection tour) between 1782 and 1785, Bishop Martínez Compañón estimated that the population of the Trujillo and Saña regions was 9 percent Spanish, 56 percent indigenous, 14 percent mixed descent, and 21 percent African and African-descent people. Obispo Baltasar Jaime Martínez Compañón y Bujanda, "Estado que demuestra el número de Abitantes del Obpdo de Truxillo del Perú con distinción de castas formade pr su actual Obpo," in *Trujillo del Perú a fines del siglo XVIII*, vol. 2.

37. This demographic shift may represent a change in the definition of mestizo rather than a rise of this population. For example, see Muriel Nazzari's discussion of Indians in São Paulo, Brazil. While in the early eighteenth century, Indians were 80 percent of the population, by the early nineteenth century the category of "Indian" no longer existed in the local census. Nazzari has suggested that this demographic shift reflected changing definitions of census categories. See Nazzari, "Vanishing Indians," 497–524.

38. Vila Vilar, *Aspectos sociales*, 118–19.

39. AGI, Lima. Leg. 54. Num. 10. No. 46 (1650), 74; and AGI, Indiferente. Leg. 2796 (1647), 1v.

40. See Appendix 1, "Origin of Slaves Sold in Trujillo over Time by Percentage (1640–1730)," in this book. For Trujillo slave sales of West Central Africans from Panama, see ARLL, Protocolos. Escobar. Leg. 146 (1645), 718; ARLL, Protocolos. Escobar. Leg. 146 (1645), 808; and ARLL, Protocolos. Escobar. Leg. 146 (1645), 814v.

41. AGI, Panamá. Leg. 31 (1646), #257, in Jopling, *Indios y negros*, 502; and AGI, Lima. Leg. 53. No. 4. Num. 15 (1646), 167–167v.

42. AGI, Lima. Leg. 53. No. 4. Num. 15 (1646), 167.

43. See the complaints of Juan Nuñez Holguiar, who was renting a Chicama hacienda in 1652. The Spanish or *creole labrador* complained that although he employed yanaconas and other Indians, he was in need of more laborers to harvest his wheat crop. ARLL, Co. Ords. Leg. 193. Exp. 1255 (1652), 4, 11.

44. Powers, *Andean Journeys*, 42; Wightman, *Indigenous Migration and Social Change*, 29–30; and Zulawski, *They Eat from Their Labor*, 53, 55.

45. Ocaña, *Viaje fascinante*, 29.

46. Postma, *Dutch in the Atlantic Slave Trade*, 33; AGI, Contaduría. Leg. 263 (1668), 2v; and AGI, Contaduría. Leg. 263 (1669), 3.

47. Vila Vilar, *Aspectos sociales*, 125; and Emmer, "Dutch and the Making of the Second Atlantic System," 73.

48. AGI, Contaduría. Leg. 263. No. 42 (1667), 1, 4, 5, 5v; and AGI, Contaduría. Leg. 236. No. 40 (1665), 1.

49. See Appendix 1, "Origin of Slaves Sold in Trujillo over Time by Percentage (1640–1730)," in this book.

50. See Appendix 2, "Price Trends of Slaves Sold in Trujillo (1640–1730)," in this book.

51. Israel, *Dutch Republic*, 934; Emmer, "Dutch and the Making of the Second Atlantic System," 83; and Law, *Kingdom of Allada*, 88.

52. ARLL, Protocolos. Álvarez. Leg. 90 (1675), 306v; and ARLL, Ca. Ords. Leg. 23. Exp. 487 (1670), 1.

53. Thirty-thousand *fanegas* of flour waited in the Chicama port of Malabrigo in 1690. AGI, Lima. Leg. 298 (1690).

54. ARLL, Ca. Cr. Leg. 83. Exp. 1481 (1720), 82v. AGI, Lima Leg. 111 (1656), 1, 2. The replacement of indigenous workers with African and criollo slaves was commonplace in colonial Latin America. For a similar situation in the Chota valley in present-day Ecuador, where African and criollo slaves replaced indigenous laborers, see Coronel, "Indios y esclavos negros," 172.

55. Ramírez, *Provincial Patriarchs*, 101, 116.

56. Ibid., 172–73.

57. ARLL, Protocolos. García Sancho. Leg. 166 (1660), 183.

58. Ramírez, *Provincial Patriarchs*, 198.

59. Ibid., 160, 172.

60. Moreno Cebrián, *Corregidor de indios*, 34, 70.

61. AGI, Escribanía. Leg. 963 (1655); ARLL. Co. Cr. Leg. 248. Exp. 2649 (1682), 1; and AGI, Lima Leg. 348 (1722).

62. AGI, Indiferente. Leg. 431. Libro 43 (1685), 15; and ARLL, Actas del Cabildo. Vol. 13 (1723), 24–25.

63. Andrien, *Crisis and Decline*, 100, 202, 204.

64. De la Fuente, "Slave Law and Claims-Making in Cuba," para. 7.

65. Stoler, *Along the Archival Grain*, 20, 24.

66. Jouve-Martín, *Esclavos de la ciudad letrada*, 80, 82.

67. Ginzburg, *Cheese and the Worms*, 1, 19, 21, 41, 100; and Ginzburg, "Microhistory," 24.

68. De Certeau, *Practice of Everyday Life*, 23, 43, 54.

69. Putnam, "To Study the Fragments/Whole," 4.

70. For a working definition of colonial discourse and its appropriation, see Seed, "Colonial and Postcolonial Discourse," 127, 139. For an exploration of the inequality of law, see Edwards, "Status without Rights," 373–74.

71. Owensby, *Empire of Law and Indian Justice*, 47; and Guevara-Gil and Salomon, "'Personal Visit,'" 13, 19.

72. Kathryn Burns provides an exciting model for understanding how colonized and enslaved people shaped legal documents with her exploration of notaries. See Burns, *Into the Archive*, 50–51.

73. For example, Jouve-Martín, "Public Ceremonies and Mulatto Identity," 190, 193, 194.

74. O'Toole, "From the Rivers of Guinea to the Valleys of Peru"; and O'Toole, "Within Slavery."

75. Bowser, *African Slave in Colonial Peru*, 37–38, 40–50; Lockhart, *Spanish Peru*, 195–

98; and Romero, *Negro en el Perú*, 62, 70. See also Tardieu, "Origins of the Slaves," 43–54.

76. Bristol, *Christians, Blasphemers, and Witches*, 153–56; McKnight, "'En su tierra lo aprendió,'" 63–84; and Bennett, *Africans in Colonial Mexico*, 87–110.

77. Gomez, *Exchanging Our Country Marks*; Sweet, *Recreating Africa*; and Thornton, *Africa and Africans in the Making of the Atlantic World*. Among the growing scholarship on African Diaspora collective articulations in the Americas, see Reis, *Slave Rebellion in Brazil*; Hawthorne, *From Africa to Brazil*; and Young, *Rituals of Resistance*.

78. Sweet, "Mistaken Identities?" 289, 299, 302. Sweet has expanded on these ideas and much more in *Domingos Álvares*. Also see David Northrup's exploration of multiple African Diaspora identities in his "Becoming African," 10, 12.

79. For compelling discussion of how to chart African Diaspora communities and individuals, see Lovejoy, "Ethnic Designations of the Slave Trade," 10, 19, 36; and Miller, "Retention, Reinvention, and Remembering," 86, 87, 90, 99. 109.

1. Between Black and Indian: Labor Demands and the Crown's Casta

1. Cárdenas, *Memorial y relación*, 49.

2. Ibid., 58.

3. Powers, *Andean Journeys*, 95.

4. Cole, *Potosí Mita*, 66.

5. Bakewell, *Miners of the Red Mountain*, 83.

6. Larson, *Cochabamba, 1550–1900*, 105–6.

7. Vila Vilar, *Aspectos sociales*, 114.

8. For more on the well-known attempts to reform the mita by this viceroy, see Mangan, *Trading Roles*, 165, 166; and Larson, *Cochabamba, 1550–1900*, 98, 108, 109.

9. Lewis, *Hall of Mirrors*, 29, 31; and Martínez, *Genealogical Fictions*, 168, 221, 235.

10. Archivo General de Indias (AGI), Escribanía. Leg. 533A. No. 2 (1659), 147.

11. Konetzke, *Colección de documentos* cites a *real cédula* of 1655, vol. 2, foma 1, pages 461–62; Ayala, *Diccionario de gobierno* cites a *real cédula* of 1680, page 316; and AGI, Lima. Leg. 104A (1685), 1.

12. Andrien, *Andean Worlds*, 65; and Cole, *Potosí Mita*, 78.

13. *Recopilación de leyes de los reynos de las Indias*, Libro Sesto, Título Segundo. Ley Primera (1526, 1530, 1532, 1540, 1542, 1548), 224. Vatican Film Library (VFL), Colección Pastells. Vol. 100. Roll 20. AGI, Charcas. Cartas y expedientes del Presidente y oidores de aquella audiencia vistos en el Consejo (1606), 405. VFL, Colección Pastells. Vol. 89. Roll 16. AGI, Lima. Cartas y expedientes del Virrey de Lima, conde de Chinchon, visto en el Consejo. No. 4 (1622), 423. AGI, Lima. Cartas y expedientes de virreyes de Perú. Leg. 63. No. 3. Num. 54 (1662), 1. AGI, Lima. Cartas y expedientes de virreyes de Perú. Leg. 68. No. 6. Num. 18 (1669), 1.

14. Solórzano Pereira, *Política Indiana*, 154; and González de Acuña, *Informe*, 20, refers to dispatches from 1570 to 1650.

15. VFL, Colección Pastells. Vol. 28. Roll 11. AGI, Lima. Cartas y expedientes de personas eclesiásticas del distrito de dicha audiencia visto en el Consejo (1625), 46.

16. AGI, Lima. Cartas y expedientes de virreyes de Perú. Leg. 63. No. 3. Num. 54 (1662), 2.

17. VFL, Colección Pastells. Roll 6. Peru. Vol. 1. 1669-7-1. Chile. 76-8-6, "Carta a SM del Obispo de Santiago de Chile" (1669), 98.

18. Glave Testino, *Trajinantes*, 194.

19. Clements Library, Peru Collection. Don Melchor de Liñán y Cisneros, "Relacion de Govierno que el exmo senor don Melchor de Liñán y Cisneros, Arzobispo de Lima, hace a su succesor el exmo senor Duque de la Palata," pages 403, 415v.

20. Konetzke, *Colección de documentos*, vol. 2, tomo 2, 729.

21. AGI, Lima. Residencia de la Audiencia de Lima. Leg. 534A. No. 1 (1672), 223v.

22. Monsalve, *Redvcion vuniversal de todo el Pirv*, 6v.

23. Larson, *Cochabamba, 1550–1900*, 98; and Saignes, "Colonial Condition in the Quechua-Aymara Heartland," 83.

24. Cárdenas, *Memorial y relación*, 29, 48.

25. VFL, Colección Pastells. Roll 6. Vol. 1 Peru. 77-6-7 (1662), 200.

26. Ibid.

27. Cárdenas, *Memorial y relación*, 58.

28. *Cedulario* tomo 37, fol. 164v, no. 110, quoted in Ayala, *Diccionario de gobierno*, 292; AGI, Indiferente 429, Libro 38, fol. 36v, in Konetzke, *Colección de documentos*, vol. 2, tomo 1, 338; AGI, Lima. Leg. 51. Lib. 4. No. 22 (1642), 220v, 221; AGI, Lima. Leg. 104A (1685), 1; and Solórzano Pereira, *Política Indiana*, 427.

29. Solórzano Pereira, *Política Indiana*, 173, 176.

30. AGI, Lima. Leg. 6 (1640), 1v.

31. Konetzke, *Colección de documentos*, cites a 1668 *real cédula*, vol. 2, tomo 2, page 541. AGI, Lima. Leg. 59 (1660), 1, 2, 2v; *Tercero Catecismo*, 73, 74; Acosta, *Tercero catecismo*, 226, 246; Solórzano Pereira, *Política Indiana*, pages 390–91; and Torres, *Crónica de la provincia*, 61, 62, 79.

32. Konetzke, *Colección de documentos*, vol. 2, tomo 1, cites a 1646 *real cédula*, page 401; and Konetzke, *Colección de documentos*, vol. 2, tomo 2, cites a 1684 *real cédula*, page 755.

33. VFL, Colección Pastells. Vol. 86, Lima 6. Roll 29 from AGI, Audiencia de Lima. Cartas y expedientes del Virrey de Lima vistos en el Consejo. "Carta del Marques de Montes Claros a S.M." Lima, April 8, 1611, page 159.

34. Ibid., 169. Ecclesiastical officials also urged the separation of blacks from Indians following royal orders. *Constitvciones synodales del arçobispado de Los Reyes en el Pirv, Hechas y ordenadas* [1614], 37.

35. Wightman, *Indigenous Migration and Social Change*, 25–27; and Mangan, *Trading Roles*, 43.

36. Archivo Regional de La Libertad (ARLL), Co. Asuntos de Gobierno. Leg. 266. Exp. 3074 (1607), 2.

37. *Recopilación de leyes de los reynos de las Indias*, Libro VI, Titulo Trece, Ley VIII, 285.

38. ARLL, Co. Asuntos de Gobierno. Leg. 266. Exp. 3074 (1607), 2.

39. Ibid., 2v, 5.

40. Ibid., 13.

41. Ibid., 3v.

42. Ibid., 6.

43. Solórzano Pereira, Política Indiana, 178; and Lane, Quito 1599, 74, 76.

44. VFL, Colección Pastells. Vol. 86. Lima 6. Roll 29. AGI, Audiencia de Lima. Cartas y expedientes del Virrey de Lima vistos en el Consejo. No. 6 (1615), 370.

45. For an assertion that the expense of black slaves made Indians indispensable, see Lewis, Hall of Mirrors, 34.

46. AGI, Lima. Leg. 59 Carta dated 1601, (1660), 1.

47. Lane, Quito 1599, 59; and Bryant, "Finding Gold, Forming Slavery," 94.

48. Lane, Quito 1599, 73–74.

49. For the need for labor in the early seventeenth century in the southern Andes, see Larson, Cochabamba, 1550–1900, 93. For the ability of indigenous laborers to find work outside of their assigned reducciones in the northern Andes, see Powers, Andean Journeys, 92. Following the work of Kenneth J. Andrien, the Andes experienced diverse local economies throughout most of the seventeenth century, including labor opportunities. Andrien, Crisis and Decline, 4. In the 1640s, if indigenous people had migrated to areas that produced commercial crops, there must have been a demand for their labor in the southern and northern Andes. Zulawski, They Eat from Their Labor, 81, 83; and Powers, Andean Journeys, 51. Reforms of indigenous wages in the 1680s indicate that Andeans were working as laborers in transportation, agriculture, and mining. Spalding, Huarochirí, 191.

50. Vila Vilar, Aspectos sociales, 118–19; AGI, Lima. Leg. 54. Num. 10. No. 46 (1650), 74; and AGI, Indiferente. Leg. 2796 (1647), 1v.

51. See Appendix 1, "Origin of Slaves Sold in Trujillo over Time by Percentage (1640–1730)," in this book. For Trujillo slave sales of West Central Africans from Panama, see ARLL, Protocolos. Escobar. Leg. 146 (1645), 718; ARLL, Protocolos. Escobar. Leg. 146 (1645), 808; and ARLL, Protocolos. Escobar. Leg. 146 (1645), 814v.

52. AGI, Panamá. Leg. 31 (1646), #257, in Jopling, Indios y negros, 502; AGI, Lima. Leg. 53. No. 4. Num. 15 (1646), 167–167v; Andrien, Kingdom of Quito, 17; and Lane, Quito 1599, 133, 135.

53. AGI, Lima. Leg. 53. No. 4. Num. 15 (1646), 167.

54. Bakewell, Miners of the Red Mountain, 32.

55. Larson, Cochabamba, 1550–1900, 96; Powers, Andean Journeys, 51; Saignes, "Indian Migration and Social Change," 173, 184; and Zulawski, They Eat from Their Labor, 81, 83.

56. Toribio Polo, Memorias de los Virreys, 19, 21.

57. AGI, Lima. Cartas y expedientes de virreyes de Peru, vistos o resueltos en el Consejo. Leg. 54. Num. 10. No. 46 (1650), 74, 74v.

58. AGI, Indiferente. Asiento de Negros: Cartas, Ordenes, etc. Leg. 2797 "Resumen" (1657), 1.

59. AGI, Indiferente. Asiento de negros: Cartas, Ordenes, etc. Leg. 2799 (1705), 6v.

60. AGI, Indiferente. Asiento de Negros. Cartas, Ordenes, etc. Leg. 2796 (1640), 1, 1v.

61. VFL, Colección Pastells. Vol. 94. Lima 15. Roll 3. AGI, Audiencia de Lima. Cartas y expedientes del virrey de Lima vistos en el Consejo (1669), 142.

62. Larson, Cochabamba, 1550–1900, 105–6.

63. Tardieu, "La mano de obra negra," 137.

64. Viceregal officials who dealt with the lack of revenue, labor, and resources on a regional level were reluctant to comply with crown mandates regarding the differences between blacks and Indians. MacLachlan, Spain's Empire in the New World, 22.

65. AGI, Lima. Cartas y expedientes: varios cabildos seculares. Leg. 111 (1656), 1, 2.

66. Mangan, Trading Roles, 165.

67. AGI, Lima. Cartas y expedientes de virreyes de Perú, vistos o resueltos en el Consejo. Leg. 54. Num. 10. No. 46 (1650), 74.

68. AGI, Indiferente. Leg. 2796 (1643), 1, 1v.

69. AGI, Indiferente. Asiento de Negros: Cartas, Ordenes, etc. Leg. 2796, "Copia de Capitulo de carta de don Pedro Capta," (1648).

70. AGI, Indiferente. Asiento de Negros: Cartas, Ordenes, etc. Leg. 2796, "Don Francisco Galindo y Çayas," (1648).

71. AGI, Indiferente. Asiento de Negros: Cartas, Ordenes, etc. Leg. 2796, "A Su Magestad Don Juan Velardo Trucino" (1647), 1v.

72. Wade, "La construcción de 'el negro,'" 145.

73. Anónimo, "Descripción del Virreinato," 40.

74. Carroll, Blacks in Colonial Veracruz, 63; and Aguirre Beltran, "El trabajo del indio," 206.

75. Lewis, Hall of Mirrors, 29; and Martínez, Genealogical Fictions, 168.

76. Wightman, Indigenous Migration and Social Change, 31–32.

77. VFL, Colección Pastells. Vol. 76, Peru. V. 7. Roll 13. 1668-4-2. Lima. 116-1-5O (1687), 342.

78. Navarra y Rocafull, Relación de govierno, 23v–24, 153.

79. Ordoñez de Zevallos, Historia, y viage, 422.

80. Wightman, Indigenous Migration and Social Change, 18; and Ramírez, World Upside Down, 116.

81. Mangan, Trading Roles, 33, 163; and Zulawski, They Eat from Their Labor, 97.

82. Archivo General de la Nación (AGN), Derecho Indigena. Leg. 7. Exp. 169 (1693), 6; and Klein, Haciendas and Ayllus, 11.

83. Cañeque, King's Living Image, 187.

84. *Recopilación de leyes de los reynos de las Indias*, Libro VI, Titulo III, 208v, cites the King, 1646.

85. AGI, Lima. Leg. 528 "Sacra y real magestad" (1713), 7.

86. Mangan, *Trading Roles*, 83, 125; and Glave Testino, *Trajinantes*, 54.

87. Ramírez, *World Upside Down*, 64; and Spalding, *Huarochirí*, 166.

88. AGN, Campesinado. Titulos de propiedad. Leg. 34. Cuad. 649 (1644), 27, cites a viceregal order from 1636; Konetzke, *Colección de documentos*, vol. 2, tomo 1, 401, cites a *real cédula* of 1646; Konetzke, *Colección de documentos*, vol. 2, tomo 2, 755, cites a royal response of 1684; AGI, Indiferente. Leg. 431. Libro 43 (1685), 15; and AGI, Escribanía. Leg. 1190 (1660), 1.

89. Bowser, *African Slave in Colonial Peru*, 23; Chang-Rodríguez, *Coloniaje y conciencia*, 35; Konetzke, *Colección de documentos*, vol. 2, tomo 1, part 2, 306; Borrego Pla, "Palenques de negros," 429, citing Real Cédula, Madrid, 23 agosto 1691; AGI, Santa Fé, Leg. 213; and Konetzke, *Colección de documentos*, vol. 2, tomo 1, 377–78.

90. AGI, Lima. Leg. 52. No. 27A (1640), 26v.

91. Konetzke, *Colección de documentos*, cites a 1681 *real cédula*, vol. 2, tomo 2, 722–23.

92. *Constitvciones synodales de el obispado de la civdad de Gvamanga, celbradas en concilio diocesano per el* [1677], 26.

93. VFL, Colección Pastells. Roll 6. Peru. AGI. 1688-1-18. Chile. 77-6-7 (1688), 241.

94. Archivum Romanum Societatis Iesu (ARSI), Peruana Litterae Annuae. Vol. 17 "Letras Annuas de la Provincia del Peru de los años 1678, 1679, 1680," 5.

95. ARSI, Nov. Reg. Historia. Ab Ann (1690), 236.

96. Konetzke, *Colección de documentos* cites a 1724 *real cédula*, vol. 3, tomo 1, 187.

97. Graubart, *With Our Labor and Sweat*, 154; and Earle, "Luxury, Clothing, and Race," 223.

98. AGI, Lima. Cartas y expedientes de virreyes de Perú. Leg. 63. No. 1. Num. 52 (1661), 1.

99. For prohibitions of arming slaves, see Konetzke, *Colección de documentos*, vol. 2, tomo 1, cites a 1696 *real cédula*, 54, cites a 1621 *real cédula*, 262, cites a 1628 *real cédula*, 317, cites a 1647 *real cédula*, 417, cites a 1647 *real cédula*, 427, cites a 1663 *real cédula*, 513.

100. AGI, Lima. Cartas y expedientes de virreyes de Perú. Leg. 63. No. 14 (1662), 1v.

101. The intentions of the crown had been clear as Dominican Antonio González de Acuña recalled royal orders forbidding the enslavement of any Indian. See González de Acuña, *Informe*, 19–20.

102. Bennett, *Africans in Colonial Mexico*, 4–5, 42–43.

103. Vinson III, *Bearing Arms for His Majesty*, 224, 225, 226, 227.

2. Working Slavery's Value, Making Diaspora Kinships

1. *Recopilación de leyes de los reynos de las Indias*, Libro VII, Título V, Ley VIII, 321; and Tardieu, *Los negros y la iglesia en el Perú*, tomo 1, 84, 85, 86, 87.

2. Miller, *Way of Death*, 390, 395; and Smallwood, *Saltwater Slavery*, 38–39, 45, 49.

3. Thornton, "Cannibals, Witches, and Slave Traders," para. 33; and Olaudah Equiano as quoted in Rediker, *Slave Ship*, 119.

4. Smallwood, *Saltwater Slavery*, 131, 140.

5. Veitia Linage, *Spanish Rule of Trade*, 159; Palacios Preciado, *La trata de negros*, 375; and García, *La diaspora de los kongos*, 22.

6. Bennett, *Colonial Blackness*, 1, 104.

7. Johnson, *Soul by Soul*, 17, 118; and Gross, *Double Character*, 3, 5, 42, 50, 52.

8. For a discussion of how race legally fixed African Americans in the nineteenth century, see Edwards, *Gendered Strife and Confusion*, 96. For a discussion of flexibilities in Spanish American racial assignations or casta categories, see O'Toole, "Castas y representación," 56, 60. For the domestic slave trade of the nineteenth-century United States, see Johnson, *Soul by Soul*, 49–52, versus the discussion of the international trade (legal and illegal) into Spanish America in the seventeenth century, see Vila Vilar, *Hispanoamérica*, 152.

9. Sweet, *Recreating Africa*, 43, 47, 123, 126–27, 132; Bennett, *Africans in Colonial Mexico*, 93–99; Karasch, *Slave Life in Rio de Janeiro*, 266, 293; and Brown, *Santería Enthroned*, 21.

10. See Appendix 1, "Origin of Slaves Sold in Trujillo over Time by Percentage (1640–1730)," in this book.

11. See Appendix 1, "Origin of Slaves Sold in Trujillo over Time by Percentage (1640–1730)."

12. Sweet, *Recreating Africa*, 116.

13. By agreeing to share property or labor skills, enslaved people formed new social ties as the act of mutually beneficial economic strategies made people into kin. Penningroth, *Claims of Kinfolk*, 86, 89. For previous approaches that assume affinities based on origins, see Gomez, *Exchanging Our Country Marks*, 6, 27; and Hall, *Africans in Colonial Louisiana*, 29, 53.

14. Sweet, "Mistaken Identities?" 289, 299, 302. Also see David Northrup's exploration of multiple African Diaspora identities in his "Becoming African," 10, 12.

15. Enslaved people who arrived together had to choose to create lasting kinship connections that were passed on to subsequent generations as evidenced by Sylviana Diouf's careful reconstruction of the relationships among a core group of Yoruba and others sold from Ouidah to Alabama in the mid-nineteenth century. Diouf, *Dreams of Africa in Alabama*, 107, 137.

16. Silverblatt, *Modern Inquisitions*, 17, 115; and Lewis, *Hall of Mirrors*, 29–33.

17. Bennett, *Colonial Blackness*, 76–77.

18. Rediker, *Slave Ship*, 116, 117–18; and Smallwood, *Saltwater Slavery*, 118–19.

19. Johnson, *Soul by Soul*, 30, 179.

20. Hawthorne, *Planting Rice and Harvesting Slaves*, 62–63.

21. Miller, *Way of Death*, 22, 28, 30, 118, 142–43.

22. Smallwood, *Saltwater Slavery*, 24, 28, 37–38.

23. Law, *Kingdom of Allada*, 70, 99, 104.

24. Smallwood, *Saltwater Slavery*, 44—45; and Miller, *Way of Death*, 390, 395.

25. Smallwood, *Saltwater Slavery*, 51.

26. Rediker, *Slave Ship*, 120.

27. Sandoval, *Un tratado sobre la esclavitud*, 152, 397.

28. Ibid., 134, 152.

29. Newson and Minchin, *From Capture to Sale*, 19, 109—10.

30. Ibid., 110; and Vila Vilar, *Hispanóamérica*, 200.

31. Newson and Minchin, *From Capture to Sale*, 144.

32. Archivo General de las Indias (AGI), Indiferente. Asiento de Negros: Cartas, Ordenes, etc. "Testimo del ajuste y quanta" (1699), 3.

33. AGI, Contaduría. Asientos de negros con diferentes compañías y particulares. Leg. 261. No. 3 "Testimo de los Autos y Visita del navio nombrado Nra Señora del Buen Subsesso y San Carlos" (1674), 5v, 11, 17.

34. AGI, Contaduría. Autos sobre el asiento de negros con Domingo Grillo. Leg. 263 (1666), ff. 52; and AGI, Indiferente. Asiento de Negros: Cartas, Ordenes etc. Leg. 2798 "Testimonio de los autos dhos sobre La Aprehenssion de treçe esclavos y dos crias en la estancia San Bartme de Pechelni por no tener marca R1 ni del asiento" (1700), 32v.

35. Navarrete, *Historia social*, 79.

36. Sandoval, *Un tratado sobre la esclavitud*, 153—54.

37. Navarrete, *Génesis y desarrollo*, 130.

38. Vila Vilar, *Hispanoamérica*, 139; and Sandoval, *Un tratado sobre la esclavitud*, 411, 440.

39. Newson and Minchin, *From Capture to Sale*, 148.

40. Ibid., 136.

41. Ocaña, *Viaje fascinante*, 23.

42. Busto Duthurburu, *Historia marítima*, 465.

43. AGI, Contaduría. Leg. 261. No. 2 (1674), 50, 51, 52v.

44. Rodríguez, "Cimarrón Revolts," 149, 151; and Newson and Minchin, *From Capture to Sale*, 194.

45. Andrade, *Varones ilustres*, 769. In 1580 the fugitive leaders on the Panamanian rivers—Juan Jolofo, Vicente Sape, and Gaspar Bran—reflected the origins of the majorities of captives sold into the Spanish Americas and forced to cross the isthmus during this period, including Senegambia, Sierra Leone, and Guinea-Bissau. Jopling, *Indios y negros*, 359, cites a document from AGI, Audiencia de Panamá, 234/1/5, dated August 30, 1580.

46. Herrera, *Historia general*, 30; and Ocaña, *Viaje fascinante*, 30.

47. Busto Duthurburu, *Historia marítima*, 471.

48. Archivo Regional de La Libertad (ARLL), Protocolos. Ortiz de Peralta. Leg. 189, #314 (1665), 519v.

49. ARLL, Co. Ords. Leg. 193. Exp. 1243 (1642), 11v.

50. ARLL, Protocolos. Toledo. Leg. 244 (1620), 25; and ARLL, Protocolos. Bernal. Leg. 94 (1620), 195v.

51. Pedro Gonzales was identified as a criollo of Mexico, age twenty-seven, sold from Lima to Trujillo. ARLL, Protocolos. Escobar, Leg. 133 (1630), 921. Juan Lorenço was identified as a criollo from Río de la Hacha (east of Cartagena), age thirty, sold by a ship's captain to a Trujillo slaveholder. ARLL, Protocolos. Bernal. Leg. 94 (1620), 178v. For Afro-Mexican communities in the first half of the seventeenth century, see Bennett, *Africans in Colonial Mexico*.

52. ARLL, Protocolos. Escobar. Leg. 143 (1640), 447v.

53. ARLL, Protocolos. Escobar. Leg. 133 (1630), 781.

54. Ibid., 87v.

55. Archivo Arzobispal de Lima (AAL), Leg. 2. Exp. 15 (1611), 2v. For trading connections between the Nicaraguan and Guatemalan coasts and Trujillo, see Busto Duthurburu, *Historia marítima*, 500.

56. ARLL, Ca. Ords. Leg. 23. Exp. 487 (1670), 1.

57. ARLL, Ca. Ords. Leg. 20. Exp. 437 (1653), 2.

58. Friars and clerics provided refuge in monasteries for enslaved men having a disagreement with their owners. Bowser, *African Slave in Colonial Peru*, 160, 169, 258.

59. For African and African-descent populations in Panama, see Archivum Romanum Societatis Iesu (ARSI), N. R. et Quit. Histor. Literae Annuae. Vol. 12. No. I and II (1604), 12v.

60. The scholar Frederick Bowser has estimated that mortality rates of the Pacific slave trade ranged between 10 and 20 percent. Bowser, *African Slave in Colonial Peru*, 66.

61. ARLL, Protocolos. Espino y Alvarado. Leg. 149, #208 (1684), 329.

62. Córdoba y Salinas, *Vida, virtudes, y milagros*, 30–31.

63. Ocaña, *Viaje fascinante*, 36. The journey between Perico and Guayaquil was estimated at fifteen days. From Perico to Paita was estimated to take thirty days. For evidence of the smaller groups of captives in the Pacific slave trade, see ARLL, Protocolos. Moto. Leg. 182, #2 (1650), 1v.

64. Customarily, slave traders appointed a captain to lead parcels of captives crossing the Panamanian isthmus. Newson and Minchin, *From Capture to Sale*, 193.

65. ARLL, Co. Ords. Leg. 196. Exp. 1317 (1662).

66. ARLL, Protocolos. Obregon. Leg. 57 (1630), 313v.

67. Newson and Minchin, *From Capture to Sale*, 211. Bowser describes traders providing mules for slaves to make this journey, yet I have found no indication that newly arrived captives rode pack animals at any part of their forced transport on the northern Peruvian coast. Bowser, *African Slave in Colonial Peru*, 64. Captains of trading ships continued to sell slaves along the Pacific coast toward Lima. See ARLL, Protocolos. Álvarez. Leg. 90, #144 (1675), 306v. ARLL, Ca. Ords. Leg. 36. Exp. 698 (1716), 1.

68. Bowser, *African Slave in Colonial Peru*, 149.

69. ARLL, Ca. Cr. Leg. 78. Exp. 1314 (1617), 2.

70. Troutman, "Grapevine in the Slave Market," 210.

71. Vázquez de Espinosa, *Compendium and Description*, 393, 395; Anónimo, *Descripción del Virreinato del Perú*, 24; and Cieza de León, *Travels of Pedro de Cieza de León*, 26.

72. ARLL, Co. Ords. Leg. 206. Exp. 1487 (1685), 2v. Local indigenous porters were more likely to save their kin or patrons than newly arrived strangers, as rescuers saved five indigenous mariners but lost six captives. The Huanchaco colonial reducción contained agriculturalists and fishing people made of particular family groups. See Calancha, *Crónica moralizada*, vol. 2, 1090; and Feijóo de Sosa, *Relación descriptiva de la ciudad*, 83.

73. ARLL, Ca. Cr. Leg. 78. Exp. 1312 (1616). I thank Juan Castañeda Murga for providing his notes of this case.

74. De la Fuente, "Slaves and the Creation of Legal Rights," 662.

75. ARLL, Co. Cr. Leg. 244. Exp. 4446 (1631), 2.

76. ARLL, Protocolos. Viera Gutiérrez. Leg. 253 (1644), 85v, lists five angola men and one angola woman out of eighteen slaves on a Chicama estate. ARLL, Co. Ords. Leg. 193. Exp. 1243 (1652), 19v, lists three angola men and one angola woman out of six slaves on the farm San Vicente Ferrer; ARLL, Co. Ords. Leg. 194. Exp. 1259 (1653), ff. 153–153v, lists ten angola men and one angola woman out of forty-three slaves on the sugar mill Tulape.

77. ARLL, Co. Cr. Leg. 248. Exp. 2662 (1686), 1.

78. Vila Vilar, *Hispanoamérica*, 223; and Appendix 2, "Price Trends of Slaves Sold in Trujillo (1640–1730)," in this book.

79. For a discussion of how slave traders created characteristics of "tradable" slaves, see Baptist, "'Cuffy,' 'Fancy Maids,' and 'One-Eyed Men,'" paras. 22–24; and Johnson, *Soul by Soul*, 119, 121.

80. Anónimo, *Descripción del Virreinato del Perú*, 40.

81. AGI, Indiferente. Leg. 2796 (1645), 1v.

82. For a discussion of slaveholders' fantasies, see Johnson, *Soul by Soul*, 119, 205. For a discussion of domination as simultaneously material and cultural, see Ortner, *Anthropology and Social Theory*, 25.

83. AGI, Indiferente. Leg. 761 (1640), 2.

84. AGI, Indiferente. Leg. 2796 (1647), 2.

85. Littlefield, *Rice and Slaves*, 13; and Bontemps, *Punished Self*, 94.

86. Sandoval, *Un tratado sobre la esclavitud*, 137. The Jesuits were slaveholders and their Cartagena house owned slaves, including those who served as translators and assistants to Sandoval. Olsen, *Slavery and Salvation*, 16.

87. Hawthorne, *Planting Rice and Harvesting Slaves*, xvi, 64.

88. Sandoval, *Un tratado sobre la esclavitud*, 137.

89. AGI, Indiferente. Asiento de Negros: Cartas, Ordenes, etc. Leg. 2796 (1650, 1652).

90. ARLL, Co. Ords. Leg. 195. Exp. 1300 (1658), f. 1; and ARLL, Ca. Ords. Leg. 23. Exp. 499 (1673), 1, 4v.

91. AGI, Indiferente. Asiento de Negros: Cartas, Ordenes, etc. Leg. 2796 "El dor. Don Joseph de los Rios y Berries," (1645), 1v.

92. AGI, Contaduría. Asientos de negros con diferentes compañías y particulares. Leg. 261. No. 9 (1663), 4.

93. Sandoval, Un tratado sobre la esclavitud, 136.

94. O'Toole, "Inventing Difference," Appendix C; and Bowser, African Slave in Colonial Peru, 40.

95. Burnard and Morgan, "Dynamics of the Slave Market," para. 7.

96. Palacios Preciado, La trata de negros, 122; and AGI, Indiferente. Leg. 2771 (1707), 3v.

97. AGI, Indiferente. Leg. 2771 (1704), 3v.

98. AGI, Indiferente. Leg. 2773 (1707), 14; and Klein, Atlantic Slave Trade, 76–77.

99. Hünefeldt, Paying the Price of Freedom, 68–69; Morgan, Laboring Women, 177, 189; and Karasch, Slave Life in Rio de Janeiro, 90.

100. ARLL, Co. Ords. Leg. 206. Exp. 1489 (1685), 30.

101. ARLL, Protocolos. Salinas. Leg. 237 (1685), 244. Salinas, an active and licensed notary in Trujillo, noted that the previous sale in Panama had not been officially recorded by a notary. Antonio Benteno had probably chosen to not seek to transfer the record of an informal transaction into an official sale, thus safeguarding his legal liability for the quality of María. For notaries and the transformation of truths after the fact, see Burns, Into the Archive, 100, 114.

102. For evidence of Juan Dávila's status and wealth, see his will in ARLL, Co. Ords. Leg. 211. Exp. 1614 (1700).

103. Another mina woman in her early twenties named María was sold by a man from Piura (along the same Pacific slave trade route) to a single woman in Trujillo, doña Angela de Bilela for seven hundred pesos. In contrast to the ladina María, the enslaved mina woman was still described as a "bozal recently arrived from Guinea," which accounts for her lower price. ARLL, Protocolos. Salinas. Leg. 234, #189 (1675), 252v.

104. For physical inspections and questioning slaves regarding their health before purchase, see Johnson, Soul by Soul, 141–50, 210.

105. Baptist, "'Cuffy,' 'Fancy Maids,' and 'One-Eyed Men,'" para. 39.

106. Jouve-Martín, Esclavos de la ciudad letrada, 80, 82.

107. ARLL, Ca. Cr. Leg. 81. Exp. 1417 (1680).

108. Gross, Double Character, 92.

109. ARLL, Co. Ords. Leg. 206. Exp. 1489 (1685), 31, 34.

110. Ibid., 58.

111. Karasch, Slave Life in Rio de Janeiro, 317; and Hünefeldt, Paying the Price of Freedom, 182.

112. Smallwood, Saltwater Slavery, 63.

113. Hartman, Scenes of Subjection, 62.

114. Smallwood, Saltwater Slavery, 186; and Gomez, Exchanging Our Country Marks, 120.

115. Bontemps, Punished Self, 87.

116. Penningroth, *Claims of Kinfolk*, 86, 88; and Olwig, "African Cultural Principles," 31.

117. Sweet, *Recreating Africa*, 46–47; Bennett, *Africans in Colonial Mexico*, 91–103; and Karasch, *Slave Life in Rio de Janeiro*, 293.

118. Sweet, "Mistaken Identities?" 289.

119. ARLL, Co. Ords. Leg. 195. Exp. 1291 (1656), 12v.

120. Larco Herrera, *Anales de cabildo*, cites ff. 366–366v, 37.

121. Ibid., cites ff. 162–164v, 34–35; Archivo General de las Indias (AGI), Gobierno. Audiencia de Lima. Consultas originales del Consejo, Cámara y Juntas Especiales correspondientes al distrito de la Audiencia de Lima. Leg. 6 (1634), 1.

122. It was possible that other groups arrived together in Trujillo, like three *arara* men who had been rescued from a shipwreck that included fifty captives brought from Panama who were sold together in Trujillo. See ARLL, Protocolos. Cortijo Quero. Leg. 100, #279 (1700), 254.

123. The slave trade created lasting memories among its survivors. Dominga, an enslaved woman, testified that she knew Barbola de Carcares, a resident of Lima and a vecina of Nicaragua, when she worked in the mines in Nicaragua. Archivo Arzobispal de Lima (AAL), Causas de negros. Leg. 2. Exp. 15 (1611), 1v, 3.

124. Vila Vilar, *Aspectos sociales*, 106–7.

125. Schwartz, *Sugar Plantations*, 174.

126. Sweet, *Recreating Africa*, 33; and Sweet, "Mistaken Identities?" 289.

127. Diouf, *Dreams of Africa in Alabama*, 107.

128. Dakubu, *Korle Meets the Sea*, 101.

129. Archivo Regional de Lambayeque (ARL), Causas eclesiásticas (1722).

130. In the early eighteenth century, English traders sold those called minas and chalas from the same general region on the eastern Ghanaian coast. Smallwood, *Saltwater Slavery*, 28–29; and Klein, *Atlantic Slave Trade*, 61–62, 80. ARLL, Protocolos. San Román. Leg. 230 (1730), 233, 235, 243, 245; and ARLL, Protocolos. Aguilar. Leg. 264 (1730), 251v, for multiple purchases of unbaptized black women and boys of castas mina and chala from the British *asiento* in Panama managed by the agent don Enrique Juanson.

131. Greene, *Gender, Ethnicity, and Social Change*, 28.

132. ARL, Causas eclesiasticas (1724).

133. Vaughan, "Slavery and Colonial Identity," 51.

134. Verger, *Trade Relations between the Gulf of Benin and Bahia*, 11.

135. Klein, *Atlantic Slave Trade*, 30, 70.

136. ARLL, Co. Ords. Leg. 220. Exp. 1787 (1730), 8v.

137. In rural areas skilled workers such as sugar masters and carpenters who could hire their labor out for a daily wage were more likely to register their marriages. ARLL, Protocolos. Cortez. Leg. 97, #99 "Inventario del tierras Llamipe" (1655), 134.

138. Archivo Arzobispal de Trujillo (AAT), Parroquias. Matrimonios. Ascope/Facala (1670–1740).

139. See also the four entries for marriages on January 2, 1678, in the Archivo Sagrario de Trujillo (AST). Libro de Casamientos de Mixtos (1619–1753). Likewise, James Sweet found that Africans in Rio de Janeiro generally tended to marry others from "the same broad cultural areas of Africa." Sweet, *Recreating Africa*, 46.

140. See Appendix 1, "Origin of Slaves Sold in Trujillo over Time by Percentage (1640–1730)," in this book.

141. AST, Libro de Casamientos de Mistos (1619–1753). The twenty-three matrimony records including Africans correspond to the surviving records from 1619, 1626, 1627, 1677, 1678, 1679, 1680, and 1681.

142. In 1627, Pablo de Olebares, a *moreno* married Cathalina Angola and in 1678, Pasqual Criollo (a widower) married María Conga (both had the same owner).

143. By employing the numbers from the estate inventories as a rough demographic estimate, it appears that women probably constituted 20 percent of the total rural enslaved populations. Of the estate inventories that included children, only the large estates sustained a sizable population of men and women, such as the sugar hacienda of Tulape, with about 20 percent of its total population below the age of fifteen. ARLL, Protocolos. López Collado y Daza. Leg. 373, #10 and #11 "Inventario de la hacienda Tulape" (1725), 23–32.

144. Cushner, *Lords of the Land*, 106.

145. Archivo Arzobispal de Trujillo (AAT), Parroquias. Bautismos. Ascope/Facala (1670–1740).

146. Sweet, "Mistaken Identities?" 302.

147. Archivo Parroquial de Cartavio (APC), Libro de Bautismos.

148. ARLL, Co. Ords. Leg. 200. Exp. 1378 (1672).

149. Burga, *De la encomienda*, 51, 52.

150. APC, Libro de Bautismos.

151. Mannarelli, *Private Passions*, 129, 131.

152. Bay, *Wives of the Leopard*, 19.

153. ARSI, Peruano Litterae Annuae. Vol. 16, "Letras Annuas de la Provincia de el Peru de los años de 1664, 1665, 1666," 129v, for discussion of the confraternity Arcangel San Miguel founded in Jesuit church for criollo slaves in Trujillo. ARSI, Peruana Litterae Annuae IV. Vol. 15, "Letras Annuas de Provincia del Peru de la compania de Jesus del ano de 1637 Roma," 100, for a discussion of confraternities in Lima's Jesuit church. Bowser, *African Slave in Colonial Peru*, 248.

154. Nuestra Señora del Rosario was a popular Dominican confraternity among free people of color in Trujillo. ARLL, Protocolos. Rosales Hoyos. Leg. 211, #131 (1655), 231v. For others, see Anómino, "Fragmento de una historia de Trujillo," 96.

155. ARLL, Protocolos. Paz. Leg. 202 (1637), 117v–118v.

156. Von Germeten, *Black Blood Brothers*, 188.

157. Brooks, *Euroafricans in Western Africa*, 73; and Rodney, "Portuguese Attempts at Monopoly," 312.

158. ARLL, Ca. Cr. Leg. 84. Exp. 1496 (1737), 2v.

159. De la Fuente, "Slaves and the Creation of Legal Rights," 675.

160. Dakubu, *Korle Meets the Sea*, 101.

161. ARLL, Ca. Cr. Leg. 84. Exp. 1496 (1737), 2.

162. Tardieu, *Los negros y la iglesia en el Perú*, tomo 1, 222, 226.

163. Graubart, *With Our Labor and Sweat*, 139, 147.

164. Tomich, "Une petite guinée," 81.

165. Macera, *Instrucciones para el manejo*, 48; and McKee, "Food Supply and Plantation Social Order," 234.

166. ARLL, Ca. Cr. Leg. 83. Exp. 1477 (1717), 45v.

167. Moreno Fraginals, *El ingenio*, 290.

168. Bay, *Wives of the Leopard*, 13.

169. Snelgrave, *New Account of Some Parts of Guinea*, 6, 31, 44; and Law, "'My Head Belongs to the King,'" 405.

170. Law, *Kingdom of Allada*, 41.

171. Hartman, *Scenes of Subjection*, 61; and Kopytoff, "Development of Jamaican Maroon Ethnicity," 35, 36.

172. Lohmann Villena, *El corregidor de indios*, 357, 359.

173. ARLL, Co. Cr. Leg. 248. Exp. 2662 (1686).

174. ARLL, Ca. Cr. Leg. 83. Exp. 1478 (1718), 72v.

175. For an initial discussion of the concept of double consciousness, see Du Bois, *Souls*, 5.

176. *Recopilación de leyes de los reynos de las Indias*, Libro Octavo. Titulo Diez y Ocho. De los derechos de esclavos.

177. In 1527, 1538, and 1541, the crown ordered that black men should marry only black women, followed by a 1563 mandate for Spanish fathers to purchase their mulato sons and free them. *Recopilación de leyes de los reynos de las Indias*, Libro VII. Título V. Ley V and Ley VI, 321; *Instrucción para remediar*, 1628.

178. *Constitvciones synodales del arçobispado de Los Reyes en el Pirv*, Libro IV, 79. In the early seventeenth century, Solórzano Pereira repeated a royal order that even if certain allowances were granted for enslaved men and women with different owners, spouses were still slaves. Solórzano Pereira, *Política Indiana*, 450; and Bennett, *Africans in Colonial Mexico*, 35;

179. Sweet, "Iberian Roots," 154; and Martínez, "Black Blood of New Spain," 1–29.

180. For more on the vibrant discussion of legal consciousness, legal agency, and legal claims-making among enslaved and freed people of African descent, see de la Fuente, "Slave Law and Claims-Making in Cuba," para. 7; de la Fuente, "Slaves and the Creation of Legal Rights," 672; Bennett, *Colonial Blackness*, 3; Bryant, "Enslaved Rebels, Fugitives, and Litigants," 11, 25; McKinley, "Fractional Freedoms," 751; and Soulodre-La France, "Los Esclavos de su Majestad," 190.

3. Acting as a Legal Indian: Natural Vassals and Worrisome Natives

1. Stern, *Peru's Indian Peoples*, 119; Larson, *Cochabamba, 1550–1900*, 129; and Spalding, *Huarochirí*, 205.

2. Solórzano Pereira, *Política Indiana*, 163, 417, 423.

3. Netherly, "Management of Late Andean Irrigation Systems," 231, 233, 239.

4. Ramírez, *World Upside Down*, 18, 21.

5. Gama, "Visita hecha en el valle de Jayanca," 217; Noack, "Relaciones políticas y la negación," 253, 257; Graubart, *With Our Labor and Sweat*, 168, 180; and Ramírez, *World Upside Down*, 34–35.

6. Lizárraga, *Descripción breve del Peru*, 77; and Angulo, "Diario de la segunda visita pastoral que hizo de su Arquidiocesis el Ilustrisimo Señor don Toribio Alfonso de Mogrovejo," 229, 232, 233, 235.

7. Zárate, *Discouerie and Conquest*, 4.

8. Bakewell, *Miners of the Red Mountain*, 162–63; and Saignes, "Colonial Condition," 63–64.

9. Stoler, *Along the Archival Grain*, 47, 53. For more on how identity is created, or made real, through repetitive actions that constitute performance, see Butler, *Gender Trouble*, 136, 140, 145. For an illuminating discussion of how colonial courts served as stages for indigenous political and legal performances, see Yannakakis, *Art of Being In-between*, 40, 47, 109.

10. Benton, *Law and Colonial Cultures*, 3, 17, 255, 258. As other scholars have demonstrated, Andeans also articulated identities and practices further removed from colonial institutions. Mills, *Idolatry and Its Enemies*, 111–36.

11. Wightman, *Indigenous Migration and Social Change*, 39, 84; and Spalding, *Huarochirí*, 182.

12. Ramírez, *Provincial Patriarchs*, 154.

13. Stern, *Peru's Indian Peoples*, 161; and Spalding, *Huarochirí*, 229.

14. Zulawski, *They Eat from Their Labor*, 173; and Powers, *Andean Journeys*, 38, 46–47.

15. Wightman, *Indigenous Migration and Social Change*, 19, 22, 27, 31.

16. Ramírez, *Provincial Patriarchs*, 45, 76.

17. For landholder demands, see Archivo General de la Nación (AGN), Derecho Indígena. Cuad. 69 (1621), f. 1; Archivo Regional de La Libertad (ARLL), Co. Asuntos de Gobierno. Leg. 266. Exp. 3069 (1604); Larco Herrera, *Anales de cabildo*, cites ff. 143–47, 13–14; Larco Herrera, *Anales de cabildo*, cites ff. 90v–91, 21; and Larco Herrera, *Anales de cabildo*, cites ff. 152–53v, 30–31. For indigenous complaints, see ARLL, Co. Asuntos de Gobierno. Leg. 266. Exp. 3072 (1606); and ARL, Protocolos. Martínez. Leg. 172 (1610), 801v.

18. Cutter, *Protector de Indios*, 6–7. Protectors were usually quite prominent in the criminal and civil cases because they filed petitions, submitted cross-examinations, and called witnesses to testify. Kellogg, *Law and the Transformation*, 40.

19. Stern, *Peru's Indian Peoples*, 98; Patch, *Maya and Spaniard in Yucatan*, 105; Farriss, *Maya Society under Colonial Rule*, 191; and AGI, Leg. 6. Lima (1640), 1.

20. Stavig, *World of Túpac Amaru*, 107; Burns, *Into the Archive*, 50–51, 130–31; and Saignes, "Colonial Condition," 74. The scholar Karen Powers has described seventeenth-century caciques as "intruders" who were "intricately woven into the local power structure and whose interests were more aligned with those of their

Spanish cohorts than with those of the communities they ruled." See Powers, *Andean Journeys*, 151. These same characteristics could also be understood as the successful adaptation of indigenous leadership to Spanish colonialism. For instance, the historian Joanne Rappaport has explained how colonial caciques became critical interpreters of indigenous pasts to Spanish colonizers. See Rappaport, *Politics of Memory*, 60.

21. Ramírez, *World Upside Down*, 80, 84–85.

22. ARLL, Protocolos. Paz. Leg. 202 (1639), 562–63.

23. Ibid., 562v.

24. Toledo, *Ordenanzas de Don Francisco de Toledo*, 379–80; and ARLL, Protocolos. Paz. Leg. 202 (1639), 562v.

25. AGI, Leg. 51. Lib. 4. No. 22 (1642), 223. This colonial adaptation of an Incan institution was also protected by other royal and colonial officials who relied on chasquis to safely and efficiently transport sealed documents, royal orders, and judicial correspondence among officials and courts throughout the viceroyalty.

26. For example, Pasqual de Mora, an enslaved *mulato*, carried letters for his owner from Lima to Trujillo. ARLL, Co. Cr. Leg. 241. Exp. 2342 (1622), 4v.

27. Yannakakis, *Art of Being In-between*, 40.

28. Aldana, *Empresas coloniales*, 55. Travelers to Piura often stopped in Mórrope for water and to contract with indigenous local guides, both necessary for crossing the desert at night. Gómez Cumpa, "Mórrope," 330. Dry and desolate, a stranger could lose his or her way in the desert and certainly never find water.

29. According to their witness, a lieutenant of the postal service in Saña, the Mórrope couriers had "brought him lawsuit documents on many occasions." AGN, Derecho Indígena. Cuad. 102 (1639).

30. ARLL, Co. Ords. Leg. 179. Exp. 890 (1630), 1.

31. Lewis, *Hall of Mirrors*, 19, 105.

32. ARLL, Co. Ords. Leg. 179. Exp. 890 (1630), 2v.

33. Solórzano Pereira, *Política Indiana*, 225, 226.

34. *Recopilación de leyes de los reynos de las Indias*, Libro VII. Titulo III. Ley XX, 230; and Benton, *Law and Colonial Cultures*, 3.

35. Instead, judicial representatives and colonial judges acted based on a continually shifting compilation of royal decrees, religious doctrine, regional practices, and local customs when asserting their cases or decisions. Herzog, *Upholding Justice*, 19–20; and Kellogg, *Law and the Transformation*, 10.

36. Herzog, *Upholding Justice*, 156.

37. Toledo, *Disposiciones gubernativas*, 32.

38. ARLL, Co. Ords. Leg. 179. Exp. 890 (1630), 2v.

39. Ibid., 1.

40. Solórzano Pereira, *Política Indiana*, 225.

41. ARLL, Co. Cr. Leg. 246. Exp. 2568 (1653), 4; and ARLL, Co. Ords. Leg. 198. Exp. 1350 (1669), 21.

42. Herzog, *Upholding Justice*, 155–56.

43. Kellogg, *Law and the Transformation*, 67.

44. AGI, Lima. Leg. 7 (1647), 2v; and AGI, Lima. Leg. 7 (1646), 2v.

45. ARLL, Co. Ords. Leg. 179. Exp. 890 (1630), 1, 2.

46. For conflicts regarding controlling cattle, see ARLL, Co. Cr. Leg. 237. Exp. 2180 (1580), 1, 2, 3; and ARLL, Ca. Cr. Leg. 77. Exp. 1258 (1580), 6. For the effects of cattle on indigenous agriculture, see Melville, *Plague of Sheep*, 121.

47. The Paypaymamo brothers appear to be renting out lands that belong to reducción members. Their father may have been renting these lands to pay the tribute of absent members in a strategy that was common for indigenous leaders throughout the seventeenth-century Andes. Powers, *Andean Journeys*, 124–31; Stern, *Peru's Indian Peoples*, 162; Ramírez, *World Upside Down*, 69, 85; and Saignes, "Indian Migration and Social Change," 173.

48. Burns, *Into the Archive*, 13.

49. ARLL, Protocolos. Escobar. Leg. 143 (1640), 240–241v.

50. Ibid., 241.

51. Stern, *Peru's Indian Peoples*, 120.

52. It is also plausible that they understood that only by behaving according to colonial standards ascribed to Indians could they address the colonial dilemma of generating necessary funds or resources. The Paypaymamo brothers, like other indigenous men and women, may have been acting within a cultural paradigm "that only a Spanish cure could counter Spanish abuse." See Lewis, *Hall of Mirrors*, 92.

53. ARLL, Protocolos. Escobar. Leg. 143 (1640), 241.

54. ARLL, Co. Asuntos de Gobierno. Leg. 266. Exp. 3074 (1607), 14, 14v; and Archivo Regional de Lambayeque (ARL), Arriola, Juan. Causas civiles. Leg. 1 "Inventario de trapiche" (1642), 2v.

55. ARLL, Ca. Cr. Leg. 78. Exp. 1284 (1609), 13.

56. Landers, "Cimarrón Ethnicity and Cultural Adaptation," 45; and McKnight, "Confronted Rituals," paras. 2, 38, 41.

57. *Recopilación de leyes de los reynos de las Indias*, Libro VI, Título X, Ley XVIII, 272; and Solórzano Pereira, *Política Indiana*, Libro II, Capítulo IV, 155.

58. Don Andrés Pay Pay Chumbi, an indigenous leader of the reducción of Magdalena de Cao in the Chicama valley, accused Joan de Grados Calderón, a fugitive *mulato* man, of stealing his wife and assaulting other indigenous women. ARLL, Co. Cr. Leg. 241. Exp. 2329 (1621), 12v, 14v; and O'Toole, "'In a War against the Spanish,'" 48–49.

59. For use of legal discourse as rhetorical tools, see Yannakakis, *Art of Being In-between*, 107.

60. ARLL, Co. Cr. Leg. 242. Exp. 2375 (1625), 1v.

61. Lewis, *Hall of Mirrors*, 69.

62. ARLL, Co. Cr. Leg. 242. Exp. 2375 (1625), 2v.

63. Ibid., 3.

64. Ibid., 4, 4v.

65. ARLL, Co. Cr. Leg. 241. Exp. 2304 (1617), 2, 4. While casual drinking was

common on the northern coast, the *borrachera* gathering had ritualized aspects that included order of drinking and perhaps arranged seating. See Harvey, "Genero, comunidad y confrontación," 120.

66. This dispute lasted into the 1660s. See ARLL, Co. Ords. Leg. 198. Exp. 1350 (1669).

67. Randall, "Los dos vasos," 75.

68. ARLL, Co. Cr. Leg. 241. Exp. 2304 (1617), 2v.

69. ARLL, Co. Cr. Leg. 243. Exp. 2401 (1626), 1v.

70. ARLL, Protocolos. Mata. Leg. 21, #143 (1590), 274v, 275v, 277v, 278; Burga, *De la encomienda*, 43; and Gómez Cumpa, "Mórrope," 325.

71. Ramírez, *World Upside Down*, 37.

72. ARLL, Co. Cr. Leg. 243. Exp. 2401 (1626), 2.

73. Yannakakis, *Art of Being In-between*, 37; and Burns, *Into the Archive*, 130–31.

74. Toribio Polo, *Memorias de los Virreys del Perú Marqués de Mancera y Conde de Salvatierra*, 7.

75. Ortiz de Cervantes, *Memorial que presenta*, 11v, 12v, 13v.

76. Torres, "Al Conde de Lemos y Andrade," 447–48; and Solórzano Pereira, *Política Indiana*, 180.

77. A cleric could have assisted Mache. Religious personnel objected to the exploitation of indigenous communities that often caused their parishioners to flee their communities. Without members, clerics were unable to provide religious services and collect their fees—a clear threat to the livelihoods of parish priests and mendicant friars. Powers, "Battle for Bodies and Souls," 32; and Marsilli, "Missing Idolatry," 399–421. It is also possible that a prosperous cacique such as don Diego Mache was capable of appropriating clerical language. See St. George, "Introduction," 25–26.

78. Before 1630 the cacique had purchased lands whose rents would fund the office of the protector. In doing so, Mache followed a crown directive that ordered noble Indians to pay the salary of their community's protector. ARLL, Protocolos. Paz. Leg. 199 (1630), 200v; and *Recopilación de leyes de los reynos de las Indias*, Libro VI. Título VI. Ley XI (1596), 250.

79. Zevallos Quiñones, *Los cacicazgos de Trujillo*, 49–50, 94.

80. ARLL, Protocolos. Paz. Leg. 199 (1630), 200v.

81. ARLL, Co. Cr. Leg. 243. Exp. 2401 (1626), 2. Again, the author (or authors) draws from clerical writings such as the memorial by Diego de Torres, who declared that Indians working in the Potosí mines did not benefit from "the fruit of their sweat which is the silver." Torres, "Al Conde de Lemos y Andrade," 453. The Jesuit's concern with Indian poverty was also reflected in ecclesiastical mandates to protect the "poor" Indians, who, as rustic and miserable people, required paternal love until they acquired more rational capacities. Solórzano Pereira, *Política Indiana*, 423, quoting the Concilio Limense. On the northern coast clerics called for an extension of parochial oversight to alleviate the "poor Indians" from the magistrate's demands. AGI, Lima. Leg. 101 (1656), 1. These clerics called for relief of indigenous suffering. In contrast, the author of the unsigned 1626 document employed clerical

concerns to bolster the claim of indigenous laborers to just compensation and timely payment as repeatedly ordered by Peruvian viceroys. Oñate, *Parecer de vn hombre docto*, 369v; and AGI, Lima. Leg. 59 (1660) [1601], 1v.

82. Stern, *Peru's Indian Peoples*, 162.

83. Sánchez Bella, *Derecho Indiano*, 72; and Herzog, *La administración como un fenómeno social*, 209–10. For examples of public announcements of municipal rulings in Trujillo, see ARLL, Protocolos. Morales. Leg. 181 (1610), 13; and ARLL, Actas del cabildo. Vol. 11 (1682), 250v–253.

84. Alaperrine-Bouyer, *La educación de las elites indígenas*, 31. For an example of a Trujillo notary present in a rural village, see ARLL, Co. Compulsas. Leg. 261. Exp. 2975 (1714).

85. Durston, *Pastoral Quechua*, 141.

86. Bhabha, *Location of Culture*, 86, 87, 90.

87. Kamen, *Spain's Road to Empire*, 410.

88. Ramírez, *Provincial Patriarchs*, 148.

89. Burga, *De la encomienda*, 100.

90. Ramírez, *Provincial Patriarchs*, 147.

91. Ibid., 148, 153.

92. Stern, *Peru's Indian Peoples*, 120.

93. ARLL, Hacienda. Compulsas. Leg. 131. Exp. 161 (1688) for the sixteenth-century counts of the Chicama valley reducciones.

94. ARLL, Co. Pedimientos. Leg. 284. Exp. 4037 (1643), 1v.

95. Stern, *Peru's Indian Peoples*, 135.

96. ARLL, Co. Ords. Leg. 191. Exp. 1184 (1643), 1.

97. Powers, *Andean Journeys*, 51.

98. Ibid., 149.

99. Stern, *Peru's Indian Peoples*, 175.

100. ARLL, Protocolos. Viera Gutiérrez. Leg. 2 (1650), 204; and ARLL, Protocolos. Viera Gutiérrez. Leg. 257 (1650), #153.

101. ARLL, Co. Cr. Leg. 246. Exp. 2541 (1643), 5.

102. Toledo, *Ordenanzas de Don Francisco de Toledo*, 344.

103. Powers, *Andean Journeys*, 86; and Wightman, *Indigenous Migration and Social Change*, 24.

104. After colonial officials reduced Ulchop to Magdalena de Cao in the sixteenth century, its members continued to govern themselves as a distinct parcialidad with separate water rights, land allocations, and tribute rolls. ARLL, Co. Juez Pesquisidor. Leg. 273. Exp. 3397 (1616); ARLL, Co. Cr. Leg. 243. Exp. 2401 (1626); ARLL, Co. Ords. Leg. 191. Exp. 1184 (1643), 3; ARLL, Ca. Asuntos de Gobierno. Leg. 105. Exp. 1808 (1644); and ARLL, Co. Ords. Leg. 196. Exp. 1312 (1661), 6.

105. Toledo, *Ordenanzas de Don Francisco de Toledo*, 350.

106. ARLL, Co. Ords. Leg. 192. Exp. 1230 (1647), 3.

107. Graubart, *With Our Labor and Sweat*, 40.

108. AGI, Lima. Leg. 100 (1648), 2; and AGI, Escribania. Leg. 511A (1648), 11.

109. Ramírez, *Provincial Patriarchs*, 151; and AGI, Leg. 167 (1648), 4.

110. ARLL, Co. Ords. Leg. 198. Exp. 1350 (1669), 15, 17v, 19.

111. AGI, Lima Leg. 101 (1654), 1; AGI. Lima. Leg. 100 (1649), doc. 2, 30v–31, 32, 33v; and AGI, Escribanía. Leg. 511A (1648), 38.

112. ARLL, Co. Ords. Leg. 198. Exp. 1350 (1669), 12; ARLL, Protocolos. Viera Gutiérrez, Leg. 253, (1644), 12v; ARLL, Protocolos. Espino y Alvarado. Leg. 149, (1684), 176v; ARLL, Protocolos. Paz. Leg. 205 (1645), 191v; and ARLL, Protocolos. Rosales Hoyos. Leg. 211, (1652), 580–580v.

113. AGI, Lima. Leg. 237. No. 14 (1645), 36v; AGN, Campesinado. Títulos de propiedad. Leg. 34. Exp. 649 (1644), 26v; ARLL, Co. Eclesiasticas Leg. 253. Exp. 2843 (1756), 18; and Zulawski, *They Eat from Their Labor*, 135.

114. Glave Testino, *Trajinantes*, 193; and Powers, *Andean Journeys*, 45, 54.

115. Larson, *Cochabamba, 1550–1900*, 96; and Powers, *Andean Journeys*, 51.

116. Wightman, *Indigenous Migration and Social Change*, 29.

117. AGI, Lima. Leg. 167 (1650), 2v.

118. AGI, Lima. Leg. 167 (1648), 1.

119. Ibid.

120. As suggested by Spanish jurists, an Aristoliean hierarchy designated the Spanish as rulers and Indians with their "more robust or vigorous bodies for work and a lesser understanding or capacity." See Solórzano Pereira, *Política Indiana*, 172.

121. Silva, *Advertencias importantes*, 43v.

122. Oñate, *Parecer de vn hombre docto*, 3v.

123. AGI, Lima. Leg. 100. No. 2. (1649), 29, 31v.

124. Ramírez, *World Upside Down*, 58, 85.

125. AGI, Lima. Leg. 167 (1648).

126. Ibid., 1v.

127. Herzog, *Upholding Justice*, 155–56.

128. AGI, Lima. Leg. 7 (147), 1.

129. *Recopilación de leyes de los reynos de las Indias*, 272; and de la Puente Luna, *Los Curacas hechiceros de Jauja*, 206.

130. Many people, indigenous and Spanish, traveled between the Americas and the Iberian peninsula without permission as indicated by the repeated orders from the crown for passengers to secure licenses to travel. Encinas, *Cedulario Indiano*, 239, 396–97.

131. AGI, Lima. Leg. 7 (1647); and AGI, Lima. Leg. 167 (1648), 1v.

132. Toribio Polo, "Relación del estado del govierno del Peru, que haze el Marqués de Mancera al señor Virrey Conde de Salvatierra," in *Memorias de los Virreys*, 26; and AGI, Lima. Leg. 7 (1647), 1.

133. Toribio Polo, "Relación del estado del govierno del Peru, que haze el Marqués de Mancera al señor Virrey Conde de Salvatierra," in *Memorias de los Virreys*, 1, 7; and AGI, Lima. Leg. 52. No. 27A (1640), 10v.

134. Moreno Cebrián, *El corregidor de indios*, 18.

135. AGI, Lima. Leg. 7 (1647), 1; and Ramírez, *World Upside Down*, 108.

136. Zevallos Quiñones, *Los cacicazgos de Trujillo*, 71; and Saignes, *Caciques, Tribute, and Migration in the Southern Andes*, 23.

137. AGI, Lima. Leg. 167 (1648), 2.

138. Spanish colonial officials assigned their indigenous allies as reducción leaders often against the wishes of local communities. Garrett, *Shadows of Empire*, 127, 153; and Ramírez, *World Upside Down*, 33–34.

139. AGI, Gobierno. Audiencia de Lima. Consultas originales del Consejo, Cámara y Juntas Especiales correspondientes al distrito de la Audiencia de Lima. 1643–1650. Leg. 7 (1646), 2v.

140. Ibid.

141. ARL, Co. Eclesiasticas. Leg. 253. Exp. 2843 (1756), 14v.

142. Silverblatt, "Political Memories and Colonizing Symbols," 187.

143. Glave Testino, *Trajinantes*, 194.

144. AGI, Lima 100 (1648), 36.

145. Garrett, *Shadows of Empire*, 167; and AGI, Escribanía. Leg. 511A (1648), 44.

146. ARLL, Co. Cr. Leg. 245. Exp. 2518 (1641), 1v, 15.

147. Ibid., 1v, 15.

148. O'Toole, "Don Carlos Chimo del Perú," 36–37.

149. AGI, Lima. Leg. 167 (1648), 9.

150. Saignes, "Indian Migration and Social Change in Seventeenth-Century Charcas," 192; and Powers, *Andean Journeys*, 169–70.

151. Powers, *Andean Journeys*, 100.

152. Cañeque, *King's Living Image*, 13.

153. Rabasa, *Writing Violence on the Northern Frontier*, 6, 20, 24.

154. For a discussion of colonialism's fractured project, see Thomas, *Colonialism's Culture*, 51.

4. Market Exchanges and Meeting the Indians Elsewhere

1. Archivo Regional de La Libertad (ARLL), Ca. Cr. Leg. 79. Exp. 1350 (1641), 23.

2. ARLL, Ca. Cr. Leg. 79. Exp. 1353 (1642), 23.

3. ARLL, Ca. Cr. Leg. 79. Exp. 1350 (1641), 8.

4. For common stereotypes of Africans and their descendants, see Lewis, *Hall of Mirrors*, 73.

5. ARLL, Ca. Cr. Leg. 79. Exp. 1351 (1641), 2.

6. Deloria, *Indians in Unexpected Places*.

7. Ibid., 4–5.

8. Powers, *Andean Journeys*, 46, 51; Wightman, *Indigenous Migration and Social Change*, 48, 126; and Zulawski, *They Eat from Their Labor*, 78, 176.

9. Deloria, *Indians in Unexpected Places*, 5.

10. Cook, *Demographic Collapse*, 133; Burga, *De la encomienda*, 120; and Ramírez, *World Upside Down*, 26–28.

11. Burga, *De la encomienda*, 120.

12. In certain regions of the Audiencia of Quito, between 50 and 80 percent of the populations from indigenous reducciones migrated to labor and market opportunities of cities and estates during this period. Powers, *Andean Journeys*, 50–51. By 1690 almost half of the indigenous population of the Cuzco bishopric was identified as forastero (migrant). Wightman, *Indigenous Migration and Social Change*, 6.

13. Wightman, *Indigenous Migration and Social Change*, 35; and Powers, *Andean Journeys*, 40.

14. Wightman, *Indigenous Migration and Social Change*, 43, 74; and Powers, *Andean Journeys*, 38, 54, 173.

15. Saignes, "Indian Migration and Social Change," 190; and Zulawski, *They Eat from Their Labor*, 84, 198, 202–5.

16. Zulawski, *They Eat from Their Labor*, 126–27, 139–40, 170, 203.

17. Saignes, *Caciques, Tribute, and Migration*, 15.

18. Ibid., 15, 25.

19. Larson, *Cochabamba, 1550–1900*, 95; and Wightman, *Indigenous Migration and Social Change*, 148.

20. Ramírez, *Provincial Patriarchs*, 148.

21. Archivo General de Indias (AGI), Lima. Leg. 54. Num. 10. No. 46 (1650), 74; AGI, Indiferente. Leg. 2796 (1647), 1v. Contraband trade probably continued as Trujillo's slaveholders continued to purchase captive West Central Africans from Panamanian merchants. See Appendix 1, "Origin of Slaves Sold in Trujillo over Time by Percentage (1640–1730)," in this book. For Trujillo slave sales of West Central Africans from Panama, see ARLL, Protocolos. Escobar. Leg. 146 (1645), 718; ARLL, Protocolos. Escobar. Leg. 146 (1645), 808; and ARLL, Protocolos. Escobar. Leg. 146 (1645), 814v. Vila Vilar, *Aspectos sociales*, 125; and Emmer, "Dutch and the Making of the Second Atlantic System," 73.

22. In 1662 the Spanish crown granted the asiento to two Genoese merchants who contracted the English Royal African Company and the Dutch West Indies Company to supply Spanish America with African slaves. Postma, *Dutch in the Atlantic Slave Trade*, 33. During the mid-seventeenth century the Dutch secured the Caribbean island of Curaçao and increased the numbers of slaves traded into Portobelo and Cartagena. AGI, Contaduría. Leg. 263 (1668), 2v; and AGI, Contaduría. Leg. 263 (1669), 3. Contraband trade continued throughout the 1660s as Portuguese, Dutch, and English slave traders sold Africans and criollos along the Caribbean borders of Spanish America. Vila Vilar, *Aspectos sociales*, 125; and Emmer, "Dutch and the Making of the Second Atlantic System," 73. The English, in particular, offered stiff competition. During the 1660s, English ships transported captives from Jamaica and Barbados to Portobelo, where the slave trading company maintained its agents. AGI, Contaduría. Leg. 263. No. 42 (1667), 1, 4, 5, 5v; and AGI, Contaduría. Leg. 236. No. 40 (1665), 1. For the rise in slave prices, see Appendix 2, "Price Trends of Slaves Sold in Trujillo (1640–1730)," in this book.

23. See Appendix 2, "Price Trends of Slaves Sold in Trujillo (1640–1730)," in this book.

24. Trujillo's buyers noted only whether captives were healthy and able-bodied even though the origins of Africans sold to the region shifted in this period. ARLL, Protocolos. Álvarez. Leg. 90 (1675), 306v; and ARLL, Ca. Ords. Leg. 23. Exp. 487 (1670), 1. At first the Dutch supplied slaves from Luanda, but gradually captives from the Gold Coast and the Bight of Benin (also traded by the English) were sold into Spanish America. Israel, *Dutch Republic*, 934; Emmer, "Dutch and the Making of the Second Atlantic System," 83; and Law, *Kingdom of Allada*, 88.

25. Burga, *De la encomienda*, 114; and Cushner, *Lords of the Land*, 82–83.

26. ARLL, Protocolos. Moto. Leg. 182 (1650), 405v; ARLL, Protocolos. Moto. Leg. 182 (1650), 108; ARLL, Protocolos. Viera Gutiérrez. Leg. 258 (1655), 205; and ARLL, Protocolos. Viera Gutiérrez. Leg. 258 (1655), 655.

27. In 1630 there were no contracts recorded. In 1620 two children were contracted but not in exchange for cash. In 1610 the contracts were mostly for indigenous women to serve as domestics in the city. In 1610 an indigenous man from Chachapoyas was contracted for five pesos and clothing. ADLL, Protocolos. Morales. Leg. 181 (1610), 303. In 1610 an indigenous man from Conchucos was contracted for ten pesos and clothing. ADLL, Protocolos. Morales. Leg. 181 (1610), 311. In 1610 an indigenous man from Popayán was contracted for twenty pesos and clothing. ADLL, Protocolos, Morales. Leg. 181 (1610), 245.

28. Polo y La Borde, "La Hacienda Pachachaca," 235, 237.

29. Biblioteca Nacional del Perú (BNP), #B357 (1668), 99, 173–173v.

30. ARLL, Protocolos. Moto. Leg. 182 (1650), 490; ARLL, Protocolos. Moto. Leg. 182 (1650), 238; ARLL, Protocolos. Viera Gutiérrez. Leg. 258 (1655), 520; and ARLL, Protocolos. Viera Gutiérrez. Leg. 258 (1655), 732.

31. Ocaña, *Un viaje fascinante*, 29; AGI, Lima. Leg. 168 (1651), 2v; and AGI, Panama. Leg. 21. Ramo 7. No. 40 (1653), 1. These high profits were magnified by a temporary agricultural sterility in Panama as well as poor wheat harvests in the Chicama valley resulting from a plague of locusts. AGI, Lima. Leg. 168 (1651), 1; ARLL, Co. Ords. Leg. 193. Exp. 1255 (1652); and Larco Herrera, *Anales de cabildo*, cites ff. 267–268 (1651), 53. ARLL, Actas del cabildo. Vol. 8 (1661), 251v–252; and ARLL, Actas del cabildo. Vol. 10 (1672), 9.

32. ARLL, Protocolos. García Sancho. Leg. 166 (1660), 551v. For coastal trade from Trujillo, see ARLL, Actas del cabildo. Vol. 8 (1660), 201v–202; ARLL, Actas del cabildo. Vol. 8 (1662), 258–258v; and ARLL, Actas del cabildo. Vol. 9 (1668), 272; Ramírez, *Provincial Patriarchs*, 174; and ARLL, Protocolos. Verde. Leg. 250 (1670), 118v, 119, 119v.

33. Ramírez, *Provincial Patriarchs*, 101, 116.

34. Ibid., 172–73.

35. ARLL, Co. Ords. Leg. 193. Exp. 1243 (1642), 201v; ARLL, Co. Ords. Leg. 196. Exp. 1307 (1660), 4; ARLL, Protocolos. Pacheco de Guevara. Leg. 197 (1663), 38v; ARLL, Ca. Ords. Leg. 22. Exp. 481 (1669), 25v; ARLL, Protocolos. Verde. Leg. 250 (1670), 162v; ARLL, Ca. Ords. Leg. 23. Exp. 493 (1671), 5; ARLL, Protocolos.

Salinas. Leg. 234 (1675), 498, 499v; and ARLL, Protocolos. Salinas. Leg. 235 (1677), 239, 243v.

36. Noack, "El cacicazgo de Huamán," 361. In addition, their cacique, don Manuel Fernandez Asmat, claimed to be "inga segunda persona," or an Inca and leader of the secondary community within Guamán. See ARLL, Co. Ords. Leg. 202. Exp. 1407 (1677), 8.

37. ARLL, Co. Asuntos de Gobierno. Leg. 268. Exp. 3159 (1659), 1.

38. Spalding, Huarochirí, 38, 84; and Wightman, Indigenous Migration and Social Change, 86. Sixteenth-century colonial officials such as Cuenca and subsequent representatives of the Spanish state had fixed coastal pre-Hispanic differences between agriculturalists and fishing people into reducción assignments as well as the contents of tribute requirements. Noack, "El cacicazgo de Huamán," 348.

39. Larco Herrera, Anales de cabildo, cites ff. 200v–202 (1602), 29–30.

40. Cushner, Lords of the Land, 52; and Ramírez, Provincial Patriarchs, 144–45.

41. AGI, Lima. Leg. 170. Petición 6 dic 1664 (1666), 2; and Cushner, Lords of the Land, 52.

42. Owners and renters recorded where farms and estates had rights to water such as the San Cristóbal hacienda and mill that was sold with intakes from the Popan canal. Archivo General de la Nación (AGN), Juzgado de aguas. Cuad. No. 3.3.3.1 (1666). The owners of San Francisco of Chicama included the names of the canals that were part of the estate in its inventory. ARLL, Protocolos. García. Leg. 166 (1661), 618v. Landholders carefully measured allocations such as a Chicama valley landholder who donated two-thirds of the water from the Colonique canals to another estate owner. ARLL, Protocolos. Ortiz. Leg. 194 (1670), 194.

43. Netherly, "Management of Late Andean Irrigation Systems," 243; and Lipsett-Rivera, To Defend Our Water, 35.

44. Ramírez, World Upside Down, 21; Netherly, "Management of Late Andean Irrigation Systems," 244; and Spalding, Huarochirí, 22.

45. ARLL, Co. Ords. Leg. 194. Exp. 1284 (1655), 4.

46. Lipsett-Rivera, To Defend Our Water, 122; and Ramírez, Provincial Patriarchs, 197–98.

47. For yanaconas lacking motivation to clean an irrigation canal, see ARLL, Co. Cr. Leg. 238. Exp. 2220 (1609), 9–9v. For an example of the Indians refusing to clean or work on irrigation systems because the labor would only benefit Spanish landholders, see Castañeda Murga, La epidemia general de agua, 27–28. To fulfill their obligations, Spanish landholders sent slaves or hired day laborers. Ramírez, Provincial Patriarchs, 213. In addition, as Sonya Lipsett-Rivera has pointed out, Spanish and creoles avoided manual labor as a sign of dishonorable or lower status but also because cleaning the irrigation ditches meant following the directions of indigenous people who were considered "social inferiors." See Lipsett-Rivera, To Defend Our Water, 122.

48. ARLL, Co. Ords. Leg. 202. Exp. 1401 (1676), 2. Rains usually fell on the

northern coast in February and March. See Aldana, *Empresas coloniales*, 55; BNP, #B1133 (1684), 1; and ARLL, Ca. Cr. Leg. 83. Exp. 1484 (1725), 9.

49. BNP, #B1737 (1669), 4v, 5.

50. ARLL, Co. Ords. Leg. 194. Exp. 1283 (1655).

51. ARLL, Cabildo. Alcalde de aguas. Leg. 111. Exp. 2087 (1681), 12.

52. ARLL, Ca. Alcalde de aguas. Leg. 111. Exp. 2087 (1681), 3. This mandate was affirmed in 1699 by another inspection of the water allocation. See BNP, #B760 (1699), 96.

53. ARLL, Ca. Ords. Leg. 28. Exp. 578 (1694), 1.

54. Powers, *Andean Journeys*, 149. As discussed in chapter 3, caciques were charged with a biannual collection, in goods and in pesos, of the amount that their community owed to crown coffers. Moreno Cebrián, *El corregidor de indios*, 238. In addition, indigenous people continued to perish from repeated epidemics that spread throughout the valleys and the highlands. Larco Herrera, *Anales de cabildo*, (1646) cites ff. 151–152, 30; ARLL, Actas del cabildo. Vol. 8 (1659), 181v–182; and ARLL, Actas del cabildo. Vol. 8 (1663), 295–295v.

55. ARLL, Protocolos. Viera Gutiérrez. Leg. 2 (1650), 204; ARLL, Protocolos. Viera Gutiérrez. Leg. 257 (1650), #153; and ARLL, Co. Ords. Leg. 194. Exp. 1278 (1654), 1, 2.

56. ARLL, Protocolos. Álvarez. Leg. 87 (1670), 50; and ARLL, Protocolos. Álvarez. Leg. 87 (1670), 50.

57. AGI, Escribanía. Leg. 534A. No. 1 (1672), 515. The Spanish created the office of *gobernador* with similar duties to a cacique. Though expected to be independent of the position of cacique, Andeans usually treated the office as inherited and filled by noble families. See Charney, *Indian Society in the Valley of Lima*, 94.

58. ARLL, Protocolos. Espino. Leg. 151 (1690), 170; and ARLL, Protocolos. Cortijo Quero. Leg. 110 (1700), 515v.

59. ARLL, Co. Ords. Leg. 202. Exp. 1397 (1675), 1.

60. ARLL, Co. Ords. Leg. 202. Exp. 1412 (1678), 2.

61. Powers, *Andean Journeys*, 5.

62. Saignes, "Colonial Condition," 88.

63. AGI, Lima. Leg. 58. No. 2. Num. 90 (1656); and Burga, *De la encomienda*, 125.

64. AGI, Escribanía. Leg. 511A (1648), 26, 30v. It also appears that the cacique of Virú had purchased lands during the same *composición de tierras*. AGI, Lima. Leg. 101 (1654). For the definition of a *fanega*, see Ramírez, *Provincial Patriarchs*, 279.

65. ARLL, Protocolos. Paz. Leg. 205 (1644), 137.

66. ARLL, Protocolos. Rosales Hoyos, Leg. 211 (1652), 580.

67. Powers, *Andean Journeys*, 126.

68. ARLL, Protocolos. Ortiz. Leg. 194 (1670), 698.

69. Ibid., 609.

70. Ibid., 698v; see Radding, *Wandering Peoples*, 176, for a definition of lands called "*pan sembrar*."

71. Ramírez, *World Upside Down*, 37.

72. ARLL, Protocolos. Ortiz. Leg. 194 (1670), 609.

73. Barragán Romano, *Etnicidad y verticalidad ecológica*, 18; and Brockington, *Blacks, Indians, and Spaniards*, 73, 97.

74. Indicating the limits of Andean market ventures, I have not found evidence of indigenous investments or activity in sugar production.

75. ARLL, Protocolos. Antolinez de Valdés. Leg. 93 (1649), 37.

76. ARLL, Protocolos. Viera Gutiérrez. Leg. 2 (1650), #136.

77. ARLL, Co. Ords. Leg. 198. Exp. 1350 (1669), 15, 17.

78. ARLL, Protocolos. Rosales Hoyos. Leg. 211 (1652), 580v.

79. ARLL, Protocolos. Viera Gutiérrez. Leg. 253 (1645), 327v.

80. ARLL, Protocolos. García. Leg. 166 (1660), 196v. Other indigenous elites were slaveholders. Doña María de Mora owned an alfalfa farm with two enslaved men, Francisco Congo and Manuel Congo. ARLL, Protocolos. Espino y Alvarado. Leg. 161 (1705), 365v. A wealthy landholder, Mora was the second wife of an indigenous migrant from the highlands who served as the alcalde of the San Sebastián parish in Trujillo. ARLL, Protocolos. Espino y Alvarado. Leg. 161 (1707), 604, 605. Captain Diego de Zárate, an "Indian native who was from the port of Paita and vecino of Huanchaco," also owned an enslaved man named Juan of *casta popo* and a young enslaved woman also of casta popo named Antonia. ARLL, Protocolos. Cortijo Quero. Leg. 115 (1705), 6.

81. Saignes, *Caciques, Tribute, and Migration*, 26.

82. ARLL, Protocolos. Rosales Hoyos. Leg. 211 (1652), 580.

83. ARLL, Ca. Ords. Leg. 20. Exp. 446 (1654), 1.

84. Ramírez, "Don Clemente Anto," 839.

85. ARLL, Co. Ords. Leg. 199. Exp. 1358 (1670), 3.

86. Powers, *Andean Journeys*, 157; and Saignes, *Caciques, Tribute, and Migration*, 27.

87. ARLL, Co. Ords. Leg. 199. Exp. 1358 (1670), 3.

88. AGI, Lima. Leg. 58. No. 2. Num. 90 (1656).

89. Powers, *Andean Journeys*, 145.

90. ARLL, Co. Ords. Leg. 199. Exp. 1358 (1670), 3.

91. ARLL, Co. Ords. Leg. 192. Exp. 1199 (1645), 2–2v.

92. ARLL, Co. Ords. Leg. 198. Exp. 1350 (1669), 14v–15.

93. ARLL, Co. Ords. Leg. 199. Exp. 1358 (1670), 3.

94. ARLL, Protocolos. Viera Gutiérrez. Leg. 258 (1655), 704–705v.

95. ARLL, Co. Ords. Leg. 199. Exp. 1358 (1670), 3.

96. Ibid., 2v, 3; and ARLL, Protocolos. Rosales Hoyos. Leg. 211 (1652), 580v. For the sixteenth century, see Ramírez, *World Upside Down*, 41.

97. Spalding, *Huarochirí*, 199.

98. Graubart, *With Our Labor and Sweat*, 20, 134–35; and Dean, *Inka Bodies and the Body of Christ*, 113–14, 123, 126, 127, 148.

99. ARLL, Protocolos. Rosales Hoyos. Leg. 211 (1652), 580.

100. ARLL, Co. Ords. Leg. 199. Exp. 1358 (1670), 3.

101. Diez Hurtado, *Fiestas y cofradías*, 156, 199; and Charney, *Indian Society in the Valley of Lima*, 79.

102. ARLL, Protocolos. Rosales Hoyos. Leg. 211 (1652), 580v.

103. ARLL, Co. Ords. Leg. 198. Exp. 1350 (1669), 15, 17v.

104. Ibid., 26.

105. ARLL, Co. Ords. Leg. 202. Exp. 1407 (1677), 3, 6, 24.

106. This was true for other northern coastal indigenous communities. Rostworowski de Diez Canseco, *Curacas y sucesiones*, 39.

107. ARLL, Co. Ords. Leg. 202. Exp. 1407 (1677), 10v, 11.

108. Stern, *Peru's Indian Peoples*, 134.

109. Ibid., 127; and Powers, *Andean Journeys*, 91.

110. Vatican Film Library (VFL), Colección Pastells, Vol. 94. Lima 15. Roll 3 from the AGI, Lima. 76-3-1. No. 6 (1669), 157.

111. Archivo Arzobispal de Lima (AAL), Apelaciones de Trujillo. Leg. 14. Exp. 1 (1670/1672), 2v; and ARLL, Actas del cabildo. Vol. 10 (1675), 104–104v.

112. Burga, *De la encomienda*, 120; and Powers, *Andean Journeys*, 111, 113.

113. Wightman, *Indigenous Migration and Social Change*, 88.

114. Archivo Parroquial de Cartavio (APC), Parroquía San José. Casimientos (Santiago de Cao), loose pages.

115. APC, Parroquía San José. Bautismos (Santiago de Cao), entries from 1675.

116. ARLL, Co. Asuntos de Gobierno. Leg. 269. Exp. 3231. (1700).

117. *Recopilación de leyes de los reynos de las Indias*, Titulo Tercero, Ley XXI, 231.

118. AGI, Escribanía. Residencia de la Audiencia de Lima. Leg. 534B (1674), 248.

119. AGI, Escribanía. Leg. 1190 (1660), 1.

120. Burns, *Colonial Habits*, 21.

121. ARLL, Co. Cr. Leg. 246. Exp. 2524 (1642), 1.

122. Ibid., 1v.

123. Ibid.

124. Konetzke, *Colección de documentos*, vol. 2, tomo 1, part 2 (1646), 401.

125. AGI, Lima. Leg. 252. No. 10 (1660), 4, 15.

126. AGI, Lima. Leg. 64. No. 7 (1663), 1. In another example, in 1660, Pedro Ruis, a native of Catacaos, spoke for "the rest of the Indians" when he complained that their assigned priest served "Spaniards, mestizos, mulatos, blacks and Indians" even though members of his community paid his salary. AGI, Lima. Leg. 252. No. 10 (1660), 4, 15.

127. Clements Library, Peru Collection. Eighteenth-century copies of four viceregal reports on the state of Peru. Conde de Santistevan, *Relación de Govierno, que hizo la Real Audiencia de Lima en vacante de el exmo señor virrey, Conde de Santistevan a su succesor el de Lemus*, 27, 36, 40v.

128. Stern, *Peru's Indian Peoples*, 162.

129. Larson, *Cochabamba, 1550–1900*, 101; and Stern, *Peru's Indian Peoples*, 162.

130. ARLL, Co. Ords. Leg. 200. Exp. 1367 (1671), 101.

131. Vegas de Cáceres, *Economía rural y estructura social*, 132.

132. Doña María de Bracamonte was from a family of landholders and colonial authorities. For Bracamontes as landholders, see ARLL, Co. Ords. Leg. 200. Exp. 1366 (1671); and ARLL, Co. Ords. Leg. 203. Exp. 1470 (1679), 1. Don Valentín del Risco was the owner of the San Joseph de Nuja and Mocan haciendas, see ARLL, Protocolos. Lopez Collado y Daza. Leg. 372 (1722), 106v. Fray Simón de Losada served in the Santiago de Cao reducción. See APC, Parroquia San José. Casamientos (1675), loose pages. Don Luis de Mora was the cacique of Santiago de Cao and Chocope. See ARLL, Co. Ords. Leg. 194. Exp. 1265; and ARLL, Protocolos. Protocolos. Cortijo Quero. Leg. 100 (1680), 191.

133. Burga, De la encomienda, 125; and Ramírez, Provincial Patriarchs, 154, 195.

134. Zulawski, They Eat from Their Labor, 54.

135. ARLL, Co. Ords. Leg. 202. Exp. 1410 (1678), 4, 4v, 5v.

136. Ibid., 4v.

137. Chambers, From Subjects to Citizens, 165.

138. ARLL, Co. Ords. Leg. 202. Exp. 1410 (1678), 5.

139. Graubart, With Our Labor and Sweat, 40.

140. ARLL, Co. Cr. Leg. 247. Exp. 2627 (1678); and Zevallos Quiñones, Los cacicazgos de Trujillo, 52.

141. Vegas de Cáceres, Economía rural y estructura social, 132.

142. Ramírez, World Upside Down, 90–91.

143. ARLL, Co. Ords. Leg. 202. Exp. 1410 (1678), 8.

144. Ibid., 5–5v.

145. Diez Hurtado, Fiestas y cofradías, 189.

146. Durston, Pastoral Quechua, 175.

147. ARLL, Ca. Ords. Leg. 25. Exp. 524 (1679), 4.

148. ARLL, Protocolos. Ortiz. Leg. 194 (1670), 247v.

149. AGN, Derecho Indígena. Leg. 102 (1639); and Vázquez de Espinosa, Compendium and Description, 396.

150. Lipsett-Rivera, To Defend Our Water, 17; Gómez Cumpa, "Mórrope," 326; Diez Hurtado, Las comunidades indígenas, 29; and Aldana, Empresas coloniales, 55.

151. ARLL, Protocolos. Viera Gutiérrez. Leg. 258 (1655), 655.

152. ARLL, Co. Asuntos de Gobierno. Leg. 268. Exp. 3179 (1672), 4v; and ARLL, Co. Cr. Leg. 247. Exp. 2603 (1675), 1v.

153. Herzog, Defining Nations, 55, 56.

154. ARLL, Co. Asuntos de Gobierno. Leg. 268. Exp. 3179 (1672), 4.

155. Recopilación de leyes de los reynos de las Indias, Título Tercero, Ley IX, 58.

156. ARLL, Co. Asuntos de Gobierno. Leg. 268. Exp. 3179 (1672), 4.

157. ARLL, Protocolos. García. Leg. 166 (1660), #19.

158. Ibid.

159. Graubart, "Creolization of the New World," 483, 486, 490, 492.

160. ARLL, Co. Asuntos de Gobierno. Leg. 268. Exp. 3179 (1672), 1.

161. Herzog, La administración como un fenómeno social, 89.

162. ARLL, Co. Asuntos de Gobierno. Leg. 268. Exp. 3179 (1672), 6.

163. ARLL, Co. Ords. Leg. 200. Exp. 1379 (1672), 1.
164. ARLL, Co. Cr. Leg. 247. Exp. 2610 (1677), 3v.
165. Glave Testino, *Trajinantes*, 61.
166. ARLL, Protocolos. Ortiz. Leg. 194 (1670), 247.
167. Cosamalón Aguilar, *Indios detrás de la muralla*, 198.
168. ARLL, Protocolos. Escobar. Leg. 146. (1644), 38.
169. ARLL, Co. Cr. Leg. 241. Exp. 2304 (1617), 1.
170. ARLL, Co. Cr. Leg. 247. Exp. 2587 (1660), 1v.
171. Konetzke, *Colección de documentos*, vol. 1, 384–88.
172. Enslaved men and women may have been able to feed themselves on the estates and farms. In some cases estate inventories include small fields of beans, garbanzos, and maize that may have been considered provision grounds for enslaved inhabitants. ARLL, Protocolos. Cortijo Quero. Leg. 125 (1715), 363; and Tardieu, *Los negros y la iglesia en el Perú*, tomo 1, 217. There are no descriptions of enslaved men and women tending their own fields on the northern Peruvian coast during the seventeenth century. In his exhaustive study of enslaved life in colonial Peru, the scholar Frederick Bowser did not find a record of slave provision grounds. See Bowser, *African Slave in Colonial Peru*, 226. It is possible that as the sugar estates expanded, landholders and overseers did not allow enslaved men and women the time required to work their plots or did not allocate water for their fields. See Tomich, "*Une petite guinée*," 82–83. In fact, the historian Pablo Macera found that the Jesuits, known as the most lenient slaveholders in colonial Peru, took away provision grounds from enslaved laborers in the mid-eighteenth century. See Macera, "Los Jesuitas y la agricultura de la caña," 219; Espinosa Descalzo, *Cartografía de Lima*, xxix, lxiv; and Cushner, *Lords of the Land*, 95.
173. Cushner, *Lords of the Land*, 90. In addition to foodstuffs, inventories of rural estates include large pots supplied to a designated cook, usually an enslaved woman, who oversaw the preparation of communal meals for all of the workers, indigenous and African, enslaved and waged. ARLL, Protocolos. Lopez Collado y Daza. Leg. 373 (1725), 24; and ARLL, Protocolos. Lopez Collado y Daza. Leg. 373 (1727), f. 782v. Meat was sometimes supplied as the administrator of the sugar mill of San Joseph de Oiutan near Saña also listed weekly purchases of a sheep or cow to be slaughtered for "workers on the estate." BNP, #B1034 (1677), 188v, 189, 189v; and Barrett, *Sugar Hacienda*, 93–95. Slaveholders were more likely to slaughter an ox for enslaved men and women on a holiday such as Easter. ARLL, Co. Ords. Leg. 220. Exp. 1787 (1730), 8; and Moreno Fraginals, *El ingenio*, 313. In the northern coastal valleys it is plausible that indigenous farmers supplied maize, beans, peppers, and other foodstuffs to estates just as they provisioned urban areas. Rubiños y Andrade, "Noticia previa por el Liz," 320. For examples of estates as markets for food and draft animals in Jamaica, see Shepherd, "Livestock and Sugar," 631.
174. For reports of markets in colonial Trujillo, see ARLL, Ca. Asuntos de Gobierno. Leg. 107. Exp. 1914 (1723), 1. For Lima and Quito, see Cosamalón Aguilar, *Indios detrás de la muralla*, 45; and Minchom, *People of Quito*, 104–5. Indigenous

people marketed goods that they purchased from their rural kin. Mangan, *Trading Roles*, 159; and Minchom, *People of Quito*, 107. In the Caribbean and in colonial South Carolina, enslaved men and women grew foodstuffs and made goods that they sold at weekly markets. Hall, "Slaves' Use of Their 'Free' Time," 725; and Olwell, *Masters, Slaves, and Subjects*, 143, 165.

175. BNP, #B1034 (1677), 188, 188v, 189; ARLL, Ca. Ords. Leg. 29. Exp. 582 (1696), 10v; and ARLL, Co. Ords. Leg. 215. Exp. 1672 (1708), 58. For enslaved mobility, see ARLL, Co. Cr. Leg. 249. Exp. 2699 (1702), 1.

176. ARLL, Co. Cr. Leg. 242. Exp. 2348 (1623), 1.

177. ARLL, Co. Asuntos de Gobierno. Leg. 266. Exp. 3074 (1607), 7.

178. The dark syrup was a by-product of sugar processing and could be used to make an alcoholic drink or to strengthen chicha. Von Wobeser, *La Hacienda Azucarera*, 229; and Barrett, *Sugar Hacienda*, 57.

179. AGN, Superior Gobierno. Juicios de Residencias. Leg. 37. Exp. 109 (1693), 508. The admonishments were echoed by ecclesiastical officials. See *Constituciones synodales del obispado de Arequipa*, 18v.

180. ARLL, Ca. Cr. Leg. 82. Exp. 1442 (1697), 2.

181. Lavallè, *Amor y opresión*, 170; and Ramírez, *Provincial Patriarchs*, 174.

182. ARLL, Ca. Cr. Leg. 82. Exp. 1448 (1698), 1.

183. Mangan, *Trading Roles*, 91.

184. Penningroth, *Claims of Kinfolk*, 94, 95.

185. Bowser, *African Slave in Colonial Peru*, 227.

186. BNP, #B1034 (1677), 190v; ARLL. Co. Ords. Leg. 200. Exp. 1366 (1671).

187. ARLL, Co. Ords. Leg. 210. Exp. 1578 (1695), 4.

188. Graubart, *With Our Labor and Sweat*, 70; and Minchom, *People of Quito*, 41.

189. ARLL, Co. Cr. Leg. 250. Exp. 2716 (1718), 2v.

190. ARLL, Co. Cr. Leg. 245. Exp. 2500 (1639), f. 13v.

191. ARLL, Ca. Ords. Leg. 21. Exp. 453 (1658), 1v–2.

192. Karasch, *Slave Life in Rio de Janeiro*, 89–90.

193. ARLL, Co. Cr. Leg. 246. Exp. 2533 (1642).

194. Ibid.

195. ARLL, Ca. Cr. Leg. 80. Exp. 1387 (1651).

196. Walker, "'He outfitted his family in notable decency,'" 394.

197. ARLL, Co. Cr. Leg. 242. Exp. 2365 (1624), 2, 3–3v.

198. Anómino, "Fragmento de una historia," 97, 98.

199. ARLL, Co. Cr. Leg. 240. Exp. 2266 (1614), 1v, 3.

200. White, "'Wearing three or four handkerchiefs.'"

201. ARLL, Ca. Cr. Leg. 79. Exp. 1350 (1641).

202. Ibid.

203. ARLL, Co. Cr. Leg. 246. Exp. 2533 (1642).

204. Enslaved men with money could purchase a jacket or ruffled shirt to express their status or style throughout the Americas. Karasch, *Slave Life in Rio de Janeiro*, 223.

205. ARLL, Ca. Cr. Leg. 79. Exp. 1344 (1636), 1.

206. Usner, *Indians, Settlers, and Slaves*, 191; Spaniards noted that Andean communities produced short skirts made of good cloth, including velvet, textiles woven with gold thread, and "painted" fabrics of various colors. Anónimo, *Descripción del Virreinato del Perú*, 24–25.

207. ARLL, Ca. Cr. Leg. 79. Exp. 1350 (1641).

208. ARLL, Co. Cr. Leg. 246. Exp. 2578 (1655), 1.

209. ARLL, Protocolos. Pacheco de Guevara. Leg. 197 (1667), 219v, 220.

210. AGI, Escribanía. Leg. 534A. No. 1 (1670), 705v, 713v.

211. ARLL, Protocolos. Pacheco de Guevara. Leg. 197 (1667), 219v, 220.

212. Mangan, *Trading Roles*, 109–10.

213. ARLL, Ca. Ords. Leg. 19. Exp. 415 (1647), 1; and ARLL, Protocolos. Paz. Leg. 205 (1644), 282v.

214. ARLL, Co. Cr. Leg. 246. Exp. 2573 (1655), 3.

215. ARLL, Ca. Cr. Leg. 80. Exp. 1388 (1652), 1v.

216. ARLL, Actas del Cabildo. Vol. 9 (1667), 221v; and ARLL, Actas del Cabildo. Vol. 8 (1658), 66–68.

217. Archivum Romanum Societatis Iesu (ARSI), Peruano Litterae Annuae. Vol. 16 "Letras annuas de la Prova del Peru del ano de 1655," 12.

218. AAL, Inmunidad Eclesiástica. Leg. 7. Exp. 23 (1646), 10v; and ARSI, Peruano Litterae Annuae (1662), 130.

219. ARLL, Ca. Cr. Leg. 80. Exp. 1376 (1646), 1v.

220. ARLL, Protocolos. Viera Gutiérrez. Leg. 253 (1645), 371v–374.

221. Mangan, *Trading Roles*, 88, 152–53.

222. ARLL, Protocolos. Rosales Hoyos. Leg. 211 (1655), 231; and ARLL, Protocolos. Álvarez. Leg. 90 (1675), 363v.

223. ARLL, Protocolos. Viera Gutiérrez. Leg. 253 (1645), 372.

224. Reis, *Death Is a Festival*, 126–27.

225. Castañeda Murga, "Notas para una historia," 166.

226. Cope, *Limits of Racial Domination*, 30–31; and Cosamalón Aguilar, *Indios detrás de la muralla*, 155, 190.

227. Feijóo de Sosa, *Relación descriptiva de la ciudad*, 30; and AAL, Apelaciones de Trujillo. Leg. 17. Exp. 2 (1679), 1.

228. Archivo Sagrario de Trujillo, Libro de Bautismos de mistos (1651–1683), entries from 1655 and 1675.

229. Mannerilli, *Private Passions and Public Sins*, 82, 91, 95; Cosamalón Aguilar, *Indios detrás de la muralla*, 155; and Cope, *Limits of Racial Domination*, 79, 81, 82.

230. ARLL, Co. Cr. Leg. 247. Exp. 2625 (1678), 1v, 2v.

231. ARLL, Ca. Ords. Leg. 23. Exp. 490 (1670), 24.

232. Ibid., 14, 20v; and Mannarelli, *Private Passions and Public Sins*, 44.

233. Mannarelli, *Private Passions and Public Sins*, 101.

234. AGI, Lima 237 (1645), 9.

235. Minchom, *People of Quito*, 10.

236. ARLL, Ca. Cr. Leg. 80. Exp. 1368 (1644), 2.

237. Deloria, *Indians in Unexpected Places*, 4.

5. Justice within Slavery

1. I collected 168 inventories from between 1590 and 1740 based on rental and purchase agreements or a list of assets of a deceased property holder from the notarial and judicial archives in the Archivo Departamental de La Libertad (ARLL) and Archivo Regional de Lambayeque (ARL). The total number of enslaved laborers listed my sample of estates was 2,544, with 2,059 as men (80.9 percent) and 485 as women (19.1 percent).

2. Hartman, *Scenes of Subjection*, 62; and Camp, *Closer to Freedom*, 39.

3. Cutter, *Legal Culture*, 40; and Herzog, *Upholding Justice*, 21.

4. Cutter, *Legal Culture*, 35.

5. Bryant, "Enslaved Rebels, Fugitives, and Litigants," 21–22, 24–25; and Cowling, "Negotiating Freedom," 383–84.

6. Bristol, *Christians, Blasphemers, and Witches*, chapter 4; Karasch, *Slave Life in Rio de Janeiro*, chapter 11; Premo, *Children of the Father King*, chapter 7; Hünefeldt, *Paying the Price of Freedom*, chapter 5; and Higgins, "Licentious Liberty," chapter 5.

7. Bennett, *Africans in Colonial Mexico*, 2–3, 33–34.

8. Bryant, "Enslaved Rebels, Fugitives, and Litigants," 20, 22, 24; Villa-Flores, *Dangerous Speech*, 133; and Soulodre-La France, "Socially Not So Dead!" 94, 96.

9. Sharp, *Slavery on the Spanish Frontier*, 130. Sweet, *Recreating Africa*, 199.

10. In this sense I find historian Herman Bennett's argument compelling that ecclesiastical law allowed for enslaved petitions, but I did not find the same encouragement in the magistrate and alcalde courts in Trujillo. See Bennett, *Africans in Colonial Mexico*, 35, 45. The historian María Elena Martínez has suggested that blacks' status as free Christian vassals was not always upheld in practice. See Martínez, *Genealogical Fictions*, 221.

11. Sharp, *Slavery on the Spanish Frontier*, 138; and Schwartz, *Sugar Plantations in the Formation of Brazilian Society*, 134.

12. The laws pertained to free people of color, questions of manumission, sale, service, curfew, and public peace as well as admonishments against arming slaves and orders for prosecuting fugitives. *Recopilación de leyes de los reynos de las Indias*, Libro VII, Título V, 320–25.

13. In the 1660s the Dutch negotiated their first slave-trading contract with the Spanish crown and intensified their illegal trade into Spanish America. Postma, "Dispersal of African Slaves," 287; and Emmer, "Dutch and the Making," 73. After a brief agreement with the French Guinea Company, the English took over the official slave trade into the Spanish Americas. Israel, *Dutch Republic*, 946, 969. Appendix 2, "Price Trends of Slaves Sold in Trujillo (1640–1730)," in this book, indicates that prices rose in the later part of the seventeenth century reflecting demand and began to drop at the beginning of the eighteenth century. By the 1720s and 1730s, the

historian Susan Ramírez has suggested, slaveholders demanded more enslaved laborers. See Ramírez, *Provincial Patriarchs*, 216.

14. Ramírez, *Provincial Patriarchs*, 169; and Cushner, *Lords of the Land*, 52.

15. Harnessing water power increased the pace of sugar processing and expanded the fields under cultivation. Cardoso, *Negro Slavery in the Sugar Plantations*, 25; and Barrett, *Sugar Hacienda*, 54–55.

16. Joseph Arara resisted being captured by enslaved men from the estate where he was enslaved. Archivo Arzobispal de Trujillo (AAT), Causas Generales. Leg. 3 (1701). Custodio, of "Portuguese nation," killed his owner when threatened with a beating. ARLL, Co. Cr. Leg. 250. Exp. 2706 (1708), 2v. The enslaved laborers of a Chicama estate killed their owner and then revolted against colonial authorities. ARLL, Co. Cr. Leg. 249. Exp. 2674 (1691), 1, 2. The fugitive known as the albino *negro* ("black") Cayetano was accused of burning sugarcane fields and destroying a bridge in Conache valley near Trujillo. ARLL, Ca. Cr. Leg. 83. Exp. 1470 (1711), 14v.

Francisco of *mina casta* resisted capture after escaping from his owner by seizing a pistol. ARLL, Ca. Cr. Leg. 82. Exp. 1466 (1710), 4. Phelipe Lucumí, Domingo Congo, and Francisco Arara escaped from Trujillo's jail. ARLL, Co. Cr. Leg. 249. Exp. 2687 (1697), 2v. For a discussion of enslaved men resisting changes in work regimes, see Morgan, "Work and Culture," 199, 207; and Morgan, "Slaves and Livestock," 70.

17. Berlin, *Many Thousands Gone*, 2–3.

18. Moreno Fraginals, *El ingenio*, 605.

19. Morgan, *Slave Counterpoint*, 389; and Camp, *Closer to Freedom*, 13.

20. The fugitive known as the albino "black" Cayetano rode horses that supposedly he stole with his fellows into Trujillo and throughout the valleys. ARLL, Ca. Cr. Leg. 83. Exp. 1470 (1711), 4, 10v. For another example of enslaved men riding horses for their own affairs, see ARLL, Co. Cr. Leg. 249. Exp. 2698 (1702), 5. For an example of an enslaved man accused of stealing mules, see ARLL, Co. Ords. Leg. 206. Exp. 1492 (1686), 1.

21. ARLL, Ca. Ords. Leg. 24. Exp. 509 (1677), 7; ARLL, Co. Cr. Leg. 250. Exp. 2716 (1718), 2; and ARLL, Ca. Cr. Leg. 82. Exp. 1441 (1697), 3v.

22. ARLL, Co. Cr. Leg. 243. Exp. 2393 (1626), 16v. This was similar to the nineteenth-century U.S. South. See Smith, *Mastered by the Clock*, 143.

23. ARLL, Co. Cr. Leg. 241. Exp. 2304 (1617), 1; Archivo Arzobispal de Lima (AAL), Causas de negros. Leg. 2. Exp. 2 (1610), 6v.

24. ARLL, Ca. Cr. Leg. 82. Exp. 1452 (1702), 4v.

25. For examples of torture employed during enslaved confessions, see ARLL, Ca. Cr. Leg. 83. Exp. 1478 (1718), 57; and Herzog, *La administración como un fenómeno social*, 226.

26. For swollen rivers on the northern coast in March, see Aldana, *Empresas coloniales*, 55; ARLL, Ca. Cr. Leg. 83. Exp. 1484 (1725), 9. For cleaning the canals in March, see ARLL, Co. Ords. Leg. 202. Exp. 1401 (1676), 2.

27. ARLL, Co. Cr. Leg. 250. Exp. 2709 (1712), 2v; and ARLL, Ca. Alcalde de aguas. Leg. 111. Exp. 2101 (1725).

28. Cope, *Limits of Racial Domination*, 62.

29. For enslaved men who stopped work to smoke, see ARLL, Ca. Cr. Leg. 83. Exp. 1484 (1725), 5v. For enslaved men who stopped work to eat, see ARLL, Ca. Cr. Leg. 77. Exp. 1265 (1598), 3.

30. ARLL, Ca. Cr. Leg. 82. Exp. 1452 (1702), 16.

31. For the expectations of local officials to look after public well-being, see Cutter, *Legal Culture*, 107.

32. In this case the head of the rural guard, or the *alcalde de la Santa Hermandad*, served as the accusing party, the court investigator, and the judge. Cutter, *Legal Culture*, 109.

33. ARLL, Ca. Cr. Leg. 83. Exp. 1470 (1711), 25v.

34. ARLL, Ca. Cr. Leg. 82. Exp. 1452 (1702), 1v.

35. Ibid., 8.

36. ARLL, Co. Cr. Leg. 247. Exp. 2616 (1677), 2.

37. For slaveholders' complaints regarding enslaved men's "arrogance," see ARLL, Ca. Cr. Leg. 82. Exp. 1454 (1704), 9.

38. ARLL, Co. Cr. Leg. 247. Exp. 2616 (1677), 2v, 13v.

39. Ibid., 13v.

40. ARLL, Ca. Cr. Leg. 83. Exp. 1470 (1711), 15; ARLL, Protocolos. Cortijo Quero. Leg. 125 (1715), 582v; and ARLL, Ca. Cr. Leg. 83. Exp. 1477 (1717), 1.

41. For a discussion of honor disputes among slaveholders and enslaved, see Gross, *Double Character*, 50–54.

42. ARLL, Co. Cr. Leg. 249. Exp. 2699 (1702), 3v.

43. *Constitvciones synodales del arçobispado de Los Reyes en el Pirv*, 4.

44. ARLL, Co. Cr. Leg. 240. Exp. 2258 (1614), 1v.

45. Gaspar, "Sugar Cultivation and Slave Life," 119, 120.

46. Bristol, *Christians, Blasphemers, and Witches*, 99, 105; and Penningroth, *Claims of Kinfolk*, 62.

47. ARLL, Ca. Cr. Leg. 80. Exp. 1400 (1662), 2v, 3.

48. ARLL, Co. Asuntos de Gobierno. Leg. 107. Exp. 1867 (1706), 1.

49. Mangan, *Trading Roles*, 91.

50. Ramírez, *Provincial Patriarchs*, 141, 132.

51. Sandoval, *Tratado sobre la esclavitud*, 141.

52. For examples of male-only drinking, see Taylor, *Drinking, Homicide, and Rebellion*, 62; and Salazar-Soler, "Embriaguez y visions en los Andes," 36.

53. Morgan, "Work and Culture," 202.

54. Macera, "Los Jesuitas y la agricultura de la caña," 215; and Cushner, *Lords of the Land*, 90.

55. ARLL, Co. Cr. Leg. 248. Exp. 2664 (1688), 7. Since the estate produced sugar, the elderly Pedro Angola probably was able to obtain some form of sugar by-product to make *guarapo* (a highly potent alcoholic beverage) and perhaps drew on his experience with distilled alcohol production in West Central Africa. Barrett, *Sugar Hacienda*, 61; Schwartz, *Sugar Plantations in the Formation of Brazilian Society*, 117; and

Vega de Cáceres, *Economía rural y estructura social*, 96. Curto, *Enslaving Spirits*, 63, 69. Many estate owners produced lower-quality syrups and molasses or miel in addition to sugar loaves that they shipped throughout the Pacific trade routes and sold to local storeowners and tavern-keepers. See the inventory for Tulape that included "loaves of sugar" as well as "jars of white mieles." ARLL, Co. Ords. Leg. 194. Exp. 1259 (1653), 152v, and the inventory for Nuestra Señora de la Concepción that included molds to make sugar and jars for the miel. ARLL, Co. Ords. Leg. 196. Exp. 1322 (1663), 19; Ramírez, "Descripción del Reyno," 29; and Lizárraga, *Descripción breve del Peru*, 77–78. Tord Nicolini, *Hacienda, comercio, fiscalidad y luchas sociales*, 22. Miel could be distilled and sold as *aguardiente*, which while varying in purity was consumed in the cities and towns throughout the coast. ARLL, Co. Pedimentos. Leg. 285. Exp. 4301 (1719), 1; Moreno Fraginals, *El ingenio*, 188; and Barrett, *Sugar Hacienda*, 61.

56. AAL, Causas de negros. Leg. 2. Exp. 2 (1610), 6v.

57. ARLL, Co. Cr. Leg. 248. Exp. 2664 (1688), 30v, 42; and *Constituciones synodales del obispado de Arequipa*, 18v.

58. Penningroth, *Claims of Kinfolk*, 58.

59. ARLL, Co. Cr. Leg. 249. Exp. 2699 (1702), 8, 12.

60. Ibid., 7.

61. Tomich, "*Une petite guinée*," 82–83.

62. Ibid., 85.

63. ARLL, Co. Cr. Leg. 249. Exp. 2699 (1702), 2v, 3v. It is also plausible that the enslaved laborers testified that they attempted to capture the accused to prove their loyalty to their slaveholder or because they were intimidated by the magistrate's court.

64. Enslaved men confronted each other for violating their trust in other circumstances. Juan Zagal, an enslaved *mulato* confronted Juan Angola with a knife and killed him. Zagal accused Angola of coming to complain to his owner "so that tomorrow they put me in shackles." ARLL, Ca. Cr. Leg. 81. Exp. 1417 (1680), 3.

65. ARLL, Co. Cr. Leg. 249. Exp. 2699 (1702), 4v.

66. For rental instructions that include the price, alfalfa and firewood allocations, and specifics on replacing enslaved laborers, see ARLL, Protocolos. Espino de Alvarado. Leg. 333 (1725), 370v–371; ARLL, Protocolos. San Román. Leg. 228 (1724), 238v– 243v.

67. In her discussion of antebellum courts in the United States, Ariela Gross explains how "putting slave character on trial allowed slaves' moral agency to intrude into the courtroom, which raised difficulties for legal transactions dealing with slaves in the same manner as other forms of property." Gross, *Double Character*, 4.

68. AAT, Causas de negros. Leg. 1 (1702), 45v.

69. Moreno Fraginals, *El ingenio*, 287; and Cushner, *Lords of the Land*, 96.

70. AAL, Inmunidad Eclesiástica. Leg. 17. Exp. 1 (1719), 9v.

71. ARLL, Co. Cr. Leg. 247. Exp. 2616 (1677), 18.

72. ARLL, Ca. Cr. Leg. 82. Exp. 1466 (1710), 1v.

73. ARLL, Ca. Cr. Leg. 79. Exp. 1353 (1642), 4v, 23v; ARLL. Ca. Cr. Leg. 83. Exp. 1470 (1711), 3v; and Lavallè, *Amor y opresión*, 155, 156.

74. ARLL, Co. Cr. Leg. 249. Exp. 2674 (1691), 2v; Archivo General de la Nación (AGN), Superior Gobierno. Juicios de Residencias. Leg. 37. Cuad. 109 (1693), 552; and ARLL, Ca. Cr. Leg. 83. Exp. 1485 (1725), 3v.

75. Camp, *Closer to Freedom*, 49.

76. ARLL, Ca. Cr. Leg. 82. Exp. 1466 (1710), 6.

77. Lavallè, *Amor y opresión*, 190.

78. ARLL, Ca. Cr. Leg. 82. Exp. 1434 (1693), 5.

79. ARLL, Ca. Cr. Leg. 82. Exp. 1432 (1692), 3v.

80. Enslaved men and women in Trujillo solicited new owners or looked for a padrino (a "godfather" or patron) when they were dissatisfied with their owners. For examples, see ARLL, Co. Ords. Leg. 207. Exp. 1513 (1687), f. 21; and ARLL, Ca. Cr. Leg. 82. Exp. 1466 (1710). Exchanging owners was not uncommon in the Americas. See Hünefeldt, *Paying the Price of Freedom*, 133; Landers, *Black Society in Spanish Florida*, 125; and Bowser, *African Slave in Colonial Peru*, 192.

81. Konetzke, *Colección de documentos*, vol. 1, 88.

82. De la Fuente, "Slaves and the Creation of Legal Rights in Cuba," 673.

83. Cutter, *Legal Culture*, 34.

84. ARLL, Co. Ords. Leg. 209. Exp. 1554 (1692), 6.

85. ARLL, Ca. Cr. Leg. 81. Exp. 1426 (1687), 11v. Northern coastal authorities also preferred that enslaved people return to slaveholders rather than remain as permanent fugitives.

86. There were instances of fugitive collectives (mobile and settled) on the northern coast during the later seventeenth and early eighteenth century. For a group led by "Cuco," see ARLL, Ca. Cr. Leg. 83. Exp. 1470 (1711). For a discussion of a group near the Chicama estate of Facala, see ARLL, Co. Cr. Leg. 249. Exp. 2674 (1691).

87. Bowser, *African Slave in Colonial Peru*, 195.

88. ARLL, Ca. Cr. Leg. 82. Exp. 1432 (1692), 1v.

89. De la Fuente, "Slaves and the Creation of Legal Rights in Cuba," 675.

90. Landers, *Black Society in Spanish Florida*, 139.

91. ARLL, Ca. Cr. Leg. 82. Exp. 1464 (1707), 1.

92. von Wobeser, *La hacienda Azucarera*, 65–66.

93. ARLL, Ca. Cr. Leg. 81. Exp. 1426 (1687), 11v.

94. Bryant, "Enslaved Rebels, Fugitives, and Litigants," 33. De la Fuente suggests that *apadrinarse* meant in nineteenth-century Cuba to seek "the patronage and protection of local authorities." See de la Fuente, "Slaves and the Creation of Legal Rights in Cuba," 673.

95. Bowser, *African Slave in Colonial Peru*, 198, 203.

96. ARLL, Co. Cr. Leg. 249. Exp. 2698 (1702), 5.

97. Bowser, *African Slave in Colonial Peru*, 103–4.

98. Only skilled laborers or foremen appeared to have received monetary or

additional compensation on rural estates. AGN, Companía de Jesus. Colegio de Trujillo. Contabilidad. Cuentas de colegio. Leg. 86 "Libro de cuentas del Colegio de Trujillo 1685–1688 visitado por los padres Diego Francisco Altamirano, Joaquin de Velasco, Francisco Javier, Diego de Candenas, Alonso Messia, provinciales del Perú" (1686).

99. ARLL, Co. Ords. Leg. 209. Exp. 1554 (1692), 2v, 6.

100. *Recopilación de leyes de los reynos de las Indias*, Libro VII, Título V, Ley VIII, 321.

101. ARLL, Co. Ords. Leg. 209. Exp. 1554 (1692), 3v. For other examples of slaveholders providing slaves with food during their imprisonment, see ARLL, Co. Cr. Leg. 242. Exp. 2371 (1625), 5. Arroyo called on the customary practice that slaveholders take care of the physical health of their slaves whose bodies represented a financial investment. For basic care provided by slaveholders, see Sharp, *Slavery on the Spanish Frontier*, 140.

102. On the northern Peruvian coast, the rural guard looked for slaves hiding in the homes of other enslaved people. ARLL, Ca. Cr. Leg. 81. Exp. 1429 (1689), 1. The rural guard also pursued enslaved men and women who were reported to be hiding in the hills or arroyos surrounding the cultivated areas. Lavallè, *Amor y opresión*, 154, 182.

103. ARLL, Co. Ords. Leg. 203. Exp. 1470 (1679), 2v, 3v.

104. Even slaveholders were aware of Bracamonte Dávila's abusive nature. In other courts cases they accused the notorious slaveholder of permanently disabling and murdering enslaved men whom he had caught as fugitives or whom he claimed had resisted his authority. In 1679 a slaveholder from Saña accused Bracamonte Dávila of holding captive his fugitive slave, Juan Romero, for months on his estate and physically abusing him until rendering the enslaved man disabled. ARLL, Co. Ords. Leg. 203. Exp. 1470 (1679), 1. In 1688 overseers from the Chicama valley accused Bracamonte Dávila of abusing his position as captain of the rural guard. ARLL, Co. Ords. Leg. 207. Exp. 1517 (1688).

105. ARLL, Co. Ords. Leg. 209. Exp. 1554 (1692), f. 1v.

106. Slaveholders sent enslaved laborers to work on rural estates as a punishment. ARLL, Ca. Cr. Leg. 81. Exp. 1425 (1687), 8v.

107. Bryant, "Enslaved Rebels, Fugitives, and Litigants," 20.

108. Pinto, *Slavery in Portuguese India*, 25, 53, 82.

109. ARLL, Co. Cr. Leg. 249. Exp. 2676 (1692), 1v.

110. Pinto, *Slavery in Portuguese India*, 116.

111. ARLL, Co. Cr. Leg. 250. Exp. 2706 (1708), 6.

112. *Recopilación de leyes de los reynos de las Indias*, Libro VII, Titulo Quinto, ley XV, ley XVI, ley XVII, ley XVIII.

113. ARLL, Co. Cr. Leg. 250. Exp. 2706 (1708), 6.

114. Luis Congo attempted to kill his overseer on a Chicama valley estate in retaliation for excessive whipping. AAL, Inmunidad Eclesiástica. Leg. 17. Exp. 1 (1719), 17v. For a discussion of how enslaved men discarded the norms and values of slaveholding, see Gaspar, *Bondmen and Rebels*, 129–30.

115. ARLL, Ca. Cr. Leg. 81. Exp. 1427 (1688), 1.

116. Ibid., 3.

117. Taylor, *Drinking, Homicide, and Rebellion*, 104–5.

118. For examples of other Trujillo fiestas in October, see ARLL, Co. Cr. Leg. 248. Exp. 2632 (1679), 5; AGN, Compania de Jesus. Colegio de Trujillo. Leg. 86. Contabilidad. Cuentas del colegio (1685), 42; ARLL, Co. Cr. Leg. 249. Exp. 2680 (1696), 1; and Diez Hurtado, *Fiestas y cofradias*, 189. The relaxation of restrictions were not limited to Spanish America, see Griffin, "'Goin' Back Over There,'" 98; and Hall, "Slaves' Use of Their 'Free' Time," 724–25.

119. Estenssoro Fuchs, "Música y comportamiento festivo," 163; and Navarrete, "Entre Kronos y Calendas," 88.

120. ARLL, Ca. Cr. Leg. 81. Exp. 1427 (1688), 2.

121. Sandoval, *Tratado sobre la esclavitud*, 139; and Nwokeji, "Atlantic Slave Trade," 621.

122. ARLL, Co. Cr. Leg. 248. Exp. 2633 (1679), 13.

123. Konetzke, *Colección de documentos*, vol. 1 (1544), 231. The orders reflected the concerns of a Catholic monarchy. The crown along with Peruvian ecclesiastical authorities sought to ensure that enslaved laborers were religiously instructed, attended Mass, and received communion. *Constitvciones synodales del arçobispado de Los Reyes en el Pirv*, 4; *Constituciones synodales del obispado de Arequipa*, Capítulo 13, 18v; Konetzke, *Colección de documentos*, vol. 1 (1587), 572; and Konetzke, *Colección de documentos*, vol. 2, tomo 1 (1603), 99.

124. ARLL, Co. Cr. Leg. 248. Exp. 2633 (1679), 12v.

125. Bennett, *Africans in Colonial Mexico*, 140.

126. ARLL, Co. Ords. Leg. 209. Exp. 1554 (1692), 19.

127. ARLL, Co. Cr. Leg. 248. Exp. 2633 (1679), 10.

128. ARLL, Protocolos. Espino de Alvarado. Leg. 333 (1725), 371; ARLL, Protocolos. San Román (1724), 240; and ARLL, Protocolos. San Román. Leg. 212 (1696), 262v.

129. For an example of enslaved laborers revolting against the overseer and appealing to the owner, see Kapsoli, *Rebeliones de esclavos*, 72.

130. ARLL, Co. Cr. Leg. 248. Exp. 2633 (1679), 12v.

131. Konetzke, *Colección de documentos*, vol. 1 (1545), 237; vol. 2, tomo 2 (1681), 722; vol. 2, tomo 2 (1683), 754; and vol. 2, tomo 2 (1685), 762.

132. For the importance of oral testimony, see Kellogg, *Law and the Transformation*, 39.

133. ARLL, Co. Cr. Leg. 248. Exp. 2633 (1679), 10, 14v–15, 19.

134. Ibid., 25v.

135. Herzog, *Upholding Justice*, 26.

136. ARLL, Co. Cr. Leg. 248. Exp. 2633 (1679), 28v.

137. Ibid., 29v.

138. Ibid., 36, 36v, 38.

139. Ibid., 58.

140. Cutter, *Legal Culture*, 107, 129.

141. ARLL, Co. Cr. Leg. 248. Exp. 2633 (1679), 30v, 32, 33, 34.

142. Macera, "Los Jesuitas y la agricultura de la caña," 215.

143. For a discussion of a moral economy among enslaved laborers, see Morgan, *Slave Counterpoint*, 332.

144. ARLL, Co. Cr. Leg. 248. Exp. 2633 (1679), 35.

145. Ibid., 41.

146. Gross, *Double Character*, 52; and Cutter, *Legal Culture*, 126.

147. ARLL, Co. Cr. Leg. 248. Exp. 2633 (1679), 10v.

148. Ibid., 13, 19.

149. Clerical mandates include discussion of baptism and marriage but did not require slaveholders to provide a Catholic funeral for enslaved laborers. *Constitvciones synodales del obispado de Arequipa*, 70, 79.

150. ARLL, Co. Cr. Leg. 248. Exp. 2633 (1679), 28v, 30.

151. Ibid., 13v.

152. Ibid., 33.

153. Hilton, *Kingdom of Kongo*, 13.

154. ARLL, Co. Cr. Leg. 248. Exp. 2633 (1679), 6, 13; and Reis, *Death Is a Festival*, 67, 92–93, 145–46.

155. Karasch, *Slave Life in Rio de Janeiro*, 279; Sweet, *Recreating Africa*, 178; and Schuler, "Alas, Alas, Kongo," 72.

156. Hilton, *Kingdom of Kongo*, 11. Unlike larger sugar estates, where men dominated and there were few children, on the San Francisco de Buenos Aires wheat estate there was a multigenerational community with older and younger men as well as women and children, some of whom were married or at least partnered. Valentin de la Madriz, a criollo, identified Antonia de Toledo as his *compañera*. ARLL, Co. Cr. Leg. 248. Exp. 2633 (1679), 19. Both were listed on an inventory of the estate from 1685. ARLL, Protocolos. Cortijo Quero. Leg. 102 (1685), 646v–647v.

157. For example, Capitán don García de Bracamonte Dávila was both the head of the rural guard and a slaveholder. The magistrate was a slaveholder. For Bracamonte Dávila as head of the rural guard, see ARLL, Co. Ords. Leg. 207. Exp. 1526 (1688). For Bracamonte Dávila as a slaveholder, see ARLL, Protocolos. Salinas. Leg. 234 (1675), #431, 516v; and ARLL, Protocolos. Espino y Alvarado. Leg. 156 (1695), #167, f. 383v. For evidence of magistrates as slaveholders, see ARLL, Protocolos. Ortiz de Peralta. Leg. 189 (1665), #61, 93v; ARLL, Protocolos. Aguilar. Leg. 262 (1715) #1, 1–2v; and ARLL, Protocolos. San Román. Leg. 221 (1715), # 248, 490.

158. Konetzke, *Colección de documentos*, vol. 2, tomo 2 (1681), 722.

159. Herzog, *Upholding Justice*, 155.

160. ARLL, Ca. Cr. Leg. 82. Exp. 1445 (1698), 1v.

161. Ibid., 10v.

162. Gross, *Double Character*, 4.

163. ARLL, Ca. Cr. Leg. 82. Exp. 1445 (1698), 5v, 7, 8v.

164. Ibid., 12.

165. ARLL, Co. Cr. Leg. 248. Exp. 2649 (1682), 1.

166. Palmer, *Slaves of the White God*, 50; ARLL, Co. Cr. Leg. 249. Exp. 2679 (1696), 1; and Archivum Romanum Societatis Iesu (ARSI), Peruano Litterae Annuae. Vol. 16, "Letras annuas de la Prova del Peru del ano de 1655" (1651), 15.

167. ARLL, Co. Cr. Leg. 248. Exp. 2662 (1686), 1.

168. ARLL, Co. Cr. Leg. 203. Exp. 1470 (1679), 9.

169. ARLL, Co. Cr. Leg. 248. Exp. 2649 (1682), 1.

170. ARLL, Co. Ords. Leg. 215. Exp. 1672 (1708), 55; ARLL, Protocolos. Cortijo Quero. Leg. 102 (1685), 647v; ARLL, Co. Ords. Leg. 213. Exp. 1645 (1704), 36v; AAT, Testamentos. Leg. 6. Exp. 1 (1695), 79; and ARLL, Protocolos. Espino y Alvarado. Leg. 149 (1684), 177v.

171. ARLL, Ca. Ords. Leg. 27. Exp. 567 (1691), 11v; ARLL, Co. Ords. Leg. 204. Exp. 1447 (1682), 118v; ARLL, Co. Ords. Leg. 214. Exp. 1662 (1706), 2; ARLL, Protocolos. Salinas. Leg. 235 (1677), 240; ARLL, Protocolos. San Román. Leg. 215 (1704), 177v; and ARLL, Protocolos. Cortijo Quero. Leg. 110 (1700), 186.

172. ARLL, Protocolos. Cortijo Quero. Leg. 102 (1685), 648; ARLL, Protocolos. Cortijo Quero. Leg. 115 (1705), 250v; ARLL, Protocolos. Espino y Alvarado. Leg. 149 (1684), 177v; ARLL, Protocolos. Salinas. Leg. 234 (1675), 499v; and ARLL, Co. Ords. Leg. 212. Exp. 1630 (1702), 29.

173. ARLL, Co. Ords. Leg. 204. Exp. 1460 (1682), 13v–14.

174. Hartman, *Scenes of Subjection*, 8.

175. ARLL, Protocolos. Ortiz. Leg. 194 (1670), 525.

176. ARLL, Co. Ords. Leg. 203. Exp. 1470 (1679), 3.

177. Rao and Pierce, "Discipline and the Other Body," 21.

178. AGI, Escribanía. Leg. 1191 (1673), 2.

179. AGI, Escribanía. Leg. 1192 (1681), 2.

180. Scardaville, "Justice by Paperwork," 990.

181. AGI, Gobierno. Audiencia de Lima. Leg. 307 (1678), 1. For the problems of water supply in Trujillo and the northern coastal valleys, see Castañeda Murga, *La epidemia general de agua*, 34. For similar water problems resulting from the expansion of the sugar estates in the Chicama valley, see ARLL, Co. Ords. Leg. 206. Exp. 1478 (1685), 11v.

182. AGI, Gobierno. Audiencia de Lima. Leg. 307 (1678), 1–1v. Ramírez, *Provincial Patriarchs*, 279.

183. The power of slaveholders may have also been growing throughout the Peruvian viceroyalty. Ecclesiastical authorities complained that estate owners did not allow enslaved and indigenous laborers to attend Mass. When confronted by local clerics, estate owners were said to "lose respect to the clerics." *Constitvciones synodales de el obispado de la civdad de Gvamanga*, 26.

184. ARLL, Ca. Ords. Leg. 35. Exp. 683 (1714), 1–1v.

185. ARLL, Co. Cr. Leg. 248. Exp. 2649 (1682), 1.

186. ARLL, Co. Cr. Leg. 249. Exp. 2679 (1696), 1. The indigenous assistants

probably inflicted Phelipe Lucumí to the "horse," a wooden rack where victims would be pulled by their arms and legs until they confessed.

187. For a discussion of crimes against slaves considered as property, see Somerville, *Rape and Race*, 78–79.

188. For the landholders' disregard of reducciones, especially their claims to water, see ARLL, Co. Ords. Leg. 209. Exp. 1553 (1692), 33; and ARLL, Ca. Ords. Leg. 35. Exp. 686 (1714), 3, 3v, 4, 4v, 5v.

189. ARLL, Protocolos. Salinas. Leg. 241 (1695), 76–78v.

190. Cañeque, *King's Living Image*, 187.

191. Garrett, *Shadows of Empire*, 36.

192. Stern, *Peru's Indian Peoples*, 93.

193. ARLL, Co. Asuntos de Gobierno. Leg. 269. Exp. 3230 (1700), 2.

194. Ibid., 1.

195. Escobedo Mansilla, *Tributo indígena en el Perú*, 61.

196. Diez Hurtado, *Fiestas y cofradías*, 82–83.

197. ARLL, Co. Asuntos de Gobierno. Leg. 269. Exp. 3267 (1699/1700), 1.

198. ARLL, Protocolos. Espino y Alvarado. Leg. 149 (1684), 329; BNP, #B411 (1681), 33–3v; Clements Library, Peru Collection. Eighteenth-century copies of four viceregal reports on the state of Peru. Don Melchor de Liñan y Cisneros, "Relación de Govierno que el exmo senor don Melchor de Liñan y Cisneros, Arzobispo de Lima, hace a su sucesor el exmo señor Duque de la Palata," 333; AGI, Lima. Leg. 298 (1685); and AGI, Lima. Leg. 298 (1690).

199. Fisher, "Creating and Contesting Community," para. 16; and Klein, *Haciendas and Ayllus*, 61.

200. Feijóo de Sosa, *Relación descriptiva de la ciudad*, 130; and ARLL, Co. Ords. Leg. 197. Exp. 1332 (1665), 16v, 21.

201. Ramírez, *Provincial Patriarchs*, 174; AGI, Lima 304 (1698); and ARLL, Ca. Ords. Leg. 35. Exp. 683 (1714), 11–11v.

202. ARLL, Co. Asuntos de Gobierno. Leg. 269. Exp. 3267 (1699), 1v.

203. AGN, Superior Gobierno. Juicios de Residencias. Leg. 37. Cuad. 108 (1693), 288; and ARLL, Co. Cr. Leg. 246. Exp. 2565 (1651), 17.

204. ARLL, Ca. Cr. Leg. 82. Exp. 1465 (1708), 4.

205. ARLL, Co. Cr. Leg. 249. Exp. 2674 (1691), 4.

206. ARLL, Co. Ords. Leg. 210. Exp. 1588 (1696), 6v.

207. King, "*Maréchausée* of Saint-Domingue," para. 31.

208. AAT, Causas Generales. Leg. 3 (1701).

209. Lavallè, *Amor y opresión*, 179.

210. AAT, Causas Generales. Leg. 3 (1701).

211. AAT, Causas de Negros. Leg. 1 (1702).

212. Schwartz, "Rethinking Palmares," 110. The relationship between indigenous men who policed Africans with their descendants and the colonial state was also fostered in the lower Mississippi valley. Usner, *Indians, Settlers, and Slaves*, 58, 139.

213. AGN, Compania de Jesus. Cuentas de hacienda. Leg. 94. "Cuentas de Tuman" (1755), 7.

214. ARLL, Ca. Cr. Leg. 82. Exp. 1454 (1704), 3.

215. Schwartz, "Rethinking Palmares," 113.

216. ARLL, Ca. Cr. Leg. 82. Exp. 1440 (1697), 5v.

217. Russell-Wood, "Ambivalent Authorities," 28.

218. ARLL, Ca. Cr. Leg. 82. Exp. 1440 (1697), 5v.

219. ARLL, Ca. Cr. Leg. 79. Exp. 1353 (1642), 1v, 2v; ARLL, Ca. Cr. Leg. 80. Exp. 1387 (1651); and AAT, Causas de Negros. Leg. 1 (1702), 45v.

220. ARLL, Co. Cr. Leg. 249. Exp. 2679 (1696), 1–1v.

221. Figueroa Luna, "Revueltas y litigios de esclavos," 23.

222. Alejandro de la Fuente reaffirmed historian Frank Tennenbaum's discussion of slaves' "moral and juridical personality." De la Fuente, "Slave Law and Claims-Making in Cuba," para. 24.

223. Gross, *Double Character*, 4; and de la Fuente, "'Su único derecho,'" 15.

224. For discussion of questions of death among the enslaved, see Karasch, *Slave Life in Rio de Janeiro*, 250; and Brown, *Reaper's Garden*.

225. Mangan, *Trading Roles*; Zulawski, *They Eat from Their Labor*; and Powers, *Andean Journeys*.

Conclusion: The Laws of Casta, the Making of Race

1. The Royal Library (Denmark), GKS 2232 4O Guaman Poma. Nueva corónica y buen gobierno (1615). Available online at http://www.kb.dk/permalink/2006/poma/info/en/frontpage.htm. Drawing 275. Devout black Christians from the stock of unacculturated black slaves from Africa ("Guinea") say the rosary before an image of the Virgin Mary. 703 [717].

2. Cummins, "Uncomfortable Image," 55; and Adorno, *Guaman Poma*, 26.

3. For a longer discussion of the distinctions between the two images, see Adorno, *Guaman Poma*, 119; and López-Baralt, *Icono y Conquista*, 386–88.

4. Archivo Regional de La Libertad (ARLL), Co. Cr..Leg. 243. Exp. 2401 (1626), f. 1v. The cacique of Santiago de Cao accused Antón, an enslaved man, of beating his son under orders of his owner.

5. Bowser, *African Slave in Colonial Peru*, 151–52; and Flores Galindo, *Aristocracia y plebe*, 233.

6. Tardieu, *El negro en el cusco*, 24, 130; Bridikhina, *Mujer negra en Bolivia*, 24–25, 30; and Lane, *Quito 1599*, 59, 68, 81.

7. In the nineteenth century, creole elites attempted to adapt European modernization techniques, including the racialization of indigenous populations whose "primitive" cultures were charged with inhibiting Andean modern development. Larson, *Trials of Nation Making*, 115, 160, 163, 207.

8. Poole, *Vision, Race, and Modernity*, 148, 164.

9. Wade, *Race and Ethnicity*, 35–36; and Poole, *Vision, Race, and Modernity*, 155, 157; and Larson, *Trials of Nation Making*, 69, 80–81.

10. For a discussion and critique of the scholarly divisions imposed on Indians and blacks, see Wade, *Race and Ethnicity*, 37–38; and de la Cadena, *Indigenous Mestizos*, 140–41.

11. Martínez, *Genealogical Fictions*, 162; and Cope, *Limits of Racial Domination*, 4.

12. ARLL, Co. Asuntos de Gobierno. Leg. 266. Exp. 3074 (1607), 2, 2v.

13. Ibid., 2v, 3v, 5.

14. Ramírez, *Provincial Patriarchs*, 162.

15. Konetzke, *Colección de documentos*, vol. 1, 237–40.

16. I thank Sherwin Bryant for pushing me to think about the work that casta does as race. Hesse, "Racialized Modernity," 652, 654.

17. Poole, *Vision, Race, and Modernity*, 23, 164; and de la Cadena, *Indigenous Mestizos*, 308, 310, 313.

18. For the historian R. Douglas Cope, casta categorization was "a hierarchical ordering of racial groups according to their proportion of Spanish blood" that governed "sexual and marital relations between castas and Spaniards." See Cope, *Limits of Racial Domination*, 24–25. The scholar Laura Lewis has identified "caste" as "an integrated system of relations and dispositions . . . a fluid pyramid, with Spanishness most associated with the Spanish elite at the top," followed by "Indianness" and then "interstitial spaces." See Lewis, *Hall of Mirrors*, 33.

19. ARLL, Co. Ords. Leg. 200. Exp. 1378 (1672), 1, 9.

20. Colonial jurists characterized indigenous people as consummate liars and rural people were commonly understood as less incorporated into the Spanish sphere. Ordoñez de Zevallos, *Historia, y viage*, 357; Navarra y Rocafull, *Relación de govierno por el Exmo*, 155; and Kellogg, *Law and the Transformation*, 66, 77.

21. ARLL, Ca. Cr. Leg. 83. Exp. 1484 (1725).

22. ARLL, Ca. Cr. Leg. 77. Exp. 1264 (1598), 3; ARLL, Protocolos. Lopez Collado y Daza. Leg. 372, #323 (1724), 771v–774; ARLL, Protocolos. San Román. Leg. 228 (1724), 351–356v; and ARLL, Co. Asuntos de Gobierno. Leg. 269. Exp. 3259 (1718).

23. ARLL, Co. Ords. Leg. 220. Exp. 1776 (1727), 10; ARLL, Co. Asuntos de Gobierno. Leg. 269. Exp. 3264 (1720); and ARLL, Co. Ords. Leg. 211. Exp. 1618 (1700).

24. ARLL, Ca. Cr. Leg. 83. Exp. 1484 (1725), 11.

25. Zulawski, *They Eat from Their Labor*, 75, 177.

26. Fisher, "Creating and Contesting Community," paras. 26, 31.

27. Vinson and Restall, "Black Soldiers," 36, 45; Lane, "Africans and Natives," 172; and Lutz and Restall, "Wolves and Sheep?" 196.

28. For a discussion of how individuals present one identity over another, see Calhoun, "Social Theory," 26. In queer theory the presentation of "self" is often understood as a conscious decision to be seen or understood publicly as a particular identity. See Takagi, "Maiden Voyage," 247; and Rak, "Digital Queer," 179.

29. For enslaved people employing slaveholders' ideals, see Johnson, *Soul by Soul*, 166–67, 179.

30. Lewis, *Hall of Mirrors*, 73, 113. Mörner, *Estratificacion social hispanoamerica*, 17, 18.

31. Martínez, *Genealogical Fictions*; and Silverblatt, *Modern Inquisitions*.

32. In this sense I agree with Cope, *Limits of Racial Domination*, 78.

33. Minchom, *People of Quito*, 155; and Espinosa Descalzo, *Cartografía de Lima*, xxxii, xxxviii.

34. Cope, *Limits of Racial Domination*, 24–25. Illustrative of the class-caste debate, see Chance and Taylor, "Estate and Class in a Colonial City," 482; and Chance and Taylor, "Estate and Class: A Reply," 432.

35. Silverblatt, *Modern Inquisitions*, 9, 18; and Lewis, *Hall of Mirrors*, 36, 40.

36. Larson, *Cochabamba, 1550–1900*, 106; Andrien, *Crisis and Decline*, 100; and Kamen, *Empire*, 142, 350.

37. Larson, *Cochabamba, 1550–1900*, 101; and Wightman, *Indigenous Migration and Social Change*, 31, 35.

38. Bowser, *African Slave in Colonial Peru*, 148, 183.

39. Stern, *Peru's Indian*, 81–82; and Twinam, *Public Lives, Private Secrets*, 190.

40. To save Cayetano (an accused fugitive bandit), his owner declared that the enslaved man had "good habits" and was quiet and peaceful. ARLL, Ca. Cr. Leg. 83. Exp. 1470 (1711), 2da quaderno, 1v. To defend Ambrosio, of casta arara, the legal representative (hired by the slaveholder) argued that the murder was a crime of passion "of the fragility of the man." ARLL, Ca. Cr. Leg. 83. Exp. 1480 (1720), 16–16v. In another case, the slaveholder underlined that Juan Joseph mandinga fought out of jealousy for Thomasa Lucumí. ARLL, Ca. Cr. Leg. 83. Exp. 1481 (1720), 19.

41. ARLL, Protocolos, Cortijo Quero. Leg. 115 (1705), 76v.

42. Fields, "Ideology and Race in American History," 152–53, 162; and Higginbotham, "African-American Women's History," 185, 186–87.

43. Burns, "Unfixing Race," 201–2; and Fischer, *Suspect Relations*, 5–6.

GLOSSARY

aguardiente: a sugar-cane alcoholic drink.

alcalde: the highest municipal colonial official.

alguacil mayor: a bailiff.

angola: used either to describe or to self-identify an African person originating from West Central Africa (presumably sold from the southern port of Luanda).

arara: used either to describe or to self-identify an African person originating from the Bight of Benin in West Africa.

asientista: a person who holds the official license for trading slaves into the Spanish Americas.

asiento: the official license for trading slaves into the Spanish Americas.

Audiencia: the highest colonial court of appointed judges; also employed to refer to a particular region.

balanta: used either to describe or to self-identify an African person originating from a particular region in West Africa's Guinea-Bissau.

bañol: used either to describe or to self-identify an African person originating from a particular region in West Africa's Guinea-Bissau.

borrachera: an Andean gathering that includes drinking but could also include decision making, dancing, and other community celebration.

bozal: employed by slaveholders and slave traders to mean an African man or a woman recently sold from the transatlantic slave trade and suggests a person who could not speak or understand Spanish or may not have been baptized.

bran: used either to describe or to self-identify an African person originating from a particular region in West Africa's Guinea-Bissau.

cabo verde: used either to describe or to self-identify an African person originating from a particular region in West Africa, presumably sold from the Cape Verde islands.

cacigazgo: Andean institution of presumably hereditary leadership.

cacique: an indigenous leader.

chasqui: an indigenous messenger.

chicha: corn beer.

cofradía: a religious confraternity or mutual aid society associated with a particular saint.

compadre: technically a godfather but used to mean a friend or companion.

compañero: a comrade or a companion.

composición de tierras: a colonial assessment of landownership in relation to indigenous population size.

congo: used either to describe or to self-identify an African person originating from West Central Africa, presumably sold from the northern region of the Kingdom of Kongo.

Consejo de Indias: the administrative, legislative, and judicial council that presided over all of the Spanish colonial holdings

corregidor: a magistrate.

creole: employed by historians to mean a man or woman of Spanish descent born in the Americas

criollo, criolla: employed by northern Peruvian notaries to mean a man or woman of African descent born in the Americas.

cuarterón: presumably a person who is of African and Spanish descent.

fanega: about 130 pounds of flour, or a measurement of land.

feria: a market day or time that includes other festivities.

forastero: a stranger or a migrant.

fray: friar.

guarapo: a sugar cane–based alcohol.

hacienda: an estate.

indio, india: an Indian.

jornal: a day's wage.

labrador: a farmer or low-status owner of an estate.

ladino, ladina: an acculturated man or woman, employed to refer to an Andean or an African person.

lucumí: used either to describe or to self-identify an African person originating from the Bight of Benin, presumably signifying a Yoruba-speaking man or woman.

mandinga: used either to describe or to self-identify an African person originating from West Africa, presumably today's Senegal and northern Guinea-Bissau.

mestizo, mestiza: a man or woman of Spanish and indigenous descent, or an acculturated indigenous man or woman.

mina: used either to describe or to self-identify an African person originating from the Gold Coast in West Africa.

mita: a rotational colonial labor requirement of indigenous men.

mitayo: a man who serves the colonial labor requirement.

moreno, morena: a man or woman of African descent.

mulato, mulata: a man or woman of presumably African and Spanish descent.

natural: a native or an indigenous person.

negro, negra: a black man or woman.

padrino: technically a godfather but often employed to mean a patron.

palenque: a settlement of fugitive slaves.

parcialidad: a moiety or a division of an indigenous community.

pardo, parda: a man or woman of African descent.

pariente: a relative or a relation.

partida: a coffle or a group of enslaved captives.

principal: a minor indigenous leader.

protector de los naturales: an assigned colonial legal representative to indigenous people.

Real Audiencia: a superior court that sometimes was employed for appeals cases.

reducción: an assigned colonial indigenous town.

revisita: a reinspection of an indigenous community to check its population size in relation to its tribute and mita assignment.

sambo, samba: a man or woman of presumably African and indigenous descent.

segunda persona: a lesser-status indigenous leader.

tambo: an inn.

tributario: an indigenous man who pays tribute and presumably is associated with a reducción.

vecino, vecina: a male or female neighbor or recognized "citizen" of a municipality.

yanacona: an indigenous laborer who works for wages or access to land and water.

yunga: the language and people of the Peruvian northern coast, or employed to refer to the coastal region.

zambo, zamba: a man or woman of presumably indigenous and African descent.

zambiago, zambiaga: a man or woman of presumably indigenous and African descent.

BIBLIOGRAPHY

Archival Sources

DENMARK
    Copenhagen
    The Royal Library

ITALY
    Rome
    Archivum Romanum Societatis Iesu (ARSI)

PERU
    Cartavio
    Archivo Parroquial de Cartavio (APC)
    Chiclayo
    Archivo Regional de Lambayeque,(ARL)
        Haciendas y comunidades
        Protocolos

Lima

Archivo Arzobispal de Lima (AAL)
- Apelaciones de Trujillo
- Causas de negros
- Causas eclesiásticas
- Inmunidad Eclesiástica

Archivo General de la Nación (AGN)
- Campesinado, Titulos de propiedad
- Compañía de Jesús, Colegio de Trujillo
- Derecho Indígena
- Juzgado de Aguas
- Real Audiencia, Causas civiles

Biblioteca Nacional del Perú (BNP)
- Manuscritos

Trujillo

Archivo Arzobispal de Trujillo (AAT)
- Causas de negros
- Causas generales
- Testamentos
- Visitas

Archivo Regional de La Libertad (ARLL)
- Actas del cabildo
- Cabildo (Ca.), Alcalde de aguas.
- Cabildo (Ca.), Asuntos de Gobierno
- Cabildo (Ca.), Causas Criminales (Cr.)
- Cabildo (Ca.), Causas Ordinarias (Ords.)
- Corregimiento (Co.), Causas Criminales (Cr.)
- Corregimiento (Co.), Causas Ordinarias (Ords.)
- Corregimiento (Co.), Compulsas.
- Corregimiento (Co.), Eclesiasticas.
- Corregimiento (Co.), Juez Pesquisidor.
- Corregimiento (Co.), Pedimientos.
- Hacienda. Compulsas.
- Protocolos

Archivo Sagrario de Trujillo (AST)

SPAIN

Seville

Archivo General de Indias
- Audiencia de Lima
- Audiencia de Panamá
- Contaduría
- Escribanía
- Indiferente

UNITED STATES
Ann Arbor
Clements Library, Peru Collection
Chicago
Newberry Library, Ayer Collection
New Haven
Yale University, Beinecke Library
New York
New York Public Library, Humanities, Rare Book Collection
Providence
John Carter Brown Library
Saint Louis
Vatican Film Library, Colección Pastells

Primary Sources

Acosta, José de. *Tercero catecismo y exposición de la doctrina christiana por sermones para que los curas y otros ministros prediquen y enseñan á los Indios, y á las demás personas conforme a lo que se proveyó en el Santo Concilio Provincial de Lima 1583.* Lima: Concilio Provincial, 1773 [1585].

Andrade, Alonso de. *Varones ilustres en santidad, letras, y zelo de las almas: De la Compañía de Iesus / tomo quinto, a los quatro que saco a luz el venerable, y erudito padre Iuan Eusebio Nieremberg.* Madrid: Ioseph Fernandez de Buendia, 1666.

Angulo, Domingo. "Diario de la segunda visita pastoral que hizo de su Arquidiócesis el Ilustrísimo Señor don Toribio Alfonso de Mogrovejo Arzobispo de los Reyes. Libro de Visitas. 1593." *Revista del Archivo Nacional del Perú* [Lima] 1, nos. 1 and 2 (1920): 49–81, 227–79.

Anómino. "Fragmento de una historia de Trujillo." *Revista histórica* [Lima] 8, no. 1 (1925): 88–118.

Anónimo. In *Descripción del Virreinato del Perú: Crónica inédita de comienzos del siglo XVII (1637).* Edited by Boleslao Lewin. Rosario: Universidad Nacional del Litoral, Facultad de Filosofía, Letras y Ciencias de la Educación, 1958.

Ayala, Manuel Josef de. *Diccionario de gobierno y legislación de Indias.* Madrid: Ediciones de Cultura Hispánica, 1991.

Calancha, Antonio de la. *Crónica moralizada del orden de San Augustin en el Peru.* 6 volumes. Lima: Universidad Nacional Mayor de San Marcos, 1974 [1638].

Cárdenas, Bernardino de. *Memorial y relación verdadera para el Rei N.S. y su Real Consejo de las Indias, de cosas del Reino del Perú, mui importantes a su real seruicio, y conciencia.* Madrid: Francisco Martinez, 1634.

Cieza de León, Pedro de. *The Travels of Pedro de Cieza de León.* London: Hakluyt Society, 1864 [1553].

Constituciones synodales del obispado de Arequipa: Hechas y ordenadas por el ilustrissimo y reverendissimo señor doctor don Antonio de Leon, su obispo, del consejo de Su Majestad: En la Synodo Diocessana que celebro año de 1684. Lima: Ioseph Contreras, 1688.

Constitvciones synodales de el obispado de la civdad de Gvamanga, celbradas en concilio diocesano per el. Lima: Geronimo de Contreras, 1677.

Constitvciones synodales del arçobispado de Los Reyes en el Pirv, Hechas y ordenadas. Lima: Francisco del Canto, 1614.

Córdoba y Salinas, Diego de. Vida, virtudes, y milagros del apostol del Perú el b.p. fr. Francisco Solano. Sacada de las declaraciones de qvinientos testigos, que juraron ante los ilustrissimos arçobispos, y obispos de Seuilla, Granada, Lima, Cordoua, y Malaga, y de otras muchas informaciones que por autoridad apostolica se han actuado en differente villas, y ciudades. Madrid: Imprenta real, 1676.

Encinas, Diego de. Cedulario Indiano (Provisiones Cedvlas, Capitvlos de ordenacas, instruciones, y cartas, libradas y despachas en diferentes tiempos por sus Magestades). Madrid: Ediciones Cultura Hispanica, 1945 [1596].

Feijóo de Sosa, Miguel. Relación descriptiva de la ciudad y provincia de Truxillo del Perú. Lima: Fondo del Libro, Banco Industrial del Perú, 1984.

Gama, Sebastian de la. "Visita hecha en el valle de Jayanca (Trujillo) (1540)." Historia y cultura [Lima] 8 (1974): 215–28.

González de Acuña, Antonio. Informe. A N. R.mo P.M. general de el Orden de Prediccadores Fr. Ihoan Baptista de Marinis. Matriti, 1659.

Herrera, Antonio de. Historia general de los hechos de los castellanos en las islas y tierra firme del Mar Oceano. Madrid: Officina Real de Nicolás Rodríguez Franco, 1730 [1601].

Instrucción para remediar, y assegurar, quanto con la divina gracia fuere posible, que ninguno de los Negros . . . carezca del sagrado Baptismo, ordered by Señor don Pedro de Castro y Quiñones, Arzbpo. de Sevilla, del Consejo del Rey. Lima: Geronymo de Contreras, 1628.

Jopling, Carol F., ed. Indios y negros en Panamá en los siglos XVI y XVII: Selecciones de los documentos del Archivo General de Indias. Antigua: Centro de Investigaciones Regionales de Mesoamérica, 1994.

Konetzke, Richard, ed. Colección de documentos para la historia de la formación social de Hispanoamérica, 1493–1810. 3 volumes. Madrid: Consejo Superior de Investigaciones Científicas, 1962.

Larco Herrera, Alberto. Anales de cabildo, ciudad de Trujillo: Extractos tomados de las actas. Lima: SanMartí y Ca., 1907–20.

Lizárraga, Reginaldo de. Descripción breve del Peru. Madrid: Atlas, 1968 [1609].

Macera, Pablo. Instrucciones para el manejo de las haciendas jesuitas del Perú, ss. XVII–XVIII. Lima: Universidad Nacional Mayor de San Marcos, Facultad de Letras y Ciencias Humanas, Departamento de Historia, 1966.

Martínez Compañón y Bujanda, Baltasar Jaime. Trujillo del Perú a fines del siglo XVIII. 9 volumes. Madrid: Ediciones Cultura Hispánica del Centro Iberoamericano de Cooperación, 1978.

Monsalve, Miguel de. Redvcion universal de todo el Pirv, y demas Indias, con otros mvchos Auisos, para el bien de los naturales dellas, y en aumento de las Reales Rentas. Compuesto por el Padre Fray Miguel de Mosalve, de la Orden de Predicadores, morador del Reyno del Piru. Dirigido a la Católica Magestad del Rey don Felipe, Tercero deste nombre nuestro Señor. Boston, 1925 [1604].

Navarra y Rocafull, don Melchor. Relación de govierno por el Exmo. Señor Dvqve de la Palata.

Virrey que fue del Reyno del Perv. al Exmo. Se or Conde de la Moclova sv svbcesor. Mexico, 1734 [1689].

Ocaña, Diego de. *Un viaje fascinante por la América Hispana del siglo XVI.* Madrid: Stvdivm, 1969 [1605].

Oñate, Alonso de. *Parecer de vn hombre docto en la facultad de teología y canones, y lector de la misma facultad, y de muchos anos de experiencia en las cosas de las Indias.* Madrid, 1600.

Ordoñez de Zevallos, Pedro. *Historia, y viage del mundo del clérigo agradecido don Pedro Ordoñez de Zevallos, natural de la insigne civdad de Jaen, á las cinco partes de la Europa, Africa, Asia, America, y Magalanica, con el Itinerario de todo él.* Madrid: Juan Garcia Infançon, 1691 [1614].

Ortiz de Cervantes, Juan. *Memorial que presenta a Su Magestad el licenciado Juan Ortiz de Cervantes, abogado, y procurador general del Reyno del Piru y encomenderos: Sobre pedir remedio del daño, y diminución de los Indios, y propone ser medio eficaz la perpetuydad de encomiendas: Presenta el parecer de los juezes comissarios, que fueron à aquel reyno à tratar de la perpetuydad.* Granata: Distribuidores Librería Sol, 1968.

Ramírez, Balthasar. "Descripción del Reyno del Piru del sitio temple. Prouincias, obispados, y ciudades, de los Naturales de sus lenguas y trage." In *Quellen zur Kulturgeschichte des präkolumbischen Amerika.* Edited by H. Trimborn. 10–67. Stuttgart: Streker and Schröder, 1936 [1597].

Recopilación de leyes de los reynos de las Indias, mandadas imprimir y publicar por la Magestad Católica del Rey don Cárlos II. Nuestro Señor. 4. impresión. *Hecha de orden del Real y Supremo Consejo de las Indias.* Madrid: La viuda de d. J. Ibarra, 1791.

Rubiños y Andrade, Modesto. "Noticia previa por el Liz. don Justo Modesto Rubiños y Andrade, cura de Mórrope, a o de 1782." *Revista histórica* [Lima] 10, no. 3 (1936 [1782]): 289–363.

Sánchez Bella, Ismael. *Derecho Indiano: Estudios.* Volume 1, *Las Visitas generales en la America Española (Siglos XVI–XVII).* Pamplona: Ediciones Universidad de Navarra, 1991.

Sandoval, Alonso de. *Un tratado sobre la esclavitud.* Madrid: Alianza Editorial, 1987 [1627].

Silva, Juan de. *Advertencias importantes, acerca del bven govierno, y administración de las Indias, assi en lo espiritual, como en lo temporal. Repartidas en tres memoriales informatiuos, dados en diferentes tiempos a Su Magestad, y Real consejo de Indias. Por el padre fray Iuan de Silua.* Madrid: Por la viuda de F. Correa Montenegro, 1621.

Snelgrave, William. *A New Account of Some Parts of Guinea and the Slave-Trade.* London: Frank Cass, 1971 [1734].

Solórzano Pereira, Juan de. *Libro primero de la Recopilación de las cedulas, cartas, Prouisiones, y ordenanzas Reales, que en diferentes tiempos sean despachado para el gobierno de las Indias Occidentales.* Lima, 1622.

———. *Política Indiana.* Madrid: Ediciones Atlas, [1647] 1972.

Toledo, Francisco de. *Disposiciones gubernativas para el virreinato de Perú.* Seville: Escuela de Estudios Hispano-Americanos, 1986.

———. *Ordenanzas de Don Francisco de Toledo, virrey del Perú, 1569–1581.* Madrid: Imprenta de San Pueyo, 1929.

Toribio Polo, José. *Memorias de los Virreys del Perú Marqués de Mancera y Conde de Salvatierra.* Lima: Imprenta del Estado, 1899 [1648].

Torres, Bernardo de. *Crónica de la provincia peruana del Orden de los ermitanos de s. Agvstin nvestro padre* Lima: Julian Santos de Saldaña, 1657.

Torres, Diego de. "Al Conde de Lemos y Andrade, Marques de Sarria, Presidente del Real Consejo de las Indias." In *El Indio Peruano y La Defensa de sus Derechos (1596–1630).* Edited by Quintín Aldea Vaquero. 435–60. Madrid: Consejo Superior de Investigaciones Científicas, 1993 [1603].

Vázquez de Espinosa, Antonio. *Compendium and Description of the West Indies.* Washington, D.C.: Smithsonian Institution, 1942 [1621].

Veitia Linage, don Joseph. *The Spanish Rule of Trade in the West Indies: Containing an Account of the Casa De Contratacion or India House, Its Government, Laws, Ordinances, Officers and Jurisdiction; of Its Inferior Courts; of the Receiving and Sending out Armadas and Flotas; Who May Go to the Indies, and Who Not; of Slaves Carry'd Over, and Many More Observations of This Nature.* London: Samuel Crouch, 1702.

Zárate, Agustin de. *The Discouerie and Conquest of the Prouinces of Peru, and the Nauigation in the South Sea, along That Coast: And also of the Ritche Mines of Potosi.* London: Richard Ihones, 1581.

Secondary Sources

Adorno, Rolena. *Guaman Poma: Writing and Resistance in Colonial Peru.* Austin: University of Texas Press, 1986.

Aguirre, Carlos. *Agentes de su propia libertad: Los Esclavos de Lima y la desintegración de la esclavitud, 1821–1854.* Lima: Pontificia Universidad Católica del Perú, 1993.

Aguirre Beltran, Gonzalo. "El trabajo del indio comparado con el del negro en Nueva España." *México agrario* 4 (1942): 203–7.

———. "Tribal Origins of Slaves in Mexico." *Journal of Negro History* 31 (July 1946): 269–352.

Alaperrine-Bouyer, Monique. *La educación de las elites indígenas en el Perú colonial.* Lima: Instituto Francés de Estudios Andinos, Instituto Riva Agüero, Instituto de Estudios Peruanos, 2007.

Aldana, Susana. *Empresas coloniales: Las tinas de jabón en Piura.* Piura: Centro de Investigación y Promoción del Campesinado, 1989.

Andrien, Kenneth J. *Andean Worlds: Indigenous History, Culture, and Consciousness under Spanish Rule, 1532–1825.* Albuquerque: University of New Mexico Press, 2001.

———. *Crisis and Decline: The Viceroyalty of Peru in the Seventeenth Century.* Albuquerque: University of New Mexico Press, 1985.

———. *Kingdom of Quito, 1690–1830: The State and Regional Development.* Cambridge: Cambridge University Press, 1995.

Bakewell, Peter. *Miners of the Red Mountain: Indian Labor in Potosí, 1545–1650.* Albuquerque: University of New Mexico Press, 1984.

Baptist, Edward E. "'Cuffy,' 'Fancy Maids,' and 'One-Eyed Men': Rape, Commodification, and the Domestic Slave Trade in the United States." *American Historical Review* 106, no. 5 (2001): 1–28.

Barragán Romano, Rossana. *Etnicidad y verticalidad ecológica de Sicasica, Ayo-Ayo y Calamarca, siglos XVI-XVII: El acceso vertical y el nacimiento de la hacienda en Palca, 1596–1644.* La Paz: Museo Nacional de Etnografía y Folklore, 1982.

Barrett, Ward J. *The Sugar Hacienda of the Marqueses del Valle.* Minneapolis: University of Minnesota Press, 1970.

Bay, Edna G. *Wives of the Leopard: Gender, Culture, and Power in the Kingdom of Dahomey.* Charlottesville: University Press of Virginia, 1998.

Bennett, Herman. *Africans in Colonial Mexico: Absolutism, Christianity, and Afro-Creole Consciousness, 1570–1640.* Bloomington: Indiana University Press, 2003.

———. *Colonial Blackness: A History of Afro-Mexico.* Bloomington: Indiana University Press, 2009.

Benton, Lauren. *Law and Colonial Cultures: Legal Regimes in World History, 1400–1900.* Cambridge: Cambridge University Press, 2002.

Berlin, Ira. *Many Thousands Gone: The First Two Centuries of Slavery in North America.* Cambridge: Belknap Press of Harvard University Press, 1998.

Bhabha, Homi K. *The Location of Culture.* London: Routledge, 1994.

Blanchard, Peter. *Slavery and Abolition in Early Republican Peru.* Wilmington: Scholarly Resources, Inc., 1992.

Bontemps, Alex. *The Punished Self: Surviving Slavery in the Colonial South.* Ithaca: Cornell University Press, 2001.

Borah, Woodrow. *Justice by Insurance: The General Indian Court of Colonial Mexico and the Legal Aides of the Half-Real.* Berkeley: University of California Press, 1983.

Borrego Plá, María del Carmen. "Palenques de negros cimarrones en Cartagena de Indias." In *Atti del XL Congresso Internazionale degli Americanisti. 3–10 settembre 1972.* Roma-Génova. Volume 3, 429–32. Genoa: Tilgher, 1975.

Bowser, Frederick. *The African Slave in Colonial Peru, 1524–1650.* Stanford: Stanford University Press, 1974.

Boyer, Richard. "Negotiating Calidad: The Everyday Struggle for Status in Mexico." *Historical Archeology* 31 (1997): 64–72.

Bridikhina, Eugenia. *Mujer negra en Bolivia.* La Paz: Protagonistas de su propia historia, 1995.

Bristol, Joan Cameron. *Christians, Blasphemers, and Witches: Afro-Mexican Ritual Practices in the Seventeenth Century.* Albuquerque: University of New Mexico Press, 2007.

Brockington, Lolita Gutiérrez. *Blacks, Indians, and Spaniards in the Eastern Andes: Reclaiming the Forgotten in Colonial Mizque, 1550–1782.* Lincoln: University of Nebraska Press, 2006.

Brooks, George E. *Eurafricans in Western Africa: Commerce, Social Status, Gender, and Religious Observance from the Sixteenth to the Eighteenth Century.* Athens: Ohio University Press, 2003.

Brooks, James F. *Captives and Cousins: Slavery, Kinship, and Community in the Southwest Borderlands.* Chapel Hill: Omohundro Institute of Early American History and Culture, University of North Carolina Press, 2002.

Brown, David H. *Santería Enthroned: Art, Ritual, and Innovation in an Afro-Cuban Religion.* Chicago: University of Chicago Press, 2003.

Brown, Vincent. *The Reaper's Garden: Death and Power in the World of Atlantic Slavery.* Cambridge: Harvard University Press, 2008.

———. "Spiritual Terror and Sacred Authority in Jamaican Slave Society." *Slavery and Abolition* 24 (April 2003): 24–53.

Bryant, Sherwin. "Enslaved Rebels, Fugitives, and Litigants: The Resistance Continuum in Colonial Quito." *Colonial Latin American Review* 13, no. 1 (2004): 7–46.

———. "Finding Gold, Forming Slavery: The Creation of a Classical Slave Society, Popayán, 1600–1800." *Americas* 63, no. 1 (2006): 81–112.

Burga, Manuel. *De la encomienda a la hacienda capitalista: El valle de Jequetepeque del siglo XVI al XX.* Lima: Instituto de Estudios Peruanos, 1976.

Burnard, Trevor, and Kenneth Morgan. "The Dynamics of the Slave Market and Slave Purchasing Patterns in Jamaica, 1655–1788." *William and Mary Quarterly,* Third Series, 58, New Perspectives on the Transatlantic Slave Trade (January 2001): 205–28.

Burns, Kathryn. *Colonial Habits: Convents and the Spiritual Economy of Cuzco, Peru.* Durham: Duke University Press, 1999.

———. *Into the Archive: Writing and Power in Colonial Peru.* Durham: Duke University Press, 2010.

———. "Unfixing Race." In *Rereading the Black Legend: The Discourses of Religious and Racial Difference in the Renaissance Empires.* Edited by Margaret R. Greer, Walter D. Mignolo, and Maureen Quilligan. 188–202. Chicago: University of Chicago Press, 2007.

Busto Duthurburu, José Antonio del. *Historia general del Perú: Descubrimiento y conquista.* Lima: Librería Studium, 1978.

———. *Historia marítima del Peru: Siglo XVI—Historia interna.* Volume 3. Lima: Editorial Ausonia, 1972.

Butler, Judith. *Gender Trouble: Feminism and the Subversion of Identity.* New York: Routledge, 1990.

Cahill, David. "Colour by Numbers: Racial and Ethnic Categories in the Viceroyalty of Peru, 1532–1821." *Journal of Latin American Studies* 26 (May 1994): 325–46.

Calhoun, Craig. J. "Social Theory and the Politics of Identity." In *Social Theory and the Politics of Identity.* Edited by Craig J. Calhoun. 9–36. Oxford: Blackwell, 1994.

Camp, Stephanie. *Closer to Freedom: Enslaved Women and Everyday Resistance in the Plantation South.* Chapel Hill: University of North Carolina Press, 2004.

Cañeque, Alejandro. *The King's Living Image: The Culture and Politics of Viceregal Power in Colonial Mexico.* New York: Routledge, 2004.

Cañizares Esguerra, Jorge. "New World, New Stars: Patriotic Astrology and the Invention of Indian and Creoles Bodies in Colonial Spanish America, 1600–1650." *American Historical Review* 10 (February 1999): 33–68.

Cardoso, Gerald. *Negro Slavery in the Sugar Plantations of Veracruz and Pernambuco 1550–1680: A Comparative Study.* Washington, D.C.: University Press of America, 1983.

Carroll, Patrick J. *Blacks in Colonial Veracruz: Race, Ethnicity, and Regional Development.* 1991; reprint, Austin: University of Texas Press, 2001.

Castañeda Murga, Juan. *La epidemia general de agua: Documentos sobre el Niño y su impacto en los valles de Trujillo.* Trujillo: Caja Rural La Libertad, 1998.

———. "Notas para una historia de la ciudad de Trujillo del Perú en el siglo XVII." In *La tradición andina en tiempos modernos.* Edited by Hiroyasu Tomoeda and Luis Millones. 159–89. Osaka: National Museum of Ethnology, 1996.

———. "Relaciones entre negros e indios en el Valle de Chicama, 1565." In *Actas del IV Congreso Internacional de Etnohistoria.* Volume 3, 240–48. Lima: Pontificia Universidad Católica del Perú, 1998.

Chambers, Sarah C. *From Subjects to Citizens: Honor, Gender, and Politics in Arequipa, Peru, 1780–1854.* University Park: Pennsylvania State University Press, 1999.

Chance, John K., and William B. Taylor. "Estate and Class in a Colonial City: Oaxaca in 1792." *Comparative Studies in Society and History* 19 (October 1977): 454–87.

———. "Estate and Class: A Reply to Robert McCaa, Stuart B. Schwartz, and Arturo Grubbesich." *Comparative Studies in Society and History* 21 (July 1979): 426–34.

Chang-Rodríguez, Raquel. "Coloniaje y conciencia nacional: Garcilaso de la Vega Inca y Felipe Guamán Poma de Ayala." *Cahiers du Monde Hispanique et Luso-Brésilien* (Caravelle) 38 (1982): 29–43.

Charney, Paul. *Indian Society in the Valley of Lima, Peru, 1532–1824.* Lanham: University Press of America, 2001.

Cole, Jeffrey A. *Potosí Mita, 1573–1700: Compulsory Indian Labor in the Andes.* Stanford: Stanford University Press, 1985.

Cook, Noble David. *Demographic Collapse: Indian Peru, 1520–1620.* Cambridge: Cambridge University Press, 1981.

Cope, R. Douglas. *The Limits of Racial Domination: Plebeian Society in Colonial Mexico City, 1660–1720.* Madison: University of Wisconsin Press, 1994.

Coronel, Rosario. "Indios y esclavos negros en el valle del Chota colonial." In *Actas del Primer Congreso de Historia del Negro en el Ecuador y sur de Colombia. Esmeraldas 14–16 de Octubre, 1988.* 171–87. Quito: Centro Cultural Afro-Ecuatoriano, 1988.

Cosamalón Aguilar, Jesús. *Indios detrás de la muralla: Matrimonios indígenas y convivencia inter-racial en Santa Ana (Lima, 1795–1820).* Lima: Pontificia Universidad Católica del Perú, 1999.

Cowling, Camillia. "Negotiating Freedom: Women of Colour and the Transition to Free Labour in Cuba, 1870–1886." *Slavery and Abolition* 26, no. 3 (2005): 373–87.

Cummins, Tom. "The Uncomfortable Image: Pictures and Words in the *Nueva corónica i buen gobierno.*" In *Guaman Poma de Ayala: The Colonial Art of an Andean Author.* 46–59. New York: Americas Society / Art Gallery, 1991.

Curto, José C. *Enslaving Spirits: The Portuguese-Brazilian Alcohol Trade at Luanda and Its Hinterland, c. 1550–1830.* Leiden: Brill, 2004.

Cushner, Nicholas P. *Lords of the Land: Sugar, Wine, and Jesuit Estates of Coastal Peru, 1600–1767.* Albany: State University of New York Press, 1980.

Cutter, Charles. *Legal Culture of Northern New Spain, 1700–1810.* Albuquerque: University of New Mexico Press, 1995.

———. *The Protector de Indios in Colonial New Mexico, 1659–1821.* Albuquerque: University of New Mexico Press, 1986.

Dakubu, M. E. Kropp. *Korle Meets the Sea: A Sociolinguistic History of Accra.* New York: Oxford University Press, 1997.

Davies, Keith. *Landowners in Colonial Peru.* Austin: University of Texas Press, 1984.

Dean, Carolyn. *Inka Bodies and the Body of Christ: Corpus Christi in Colonial Cuzco, Peru.* Durham: Duke University Press, 1999.

de Certeau, Michel. *The Practice of Everyday Life.* Berkeley: University of California Press, 1984.

de la Cadena, Marisol. *Indigenous Mestizos: The Politics of Race and Culture in Cuzco, Peru, 1919–1991.* Durham: Duke University Press, 2000.

de la Fuente, Alejandro. *Havana and the Atlantic in the Sixteenth Century.* Chapel Hill: University of North Carolina Press, 2008.

———. "Slave Law and Claims-Making in Cuba: The Tannenbaum Debate Revisited." *Law and History Review* 22 (Summer 2004): 339–69.

———. "Slaves and the Creation of Legal Rights in Cuba: *Coartación* and *Papel.*" *Hispanic American Historical Review* 87, no. 4 (2007): 659–92.

———. "'Su único derecho': Los esclavos y la ley." *Debate y Perspectivas* 4 (2004): 7–22.

de la Puente Luna, Jose Carlos. *Los Curacas hechiceros de Jauja: Batallas magicas y legales en el Perú colonial.* Lima: Fondo Editorial Pontificia Universidad Católica, 2007.

Deloria, Philip Joseph. *Indians in Unexpected Places.* Lawrence: University Press of Kansas, 2004.

Deyle, Steven. *Carry Me Back: The Domestic Slave Trade in American Life.* New York: Oxford University Press, 2005.

Diez Hurtado, Alejandro. *Las comunidades indígenas de Bajo Piura: Catacaos y Sechura, siglo XIX.* Piura: Centro de Investigación y Promoción del Campesino (CIPCA), 1992.

———. *Fiestas y cofradias: Asociaciones religiosas e integración en la historia de la comunidad de Sechura siglos XVII al XX.* Piura: Centro de Investigación y Promoción del Campesino (CIPCA), 1994.

Diouf, Sylviane. *Dreams of Africa in Alabama: The Slave Ship Clotilda and the Story of the Last Africans Brought to America.* Oxford: Oxford University Press, 2007.

Du Bois, W. E. B. *The Souls of Black Folk.* New York: Dover, 1994 [1903].

Durston, Alan. *Pastoral Quechua: The History of Christian Translation in Colonial Peru, 1550–1650.* Norte Dame: University of Notre Dame Press, 2007.

Earle, Rebecca. "Luxury, Clothing, and Race in Colonial Spanish America." In *Luxury in the Eighteenth Century: Debates, Desires, and Delectable Goods.* Edited by Maxine Berg and Elizabeth Eger. 219–27. London: Palgrave, 2003.

Edwards, Laura. *Gendered Strife and Confusion: The Political Culture of Reconstruction.* Urbana: University of Illinois Press, 1997.

———. "Status without Rights: African Americans and the Tangled History of Law and Goverance in the Nineteenth-Century U.S. South." *American Historical Review* 112 (April 2007): 365–93.

Emmer, P. C. "The Dutch and the Making of the Second Atlantic System." In *Slavery and the Rise of the Atlantic System*. Edited by Barbara L. Solow. 75–96. Cambridge: Cambridge University Press, 1991.

Escobedo Mansilla, Ronald. *Tributo indígena en el Perú: Siglos XVI y XVII*. Pamplona: Ediciones Universidad de Navarra, Oficina de Educación Iberoamericana, 1979.

Espinosa Descalzo, Victoria. *Cartografía de Lima (1654–1893)*. Lima: Universidad Nacional Mayor de San Marcos, Seminario de Historia Rural Andina, 1999.

———. "Cimarronaje y palenques en la costa central del Perú: 1700–1815." In *Primer seminario sobre poblaciones inmigrantes. Actas. Lima, 9 y 10 de mayo de 1986*. Volume 2, 29–42. Lima: Consejo Nacional de Ciencia y Tecnología, 1988.

Estenssoro Fuchs, Juan Carlos. *Del paganismo a la santidad: La incorporación de los indios del Perú al catolicismo, 1532–1750*. Lima: Instituto Francés de Estudios Andinos, 2003.

———. "Música y comportamiento festivo de la población negra en Lima colonial." *Cuadernos hispanoamericanos* 451–52 (1988): 161–68.

Farriss, Nancy M. *Maya Society under Colonial Rule: The Collective Enterprise of Survival*. Princeton: Princeton University Press, 1992.

Fields, Barbara. "Ideology and Race in American History." In *Region, Race, and Reconstruction: Essays in Honor of C. Vann Woodward*. Edited by J. Morgan Kousser and James M. McPherson. 143–77. New York: Oxford University Press, 1982.

Figueroa Luna, Guillermo. "Revueltas y litigios de esclavos en Lambayeque, 1750–1850." *Historia y cultura* 24 (2001): 77–108.

Fischer, Kristen. *Suspect Relations: Sex, Race, and Resistance in Colonial North Carolina*. Ithaca: Cornell University Press, 2002.

Fisher, Andrew B. "Creating and Contesting Community: Indians and Afromestizos in the Late-Colonial Tierra Caliente of Guerrero, Mexico." *Journal of Colonialism and Colonial History* 7, no. 1 (Spring 2006). doi: 10.1353/cch.2006.0030. Available online at https://vpn.nacs.uci.edu/+CSCO+dh756767633A2F2F7A6866722E7 775682E727168++/journals/journal_of_colonialism_and_colonial_history/ v007/7.1fisher.html.

———, and Matthew D. O'Hara. "Introduction: Racial Identities and Their Interpreters in Colonial Latin America." In *Imperial Subjects: Race and Identity in Colonial Latin America*. Edited by Andrew B. Fisher and Matthew D. O'Hara. 1–38. Durham: Duke University Press, 2009.

Flores Galindo, Alberto. *Aristocracia y plebe: Lima, 1760–1830 (Estructura de clases y sociedad colonial)*. Lima: Mosca Azul Editores, 1984.

Franklin, John Hope, and Loren Schweninger. *Runaway Slaves: Rebels on the Plantation*. New York: Oxford University Press, 1999.

García, Jesus Alberto. *La diaspora de los kongos en las Americas y los Caribes*. Caracas: Editorial APICUM and UNESCO, 1995.

Garofalo, Leo. "Conjuring with Coca and the Inca: The Andeanization of Lima's

Afro-Peruvian Ritual Specialists, 1580–1690." *The Americas* 63 (July 2006): 53–80.

Garrett, David. *Shadows of Empire: The Indian Nobility of Cusco, 1750–1825.* Cambridge: Cambridge University Press, 2005.

Gaspar, David Barry. *Bondmen and Rebels: A Study of Master-Slave Relations in Antigua, with Implications for Colonial British America.* Baltimore: Johns Hopkins University Press, 1985.

———. "Sugar Cultivation and Slave Life in Antigua before 1800." In *Cultivation and Culture: Labour and the Shaping of Slave Life in the Americas.* Edited by Ira Berlin and Philip D. Morgan. 101–23. Charlottesville: University Press of Virginia, 1993.

Ginzburg, Carlo. *The Cheese and the Worms: The Cosmos of a Sixteenth-Century Miller.* New York: Penguin Books, 1982 [1976].

———. "Microhistory: Two or Three Things That I Know about It." *Critical Inquiry* 20 (Fall 1993): 10–35.

Glave Testino, Luis Miguel. *Trajinantes: Caminos indígenas en la sociedad colonial, siglos XVI–XVII.* Lima: Instituto de Apoyo Agrario, 1989.

Gomez, Michael. *Exchanging Our Country Marks: The Transformation of African Identities in the Colonial and Antebellum South.* Chapel Hill: University of North Carolina Press, 1998.

Gómez Cumpa, José. "Mórrope, una cultura en el desierto de la costa norte del Perú." *Actas del IV congreso internacional de etnohistoria.* Volume 3, 294–345. Lima: Pontificia Universidad Católica del Perú, 1998.

Graubart, Karen B. "The Creolization of the New World: Local Forms of Identification in Urban Colonial Peru, 1560–1640." *Hispanic American Historical Review* 89 (August 2009): 471–99.

———. "Weaving and the Construction of a Gender Division of Labor in Early Colonial Peru." *American Indian Quarterly* 24, no. 4 (2001): 537–61.

———. *With Our Labor and Sweat: Indigenous Women and the Formation of Colonial Society in Peru, 1550–1700.* Stanford: Stanford University Press, 2007.

Greene, Sandra E. *Gender, Ethnicity, and Social Change on the Upper Slave Coast: A History of the Anlo-Ewe.* Portsmouth: Heinemann, 1996.

Griffin, Rebecca J. "'Goin' Back Over There To See That Girl': Competing Social Spaces in the Lives of the Enslaved in Antebellum North Carolina." *Slavery and Abolition* 25 (April 2004): 94–113.

Gross, Ariela J. *Double Character: Slavery and Mastery in the Antebellum Southern Courtroom.* Princeton: Princeton University Press, 2000.

Guevara-Gil, Armando, and Frank Salomon, "A 'Personal Visit': Colonial Political Ritual and the Making of Indians in the Andes." *Colonial Latin American Review* 3 (1994): 3–36.

Gutiérrez Brockington, Lolita. "The African Diaspora in the Eastern Andes: Adaptation, Agency, and Fugitive Action, 1573–1677." *The Americas* 57 (October 2000): 207–24.

———. *Blacks, Indians, and Spaniards in the Eastern Andes: Reclaiming the Forgotten in Colonial Mizque, 1550–1782.* Lincoln: University of Nebraska Press, 2006.

Hall, Gwendolyn Midlo. *Africans in Colonial Louisiana: The Development of Afro-Creole Culture in the Eighteenth Century*. Baton Rouge: Louisiana State University Press, 1992.

Hall, Neville. "Slaves' Use of Their 'Free' Time in the Danish Virgin Islands in the Late Eighteenth and Early Nineteenth Century." *Journal of Caribbean History* 13 (1979): 21–43.

Hanger, Kimberly S. *Bounded Places: Free Black Society in Colonial New Orleans, 1769–1803*. Durham: Duke University Press, 1997.

Harth-Terré, Emilio. *Negros e indios: Un estamento social ignorado del Perú colonial*. Lima: Editorial Juan Mejía Baca, 1973.

Hartman, Saidiya. *Scenes of Subjection: Terror, Slavery, and Self-Making in Nineteenth-Century America*. New York: Oxford University Press, 1997.

Harvey, Penelope. "Genero, comunidad y confrontación: Relaciones de poder en la embriaguez en Ocongate, Perú." In *Borrachera y Memoria: La experiencia de lo sagrado en los Andes*. Edited by Thierry Saignes. 113–38. Lima: HISBOL/IFEA, 1993.

Hawthorne, Walter. *From Africa to Brazil: Culture, Identity, and an Atlantic Slave Trade, 1600–1830*. Cambridge: Cambridge University Press, 2010.

———. "The Production of Slaves Where There Was No State: The Guinea-Bissau Region, 1450–1815." *Slavery and Abolition* 20 (August 1999): 97–124.

———. *Planting Rice and Harvesting Slaves: Transformations along the Guinea-Bissau Coast, 1400–1900*. Portsmouth: Heinemann, 2003.

Herzog, Tamar. *La administración como un fenómeno social: La justicia penal de la ciudad de Quito (1650–1750)*. Madrid: Centro de Estudios Constitucionales, 1995.

———. *Defining Nations: Immigrants and Citizens in Early Modern Spain and Spanish America*. New Haven: Yale University Press, 2003.

———. *Upholding Justice: Society, State, and the Penal System of Quito (1650–1750)*. Ann Arbor: University of Michigan Press, 2004.

Hesse, Barnor. "Racialized Modernity: An Analytics of White Mythologies." *Ethnic and Racial Studies* 30, no. 4 (July 2007): 643–63.

Heywood, Linda M., and John K. Thornton. *Central Africans, Atlantic Creoles, and the Foundation of the Americas, 1585–1660*. Cambridge: Cambridge University Press, 2007.

Higginbotham, Evelyn Brooks. "African-American Women's History and the Metalanguage of Race." In *Feminism and History*. Edited by Joan Wallach Scott. 183–207. Oxford: Oxford University Press, 1996.

Higgins, Kathleen. *"Licentious Liberty" in a Brazilian Gold-Mining Region: Slavery, Gender, and Social Control in Eighteenth-Century Sabará, Minas Gerais*. University Park: Pennsylvania State University Press, 1999.

Hilton, Anne. *The Kingdom of Kongo*. Oxford: Oxford University Press, 1985.

Hünefeldt, Christine. *Paying the Price of Freedom: Family and Labor among Lima's Slaves, 1800–1854*. Berkeley: University of California Press, 1994.

Israel, Jonathan I. *The Dutch Republic: Its Rise, Greatness, and Fall, 1477–1806*. Oxford: Clarendon Press, 1995.

Johnson, Walter. *Soul by Soul: Life Inside the Antebellum Slave Market*. Cambridge: Harvard University Press, 1999.

Jouve-Martín, José R. *Esclavos de la ciudad letrada: Esclavitud, escritura y colonialismo en Lima (1650–1700)*. Lima: Instituto de Estudios Peruanos, 2005.

———. "Public Ceremonies and Mulatto Identity in Viceregal Lima: A Colonial Reenactment of the Fall of Troy (1631)." *Colonial Latin American Review* 16 (December 2007): 179–201.

Kamen, Henry. *Empire: How Spain Became a World Power, 1492–1763*. New York: Harper Collins, 2003.

———. *Spain's Road to Empire: The Making of a World Power, 1492–1763*. London: Penguin Books, 2002.

Kapsoli, Wilfredo. *Rebeliones de esclavos en el Perú*. Lima: Purej, 1990.

Karasch, Mary C. *Slave Life in Rio de Janeiro, 1808–1850*. Princeton: Princeton University Press, 1987.

Keith, Robert G. *Conquest and Agrarian Change: The Emergence of the Hacienda System on the Peruvian Coast*. Cambridge: Harvard University Press, 1976.

Kellogg, Susan. "Depicting *Mestizaje*: Gendered Images of Ethnorace in Colonial Mexican Texts." *Journal of Women's History* 12 (Fall 2000): 69–92.

———. *Law and the Transformation of Aztec Culture, 1500–1700*. Norman: University of Oklahoma Press, 1995.

King, Stewart. "The Maréchausée of Saint-Domingue: Balancing the Ancien Régime and Modernity." *Journal of Colonialism and Colonial History* 5 (2004). doi: 10.1353/cch.2004.0052. Available online at https://vpn.nacs.uci.edu/+CSCO+dh756767633A2F2F7A6866722E7775682E727168++/journals/journal_of_colonialism_and_colonial_history/v005/5.2king.html.

Klein, Herbert S. *The Atlantic Slave Trade*. Cambridge: Cambridge University Press, 1999.

———. *Haciendas and Ayllus: Rural Society in the Bolivian Andes in the Eighteenth and Nineteenth Centuries*. Stanford: Stanford University Press, 1993.

Kopytoff, Barbara. "The Development of Jamaican Maroon Ethnicity." *Caribbean Quarterly* 22, no. 2–3 (1976): 33–50.

Kuznesof, Elizabeth. "More Conversation on Race, Class, and Gender." *Colonial Latin American Review* 5 (June 1996): 129–33.

Landers, Jane. *Black Society in Spanish Florida*. Urbana: University of Illinois Press, 1999.

———. "Cimarrón Ethnicity and Cultural Adaptation in the Spanish Domains of the Circum-Caribbean, 1503–1763." In *Identity in the Shadow of Slavery*. Edited by Paul E. Lovejoy. 30–54. London: Continuum, 2000.

Lane, Kris. "Africans and Natives in the Mines of Spanish America." In *Beyond Black and Red: African-Native Relations in Colonial Latin America*. Edited by Matthew Restall. Albuquerque: University of New Mexico Press, 2005.

———. *Quito 1599: City and Colony in Transition*. Albuquerque: University of New Mexico Press, 2002.

Larson, Brooke. *Cochabamba, 1550–1900: Colonialism and Agrarian Transformation in Bolivia.* Durham: Duke University Press, 1998 [1988].

———. *Trials of Nation Making: Liberalism, Race, and Ethnicity in the Andes, 1810–1910.* Cambridge: Cambridge University Press, 2004.

Lavallè, Bernard. *Amor y opresión en los Andes coloniales.* Lima: Instituto de Estudios Peruanos, 1999.

Law, Robin. *The Kingdom of Allada.* Leiden: Research School, Centre of Non-Western Studies, School of Asian, African, and Amerindian Studies, 1997.

———. "'My Head Belongs to the King': On the Political and Ritual Significance of Decapitation in Pre-Colonial Dahomey." *Journal of African History* 30 (1989): 399–415.

Lewis, Laura. *Hall of Mirrors: Power, Witchcraft, and Caste in Colonial Mexico.* Durham: Duke University Press, 2003.

Lipsett-Rivera, Sonya. *To Defend Our Water with the Blood of Our Veins: The Struggle for Resources in Colonial Puebla.* Albuquerque: University of New Mexico Press, 1999.

Littlefield, Daniel. *Rice and Slaves: Ethnicity and the Slave Trade in Colonial South Carolina.* Baton Rouge: Louisiana State University Press, 1981.

Lockhart, James. *Spanish Peru, 1532–1560: A Social History.* Madison: University of Wisconsin Press, 1994 [1968].

Lohmann Villena, Guillermo. *El corregidor de indios en el Perú bajo los Austias.* Madrid: Cultura Hispánica, 1957.

López-Baralt, Mercedes. *Icono y Conquista: Guamán Poma de Ayala.* Madrid: Hiperión, 1988.

Lovejoy, Paul. "Ethnic Designations of the Slave Trade and the Reconstruction of the History of Trans-Atlantic Slavery." In *Trans-Atlantic Dimensions of Ethnicity in the African Diaspora.* Edited by Paul Lovejoy and David Trotman. 9–42. London: Continuum, 2003.

Lowry, Lyn. "Forging an Indian Nation: Urban Indians under Spanish Colonial Control (Lima, Peru, 1535–1765)." PhD diss., University of California, Berkeley, 1991.

Lutz, Christopher, and Matthew Restall. "Wolves and Sheep? Black-Maya Relations in Colonial Guatemala and Yucatan." In *Beyond Black and Red: African-Native Relations in Colonial Latin America.* Edited by Matthew Restall. 185–221. Albuquerque: University of New Mexico Press, 2005.

Macera, Pablo. "Los Jesuitas y la agricultura de la caña." In *Nueva visión del Perú.* Edited by Luis Guillermo Lumbreras. 201–20. Lima, 1988.

MacLachlan, Colin M. *Spain's Empire in the New World: The Role of Ideas in Institutional and Social Change.* Berkeley: University of California Press, 1988.

Mangan, Jane. *Trading Roles: Gender, Ethnicity, and the Urban Economy in Colonial Potosí.* Durham: Duke University Press, 2005.

Mannarelli, Maria Emma. *Private Passions and Public Sins: Men and Women in Seventeenth-Century Lima.* Albuquerque: University of New Mexico Press, 2007 [1993].

Manrique, Nelson. *La piel y la pluma: Escritos sobre literatura, etnicidad y racismo.* Lima: Sur

Casa de Estudios del Socialismo and Centro de Información y Desarrollo Integral de Autogestión, 1999.

Marsilli, Maria. "Missing Idolatry: Mid-Colonial Interactions between Parish Priests and Indians in the Colonial Diocese of Arequipa." *Colonial Latin American Historical Review* 13, no. 4 (Fall 2004): 399–421.

Martínez, María Elena. "The Black Blood of New Spain: *Limpieza de Sangre*, Racial Violence, and Gendered Power in Early Colonial Mexico." *William and Mary Quarterly* 61 (July 2004): 479–520.

———. *Genealogical Fictions: Limpieza de Sangre, Religion, and Gender in Colonial Mexico.* Stanford: Stanford University Press, 2008.

McCaa, Robert, Stuart Schwartz, and Arturo Grubessich. "Race and Class in Colonial Latin America: A Critique." *Comparative Studies in Society and History* 21 (July 1979): 421–33.

McClintock, Anne. *Imperial Leather: Race, Gender, and Sexuality in the Colonial Context.* New York: Routledge, 1995.

McKee, Larry. "Food Supply and Plantation Social Order: An Archaeological Perspective." In *"I, Too, Am America": Archaeological Studies of African-American Life.* Edited by Theresa A. Singleton. 218–39. Charlottesville: University Press of Virginia, 1999.

McKinley, Michelle. "Fractional Freedoms: Slavery, Legal Activism, and Ecclesiastical Courts in Colonial Lima, 1593–1689." *Law and History Review* 28, no. 3 (2010): 749–90.

McKnight, Kathryn Joy. "Confronted Rituals: Spanish Colonial and Angolan 'Maroon' Execution in Cartagena de Indias (1634)." *Journal of Colonialism and Colonial History* 5 (Winter 2004). doi: 10.1353/cch.2004.0082. Available online at https://vpn.nacs.uci.edu/+CSCO+dh756767633A2F2F7A6866722E7775682E 727168++/journals/journal_of_colonialism_and_colonial_history/v005 /5.3mcknight.html.

———. "'En su tierra lo aprendió': An African *Curandero's* Defense before the Cartagena Inquisition." *Colonial Latin American Review* 12 (June 2003): 63–84.

Meiklejohn, N. A. "The Implementation of Slave Legislation in Eighteenth-Century New Granada." In *Slavery and Race Relations in Latin America.* Edited by Robert Brent Toplin. 176–203. Westport: Greenwood Press, 1974.

Melville, Elinor G. K. *A Plague of Sheep: Environmental Consequences of the Conquest of Mexico.* Cambridge: Cambridge University Press, 1997.

Miles, Tiya. *Ties That Bind: The Story of an Afro-Cherokee Family in Slavery and Freedom.* Berkeley: University of California Press, 2005.

Miller, Joseph. *Way of Death: Merchant Capitalism and the Angolan Slave Trade, 1730–1830.* Madison: University of Wisconsin Press, 1988.

Miller, Joseph C. "Retention, Reinvention, and Remembering: Restoring Identities through Enslavement in Africa and under Slavery in Brazil." In *Enslaving Connections: Changing Cultures of Africa and Brazil during the Era of Slavery.* Edited by José Curto and Paul Lovejoy. 81–122. Amherst: Humanity Books, 2003.

Millones Santagadeo, Luis. "Población negra en el Peru: Analisis de la posicion social del negro durante la dominacion espa ola." In Minorías étnicas en el Perú. Lima: Pontificia Universidad Católica del Perú, 1973.

Mills, Kenneth R. Idolatry and Its Enemies: Colonial Andean Religion and Extirpation, 1640–1750. Princeton: Princeton University Press, 1997.

Minchom, Martin. The People of Quito, 1690–1810: Change and Unrest in the Underclass. Boulder: Westview Press, 1994.

Mintz, Sidney W., and Richard Price. An Anthropological Approach to the Afro-American Past: A Caribbean Perspective. Philadelphia: Institute for the Study of Human Issues, 1976.

Moreno Cebrián, Alfredo. El corregidor de indios y la economía peruana del siglo XVIII: Los repartos forzosos de mercancías. Madrid: Consejo Superior de Investigaciones Científicas, 1977.

Moreno Fraginals, Manuel. El ingenio. Barcelona: Crítica, 2001.

Morgan, Jennifer L. Laboring Women: Reproduction and Gender in New World Slavery. Philadelphia: University of Pennsylvania Press, 2004.

Morgan, Philip. Slave Counterpoint: Black Culture in the Eighteenth-Century Chesapeake and Low-country. Chapel Hill: University of North Carolina Press and Institute of Early American History and Culture, 1998.

———. "Slaves and Livestock in Eighteenth-Century Jamaica: Vineyard Pen, 1750–1751." William and Mary Quarterly 52 (1995): 47–76.

———. "Work and Culture: The Task System and the World of Lowcountry Blacks, 1700 to 1880." William and Mary Quarterly, third series, 39 (October 1982): 564–99.

Mörner, Magnus. Estratificación social hispanoamerica durante el período colonial. Stockholm: Institute of Latin American Studies, 1980.

———. Race Mixture in the History of Latin America. Boston: Little, Brown, and Company, 1967.

Navarrete, María Cristina. "Entre Kronos y Calendas: Aproximaciones al concepto de tiempo de grupos negros en la Colonia (Cartagena de Indias)." América Negra 10 (1995): 85–96.

———. Génesis y Desarrollo de la Esclavitud en Colombia Siglos XVI y XVII. Santiago de Cali: Universidad del Valle, 2005.

———. Historia Social del Negro en la Colonia Cartagena, siglo XVII. Santiago de Cali: Editorial de la Facultad de Humanidades de la Universidad del Valle, 1995.

Nazzari, Muriel. "Vanishing Indians: The Social Construction of Race in Colonial São Paulo." The Americas 57, no. 4 (2001): 497–524.

Netherly, Patricia J. "The Management of Late Andean Irrigation Systems on the North Coast of Peru." American Antiquity 49 (April 1984): 227–54.

Newson, Linda, and Susan Minchin. From Capture to Sale: The Portuguese Slave Trade to Spanish South America in the Early Seventeenth Century. Leiden: Brill, 2007.

Noack, Karoline. "El cacicazgo de Huamán dentro de la jurisdicción de Trujillo, siglo XVII: Desarrollo de su estructura y principios de organización." Boletín del Instituto Riva-Agüero 24 (1997): 343–67.

————. "Relaciones políticas y la negación de una 'nueva' sociedad colonial en el valle de Pacasmayo, costa norte del Perú (s. XVI)." In *Culturas en movimiento: Contribuciones a la transformación de identidades étnicas y culturas en América*. Edited by Wiltrud Dresler, Bernd Fahmel, and Karoline Noack. Mexico City: Universidad Nacional Autónoma de México, Instituto de Investigaciones Antropológicas, 2007.

Northrup, David. "Becoming African: Identity Formation among Liberated Slaves in Nineteenth-Century Sierra Leone." *Slavery and Abolition* 27 (April 2006): 1–21.

Nwokeji, G. Ugo. "The Atlantic Slave Trade and Population Density: A Historical Demography of the Biafran Hinterland." *Canadian Journal of African Studies* 34 (2000): 617–55.

Olsen, Margaret. *Slavery and Salvation in Colonial Cartagena de Indias*. Gainesville: University Press of Florida, 2004.

Olwell, Robert. *Masters, Slaves, and Subjects: The Culture of Power in the South Carolina Low Country, 1740–1790*. Ithaca: Cornell University Press, 1998.

Olwig, K. F. "African Cultural Principles in Caribbean Slave Society: A View from the Danish West Indies." In *Slave Cultures and the Cultures of Slavery*. Edited by S. Palmer. Knoxville: University of Tennessee Press, 1995.

Ortner, Sherry B. *Anthropology and Social Theory: Culture, Power, and the Acting Subject*. Durham: Duke University Press, 2006.

O'Toole, Rachel Sarah. "Castas y representación en Trujillo colonial." In *Más allá de la dominación y la resistencia: Estudios de historia peruana, siglos XVI–XX*. Edited by Paulo Drinot and Leo Garofalo. 48–76. Lima: Instituto de Estudios Peruanos, 2005.

————. "Don Carlos Chimo del Perú: ¿del Común o cacique?" *Revista secuencia* (Mexico) 81 (September–December 2011): 13–41.

————. "From the Rivers of Guinea to the Valleys of Peru: Becoming a *Bran* Diaspora within Spanish Slavery." *Social Text* 92 (Fall 2007): 19–36.

————. "'In a War against the Spanish': Andean Protection and African Resistance on the Northern Peruvian Coast." *The Americas* 63 (July 2006): 19–52.

————. "Inventing Difference: Africans, Indians, and the Antecedents of 'Race' in Colonial Peru (1580s-1720s)." PhD diss., University of North Carolina at Chapel Hill, 2001.

————. "Within Slavery: Marking Property and Making Men in Colonial Peru." In *Power, Culture, and Violence in the Andes*. Edited by Christine Hünefeldt and Misha Kokotovic. 29–49. Brighton, UK: Sussex Academic Press, 2009.

Owensby, Brian. *Empire of Law and Indian Justice in Colonial Mexico*. Stanford: Stanford University Press, 2008.

Palacios Preciado, Jorge. *La trata de negros por Cartagena de Indias*. Tunja: Universidad Pedagógica y Tecnológica de Colombia, Fondo Especial de Publicaciones, Ediciones "La Rana y El Aguila," 1973.

Palmer, Colin. *Slaves of the White God: Blacks in Mexico, 1570–1650*. Cambridge: Harvard University Press, 1976.

Patch, Robert. *Maya and Spaniard in Yucatan, 1648–1812.* Stanford: Stanford University Press, 1993.

Penningroth, Dylan. *The Claims of Kinfolk: African American Property and Community in the Nineteenth-Century South.* Chapel Hill: University of North Carolina Press, 2003.

Pérez-Maillaína, Pablo E. "La fabricación de un mito: El terremoto de 1687 y la ruina de los cultivos de trigo en el Perú." *Anuario de Estudios Americanos* 57, no. 1 (2000): 69–88.

Pinto, Jeanette. *Slavery in Portuguese India, 1510–1842.* Bombay: Himalaya Publishing House, 1992.

Polo y La Borda, Jorge. "La Hacienda Pachachaca (Segunda Ruta del s. XVIII)." *Historica* 1, no. 2 (December 1977): 223–47.

Poole, Deborah. *Vision, Race, and Modernity: A Visual Economy of the Andean Image World.* Princeton: Princeton University Press, 1997.

Postma, Johannes. "The Dispersal of African Slaves in the West by Dutch Slave Traders, 1630–1803." In *The Atlantic Slave Trade: Effects on Economies, Societies, and Peoples in Africa, the Americas, and Europe.* Edited by Joseph E. Inikori and Stanley L. Engerman. 283–99. Durham: Duke University Press, 1992.

———. *The Dutch in the Atlantic Slave Trade, 1600–1815.* Cambridge: Cambridge University Press, 1990.

Powers, Karen Vieira. *Andean Journeys: Migration, Ethnogenesis, and the State in Colonial Quito.* Albuquerque: University of New Mexico Press, 1995.

———. "Battle for Bodies and Souls in the Colonial North Andes: Intraecclesiastical Struggles and the Politics of Migration." *Hispanic American Historical Review* 75, no. 1 (1995): 31–56.

Premo, Bianca. *Children of the Father King: Youth, Authority, and Legal Minority in Colonial Lima.* Chapel Hill: University of North Carolina Press, 2005.

Putnam, Lara. "To Study the Fragments/Whole: Microhistory and the Atlantic World." *Journal of Social History* 39 (Spring 2006): 615–30.

Rabasa, José. *Writing Violence on the Northern Frontier: The Historiography of Sixteenth-Century New Mexico and Florida and the Legacy of Conquest.* Durham: Duke University Press, 2000.

Radding, Cynthia. *Wandering Peoples: Colonialism, Ethnic Spaces, and Ecological Frontiers in Northwestern Mexico, 1700–1850.* Durham: Duke University Press, 1997.

Rak, Julie. "The Digital Queer: Weblogs and Internet Identity." *Biography* 28, no. 1 (Winter 2005): 166–82.

Ramírez, Susan. "Don Clemente Anto, procurador del común del pueblo de Lambayeque." In *El hombre y los Andes: Homenaje a Franklin Pease G. Y.* Edited by Javier Flores Espinoza and Rafael Varón Gabai. 831–40. Lima: Pontificia Universidad Católica del Perú, Instituto Francés de Estudios Andinos, 2002.

———. *Provincial Patriarchs: Land Tenure and the Economics of Power in Colonial Peru.* Albuquerque: University of New Mexico Press, 1986.

———. *The World Upside Down: Cross-Cultural Contact and Conflict in Sixteenth-Century Peru.* Stanford: Stanford University Press, 1996.

Randall, Robert. "Los dos vasos: Cosmovisión y política de la embriaguez desde el inkanato hasta la colonia." *Borrachera y memoria: La experiencia de lo sagrado en los Andes.* Edited by Thierry Saignes. 73–112. Lima: HISBOL/IFEA, 1993.

Rao, Anupama, and Steven Pierce. "Discipline and the Other Body: Humanitarianism, Violence, and the Colonial Exception." In *Discipline and the Other Body: Correction, Corporeality, Colonialism.* Edited by Anupama Rao and Steven Pierce. 1–35. Durham: Duke University Press, 2006.

Rappaport, Joanne. *The Politics of Memory: Native Historical Interpretation in the Colombian Andes.* Durham: Duke University Press, 1998.

Rediker, Marcus. *The Slave Ship: A Human History.* New York: Viking, 2007.

Reis, João José. *Death Is a Festival: Funeral Rites and Rebellion in Nineteenth-Century Brazil.* Chapel Hill: University of North Carolina Press, 2003.

———. *Slave Rebellion in Brazil: The Muslim Uprising of 1835 in Bahia.* Baltimore: Johns Hopkins Press, 1993 [1986].

Restall, Matthew. *The Black Middle: Africans, Mayas, and Spaniards in Colonial Yucatan.* Stanford: Stanford University Press, 2009.

———. "Black Slaves, Red Paint." In *Beyond Black and Red: African-Native Relations in Colonial Latin America.* Edited by Matthew Restall. 1–13. Albuquerque: University of New Mexico Press, 2005.

Rodney, Walter. "Portuguese Attempts at Monopoly on the Upper Guinea Coast, 1580–1650." *Journal of African History* 6 (1965): 307–22.

Rodríguez, Frederick. "Cimarrón Revolts and Pacification in New Spain: The Isthmus of Panama and Colonial Columbia, 1503–1800." PhD diss., Loyola University of Chicago, 1979.

Romero, Fernando. *El negro en el Perú y su transculturación lingüística.* Lima: Editorial Milla Bartes, 1987.

Rostworowski de Diez Canseco, María. *Curacas y sucesiones, Costa Norte.* Lima: Lib. Imp. Minerva, 1961.

Russell-Wood, A. J. R. "Ambivalent Authorities: The African and Afro-Brazilian Contribution to Local Governance in Colonial Brazil." *The Americas* 57 (July 2000): 13–36.

Saignes, Thierry. "Borracheras andinas: ¿Por qué los indios ebrios hablan en español?" In *Borrachera y memoria: La experiencia de lo sagrado en los Andes.* Edited by Thierry Saignes. 43–74. La Paz: HISBOL/IFEA, 1993.

———. *Caciques, Tribute, and Migration in the Southern Andes: Indian Society and the Seventeenth Century Colonial Order (Audiencia de Charcas).* London: University of London, Institute of Latin American Studies, 1985.

———. "The Colonial Condition in the Quechua-Aymara Heartland (1570–1780)." In *The Cambridge History of the Native Peoples of the Americas.* Volume 3, South America. Part 2. Edited by Frank Salomon and Stuart Schwartz. 59–137. Cambridge: Cambridge University Press, 1999.

———. "Indian Migration and Social Change in Seventeenth-Century Charcas." In *Ethnicity, Markets, and Migration in the Andes: At the Crossroads of History and Anthropology.*

Edited by Brooke Larson and Olivia Harris. 167–95. Durham: Duke University Press, 1995.

Salazar-Soler, Carmen. "Embriaguez y visiones en los Andes: Los Jesuitas y las 'borracheras' indígenas en el Perú (Siglos XVI y XVII)." In *Borrachera y memoria: La experiencia de lo sagrado en los Andes*. Edited by Thierry Saignes. 23–42. Lima: HISBOL/IFEA, 1993.

Scardaville, Michael C. "Justice by Paperwork: A Day in the Life of a Court Scribe in Bourbon Mexico City." *Journal of Social History* 36, no. 4 (2003): 979–1007.

Schuler, Monica. *"Alas, Alas, Kongo": A Social History of Indentured African Immigration into Jamaica, 1841–1865*. Baltimore: Johns Hopkins University Press, 1980.

Schwartz, Stuart. "Rethinking Palmares: Slave Resistance in Colonial Brazil." In *Slaves, Peasants, and Rebels: Reconsidering Brazilian Slavery*. 103–36. Urbana: University of Illinois Press, 1992.

———. *Sugar Plantations in the Formation of Brazilian Society: Bahia, 1550–1835*. Cambridge: Cambridge University Press, 1985.

Seed, Patricia. "Colonial and Postcolonial Discourse." *Latin American Research Review* 26 (1991): 181–200.

———, and Philip Rust. "Estate and Class in Colonial Oaxaca Revisited." *Comparative Studies in Society and History* 25 (October 1983): 703–24.

Sharp, William. *Slavery on the Spanish Frontier: The Colombian Choco, 1680–1810*. Norman: University of Oklahoma Press, 1976.

Shepherd, Verene A. "Livestock and Sugar: Aspects of Jamaica's Agricultural Development from the Late Seventeenth to the Early Nineteenth Century." *Historical Journal* 34, no. 3 (September 1991): 627–43.

Silverblatt, Irene. *Modern Inquisitions: Peru and the Colonial Origins of the Civilized World*. Durham: Duke University Press, 2004.

———. "Political Memories and Colonizing Symbols: Santiago and the Peruvian Mountain Gods of Colonial Peru." In *Rethinking History and Myth: Indigenous South American Perspectives on the Past*. Edited by Jonathan David Hill. 174–94. Urbana: University of Illinois Press, 1988.

Smallwood, Stephanie. *Saltwater Slavery: A Middle Passage from Africa to American Diaspora*. Cambridge: Harvard University Press, 2007.

Smith, Mark. *Mastered by the Clock: Time, Slavery, and Freedom in the American South*. Chapel Hill: University of North Carolina Press, 1997.

Somerville, Diane Miller. *Rape and Race in the Nineteenth-Century South*. Chapel Hill: University of North Carolina Press, 2004.

Soulodre-La France, Renée. "Los Esclavos de su Majestad: Slave Protest and Politics in Late Colonial New Granada." In *Slaves, Subjects, and Subversives: Blacks in Colonial Latin America*. Edited by Jane Landers and Barry Robinson. 175–208. Albuquerque: University of New Mexico Press, 2006.

———. "Socially Not So Dead! Slave Identity in Bourbon New Granada." *Colonial Latin American Review* 4, no. 1 (June 2001): 87–103.

Spalding, Karen. *Huarochirí: An Andean Society under Inca and Spanish Rule*. Stanford: Stanford University Press, 1984.

Stavig, Ward. *The World of Túpac Amaru: Conflict, Community, and Identity in Colonial Peru*. Lincoln: University of Nebraska Press, 1999.

Stern, Steve J. *Peru's Indian Peoples and the Challenge of Spanish Conquest: Huamanga to 1640*. Madison: University of Wisconsin Press, 1982.

St. George, Robert Blair. "Introduction." In *Possible Pasts: Becoming Colonial in Early America*. Edited by Robert Blair St. George. 1–29. Ithaca: Cornell University Press, 2000.

Stoler, Ann L. *Along the Archival Grain: Epistemic Anxieties and Colonial Common Sense*. Princeton: Princeton University Press, 2009.

———. *Race and the Education of Desire: Foucault's History of Sexuality and the Colonial Order of Things*. Durham: Duke University Press, 1995.

Sweet, James. *Domingos Álvares, African Healing, and the Intellectual History of the Atlantic World*. Chapel Hill: University of North Carolina Press, 2011.

———. "The Iberian Roots of American Racist Thought." *William and Mary Quarterly*, third series, 54, no. 1 (January 1997): 143–66.

———. "Mistaken Identities? Olaudah Equiano, Domingos Álvares, and the Methodological Challenges of Studying the African Diaspora." *American Historical Review* 114 (2009): 279–306.

———. *Recreating Africa: Culture, Kinship, and Religion in the African-Portuguese World, 1441–1770*. Chapel Hill: University of North Carolina Press, 2003.

Takagi, Dana. "Maiden Voyage: Excursion into Sexuality and Identity Politics in Asian America." In *Queer Theory/Sociology*. Edited by Steven Seidman. Cambridge: Blackwell, 1996.

Tardieu, Jean Pierre. "La mano de obra negra en las minas del Perú colonial (fines del s. XVI–comienzos del s. XVII): De los principios morales al oportunismo." *Historica* 19 (July 1995): 119–44.

———. *El negro en el Cusco: Los caminos de la alienación en la segunda mitad del siglo XVII*. Lima: Pontificia Universidad Católica del Perú and Banco Central de Reserva del Perú, 1998.

———. *Los negros y la iglesia en el Perú: Siglos XVI– XVII*. 2 volumes. Quito: Centro Cultural Afroecuatoriano, 1997.

———. "Origins of the Slaves in the Lima Region in Peru (Sixteenth and Seventeenth Centuries)." In *From Chains to Bonds: The Slave Trade Revisited*. Edited by Doudou Diène. 43–54. New York: Berghahn Books, 2001.

Taylor, William. *Drinking, Homicide, and Rebellion in Colonial Mexican Villages*. Stanford: Stanford University Press, 1979.

Thomas, Nicholas. *Colonialism's Culture: Anthropology, Travel, and Government*. Princeton: Princeton University Press, 1994.

Thornton, John K. *Africa and Africans in the Making of the Atlantic World, 1400–1800*. Cambridge: Cambridge University Press, 1998 [1992].

———. "Cannibals, Witches, and Slave Traders in the Atlantic World." *William and Mary Quarterly* 60, no. 2 (2003): 1–15.

Tomich, Dale. "*Une petite guinée*: Provision Ground and Plantation in Martinique, 1830–1848." *Slavery and Abolition* 12 (May 1991): 68–91.

Tord Nicolini, Javier. *Hacienda, comercio, fiscalidad y luchas sociales (Perú colonial)*. Lima: Biblioteca Peruana de Historia, Economía y Sociedad, 1981.

Trouillot, Michel-Rolph. *Silencing the Past: Power and the Production of History*. Boston: Beacon Press, 1995.

Troutman, Phillip. "Grapevine in the Slave Market: African American Geopolitical Literacy and the 1841 Creole Revolt." In *The Chattel Principle: Internal Slave Trades in the Americas*. Edited by Walter Johnson. 203–33. New Haven: Yale University Press, 2004.

Twinam, Ann. *Public Lives, Private Secrets: Gender, Honor, Sexuality, and Illegitimacy in Colonial Spanish America*. Stanford: Stanford University Press, 1999.

Usner, Daniel H. *Indians, Settlers, and Slaves in a Frontier Exchange Economy: The Lower Mississippi Valley before 1873*. Chapel Hill: University of North Carolina Press, 1992.

Vaughan, Megan. "Slavery and Colonial Identity in Eighteenth-Century Mauritius." *Transactions of the Royal Historical Society* 8 (1998): 189–214.

Vegas de Cáceres, Ileana. *Economía rural y estructura social en las haciendas de Lima durante el siglo XVIII*. Lima: Pontificia Universidad Católica del Perú, 1996.

Verger, Pierre. *Trade Relations between the Gulf of Benin and Bahia from the Seventeenth to Nineteenth Century*. Ibadan, Nigeria: Ibadan University Press, 1976 [1968].

Vila Vilar, Enriqueta. *Aspectos sociales en America colonial: De extranjeros, contrabando y esclavos*. Bogotá: Instituto Caro y Cuervo, Universidad Jorge Tadeo Lozano, 2001.

———. *Hispanoamérica y el comercio de esclavos*. Seville: Escuela de Estudios Hispano-Americanos, 1977.

Villa-Flores, Javier. *Dangerous Speech: A Social History of Blasphemy in Colonial Mexico*. Tucson: University of Arizona Press, 2006.

Vinson III, Ben. *Bearing Arms for His Majesty: The Free-Colored Militia in Colonial Mexico*. Stanford: Stanford University Press, 2001.

———, and Matthew Restall. "Black Soldiers, Native Soldiers: Meanings of Military Service in the Spanish American Colonies." In *Beyond Black and Red: African-Native Relations in Colonial Latin America*. Edited by Matthew Restall. Albuquerque: University of New Mexico Press, 2005.

Von Germeten, Nicole. *Black Blood Brothers: Confraternities and Social Mobility for Afro-Mexicans*. Gainesville: University Press of Florida, 2006.

von Wobeser, Gisela. *La Hacienda azucarera en la época colonial*. México: Universidad Nacional Autónoma de México, 2004.

Wade, Peter. "La construcción de 'el negro' en América Latina." In *La construcción de las Américas*. Edited by Carlos Alberto Uribe Tobón. 141–58. Bogotá: Universidad de los Andes, 1993.

———. *Race and Ethnicity in Latin America*. London: Pluto Press, 1997.

Walker, Tamara J. "'He outfitted his family in notable decency': Slavery, Honour, and Dress in Eighteenth-Century Lima, Peru." *Slavery and Abolition* 30 (September 2009): 383–402.

Weismantel, Mary. *Cholas and Pishtacos: Stories of Race and Sex in the Andes.* Chicago: University of Chicago Press, 2001.

White, Sophie. "'Wearing three or four handkerchiefs around his collar, and elsewhere about him': Slaves' Constructions of Masculinity and Ethnicity in French Colonial New Orleans." *Gender and History* 15, no. 3 (2003): 528–49.

Wightman, Ann. *Indigenous Migration and Social Change: The Forasteros of Cuzco, 1570–1720.* Durham: Duke University Press, 1990.

Yannakakis, Yanna. *The Art of Being In-between: Native Intermediaries, Indian Identity, and Local Rule in Colonial Oaxaca.* Durham: Duke University Press, 2008.

Young, Jason. *Rituals of Resistance: African Atlantic Religion in Kongo and the Lowcountry South in the Era of Slavery.* Baton Rouge: Louisiana State University Press, 2007.

Zevallos Quiñones, Jorge. *Los cacicazgos de Trujillo.* Trujillo: Gráfica Cuatro, 1992.

Zulawski, Ann. *They Eat from Their Labor: Work and Social Change in Colonial Bolivia.* Pittsburgh: University of Pittsburgh Press, 1995.

INDEX

Achache, Andrés, 83
Africans: Andeans contrasted with, 20–22,
    164; as blacks, 1; captive status of,
    35–36; Catholic Church and, 22, 32,
    36, 52, 57–58, 63; contributions of, to
    colonial Andes, 161–64; demographics
    of, 9; and discourse regarding climatic
    conditions, 18, 26–27; identities of, 16,
    47, 59; legal rights of, 35; legal status
    of, 1, 2, 5–6, 11–16, 63, 122–56, 163;
    mortality of, 36, 38, 39, 187n60; official
    Spanish view of, 31–32, 34; scholarship
    on, 2–4; spiritual beliefs of, 143–44;
    stereotypes of, 18, 160. See also Andean-
    African relations; enslaved people
Agustín, Juan, 112
Alonso, Miguel, 114
Alto Peru, 90
Alvarado, María Magdalena de, 118–19
Andean-African relations, 2–5; beneficial,
    4, 74, 89; colonial Andes constituted
    by, 161–64; discussion of hostility in,
    3, 4, 18, 23–24, 73–75; inversion of
    hierarchy in, 157–60; labor-related,
    23–24, 73, 89; in the market, 111–16;
    marriage and cohabitation, 118;
    migrants and enslaved people, 57;
    slave/free status and, 17; social mixing
    in, 116–20; supervisory, 152–56
Andeans: accused predators of, 23;
    Africans contrasted with, 20–22,
    164; in authority positions, 152–56;
    Catholic Church and, 21, 22, 32, 101,
    196n77; clothing of, 106–7, 209n206;
    demographics of, 5, 9, 26, 90; and
    discourse regarding climatic conditions,
    26–27; discussion of enslavement of,
    20–21; identities of, 66, 90, 106–7;
    illness among, 203n54; as Indians, 1,
    65–77, 82, 152, 160; labor of, 8, 11, 17–

Andeans (continued): labor of (continued), 20, 25–29, 92–96, 179n54; languages of, 65; leaders of (see caciques); legal status of, 1, 2, 5–6, 11–16, 24–25, 64–87, 124–25, 149–55, 163; policing duties of, 153–55; poverty of, 196n81; precolonial society of, 65; scholarship on, 2–4; self-governance of, 150–52; as slaveholders, 99, 204n80; status symbols of, 106–7; weak, miserable, and vulnerable character ascribed to, 18, 22, 28–29, 30, 33, 65, 160. See also Andean-African relations; forasteros (migrants); Indians

Andrés of casta arara, 135

Andrien, Kenneth J., 175n1

Angola, 37, 38–39, 47

Angola, Anton, 113

Angola, Blas, 113

Angola, Francisco, 52–54

Angola, Juan, 213n64

Angola, Pedro, 114, 130, 212n55

angola, 45, 53

arara, 15, 37, 39, 53, 55, 60–61

Arara, Agustín, 53–54

Arara, Antonio, 57

Arara, Domingo, 129, 130–32

Arara, Francisco, 112

Arara, Josef, 148

Arara, Joseph, 55, 211n16

Arara, Juan (Melchor) de, 146, 148

Arara, Simon, 55

Ariju, Francisco, 141

Arroyo, Andrés de, 134, 136–37, 140

Asavache, Pedro, 98

Asmat, Gregorio, 94–95

asylum, 61, 153

Avila, Juan de, 116

Azabeche, Francisco, 94

Azavache, Pedro, 98

balanta, 38, 48

Balanta, Francisco, 42–43

baptism, 56–57, 118

Barta, Juan, 117–18

Bartolo, Diego, 111

Beltrán, Miguel, 165–66

Bennett, Herman, 36, 210n10

Bernabe, Pedro, 108, 110

Bight of Benin, 15, 37, 39, 47, 53, 55, 56, 60, 62, 201n24

Bight of Biafra, 47, 139

blacks. See Africans; enslaved people

Bolivia, 90

Bontemps, Alex, 51

borrachera gatherings, 74, 129, 195n65. See also drinking

Bowser, Frederick, 3, 187n60, 187n67, 207n172

bozales, 43

Bracamonte Dávila, García de, 110, 136–37, 147–48, 215n104, 217n157

bran, 15, 38, 47, 48

Bran, Pedro, 58, 110

branding, 40

Brazil, 53

Brooks, James, 176n18

Burns, Kathryn, 179n72

Cabero, Francisco, 113

cabo verde, 48

caciques (indigenous leaders): adoption of Spanish culture by, 100–101; alleged abuses of, 21; alliances between, 100–101; leadership of, 65, 193n20; and the market, 96–102; as slaveholders, 99, 204n80; susceptibility of, 101–2

Calabar, 139

Camacho, María, 55

Canegue, Phelipe, 155

Cano, Lorenso, 111

carabalí, 139

Cárdenas, Bernardino de, 17–18, 21–22

Cartagena, 10, 28, 39–40, 48

Castañeda Murga, Juan, 176n13

castas: characteristics of the enslaved attributed to, 45–48; claiming or performing of locations in, 14–15, 167–68; as constructed categories, 2, 4, 19–20, 22, 27, 29, 33, 66, 167–68; elites' relations with, 11; exchanges across, 111–16; function of, 164–67, 221n18; labor as significant for, 11; legal locations of, 2, 6; mixing across, 116–20; race compared to, 164–65, 170; reconception of, 32; Spanish regulations concerning, 11

Castro, Domingo de, 154

Castro, Lucas de, 141, 143

Catholic Church: absence of documentation from, 15–16; Africans and, 22, 32, 36, 52, 57–58, 63; Andeans and, 21, 22, 32, 101, 196n77; baptism in, 56, 118; confraternities sponsored by, 57–58; enslaved people and, 124, 139–40,

216n123, 217n149, 218n183; marriage in, 54–55
cattle, 8, 10, 11, 69–71
Cayetano, albino ("black"), 211n16, 211n20
Cecoram, Lorenço, 69
Central Africa, 62
chains, 146
chala, 54, 59, 190n130
chasquis, 68–69, 194n25
Chaybac, Antonio, 68, 97–100
Chayguac, Pedro Rafael, 96
Chérrepe port, Saña, 6
Chicama valley, 81–82, 94, 95, 96
chicha (corn beer), 58, 74, 95, 112, 116, 129
Chimo, 105–6
Chimu, Carlos, 84–86
Chiquitoy, 95, 96
Chuburría, Antonio de, 54
Chumbi Guaman, Juan, 79–80
Cipirán, Juan, 73–74
class, 175n4
clothing: of Andeans, 106–7, 209n206; as commodity, 113–15; of enslaved people, 59, 113, 208n204; fugitive slaves and, 114; royal regulation of, 32; social meanings of, 32, 106–7, 115–16, 208n204; stolen, 113–15
Cobec, Pedro, 142
Cochabamba, 81
cohabitation, 118
colonial markets. See market
compañeros (companions), 37, 42
composición de tierras, 8, 66, 77, 97. See also land inspections; land privatization
Conde de Chinchón, Viceroy, 31
confraternities, 57–58, 101, 107, 117
congo, 57
Congo, Anton, 113
Congo, Garcia, 146
Congo, Manual, 42
Congo, Manuel, 141, 143
Consejo de Indias, 148
Cope, R. Douglas, 221n18
Coronado, Carlos, 97
Cosamalón Aguilar, Jesús, 5
couriers, 68–69
Criolla, Ana, 145–46
Criollo, Diego, 114–15
Criollo, Juan, 114–15, 116
criollo/a, marriages to, 55–56
crown: Andeans' direct appeals to, 83–84; attitudes and policies concerning

Africans, 31–32, 34; attitudes and policies concerning Indians, 18, 20–25, 29–34, 66–77; land policy of, 8, 66, 77
Cruz, Francisco de la, 26
cuarterones, 31
Cuebas, Pedro de, 165
Cumozan, Salvador, 74
Curaçao, 10, 48, 200n22
Custodio (enslaved man), 138, 211n16

Dávila, Juan, 49–50, 116
De la Cruz Biafra, Gregorio, 138–39
De la Cruz, Juan, 111
De la Cruz, Lorenza, 116
De la Cruz, Sebastian, 152
De la Fuente, Alejandro, 134, 214n94, 220n222
De los Reyes, Phelipe, 140–44
Deloria, Philip, 89–90
Diego Nicolas (indigenous laborer), 165
Diego of casta angola, 116
Dios, Juan de, 138
Domingo (fugitive slave), 88, 113, 115
Dominicans, 57
drinking, 74, 129–30, 139, 195n65, 212n55
Dutch slave trade, 9, 200n22, 201n24, 210n13
dysentery, 41

elites: landholding and labor needs of, 8–11; power of, 11
English slave trade, 190n130, 200n22, 201n24, 210n13
enslaved people: Andean power over, 152–56; Andeans replaced by, 179n54; Catholic Church and, 124, 139–40, 216n123, 217n149, 218n183; clothing of, 59, 113, 208n204; commodification of, 36, 39–41, 48–51; differences among, 46–48; entries into slavery of, 38–39; escapes of, 41; extralegal claims of, 133–44; food of, 111–12, 207n172, 207n173; foremen among, 128; as hired laborers, 135–36; illness among, 40, 41, 43; Indians contrasted with, 17–19, 21–22, 23, 25–29, 183n64; and justice, 122–56; learning opportunities for, 44–45; living/working conditions of, 22, 123–24; "looking for a patron," 134–36; male-female ratio of, 122; manipulation of locations by, 48–52; and the market, 111–16, 207n174;

enslaved people (continued): mitayos and, 73; movements of, 126; muleteers and, 110–11; origins of, 171; physical capacity of, 28–29; price of, 10, 172; as property, 36, 38, 45–52; rebellion of, 46–47; Spanish view of, 18; trade in, 9–10; value of, 28, 38, 45
escapes, 41, 42, 44. See also truancy
Escobar, Juana, 119
Escuría, Cayetano de, 55
Escurra, Fermin de, 54
Espejo, Gregorio, 112–13

farmers, 98–99
Felipe, Prince, 117
Fernandez Asmat, Manuel, 101–2
festivals, 117, 129
flour, 10, 94
folupa, 38
Folupo, Anton, 58, 117
food, of enslaved people, 111–12, 207n172, 207n173
forasteros (migrants): enslaved people and, 57, 90; kinship and marriages of, 103–4; land privatization as spur to, 8–11; market opportunities for, 11, 91, 103; mita as spur to, 30; numbers of, 200n12; official obligations of, 103; rejuvenation of towns by, 90, 103; tribute payments sought from, 85
foremen, enslaved, 128
Francisco of casta mina, 133–34
French Guinea Company, 210n13
fugitive slaves, 41, 58, 73, 88–89, 111, 113, 133, 154–55, 215n102. See also palenques; truancy
funerals, 217n149

Gabriel (enslaved man), 115
Gabriel (fugitive slave), 88, 113, 115
Gamarra Zaseretta y Ortis, Miguel, 137–38
García of casta congo, 113
Garofalo, Leo, 5
Ghana, 190n130
gobernador, 203n57
godparents, 56–57, 103
Gold Coast, 37, 39, 48, 55, 62, 201n24
Gonçalo (fugitive slave), 134
Gonzales de Careaga, Juan, 139–42
Gonzalez, Bartolomé, 96
González, Gerónimo de, 50–51
Grande, Juan, 114

Graubart, Karen, 176n13
Gravero, Alonso, 20
Gross, Ariela, 36, 213n67
Guachin, Gaspar, 108–9
Guamán, 94–95
Guaman, Antonio, 111
Guaman, Domingo de, 110
Guaman, Luis, 98
Guaman, Pedro, 69
Guaman, Salvador, 69
Guaman Poma de Ayala, Felipe, 157–60
Guañape, 150–51
Guayaquil, 41
Guinea-Bissau, 15, 38, 42, 43, 47, 48, 57, 186n45

Hapsburg colonialism, 168
Herrera, Antonio de, 25
Herzog, Tamar, 82
holidays, 117, 129, 139–40
Horra, Josepha de, 134
Huanchaco port, Trujillo, 6, 44, 95
Hurtado, Juan, 126–27

Iberian peninsula, travel to, 198n130
"in company" ownership, 106, 107
Indians: Andeans as, 1, 65–77, 82, 152, 160; as appointed officials, 79–80; as census category, 178n37; enslaved laborers contrasted with, 17–19, 21–22, 23, 25–29, 183n64; failures of status of, 9; harms to, 31; meanings of category of, 86, 89–90; mestizos passing as, and vice versa, 119; modification of castas by, 31; obligations of, to crown, 1, 20, 31, 65; official Spanish view of, 18, 20–25, 29–34, 67–77; protection of, 20–25, 30–31, 33, 70, 75, 77; "restless," 71, 81, 84–85; Spanish as superior to, 198n120; stereotypes of, 18, 160; weak, miserable, and vulnerable character ascribed to, 72. See also Andeans; mitayos
indigenous leaders. See caciques
indigenous peoples. See Andeans
Inquisitorial Tribunal, 15
irrigation systems: contamination of, 148; importance of, 31, 67, 70, 75, 95; labor on, 24, 95–96, 127, 202n47
Isla Guaman, Diego, 99–102

Jaratán, Alonso, 79–80
Jesuits, 32, 57, 130, 142, 188n86, 207n172

írón, Juan Antonio, 102
Johnson, Walter, 36
Joseph of casta arara, 153
judicial cases, 12, 14
justice: labor-related issues of, 123–33;
    slavery and, 122–56

king. *See* crown
kinship: African-Andean, 57; baptism and,
    56–57; creation of, 36–37, 52–62;
    criminal cases as evidence of, 59–60;
    destruction of, 39; economic basis
    of, 185n13; functions of, 62; market
    in relationship to, 37, 38; marriage
    and, 55–56; migrants and, 103–4;
    multigenerational, 55; shipmate, 53–54
Kongo, 47

labor: of Andeans, 8, 11, 17–20, 25–29,
    179n54; black vs. Indian, 18–19, 21–22,
    23, 25–29; castas defined by, 11; of
    the enslaved, 9–11; enslaved people as
    hired, 135–36; enslaved people's justice
    demands concerning, 123–33; initiative
    in, 127–28; need of, 8–11, 18–19, 26–27,
    91–94, 182n49; on Northern Peruvian
    coast, 8–11; rest from, 129–33, 139–40;
    time issues concerning, 127. *See also*
    enslaved people
labradores (farmers), 98–99
land inspections, 77–84, 97, 102
land privatization: and cacique land
    ownership, 97–99, 101; crown policy
    and, 8, 66, 77; effects of, on Andeans,
    65, 66–67, 77–82, 86–87; effects
    of, on landholders, 92; indigenous
    communities' land ownership and,
    105–6
landholders, labor needs of, 92–94
law: Andean use of, 67–77; customary usage
    and practice vs., 123; slaveholders and,
    123, 136–37; slavery and, 124
leaders. *See* caciques
legal locations: of Africans, 1, 2, 5–6, 11–16,
    63, 122–56, 163; of Andeans, 1,
    2, 5–6, 9, 11–16, 24–25, 64–87, 124–25,
    149–55, 163; of castas, 2, 6; claiming or
    performing of, 5, 12–13, 66
Lewis, Laura, 167, 221n18
Lima, 6, 28, 32, 57, 94
Lipsett-Rivera, Sonya, 202n47
Loxa, Alonso, 88–89

Luanda, 38, 53, 201n24
lucumí, 53
Lucumí, María, 53–54
Lucumí, Phelipe, 148, 219n186
Lureño, Blas de, 135

Macera, Pablo, 207n172
Mache, Diego, 75–76
Mache, Diego Matias, 107
Magdalena de Cao, 69–71, 78–79, 81, 96
Malabrigo port, Chicama, 6, 44
Malemba, Juanillo, 116
mandinga, 48
Mandinga, Bartolomé, 140–43
Mandinga, Francisco, 74
Mangan, Jane, 5
Mansiche, 68
María Josepha (indigenous woman), 112
Marcelo of casta arara, 153
María of casta mina, 48–51
market, 88–121; caciques and, 96–102; and
    cross-casta exchanges, 111–16; enslaved
    people and, 207n174; opportunities of,
    91–96. *See also* slave market
marriage: Catholic institution of, 54–55;
    of enslaved people, 54–56, 192n178;
    intermarriages, 118; of migrants, 103;
    regulations on, 192n177; witnesses to,
    55
Martínez, Antonia, 119
Martínez, Lorenzo, 151–52
Martínez, María Elena, 210n10
Martínez Compañón, Baltazar Jaime, 11,
    178n36
Mateo of casta congo, 73–74
Melchora (Andean), 118
Mendosa, Miguel Rafael de, 108
Meneses, Pedro de, 78, 80–82, 84–85
mestizos, Indians passing as, and vice versa,
    119
microhistory, 13
Middle Passage, 39–40
miel (syrups and molasses), 213n55
migrants. *See* forasteros
Miles, Tiya, 176n18
Mills, Kenneth, 175n1
mina, 37, 45, 48, 50–51, 55, 58–59, 190n130
Mina, Antonio, 112
Mina, Baltasar, 132–33, 153
Mina, Francisco, 130–32
Mina, Pedro, 112
mining, 18–19

Miranda, Bartolomé, 69–71, 74
mita (forced labor system): avoidance
    of, 9, 18, 67, 149; defense of, 18;
    establishment of, 8; failure of, 19,
    26, 92; and irrigation work, 96;
    mining and, 19; pressures of, 21, 30;
    requirement of, 20, 67, 68, 78; revival
    of, 27; slavery likened to, 18; types of
    labor for, 70
mitayos (laborers serving mita): enslaved
    people and, 73; legal dispute involving,
    69–71; obligation to supply, 68; short
    supply of, 22
mitimaes, 94–95
Moche, 94–95
modernization, 220n7
Mora y Ulloa, Joan de, 97, 99, 101
morenos, 117
Morgan, Philip, 130
Mozanga, Anton, 52–54
muleteers, 107–11

Nazzari, Muriel, 178n37
Nicolas of casta malamba, 115–16
Northern Peruvian coast: agriculture and
    animal husbandry of, 6; demographics
    of, 8–9, 178n36; economy and trade of,
    6–8; geography of, 6; labor needs of,
    8–11, 26–27, 182n49; map of, 7

Ocampo, Miguel de, 54
officials, appointed, 79–80, 150
Ortega, Andrés de, 82–86
Our Lady of the Angels (ship), 43

Pablo, Juan, 108–9
padrinos (patrons), 134–36
Paiján, 72, 80
Paita, 41, 45
Palata, Duque de la, 19, 30
palenques (communities of escaped slaves),
    88–89, 113–15, 133, 214n86
Panama, 9, 10, 25–26, 41–42, 48, 94
pardos, 31
Pasqual (criollo black), 117
Pasqual (foreman), 132–33
Pasqual of casta angola, 115
Paypaymamo, Jacinto, 72, 195n47, 195n52
Paypaymamo, Pablo, 72, 195n47, 195n52
Pedro (herder), 115
Pedro Lucas (ladino Indian), 117

Peñarán, Pedro Esteban, 13, 106–7
Perez Timón, Juan, 100
Peru. See Northern Peruvian Coast
pirates, 43, 81, 150
Pisanquiliche, Juan, 109
popo, 55
Portobelo, 40
Portuguese slave trade, 9, 25, 38–39, 41–42,
    53
Poses, Diego de, 73–74
poverty, Andean, 196n81
Powers, Karen, 193n20
punishment, 146–47, 215n106
Puyconssoli, Geronimo, 97

Quepse, Pedro, 97
Quispi, Juana, 73–74

race, 175n4
race and racism, 161–62, 164–65, 170,
    220n7
Ramírez, Susan, 211n13
Ramos, Lázaro, 110
Rappaport, Joanne, 194n20
Real Audiencia, 20, 32, 83, 137
rebellions, slave, 46–47
reducciones (indigenous towns):
    abandonment and decline of, 9–11,
    19, 29–30, 77, 81, 90; agricultural vs.
    fishing, 202n38; attachment to, 86;
    establishment of, 65; land taken from,
    8, 65, 66–67, 77–81, 86–87; leadership
    of, 199n138; new roles played by,
    102–7; segregation policy for, 104–5;
    tensions involving, 77–81
refuge, 61, 153
Reyes, Melchor de los, 108
Rodríguez, Agustina, 112–13
Romero, Juan, 147, 215n104
rural estates: Andean policing of, 154; casta
    angola on, 45; enslaved labor on, 9, 26,
    215n98, 215n106; indigenous labor on,
    73; kinships on, 52; living/working
    conditions on, 4, 113, 123–24, 129–30,
    137, 139–40, 146; male-female ratio on,
    15; traffic of goods and labor to, 121
rural guard, 44, 89, 111, 122, 126–27, 135–
    37, 152, 154–55, 215n102

Saavedra, María Rosa de, 54
Saignes, Thierry, 90

n Francisco de Buenos Aires (wheat estate), 217n156
San Pedro de Mórrope, 68–69
Sandoval, Alonso, 47, 48
Santiago de Cao, 72, 74–75, 80–81, 103, 153, 155
Sanz de la Vega, Nicolas, 145–46
Sebastian of casta arara, 12–13, 127–28, 133
Sebastian of casta congo, 140–44
Senegambia, 62, 186n45
shackles, 146
shipmate kinship, 53–54
Siba, Francisco, 109
Siccha, Juan, 107
Sichaguaman, Gonzalo, 98–101
Sierra Leone, 186n45
Silva, Juan de, 81
slave market: kinship in relationship to, 37, 38; prices in, 10, 172. See also enslaved people: commodification of; slave trade
slave trade: Caribbean to Pacific journey in, 40–45; contraband, 9, 10, 25, 200n21, 200n22; ending of (1640s), 9, 19, 25–26, 92; experience of, 38–45; journeys in, 39–41; resumption of (1660s), 10, 28, 46, 48, 92. See also Dutch slave trade; English slave trade; Portuguese slave trade
slaveholders: abusive treatment by, 136–37, 140–49, 215n104; Andean service to, 152–56; as colonial officials, 147–48; enslaved people looking for new, 134–36; labor supervision by, 125–33; and the law, 123, 136–37; political role of, 11; power and authority of, 124–26, 144–49, 218n183; preferences of, 48; slaveholder claims against fellow, 147
slavery, Andeans and, 20–22. See also enslaved people
Solano, Francisco, 43
Solórzano Pereira, Juan de, 25
Spain. See crown
Spain, travel to, 198n130
stereotypes, 18, 160
stocks, 146–47
stolen goods, 112–15
sugar, 125, 148, 212n55
sugar production, 8, 10, 11, 25, 95

sugarcane syrup, 112, 130, 208n178
Sundays, as day of rest, 129, 139–42

Tannenbaum, Frank, 220n222
textile production, 25
Timón, Diego, 99–100
Toledo, Francisco de, 70
Toledo Congo, Salvador de, 142–43
torture, 61, 136, 146, 148, 155, 218n186. See also slaveholders: abusive treatment by
tribute payment, 1, 9, 20, 21, 23, 24, 30, 31, 68, 76, 78, 81, 90, 96–97, 149
truancy, 133–36
Trujillo, 6, 8–11, 25, 27, 57, 61
Trujillo valley, 94, 95, 96
Tupí, Gaspar, 69

Ulchop, 75, 78–80, 197n104
United States, 36

Valencia, Cristobal, 118
Valentín of casta arara, 130
Vallejo, Pasqual, 134
Vanegas, Antonio, 135
Velasco, Luis de, 68
Verde, Antonio, 148
Vergara, Alonso de, 100

wages, 92–94
water, spiritual associations of, 143–44
weapons, prohibition of, 33, 138
West Africa, 1, 35, 36, 39
West Central Africa, 1, 9, 25, 35, 36, 37, 39, 42, 53, 143–44
wheat, 8, 10, 11, 94
women: occlusion of, in the historical record, 15; sharing of households by, 118–19

Ximenez, Martín, 49–50
Xofre, Juana, 118–19

yanaconas (hired indigenous laborers), 24, 30, 91, 92–93
Yoruba, 37

Zagal, Juan, 213n64
Zulawski, Ann, 90, 175n1, 176n9